Competitive Government: Public Private Partnerships

Series Editors

More information about this series at http://www.springer.com/series/16085

Oleg V. Ivanov · Agnessa O. Inshakova
Editors

Public-Private Partnerships in Russia

Institutional Frameworks and Best Practices

Springer

Editors
Oleg V. Ivanov
Moscow State Institute of International
Moscow, Russia

Agnessa O. Inshakova
Institute of Law
Volgograd State University
Volgograd, Russia

ISSN 2524-4183 ISSN 2524-4191 (electronic)
Competitive Government: Public Private Partnerships
ISBN 978-3-030-56351-6 ISBN 978-3-030-56352-3 (eBook)
https://doi.org/10.1007/978-3-030-56352-3

This Springer imprint is published by the registered company Springer Nature Switzerland AG
The registered company address is: Gewerbestrasse 11, 6330 Cham, Switzerland

Introduction

Over the past decades, the institute of public-private partnership has become an integral part of world economic theory and practice, proved its viability as an effective tool for infrastructure development in many countries with various political systems and different levels of socio-economic development. The number of PPP projects in the world is counted in the thousands, the volume of private investments in these projects amounts to billions of dollars. The results of partnership have been embodied in numerous objects of transport infrastructure, energy, utilities, communications and telecommunications, state and municipal administration, health, education, and culture.

As a result, the world has accumulated a wealth of experience in the development of public-private partnership, covering many aspects related to organizational, institutional, managerial, legal, technical, financial, engineering, and other issues. At the same time, the world experience in development of public-private partnership is very diverse. There are no two countries in the world with the same PPP legislation or governance systems in this sphere; each of them has its own institutional environment, level of PPP development, specifics of public administration, business traditions, cultural, national, and psychological characteristics, which cannot but affect the formation of models of partnership between the state and business.

Russia did not stay away from global trends associated with the development of public-private partnership, although she entered this path with some delay. In recent years, especially the last 5 years, the use of public-private partnership mechanisms in the Russian Federation has become increasingly large-scale and intensive; efforts are being made to bring the development of this institution under a systematic basis. The number of PPP projects has increased significantly (in some areas, for example, housing, and communal services, this growth is literally explosive), their geography is expanding, and the sectoral range of use of PPP mechanisms is becoming more diverse. According to classifications of PPP phased development models used by international organizations, there are reasons to say Russia has passed the stage of PPP origin and moved to the stage of "formation and maturation." At the same time, we should be aware that this is only the beginning of the way and much more needs to be done to make the PPP institute work more effectively than it has been so far. With this in mind, the issue of creating a unified integrated system of PPP governance is becoming increasingly important on the agenda.

The presented study is the result of collective work of the Moscow State Institute of international relations of the Foreign Ministry (MGIMO University) and the National PPP center of PPP of the Russian Federation. This is the first comprehensive and most complete study of issues related to establishment, development, and application of public-private partnership mechanisms in the Russian Federation. It introduces the history and current state of PPPs in Russia, and analyzes PPP legal and institutional framework, PPP policies, and governance at the Federal and regional levels. Special attention is paid to the management of PPP projects at various stages of life cycle, legal and financial structuring of projects, analysis of practical examples in leading sectors—from transport infrastructure to information technologies. International aspects of public-private partnership of most importance for Russia are also explored in the work.

Study of PPP development in the Russian Federation seems to be essential due to a number of reasons.

First, it provides valuable material for theoretical understanding of trends in the development of modern Russian economy, evolution of "state–business relationship" as well as tools, organizational mechanisms and methods used by the state to establish cooperation with business in addressing important socio-economic issues.

Secondly, the study of Russian experience of public-private partnership, its regulatory framework, models of public administration, mechanisms, and tools can be useful in terms of the search for new algorithms of economic cooperation between the state and the private sectors for improving the efficiency of public property management, development of market institutions, stimulating private initiative, etc.

Finally, knowledge PPP practices in Russia may be of interest to foreign readers in terms of opportunities for establishing fruitful mutually beneficial international cooperation in infrastructure on both bilateral and multilateral bases. The vastness of the territory of Russia, its unique geographical position as a "bridge between Europe and Asia," and infrastructure development in a wide range of sectors form an objective background. International tensions, disputes, the use of sanctions, etc. —not forever, but it is necessary to be guided and proceed from the eternal values, which certainly include peace, good-neighborliness, and mutually beneficial cooperation.

The authors hope that this work will allow the reader to learn something new about modern Russia and its economy and will be useful not only for those interested in modern trends in the economic life of Russia and its public administration, as well as the development of the infrastructure complex. The presented study is the result of collective work of the teaching staff of the Moscow State Institute of international relations (MGIMO) of the Russian Foreign Ministry and the National Center of PPP of Russia. This is the first comprehensive study of issues related to the establishment and development of the Institute of public-private partnership in the Russian Federation. It presents the history and current state of the

PPP sector in Russia, analyzes the legal and institutional framework of PPP, and approaches to the formation of public administration in this area at the Federal and regional levels. Particular attention is paid to the management of PPP projects at various stages of their life cycle, legal and financial structuring of projects, analysis of practical examples of PPP projects in leading industries—from transport infrastructure to information technology. The international aspects of public-private partnership, which are the most important for Russia, have not been left out of the authors' field of view.

The study of the development of public-private partnership in the Russian Federation is important for a number of reasons.

First, it provides valuable material for theoretical understanding of trends in the development of the modern Russian economy, the evolution of both the model of relations between the state and business, and tools, organizational mechanisms and methods used by the state to establish cooperation with business in addressing important socio-economic issues.

Secondly, the study of the Russian experience in the field of public-private partnership, its regulatory framework, models of public administration, the mechanisms and tools used in this case can be useful in terms of the formation of new algorithms of economic cooperation between the state and the private sectors, improving the efficiency of public property management, the development of market institutions, stimulating private initiative, etc.

Finally, acquaintance with practices of PPP development in Russia may be of interest to foreign readers in terms of opportunities for establishing fruitful mutually beneficial international cooperation in the field of infrastructure on both bilateral and multilateral bases. The vastness of the territory of Russia, its unique geographical position of the "bridge between Europe and Asia", the development of a wide range of infrastructure, and much more forms objective preconditions for establishments of such cooperation. International tensions, disputes, use of sanctions, etc. are not forever, but one should be guided and proceed from eternal values, which certainly include peace, good-neighborliness, and mutually beneficial cooperation.

The authors hope that this study will help readers to learn something new about modern tends in Russian economy and will be useful for anyone interested in public administration and development of infrastructure complex.

Oleg V. Ivanov
Agnessa O. Inshakova

Contents

Contributors

Natalia Chubaeva MGIMO University, Moscow, Russia

Agnessa O. Inshakova Doctor of Law, Department of Civil and Private International Law (the Basic Department of the Southern Scientific Center of the Russian Academy of Sciences), Volgograd State University, Volgograd, Russia

Maria A. Ivanova MGIMO University, Moscow, Russia

Oleg V. Ivanov Department of economic policy and public–private partnership, MGIMO University, Moscow, Russia

Vasily A. Marinin Strategic Development, Analytical and Information Support for PPPs', Center for PPP Projects, JSC "Avtodor-invest", Moscow, Russia

Evgeny Y. Moiseichev Strategic Development, Analytical and Information Support for PPPs, Center for PPP Projects, AVTODOR-invest, Moscow, Russia

Vladimir V. Piskunov Consultant, the National PPP Center, Moscow, Russia

Alexander V. Poroshin Strategic development, analytics and information support of PPP, Center of PPP projects, JSC "Avtodor-invest", Moscow, Russia

Pavel L. Seleznev National PPP Center, Chairman of the Board of JSC "Avtodor-invest", Moscow, Russia

Ellina A. Shamanina MGIMO University, Moscow, Russia

Evgenia A. Starikova MGIMO University, Moscow, Russia

Nikolai V. Studenikin MGIMO University, Moscow, Russia

Maxim V. Tkachenko Executive Director of the National PPP Center, Moscow, Russia

Elena B. Zavyalova Department of economic policy and public-private partnership, MGIMO University, Moscow, Russia

Part I
History and the Current State of Public-Private Partnership in Russia

Chapter 1
Concession Agreements in the Russian Empire. History of Concessions in the USSR. Evolution of Approaches to PPP in the Modern History of the Russian Federation

Pavel L. Seleznev and Maria A. Ivanova

Abstract Development of the Public-Private Partnership institute in Russia in different historical periods is explored. Key stages and principal forms of PPP mechanisms in the Russian Empire, the USSR and in modern Russian Federation are investigated. Concession practices in its historical perspective, the impact of PPP projects on the development of various industries, as well as on the economy as a whole, is estimated. The paper also analyzes the evolution of legal and regulatory framework of concessions in post-revolution Russia.

Keywords Public-private partnership · Payoffs · Concessions · Public administration · NEP (new economic policy) · Introduction of foreign capital · Transition to market economy

JEL-Codes H44 · O21 · R58

Introduction

Public-private partnership (PPP) as a specific form of interaction between the state and private entrepreneurship has been used in various historical periods and has a rich history. The prototype of public-private partnership and, in particular, of such of its form as a concession (from the Latin *concessio*—permission, assignment, privilege)

P. L. Seleznev (✉)
National PPP Center, Chairman of the Board of JSC "Avtodor-invest", Shabolovka str. 23 119049, Moscow, Russia
e-mail: pseleznev@pppcenter.ru

M. A. Ivanova
MGIMO University, Vernadsky Ave. 76, 119454 Moscow, Russia
e-mail: ivmariam@mail.ru

O. V. Ivanov and A. O. Inshakova (eds.), *Public-Private Partnerships in Russia*, Competitive Government: Public Private Partnerships,
https://doi.org/10.1007/978-3-030-56352-3_1

was the payoff, that is, the transfer by the state to a private individual for a fee and under certain conditions the right to levy taxes and other state revenues. The payoff was applied in the conditions of subsistence economy, underdevelopment of credit, financial difficulties of the state, weakness of communications.

The institute of public-private partnership in Russia is more than 400 years old. The very first agreements based on the principles of PPP were concluded in the mid-XVI century during the reign of Ivan IV the Terrible. For almost three centuries these were isolated cases in the manufacturing industry. Exploring those times, Russian historians and lawyers often use the term "concession" in order to most accurately convey the essence of some of the economic life phenomena of the Moscow state and Russia of XVI–XVIII centuries, although the term "concession", of course, was not used at those times, and began to be used only from the XIX century. And already in the XIX century, thanks to concessions, some entire industries made a breakthrough. The rapid construction of railways and, as a result, ensuring the economic recovery of the country were actually provided by attracting private investors through the use of a concession model of partnership with the state. The development of telegraphic communication in the country was also based on the principles of public-private partnership.

The Soviet government, despite ideological restrictions, also considered it necessary to use PPP mechanisms for the forced recovery of industries after the Civil war (1917–1922). Until 1937, more than a hundred concessions with foreign investors, including from the United States, Great Britain and Germany, were signed in the USSR. Before the Second World War, the Soviet Union curtailed all concessions and there was a more than half a century break in the use of this tool in the country.

Public-private partnership as a systemically working mechanism returned to the country only in the 2000s, after preparation of relevant legislative framework and implementation of the first pilot projects in the new market conditions.

Methodology

To solve the tasks of the study, method of periodization, chronological and historical-typological methods, as well as system analysis, are used.

Methodological basis of the study is the generally accepted principles of historicism, consistency and complexity in historical and economic research. The principle of historicism made it possible to conduct a cross-cutting study of concession relations that existed in Russian history, that is, to consider them in constant development and modification over several centuries (XVI century—early 2000s), to consider the history of concession relations in Russia as an integral (albeit discrete) system of partnership between the state and entrepreneurship, due to the desire of the state to create new or modernize the existing production and industries. The principle of consistency is manifested in taking into account the simultaneous impact on the process of origin, development and collapse of concession relations of various factors of subjective, objective, economic and non-economic nature. Complexity realized itself through the use of a wide array of sources.

Results

Concession Agreements in the Russian Empire

In Russia, as in the world practices, the first cases of public-private partnership were essentially similar to land concessions that the state gave to individuals for long-term use. Since the XVI century, in fact, the first concessionaires were Stroganov family merchants and cossack ataman (chieftain) Ermak. In early April, 1558, Tsar Ivan the Terrible granted the Stroganovs with lands from the mouth of the Lysva river down on the banks of the Kama river to the mouth of the Chusovaya river. Afterwards, other lands on the banks of Kama and Ocher rivers, as well as Siryanski salt pans, became the gifts of the Tsar to boyars (nobility). For many people, it seemed (and seems now) strange, because the Tsar led a tough fight with boyars, who for the time being were full masters in their fiefdoms, and sometimes just ignored the Central government. Boyars judged, collected taxes and had their own squads. And suddenly huge lands and huge rights were granted to the Stroganovs. However, it should be remembered that a lot was decided by origin at those times: the Ruriks, the Gediminoviches, the Genghisides (descendants of the famous Genghis Khan)—were one thing, but just rich and noble—quite another, not so dangerous for the Tsar and his supreme power. For the Stroganovs a special title—"eminent persons"—was introduced.

Although the struggle with the Kazan khanate ended in victory and Tatar Kazan was conquered in 1552, the country remained turbulent, riots broke out one after another. In the west, the country led a tough Livonian war, in the south at any time the threat from the Crimean khanate could come. The state simply did not have the strength to protect the eastern borders and to arrange them. So, Ivan the Terrible decided to use, as it became customary to say later, a private initiative. The choice of the Tsar was truly lucky: the Stroganovs proved to be skillful managers and did a lot for the settlement and development of the region, as well as for the education of its inhabitants.

Even closer to the modern understanding of PPP can be considered a concession received in 1632, by the Dutch merchant Andrei Vinius and his colleges for construction and operation of iron and cast-iron manufacture plants near Tula (200 km South of Moscow). And in 1644, another foreign company headed by a Hamburg merchant Peter Marselis was granted a 20-year concession for construction of ironworks at the banks of Vaga, Kostroma and Sheksna rivers (European part of Russia, North of Moscow).

In 1717, during the reign of Peter the Great miller Serdyukov was granted a concession for construction of mills at the banks of Una and Shlina rivers (North of Moscow). During the same period, creation of domestic concession law began (Bulatov 2012).

The first railway in Russia was built on the basis of a concession. On April 15, 1836, the Government of the Russian Empire and the "Shareholders Company for the construction of the railway from St. Petersburg to Tsarskoye Selo (continued to Pavlovsk)" signed a concession agreement on construction and operation of the railway.

Since the end of the 1850s, the pace of railway construction increased significantly in order to meet the growing needs of the economy against the background of a booming industry. From 1837 to the end of the 1850s, 3000 km of railways were built, and during the next 20 years, the length of railways in Russia increased by another 20000 km. Russian statistics 2/3 of all railway mileage opened to traffic in 1841–1913 were put into operation due to the concluded concession agreement (Vysotsky 2010).

On January 27, 1857, the Russian Government issued a Decree on the establishment of the Head Society of Russian Railways, and two days later a relative concession agreement was signed. According to the agreement, the Society was to build within 10 years four railway lines with a total length of 4 000 versts[1] with the right to operate them for 85 years, after which the lines were to be transferred to the state free of charge. In 1887, the law that gave the government the right to set railway tariffs was passed.

Concessions for construction of the railway from Moscow to Saratov were granted in 1859, to descendants of Russified Germans Pavel von Derviz and Karl von Meck. For the first time in Russian practices, concession bonds were issued, the yield of which (18% per share in 1869), exceeded all expectations and contributed to a sharp rise in railway construction.

During the period of the railway boom, the so-called "railway kings" (new rich) appeared: they were yesterday's officials, tax-collectors, contractors, etc. drawn by the opportunity to earn. Concessions in the railway industry were important for the state, but there was the reverse side of the medal too. Concessionaires planted corruption, bribed officials and nobility especially those who lobbied their interests in the government. The rapid development of capitalism in Russia after the abolition of serfdom in 1861, required a significant restructuring of the established system of transport infrastructure, finance and legislation.

Sergei Witte, an outstanding Russian statesman, who in 1889, became the head of the Department of Railway Affairs under the Ministry of Finance, tried to put the industry in order. His main goal in this position was to eliminate a myriad of private railways and to create a unified system of state railways, which was essential for improving the efficiency of cargo transportation.

The state began to buy out private railways and to build new ones on its own. S. Witte explained that he agreed to a buy out of private roads because further tolerance of lobbying, corruption, write-offs was impossible. He launched a buy out choosing the lesser of evils. At the same time, S. Witte was and remained for the

[1] Versta—a measure of length in the Tsarist Russia, equal to about 1066 m.

rest of his life an ardent supporter of the private management of infrastructure. He explored how often in history in the modern period of Western countries purchase of an infrastructure object for debts from the private sector was used as a method of infrastructure management. Examples were found all over the world. The public-private partnership provides that a public partner (a government) may cancel the contract or nationalize the object but accordingly must provide compensation to the concessionaire. In this case, a private partner should, of course, be reimbursed not only for his investments, but also for the profits he missed (Vysotsky 2010).

The use of concessions was not limited to railway infrastructure. In 1869, the Government of Russia signed with Englishman John Hughes the concession agreement on construction of metallurgical plant in Donbass. On January 24, 1872, a blast furnace was successfully put into operation and a year later the manufacture of iron rails began.

On October 13, 1869, a concession agreement between the Russian Government and Karl Frederick Tietgen, the founder of the Great Northern Telegraph Community, to lay a telegraph cable from Copenhagen to Libava and further to St. Petersburg, was signed.

In 1872, land telegraph lines connecting the European part of Russia with Vladivostok were connected by underwater cables with Shanghai, Hong Kong and Nagasaki, which made it possible to open telegraph communication between Europe and East Asia.

On November 2, 1881, the Telegraph Department of the General Imperial Post and Telegraph Agency concluded a concession agreement with von Baranov on construction and operation of the first five public telephone networks in St. Petersburg, Moscow, Odessa, Warsaw and Riga. But the concession was ceded to the International Bell Telephone Company, which in the early 90 s of the nineteenth century began the construction of a new telephone station with 3000 numbers and expansion of linear structures.

The share of concessionaires' capital in the municipal economy of Tsarist Russia was significant. Thus, by the beginning of the first World War in 1914, in a total amount of industrial investments, concessionaires' share accounted for 75% of the funds invested in tramway enterprises; almost 50% in the electric power industry; 30% in water supply; 90% in gas supply (Ocherki 2012).

In the medium term, the expectations proved to be untenable. In the 1880s, embezzlement, corruption among officials and concessionaires were realities of Russian economic life. The government changed its priorities, abandoning concessions and moving to construction at the expense of the Treasury and to the formation of public railways by compensating nationalization of concessions.

The final chord in the history of the use of PPP mechanisms in Tsarist Russia can be considered a secret agreement on the Russian-Chinese military union concluded in May 1896, in Moscow. According to the agreement, the rights for construction and operation of the Chinese Eastern Railway (KVZHD) were granted to the Russian-Chinese Bank, created in 1895, on the initiative of the Minister of Finance of Russia Sergei Witte. On 1 July, 1903, the Chinese Eastern Railway was put into operation (Ocherki 2012).

High level of competition in the world markets and the possibility of exploitation of Russian rich natural resources became a powerful incentive for foreign and Russian investors. Historical experience shows that the problem of effective investment management can be solved only if national and regional markets for investment projects provided with appropriate legal and financial mechanisms are created in Russia.

History of Concessions in the USSR

The next round of history, concessions came to Russia in the early 1920s, during the NEP.[2] As a result of the Bolsheviks' nationalization of foreign property in 1918, and refusal of the Soviet authorities to pay the debts of the former governments to the Western countries, import of foreign capital in the form of credit resources for Soviet Russia became unlikely. This predetermined import foreign capital mainly in the form of concessionsduring the formation of Soviet power. The crisis affected all industries and sectors of the economy. The failure of the "war communism" policy led to a sharp turn in economic policies and restoration of market relations (Orlov 1999).

Introduction of new forms of public administration took place in difficult political conditions. Many in the country considered it as a retreat from the conquests of the revolution, a step towards an agreement with the bourgeoisie. For example, here are the words one could hear from representatives of peasantry and workers at that time: "We, the peasants, are ready to starve for another three years, to be cold, to incur duties, only do not sell mother Russia for concessions".[3]

In the USSR during the NEP period concessions played an important role in stabilizing the economy after the revolutionary upheavals, drew foreign investment and expertise to modernization of industrial production, brought considerable income to the Treasury in the form of equity contributions of concession companies, payment of concession fees, taxes, rents, duties, levies, etc.

In 1920, the Council of People's Commissars of the Russian Soviet Federative Republic adopted a Decree on concessions, according to which quite a number of infrastructure projects involving foreign capital were implemented during the NEP period. From that moment on, Western companies received concessions for a huge part of the country's wealth.

V. I. Lenin, who was the head of the state at that time, explained the necessity of the Decree on concessions by concern for national economy for the restoration of which raw materials were necessary. He wrote: "Our task is to save the worker, to save the working man. If we solve this problem—we will save and restore everything."

---

[2]New economic policy – a new course of Soviet power in the economy, aimed at expanding economic freedoms and introduction of certain elements of the market economy.

[3]From the statement of a non-party peasant at the Arzamas County Congress of the Nizhny Novgorod province, the end of 1921.

"Isn't it dangerous to invite capitalists, doesn't it mean to develop capitalism? Yes, it means to develop capitalism, but it is not dangerous, because the power remains in the hands of workers and peasants, and the property of landowners and capitalists is not restored," he noted. (Lenin 1920; Shishkin 1968).

The attempt to liberate the domestic potential and attract foreign capital was really one of the powerful tactics to get out of the critical situation (Inshakova Agnessa et al. Inshakova Agnessa et al. 2017).

An important feature of concession relations in the USSR was that in the mid-1920s, concessions began to be included in the system of long-term planning of the national economy of the USSR. It was planned to transfer forests of Western Siberia within the Tyumen, Omsk and Tomsk provinces, forests in the North of the European part of Russia, in the Arkhangelsk, Vologda, Olonets, Perm and Vyatka provinces, as well as minings in Siberia, including coal mines near the city of Kuznetsk to concessions. It was also supposed to lease a part of Baku and Grozny oil, coal in Donetsk, iron ore in the region of Krivoy Rog, Don, near the city of Kerch, etc.

In autumn 1922, the first Soviet international Bank, Roskombank, was created in the USSR. Olof Ashberg, the owner of the Stockholm Bank Nya Banken, became the head of the bank and Max May, Vice-President of American Guaranty Trust Company became the Head of the Foreign Department.

In 1923–1937, the Main Concession Committee under the Government of the USSR—the Agency engaged in granting concessions to foreign individuals and legal entities for trade and production activities—operated. Similar bodies operated in the Soviet Union republics. They received and considered more than 2200 applications for concessions and more than 10% of them were implemented. From 1922 to 1928, 124 major concession agreements were signed between the Government of the USSR and foreign companies, of which 64 were in industry, including 28 in mining, 21 in trade and 11 in agriculture. In total 24 concessions were signed with firms from Germany, 16—from the United States, with 61 concessions then ranked to the Federal level, and 53—to the republican (regional). In terms of the number of concessions and capital invested, the first place was occupied by the manufacturing industry (24 concessions), and the second and third places were divided between agriculture and trade (Kasyanenko 1959).

In the period from 1926 to 1927, the total amount of foreign investment attracted to the economy of the USSR using concession model amounted to 62.5 million rubles. England accounted for 14.625 million rubles (28%), the USA—12.272 million rubles (23.6%), Germany—7.096 million rubles (13.5%), Sweden—6.466 million rubles (12.5%) and the remaining 22.4% were distributed among 13 countries, ranging from Poland (3.3 million rubles) to Italy (70 thousand rubles). By the end of 1927, concession enterprises produced 40% of the total production of manganese in the country, 35% of gold, 12% of copper, 22% of ready-made dresses. Concessions in Russia during this period were also established in the field of urban economy (Khromov 2006).

On November 14, 1925, the Soviet government and the British joint stock company "Lena Goldfields" concluded a concession agreement for a period of 50 years. Under the agreement, the company, which controlled at that time over a 1/3 of gold mining in Yakutia, was also granted coal mines in the Kuzbass region, Zyryano-Zmeinogorsk deposit of zinc and lead in the Altai region.

No less famous is the concession for production of pencils, concluded between the Government of the Russian Federation and Armand Hammer, a businessman from the United States, who created the A. Hammer Pencil Company for this project. In the 1930s, when the "curtailing" of the NEP policies began and the state began to seize business from private owners, A. Hammer's concessions were bought out by Soviet authorities.

During the Soviet period of concessions development, the legal nature of concessions was mixed, i.e. the nature of an administrative act on the one hand, and a contract based on equality of property interests of the authority and the concessionaire, on the other. The time of return of the object under the agreement was not regulated in detail. In fact, the state could, under any pretext and at any time, reclaim the object of the concession.

Since 1937, in connection with a change of general priorities of the Soviet economy and intense preparation for war concessions were cancelled (Chart. 1.1).

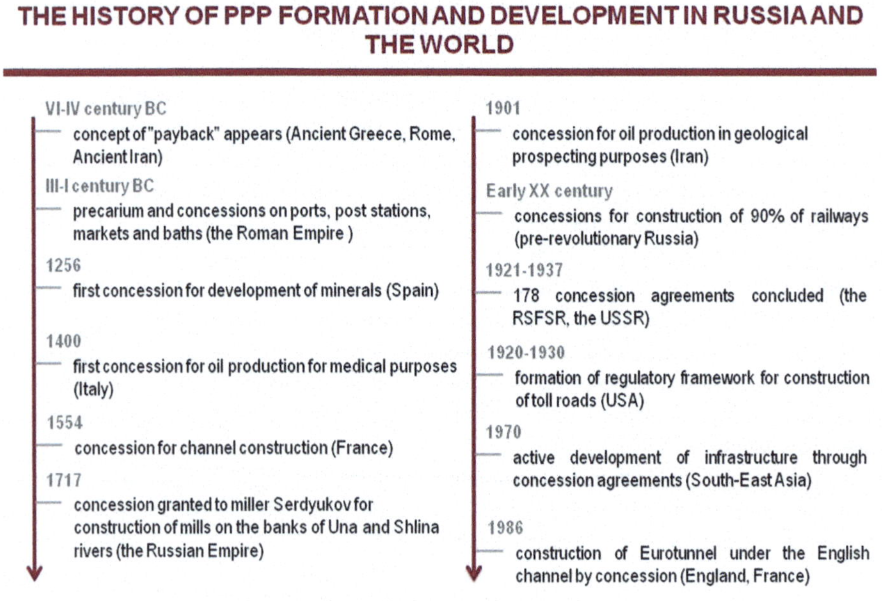

Chart 1.1 Main events in the history of PPP formation in Russia and the world (up to 2000)

Concession Agreements in the Modern History of the Russian Federation

After more than 50 years of interruption, history of PPP in Russia continued with an attempt to adopt a new law on concessions.

On July 21, 1993, the Supreme Council of the Russian Federation adopted the Law "On concession and other contracts concluded with foreign investors". However, on August 18, 1993, the President of the Russian Federation vetoed the adopted law and instructed to radically revise it.

The government of the Russian Federation instructed the Ministry of economy of Russia and other agencies to finalize the Law "On concession agreements, agreements on the provision of services and production sharing agreements concluded with foreign investors". In November 1994, the Ministry of economy of the Russian Federation sent its version of the draft law entitled "On concession and other agreements concluded by the Russian state with Russian and foreign investors" to the agencies for approval. This bill was approved in the first reading by the State Duma of the second convocation only in April 1996, and afterwards, for subjective and objective reasons, the bill lay unclaimed until 2000, then was again considered by the State Duma and re-sent for revision.

Intense work on the bill continued until 2004. During 2004, and the first half of 2005, the draft law, entitled "On concession agreements", was radically revised and adopted by the State Duma in the second and third readings, approved by the Council of the Federation and after signing by the President of the Russian Federation and official publication entered into force.

Since then, the Federal law "On concession agreements" has undergone many significant amendments, which, however, have yielded results: today concessions are the most popular form of public-private partnership in Russia, and the number of concession agreements is measured in thousands (Inshakova Agnessa et al. 2017).

However, one of the first major projects implemented with the use of PPP mechanisms in modern Russia can be considered the project for construction and operation of an aeration station in southern Moscow opened in 1998 (i.e. 7 years before the adoption of the law on concession agreements). Its construction was carried out entirely by private investments. The applied scheme was a BOOT (Build, Own, Operate, Transfer) type. This form of interaction allowed to implement expensive projects without large one-time budget costs. During the first 12 years, the station belonged to the joint venture established by the German company SHV Holter and Moscow Mosvodokanal company. Investments of the German company were gradually reimbursed from Moscow city budget, and after 12 years the object became the property of Moscow city government.

The first federal level concession agreement in modern Russia was signed in July 2009, between the Federal road Agency (Rosavtodor) and JSC "Main road" for implementation of the project "Construction of a new exit to the Moscow ring road from the Federal highway M-1 "Belarus" Moscow—Minsk". The duration of the concession is 30 years, the total costs of construction was estimated as 32.47 billion

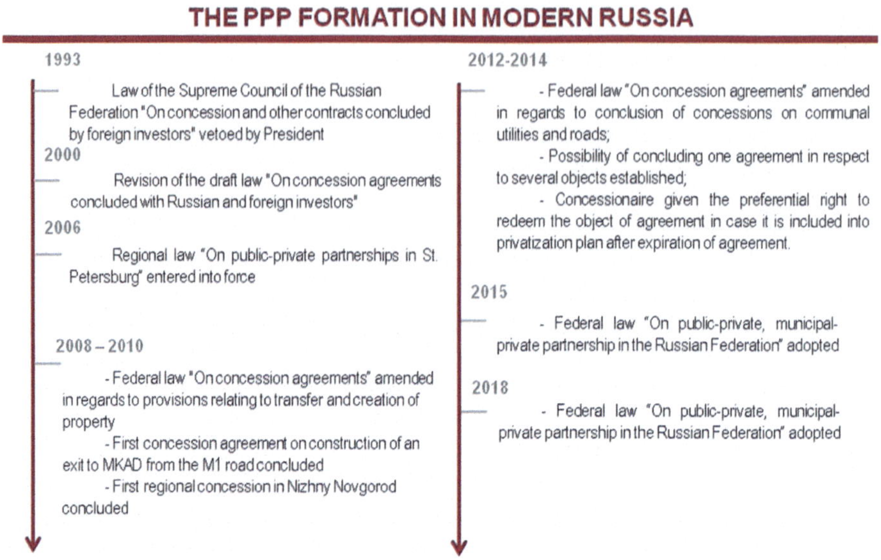

Chart 1.2 Main events in the history of PPP formation in modern Russia

rubles (about $1 billion at the time of conclusion). Of these, 11 billion (33.87%) were allocated from the Investment Fund of the Russian Federation, and the remaining part was invested by the concessionaire (Chart 1.2).

Conclusion

The use of various mechanisms similar in essence to PPP has a long, in fact, almost 500 years, history in Russia and started around the same time when such mechanisms began to be applied by leading European powers.

PPP mechanisms played an important and in some periods a key role in the economic history of Russia. In fact development of the Urals and Siberia would have been either impossible or would have been much slower, rates of construction of railways in the twentieth century would have been significantly lower, development of telegraph communication and electrification of urban economy would have gone at a completely different pace without attracting private investment and without partnership with foreign and domestic commercial companies in pre-revolutionary Russia.

In the Soviet period, it is the concession mechanisms the USSR was obliged to for the rapid revival of entire sectors of mining and processing industries of the country ravaged by the civil war of 1920s.

Modern Russia began to revive PPP mechanisms not so long ago, by global standards. At the same time, over the past 14 years since the adoption of the Federal law "On concession agreements", the Russian Federation has managed to make a serious breakthrough in regulation and practical application of PPP mechanisms, equaling in quantitative and qualitative indicators with many countries of the world and moving from countries in which PPP is at the stage of "formation" to countries where PPP is actively used and methodically developed.

References

Bernstein I. N. (1930). *Ocherk kontsessionnogo prava SSSR (Essay on concession law of the USSR)* (192 p.). Moscow; Leningrad: State Publishing House.

Bulatov V. V. (2012). Kontsessionniye otnosheniya v SSSR. (Concession relations in the USSR). Abstract of the thesis for the degree of Doctor of historical Sciences). Volgograd.

Butkovskii, V. (1928). Inostranniye kontsessii v narodnom khozyaistve SSSR (Foreign concessions in the national economy of the USSR). – Moscow, Leningrad.

Dekret SNK ot 23 noyabrya 1920. (1920). "Obtshie ekonomicheskie i yuridicheskie usloviya kontsessii" (Decree of SNK of November 23, 1920 "General economic and legal conditions of concessions"). Set of Laws of the RSFSR, 1920. No. 91. p. 481.

Inshakova Agnessa, O., Goncharov Alexander, I., & Kazachenok Olesya, P. (2018) Legal regulation of the syndicated lending: banking innovations in contemporary Russia. In: E. Popkova, V. Ostrovskaya (Eds), *Perspectives on the Use of New Information and Communication Technology (ICT) in the Modern Economy* (pp. 368–377). Cham: Springer.

Inshakova Agnessa, O., Goncharov Alexander, I., & Sevostyanov Maxim, V. (2017). Institutional ambiguity of regulation of possessory relations in modern Russia. *Overcoming Uncertainty of Institutional Environment as a Tool of Global Crisis Management, 1*, 207–212.

Kasyanenko V. I. et al. (1959). Iz istorii kontsessionnoi politiki Sovetskogo gosudarstva (From the history of concession policy of the Soviet state). History of the USSR. No. 4. 1959.

Khromov, S. S. (2006). Inostrannie kontsessii v SSSR: Istoricheskii ocherk. Dokumenti. (Foreign concessions in the USSR: Historical sketch. Documents). Part I, II. Russian Academy of Sciences, Moscow.

Lenin, V. I. (1969). *Doklad o kontsessiyakh na VII Vserossiiskom s'ezde Sovetov (Report on concessions at the VII-th All-Russian Congress of Soviets*, December 22–29, 1920. Full collection of works. 5-th edition. T. 31 (pp. 433–455). Moscow: State publishing house of political literature.

Lisovskaya, E. G. (2006). *Kontsessii i formirovanie sovetskoi ekonomiki (Concessions and the formation of the Soviet economy)*. Moscow.

Ocherki istorii kontsessii v imperatorskoi Rossii 1836–1917 (Essays on the history of concessions in Imperial Russia) V. V. Bulatov, & M. M. Zagorulko (Eds.). (2012) (166 pp.). Saarbrucken, Germany: LAP Lambert Academic Publishing.

Orlov, I. B. (1999). *Novaya ekonomicheskaya politika: istoriya, opit, problem (New economic policy: history, experience, problems)* Moscow.

Praktika primeneniya kontsessionnikh soglashenii v Rossiiskoi Federatsii (Practice of application of concession agreements in the Russian Federation) Seleznev, P. L. (Ed.). Center of the development of public-private partnership. M.

Rogachevskii, A. M. (1970). *Iz istorii kontsessionnogo predpriyaiya "Lena Goldfields limited" (1925–1930) (From the history of the concession company "Lena Goldfields limited" (1925–1930)*. Novosibirsk institute of water transport engeneers. Issue 51. Novosibirsk.

Shishkin, V. A. (1968). *Lenin i razrabotka kontsessionnoi politiki (1918–1921) (V. Lenin and development of concession policy (1918–1921)*. Issues of history of the CPSU. No. 6.

Vysotsky, A. E. (2010). *Razvitie gosudarstvenno-chastnogo partnyorstva v zheleznodorozhnom khozyaistve Rossii (Development of public-private partnership in the railway sector of Russia)* (the second half of the XIX – early XX centuries). Abstract of the thesis for the degree of candidate of economic Sciences. Saint Petersburg.

Yumashev, Yu. M. (1993). *Inostrannie kontsessii v Rossii i SSSR (1920–1930) (Foreign concessions in Russia and the USSR (20–30-ies)*. State and law. No. 7.

Chapter 2
Infrastructure Gaps and Investment Needs. Current State and Key Trends of PPP Development

Pavel L. Seleznev, Alexander V. Poroshin, and Natalia Chubaeva

Abstract The present state of infrastructure in Russia is reviewed in detail. On the basis of assessment of investment needs in infrastructure sectors the degree of sufficiency of the current and projected levels of investments required to eliminate existing infrastructure gaps is investigated and evaluated. Key factors behind PPP market development are identified. Current situation of PPP in Russia is analyzed from different angles—dynamic of project number, projects investment capacity, sectoral structure, implementation level, organizational and legal forms of PPP projects, etc. Major trends in PPP development are systematized and revealed. Conclusions on Russia's compliance with global PPP development trends are presented. Estimates of demand for PPP mechanisms in development of infrastructure in Russia are made. At the same time, an analysis of specific issues impeding the development of PPPs in Russia is conducted and recommendations on elimination of existing barriers and dynamization of further development of PPP are suggested.

Keywords Public–private partnership · Infrastructure · Infrastructure gap · Investment project · Concession agreement · PPP/MPP agreement

JEL-Codes H42 · H44 · H57 · L80 · L90 · O10

P. L. Seleznev (✉)
National PPP Center, Chairman of the Board of JSC "Avtodor-invest", Shabolovka str. 23, 119049 Moscow, Russia
e-mail: pseleznev@pppcenter.ru

A. V. Poroshin
Strategic development, analytics and information support of PPP, Center of PPP projects, JSC "Avtodor-invest", Malaya Dmitrovka str. 16-6, 127006 Moscow, Russia
e-mail: caunte@gmail.com

N. Chubaeva
MGIMO University, Vernadsky Ave., 76, 119454 Moscow, Russia
e-mail: Nn1042781@yandex.ru

O. V. Ivanov and A. O. Inshakova (eds.), *Public-Private Partnerships in Russia*, Competitive Government: Public Private Partnerships,
https://doi.org/10.1007/978-3-030-56352-3_2

Introduction

Russia has low and continue to decline the level of infrastructure. Infrastructure is systematically underfunded and infrastructure gaps as well as investment needs continue to increase.

At the present stage of development of the Russian economy, demand for PPP mechanisms is objectively growing. The Government's goals for achieving high rates of economic growth and ensuring quality of life require accelerated development and renovation of a significant number of infrastructure facilities. Insufficient development of transport, energy, housing and communal and social infrastructure becomes an obstacle both for the state to fulfill its duties and for business to implement its plans.

At the same time development of PPP in the country faced both general problems related to the model of "state-business" relationship and systemic gaps in the sphere of PPP.

Results

Infrastructure Investment in Russia: Level and Needs

The level of infrastructure development in Russia remains low. Infrastructure availability in Russia is insufficient and its quality is poor, similar to the level of developing countries. Despite some improvement in Russia's position in the international infrastructure quality rankings (currently, according to the World Economic Forum, Russia ranks 35th out of 137 countries), the state of infrastructure in many important components leaves much to be desired—114th place in road infrastructure, 66th—in seaports infrastructure, and 59th—in airport infrastructure (World Economic Forum 2018).

InfraONE, a credible Russian investment consulting company, considers Russian infrastructure that has been in dire need of investment for decades, the current investment does not cover minimum needs and poor state of infrastructure in Russia is typical for all sectors and all regions of the Russian Federation. InfraONE estimates that national average index of infrastructure development is only 5.70 of possible 10. Transport infrastructure is the worst in Russia—average development index is only 3.24 points out of 10.

Leading regions in terms of infrastructure development (Moscow, Saint-Petersburg, Khanty-Mansi Autonomous District) ensured their leadership are primarily due to the developed transport infrastructure, but even these regions all have a relatively weak social infrastructure, the capacity of which does not keep up with the growing load.

The poorest infrastructure is in the Chechen Republic, Tuva, and Dagestan. To a large extent, the infrastructure lag of these regions is due to difficult accessibility of respective territories, caused by mountainous terrain, and predominance of rural population.

There are significant gaps between the leading, middle, and lagging regions in terms of infrastructure development. Thus, Moscow's index is 36.5% higher than average value of the index in all regions and 78.9% higher than in Dagestan which is in the last place (InfraONE 2018; InfraONE 2019).

Russia invests in infrastructure significantly less than, for example, such a developed country as Japan, which is comparable to Russia in population, but less in area by 45 thousand times. Among the BRICS countries, Russia is ahead of only South Africa and lags far behind Brazil and India (Chart 2.1).

In Russia, the share of infrastructure financing in GDP is not high (about 2.8%). By this indicator, China is a leader: its infrastructure spending is 6% of GDP. But the US is not in second or even third place—the country spends less than 2% of GDP on infrastructure (Proekt nacional'nogo doklada 2018) (Chart 2.2).

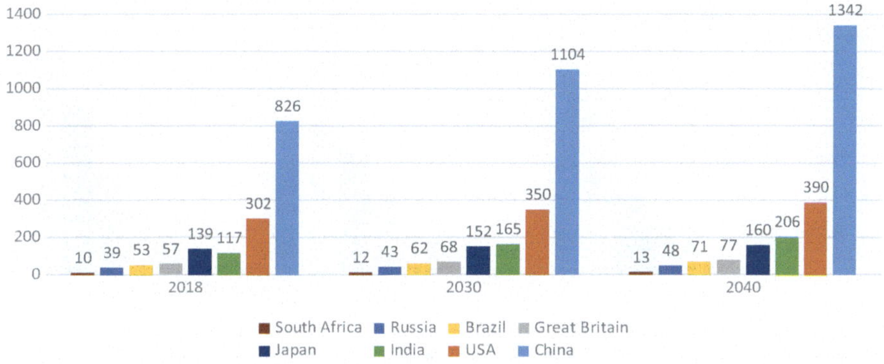

Chart 2.1 Dynamics of infrastructure investments up to 2040 ($ billion). *Source* compiled on the basis of data of Global Infrastructure Hub, OECD and the World Bank

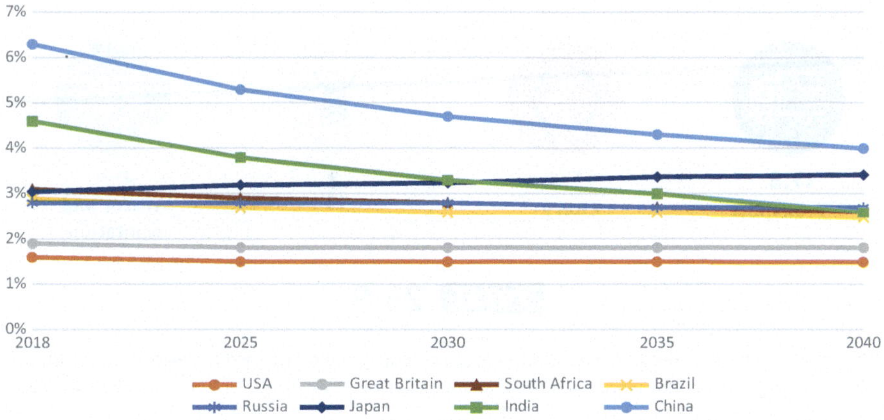

Chart 2.2 Infrastructure investments in relation to GDP until 2040 (%). *Source* compiled on the basis of data of Global Infrastructure Hub, OECD and the World Bank

Russia has a deficit in infrastructure financing higher than India, where 10 times more people live. Oddly enough, the USA infrastructure financing deficit is ahead of everyone. The uncovered need for infrastructure in the USA is twice as great as in China (Chart 2.3).

The Russian Federation expenses for infrastructure are 2.8% of GDP but according to experts' estimates should be at least 4.2% and by 2024 spending should reach 5%. In absolute figures the country needs to spend 25.9 trillion rubles for six years. Investments of all national projects are 25.7 trillion rubles. Of this figure, according to expert estimates, on infrastructure can be directed about 15.3 trillion rubles, the deficit will be 10.6 trillion rubles (Chart 2.4).

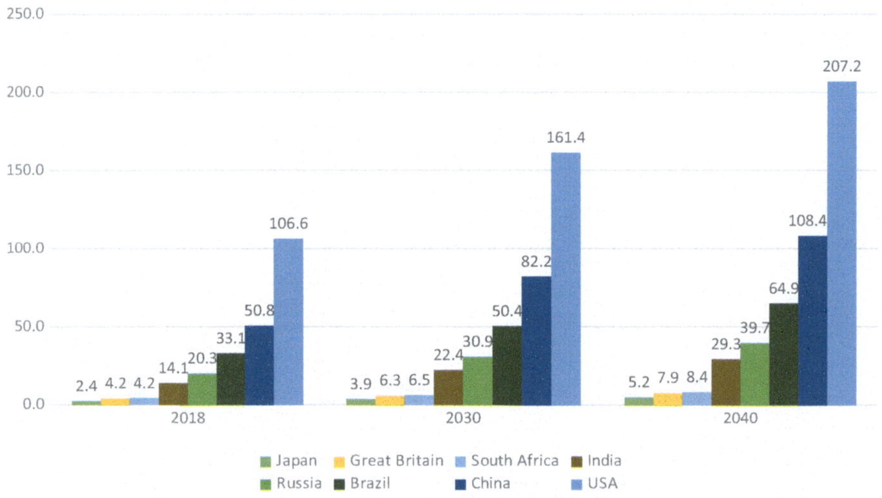

Chart 2.3 The dynamics of the infrastructure gap until 2040 ($ billion). *Source* compiled on the basis of data of Global Infrastructure Hub, OECD and the World Bank

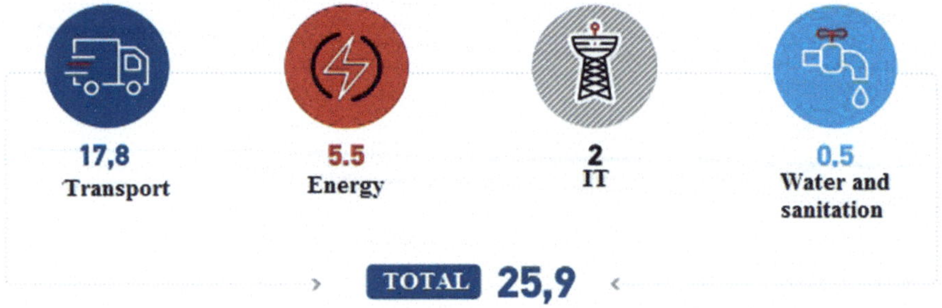

Chart 2.4 Cumulative projected investment requirement by sector to 2024 in Russia (RUB biilion). *Source* calculations of the National PPP Center based on data from Global Infrastructure Hub, Rosstat, Bank of Russia

Use of PPPs to Attract Private Investment in Infrastructure in Russia: Current Status and Key Trends

In recent years, the PPP market in Russia has gone an impressive way from a fragmented set of individual projects to an integrated market with established rules of the game, a wide industry coverage, a large number of participants, thereby creating a fundamentally new field of interaction between the state and business in infrastructure development.

Let us reveal the key trends and patterns that most clearly reflect development of PPP market in Russia and its current state.

- *Sharply increased demand for PPP in Russia in the 2010-s is primarily due to the opportunity provided within the framework of relevant mechanisms to shift part of obligations to finance infrastructure development from the state to the private sector in the conditions of long-term economic stagnation and "impoverishment" of regional budgets.*

After the crisis of 2008–2009, the Russian economy changed its development trajectory—in 1999–2008 the economic growth rate averaged 6–7% per year, in the next decade it was only 1–2% per year. On the one hand, low rates of economic growth are long-term stable, as, first of all, determined by the unwillingness of the government to carry out structural reforms in economy and change its foreign policy course to lift foreign sanctions. On the other hand, among the priorities of socio-economic development, the authorities are most concerned with ensuring macroeconomic and budgetary stability. Under these conditions, the state refuses to increase funding for many areas and tasks of socio-economic development that are not related to the basic or priority obligations.

Moreover, significant, if not primary, part of the required infrastructure is of regional/local scale and relates to sectors the powers of which is assigned to regional or municipal authorities. Budgetary centralization and redistribution of budget revenues from regional budgets to the Federal budget carried out by the state in the mid-2000s deprived the regions of a significant part of budget revenues. As a result, the regions found themselves in an even more difficult situation, suffering not only of a negative macroeconomic situation, but also of a significantly reduced amount of budget revenues, which is clearly insufficient to fulfill the entire set of obligations. In this context, a wide range of development plans and objectives, including investment in infrastructure, have become quite an expected "victim".

Configuration of these conditions determined the demand for PPP mechanisms in infrastructure development, allowing to replace the falling amounts of budget financing by private investment.

– *Increase in the number of ongoing projects*

Demand for PPP mechanisms is largely due to the difficult financial situation of the regions and inability to solve important socio-economic problems without involvement of the private sector. In addition, in PPP authorities see a way to improve poor management of state and municipal property.

Just 5–10 years ago, the number of PPP projects launched annually was several tens, now it increased to hundreds. Despite the reduction and obvious lack of budget funding for public infrastructure in Russia, the number of infrastructure projects implemented using PPP mechanisms is growing. Since 2014, in average more than 600 PPP projects have been launched annually, providing an annual inflow of private investment of 317.0 billion rubles (Gosudarstvenno-chastnoe partnyorstvo 2019) (Chart 2.5).

As of the beginning of 2019, the number of PPP projects that have passed the stage of commercial closure (signing agreements/contracts) reached 3422. Since 2014, the number of PPP projects that have passed the stage of commercial closure has increased more than 8 times. Besides, more than 1 000 projects, according to expert estimates, are at different stages of preparation by authorities.

Contracted PPP projects (3422) draw total volume of private investment obligations of about 2 180 billion rubles. And this is not little. For example, in China at the end of 2018, 4691 PPP projects were under implementation, although with a larger volume of contracted investments (about $1 trillion). In Kazakhstan 473 projects with investment of 90 billion rubles are under implementation (Prosto i chestno 2019).

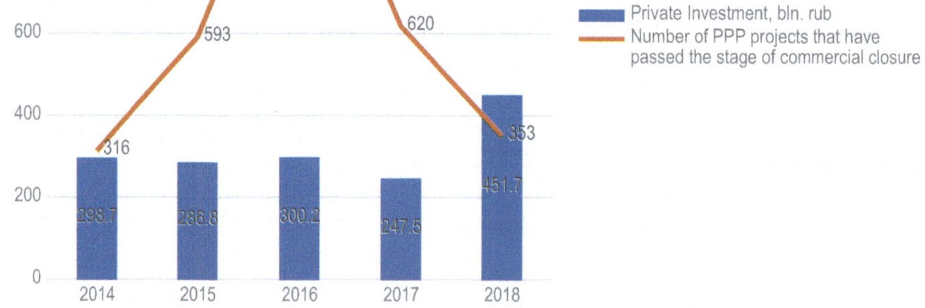

Chart 2.5 Number of PPP projects passed the stage of commercial closure and volume of private investment (RUB billion). Source data and calculations of the National PPP Center

– *Growth of capital intensity in the PPP market*

The PPP market in Russia shows intensive growth not only in number of projects, but also in monetary terms. Under PPP projects that have passed the stage of commercial closure, total investment obligations (obligations to finance construction/reconstruction) of the public and private partners are 3 065.9 billion rubles, of which the obligations of private partners are 71.2% of the total. Since 2013, total volume of investments in PPP projects has increased 3.5 times, and investment obligations of private partners—about 3.7 times (Chart 2.6).

– *Projects of more than 1 billion rubles represent the bulk of investments*

92% of all private investments in PPP projects account for projects of more than 1 billion rubles. At the same time, in quantitative terms, there are only 193 such projects, or 6% of the total number. Such proportions have been maintained for many years, and it is unlikely that the picture will change soon. Investors and banks are more interested in investing in large scale projects. Consolidation of projects is also taking place in sectors where traditionally investments were small (sometimes with a volume of <1 million rubles): heat supply, water supply, improvement of public spaces, social and consumer services, tourism, etc (Chart 2.7).

– *Most projects and investments take the form of "classic" PPP, primarily concessions*

The whole set of PPP mechanisms used in Russia can be divided into three groups: concessions, PPP/MPP agreements and "quasi-PPP", which includes life cycle contracts, investment agreements, lease with investment obligations and other forms of "non-classical" PPP (Ivanov et al. 2018).

Chart 2.6 "Contracted" investment obligations of private partners in PPP projects (RUB billion, accumulated total by relevant year). Source data and calculations of the National PPP Center

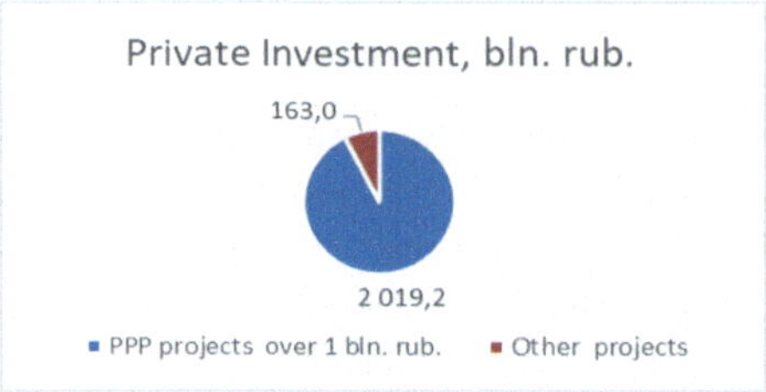

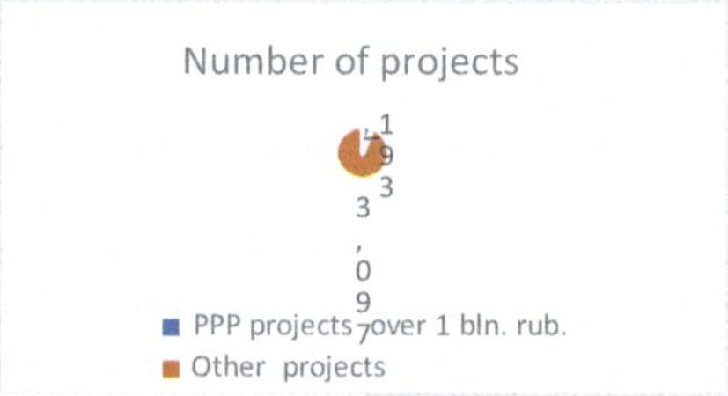

Chart 2.7 Number of projects and volume of private investment in PPP projects by degree of investment capacity. Source data and calculations of the National PPP Center

The lion's share in both number of projects and volume of investments is taken by concessions. 2939 projects (85.9% of the total number of projects) are implemented under concession agreements with a total volume of private investment of 1 trillion rubles (47% of the total). "Quasi-PPP" account for 12% of projects number and 38% of investments. PPP/MPP agreements, including the framework of regional legislation, is the youngest and so far is only a gaining popularity form (3% by number and 15% by investment).

Concessions and PPP/MPP agreements are two forms of public–private partnership regulated by Federal laws—115-FZ and 224-FZ, respectively. Concession is generally one of the oldest PPP mechanisms in the country. Actually, acccording to concession agreements in Russia formation of the railway industry took place in the nineteenth century. Even the Soviet Union used concessions for economic development until 1937.

In terms of number of projects implemented under concession agreements and PPP agreements, energy and communal utilities sector is leading with 2656 projects. Social sphere follows with 266 projects. There are 69 concessions and PPP agreements in the transport sector (Chart 2.8).

Unlike concessions, which have already settled, PPP/MPP agreements continue to shape. Previously, PPP/MPP agreements were implemented within the framework of regional legislation. However, since 2018, they began to be concluded under Federal Law 224-FZ "On PPP/MPP agreements in the Russian Federation" of 2015 (Chart 2.9).

- *Expansion of the range of PPP mechanisms used, active development of new "non-classical" forms of project implementation*

Public and private partners are increasingly taking different formats of infrastructure projects, including "non-classical", or "quasi-PPP". As the market develops and PPP enters new sectors, authorities and investors continue to search for such mechanisms that would be most adequate to specific project practice and would allow to fine-tune the contract mechanism in fullest accordance with unique features of the project and goals of its participants (Tarakanov et al. 2019). By the beginning of 2019, besides "classical" concessions and PPP agreements seven forms of "quasi-PPPs were also widely used in PPP practices in Russia. They are

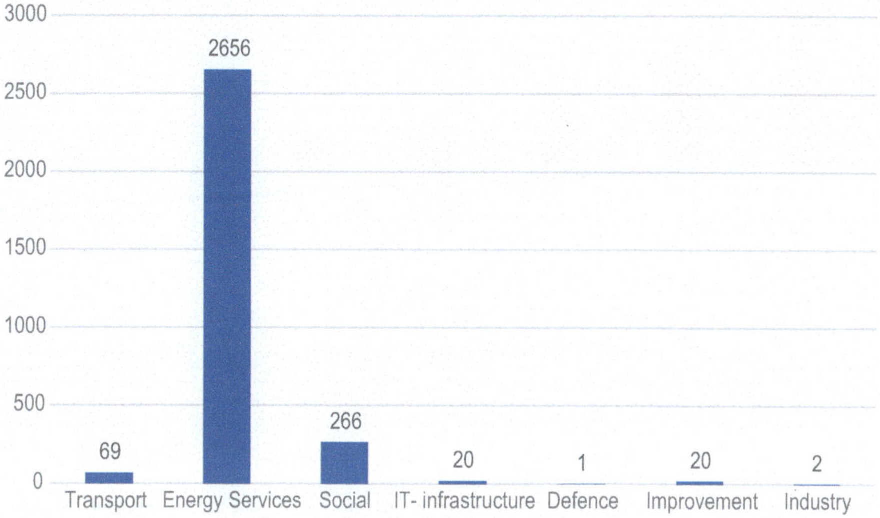

Chart 2.8 Sectoral structure of concession agreements and PPP/MPP agreements by number (2018). Source data and calculations of the National PPP Center

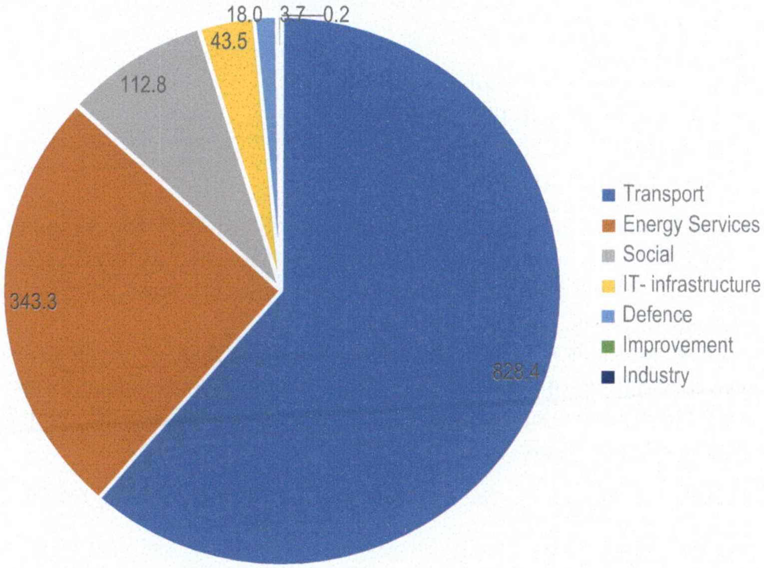

Chart 2.9 Sectoral structure of concession agreements and PPP/MPP agreements by volume of private investments (2018, RUB billion). Source data and calculations of the National PPP Center

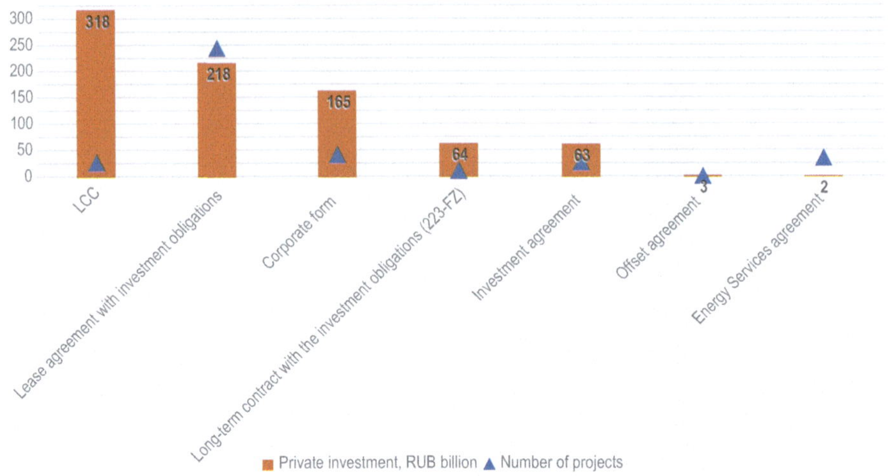

Chart 2.10 Form of quasi-PPP projects in terms of private investment and number of projects. Source data and calculations of the National PPP Center

- life cycle contract;
- lease with investment obligations;
- corporate partnership;
- long-term contract with investment obligations
- investment agreement with PPP features;
- offset purchasing;
- energy service contract (Ivanov et al, 2018).

The largest in investment volume projects among "quasi-PPP" forms are life cycle contracts (LCC). Under this mechanism, for example, Moscow city buys buses, trams, and subway cars. Along with LCC, investors also often use lease with investment obligations and corporate partnerships (Chart 2.10).

If we look at "quasi-PPP" projects by sector, the largest share of private investment is held by transport (56% of the total, or 464 billion rubles). communal utilities sector goes second (26%), and social sector—the third. All other sectors account for 2% (Charts 2.11 and 2.12) (Table 2.1).

- *Communal utilities sector is the leader in number of PPP projects, transport—in terms of investment volume*

Among the sectors there are two leaders—transport and communal utilities. Transport is the leader in terms of investment volume (59% of total investment, or 1.3 trillion rubles), but by number of projects the transport industry accounts for only 4%. In communal utilities sector we have a vice versa picture: 80% of all PPP projects (or 2 731) were launched in this sector, although in monetary terms it is only a 1/4 of the total investment. To put it simply, communal utilities projects are small and not expensive (Charts 2.13 and 2.14).

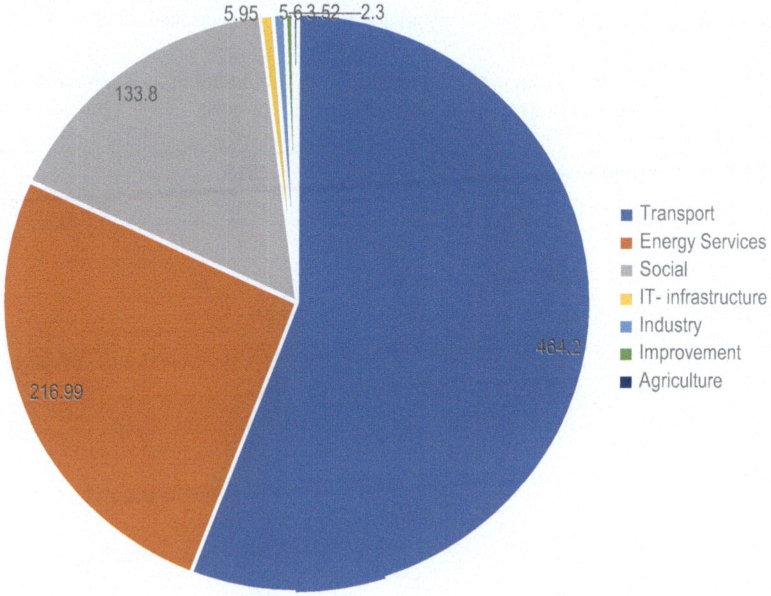

Chart 2.11 Sectoral structure of quasi-PPP projects in terms of private investment (RUB billion). Source data and calculations of the National PPP Center

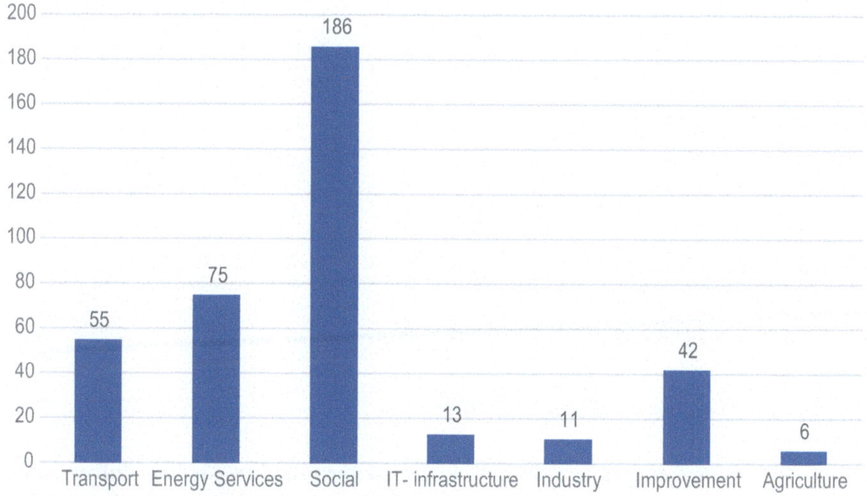

Chart 2.12 Sectoral structure of "quasi-PPP" projects by number of projects. Source data and calculations of the National PPP Center

Table 2.1 Structure of the PPP market by major forms of projects and categories of private investment

	Private investment (RUB billion)	Private investment (%)	Number of projects	Number of projects (%)
Concessions	**1020,5**		**2815**	
Less than 10 mln	3,6	0,4	1939	68,9
10–100 mln	18,5	1,8	524	18,6
100–500 mln	51,5	5,0	208	7,4
500–3000 mln	109,3	10,7	97	3,4
3000–10,000 mln	127,9	12,5	25	0,9
More than 10,000 mln	709,7	69,5	22	0,8
PPP/MPP argreements	**329,21**		**95**	
Less than 10 mln	0,04	0,01	4	4,2
10–100 mln	0,47	0,1	20	21,1
100–500 mln	13,9	4,2	52	54,7
500–3000 mln	8,3	2,5	6	6,3
3000–10,000 mln	41,1	12,5	8	8,4
More than 10,000 mln	265,4	80,6	5	5,3
Quasi-PPP	**832,36**		**380**	
Less than 10 mln	0,45	0,05	88	23,2
10–100 mln	5,21	0,6	124	32,6
100–500 mln	15,5	1,9	64	16,8
500–3000 mln	62,2	7,5	45	11,8
3000–10,000 mln	218,3	26,2	38	10,0
More than 10,000 mln	530,7	63,8	21	5,5

Source Data and calculations of the National PPP Center

– *Expansion of the sectoral scope of PPP*

Not only emergence of projects in new infrastructure sectors, such as information and communication (photo and video recording systems of traffic violations, traffic management systems, parking spaces, smart stops), agriculture, industry, defense and security, but also emergence of new segments within traditional sectors—for example, in transport (port development, construction of transport hubs)—is becoming a remarkable phenomenon (Prosto i chestno 2019).

Traditionally, PPP projects in Russia are implemented in three sectors—transport, social, and communal utilities (including energy, solid waste treatment, and territory

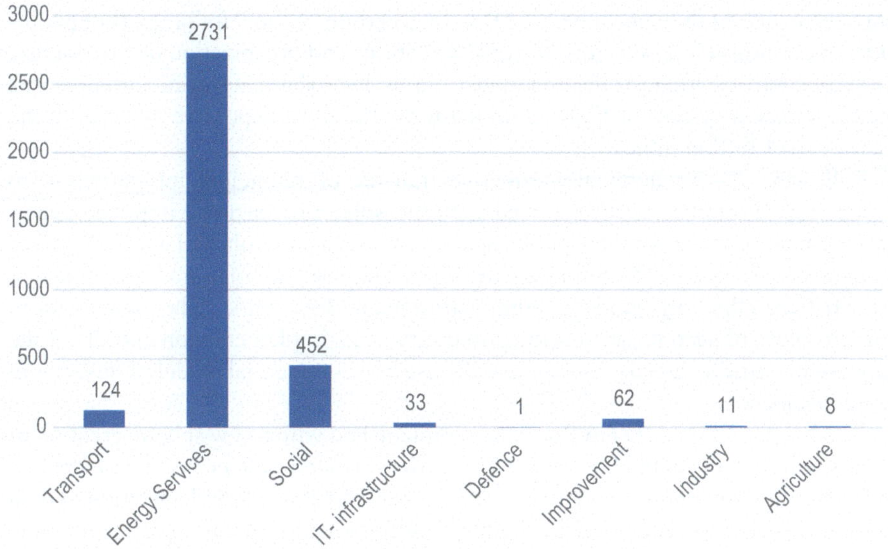

Chart 2.13 Sectoral structure of PPP projects by number of projects

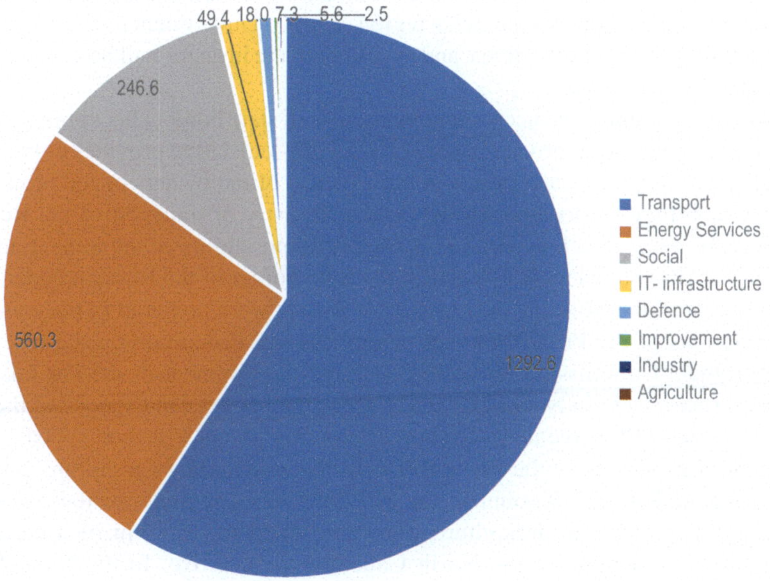

Chart 2.14 Sectoral structure of PPP projects by volume of private investment. Source data and calculations of the National PPP Center

improvement). At the same time, in 2014–15, a certain "boom" for projects of photo-video recording (PVR) systems of traffic violations and organization of road weight and size control started. At the end of 2017 in St. Petersburg, a private initiative was filed to create a system of PVR, claiming to be the most expensive contract in the sector—10.1 billion rubles.

Following the economically effective transfer of municipal infrastructure to concession, a similar practice extended to the sphere of territory improvement—arrangement of embankments, public spaces, parks. In particular, a large PPP agreement on creation of the "Central Park of culture and rest" in Volgograd was signed in 2017 between the Volgograd city administration and JSC "Park". The main factor in attractiveness of such projects is the possibility of its implementation entirely at the expense of extra-budgetary sources and the use of a commercial model of investment reimbursement.

In 2018, the PPP market in Russia was replenished with a new sphere: creation of infrastructure in the field of defense and security. The first such project was launched in 2018 following the introduction of amendments to concession legislation, which made it possible to conclude agreements on infrastructure for storage, keeping and repair of property of the Armed Forces. In September 2018 the Ministry of defense and JSC "Arkhangelsk" signed a concession agreement on construction of a logistics complex for storage, keeping and repair of property of the Armed Forces of the Russian Federation in the Arkhangelsk region. The total investment in construction of the facility will be 15 billion rubles, and expenses of the investor will be compensated by "availability payments".

Currently, investment projects for construction of state border checkpoints are not of commercial interest to private investors, since the legislation provides only for the possibility of equipping such points at the expense of the owners of the infrastructure on which they are located. However, the Ministry of transport of the Russian Federation began to develop a draft Federal law on possibility of implementing PPP projects in relation to checkpoints across the state border of the Russian Federation. The proposals of the Ministry of transport of Russia were prepared in pursuance of the instructions of the Prime Minister of the Russian Federation on the results of the government Commission on socio-economic development of the Far East and the Baikal region held in November 2017. Thus, the market can expect that the first concessions and PPP agreements for border crossing points will soon appear.

In light of expansion of the list of PPP objects by including agriculture, relevant projects were taken into account in the PPP ranking of regions for the first time. In 2017, PPP projects in agriculture were concluded in the form of a corporate partnership. The regions of the North Caucasus were active. In the Republic of Dagestan, two agreements were concluded in regard to the greenhouse complex facilities. At the end of 2017, in the Yamal-Nenets Autonomous district, a concession agreement was concluded in regard to the livestock and agricultural products storage facility—the point of deer slaughter in the Nyda village of the Nadym district.

So, the sectoral scope of PPP projects is gradually expanding due to many reasons: the need to ensure demand and availability of public services, simplification of legislative environment, opening of new niches for cost recovery of PPP projects, and expansion of sectoral lists of objects that can be transferred to private investors.

- *Regional projects provide the largest amount of investment*

Federal projects, despite their scale, are still inferior to regional ones in terms of total investment. At the Federal level, 24 PPP projects with investment volume of 496 billion rubles are being implemented. There are large projects such as the Central ring road, the system of weight and size control "Platon" and others. At the regional level, volume of private investments is more than twice as much—1.3 trillion rubles, also there are much more projects—356. At the municipal level, there is a large number of small projects (3042) with total volume of private investment of 368 billion rubles (Prosto i chestno 2019) (Chart 2.15).

- *PPP market in Russia has a significant potential and therefore will continue to grow dynamically*

We estimate that there are now more than 1000 potential projects at different stages of preparation where PPP mechanisms can be used. The volume of investment planned to be attracted into these projects amounts to more than 3 trillion rubles.

At the stage of initiation, there are such large Federal projects as high-speed railway Yekaterinburg-Chelyabinsk (180 billion rubles of private investments) and deep-water port in Arkhangelsk (123 billion rubles). There are no less large projects

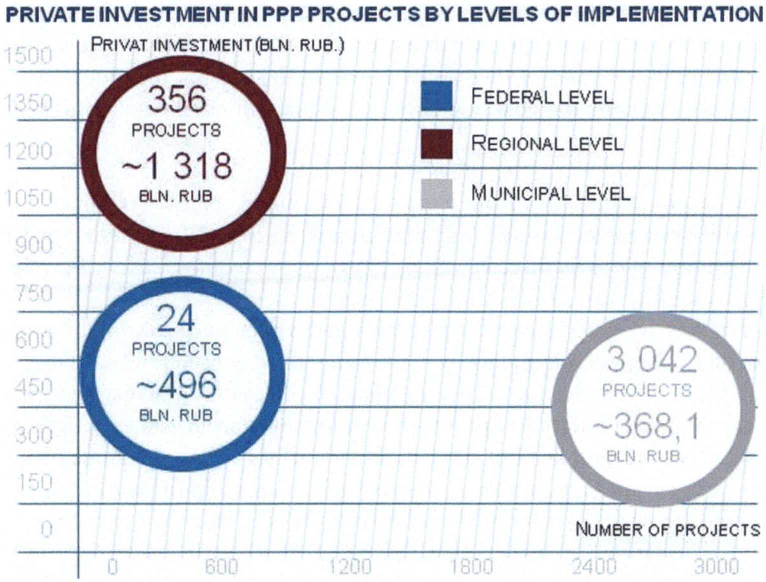

Chart 2.15 PPP projects by levels of implementation. Source data and calculations of the National PPP Center

at the municipal level, for example, modernization of centralized cold water supply and sanitation facilities in Samara city (total investment of 22 billion rubles, 100% private investment).

– *Implementation of "package" solutions for unification and typology of projects*

Unification and typology of PPP projects is an international trend that allows to save resources at the preparatory stage, which is especially important for projects with low capital intensity (small municipal projects in communal services) and/or low profitability (projects in social sphere—schools and kindergartens, primary health care, gerontological centers, and other social service facilities). In recent years, the PPP market in Russia has made significant progress toward standardization of project practices. In particular, Sberbank developed and began to apply "package" solutions for communal utilities sector, and the Fund for development of Khanty-Autonomous District—for schools (Sberbank zapustit 2019).

– *Use of new mechanisms of financing implementation of projects*

Provision of a capital grant (co-financing of part of the costs of creating an infrastructure object at the investment stage) is the mechanism for financing infrastructure projects with "budget leverage" in Russia. Payment mechanisms (private investment reimbursement models) used in PPP projects in Russia can be divided into three groups:

- *direct collection of fees* from users (consumers) and/or other commercial activities—this mechanism is used if payments from the budget at the operational stage are not expected, return on investment is carried out exclusively at the expense of commercial activities of the private investor (this model, like others, may well involve co-financing the cost of creating an object of agreement from the budget at the investment stage).
- *"availability payment"*—the main source of return on investment of a private partner are payments from the budget of the public partner (Concedent). The "availability payment" usually includes compensation of the cost of construction and operation of the facility, as well as ensuring the required level of profitability and covering the cost of servicing debt financing;
- *mixed return on investment model*—this model presumes two main sources of return on investment: payments from the budget and commercial activities (availability fee + consumer fee). This mechanism of return on investment may also include compensation for lost profits (minimum revenue guarantee, MRG), as well as providing a certain level of implementation of services (guarantee of loading) or the right of a private partner to create/retain ownership of part of the property in order to provide commercial services with its help (Ivanov et al. 2018).

In addition, today in Russia a mechanism to protect the investor from the risks of non-repayment of investments is actively used.

– *Significant strengthening of PPP regulatory framework*

In 2014–2016, important amendments to the Federal law "On concession agreements" were adopted, the law on PPP and MPP in Russia was developed and adopted and a new regulatory framework for the PPP law has been formed. Large-scale work to reconstruct PPP legal framework in the regions is under way.

Among important changes in PPP regulatory framework in recent years there are the following:

- IT-objects in concessions and PPP agreements. Since mid-2018, it is possible to conclude concession agreements and PPP agreements for IT-infrastructure facilities in Russia. In fact, this is a small revolution that significantly expands the boundaries of the use of PPP mechanisms (Federal Law № 224-FZ 2019).
- Improvement of tax legislation. In 2017, the practice of submission of tax deductions by concessionaires to the state for the amount of VAT paid at the expense of budgetary funds was abolished. For road concessionaires, the previous tax deduction conditions were restored and extended for another six years until 2022. In relation to concessions in the communal utilities sector re-charging of VAT when converting lease contracts into concession agreements was excluded. In 2018, new procedure of recognition of the grantor's payment obtained in the form of cash for the purposes of taxation for the tax on profit was established. In 2018, the list of cases of obtaining budget financing, in which the taxpayer has no right to reimburse incoming VAT, or is obliged to restore previously deducted VAT, was expanded.
- Regulation of syndicated lending. In 2018, activities to provide the borrower with loan by several co-acting creditors were put under regulation. Under the syndicated loan agreement, several creditors undertake to provide the borrower with funds in the amount and terms stipulated by the agreement for each lender, and the borrower undertakes to return the funds received from the creditors (to pay interest for the use of money and other stipulated payments) (Federal Law №486-FZ "On sindicated loan" of 31.12.2017).
- Regulation of SPIC. In 2017, a new version of rules of conclusion of the special investment contract (SPIC) was approved. It is established that the SPIC may be concluded in respect to an investment project that is already being implemented or is only planned for launch (as well as in respect to a new stage of such a project). Requirements to the investor for the purposes of the conclusion of the SPIC, as well as to the persons involved in the implementation of the project are defined.
- Regulation of municipal solid waste treatment. Obligations of regional authorities to identify regional operators and territorial waste treatment schemes have been approved. The company "Russian ecological operator" (REO) that will formulate proposals for amending legislation, develop projects, issue bonds, buy land, businesses, equipment, and equity of other companies was established. REO will also form a database of best standard projects for the industry, and develop and promote new technologies.

- Improvement of legislation in communal services. In 2016, the subject of the Russian Federation was defined as an independent party to PPP agreement in communal utilities projects (along with the municipality as the Concedent and the investor). A ban on participation of foreign investors in communal utilities projects, possibility of holding a joint (regional-municipal) tender, the right to transfer to concession water, heat and sanitation facilities with unregistered real estate in their composition, etc. were installed. In 2017, the specifics of entering into concession projects of unified heat supply organizations, which were endowed with a preferential right to conclude a concession in respect to heat and water supply facilities in the area of activity of such an organization (without a tender), were determined.
- Improvement of legislation in healthcare. In 2018, the list of cases of participation of public institutions on the side of the Concedent was expanded. It is determined that Federal healthcare institutions will be able to act in concession agreements on the side of the Concedent.
- Improvement of legislation in agriculture. In 2017 (2 years after inclusion of agricultural infrastructure objects in the list of possible concession objects and PPP/MPP), the criteria for relevant objects to be classified as concession or PPP/MPP objects were approved.

– *Creation of the Platform to support infrastructure projects*

In 2015, as a result of implementation of the agreement on information cooperation between the National PPP Center and the Ministry of economic development of Russia, the "ROSINFRA" Platform for supporting infrastructure projects was launched (pppi.ru). The purpose of the Platform is to provide market participants with up-to-date information on the development of PPP mechanisms and projects implemented on the basis of PPP in the regions of the Russian Federation. The key service of the Platform is assistance to find potential partners for implementation of PPP projects. The service was launched within the framework of project initiatives support program implemented by the National PPP Center with support of the Federation Council and the Agency for strategic initiatives. The largest database of PPP projects implemented on the territory of the Russian Federation operates on the ROSINFRA Platform. Moreover, the Platform hosts daily announced tenders for the right to conclude concession agreements and PPP agreements.

– *Russia partly complies with international trends in approaches to PPP governance*

Recently, several interesting trends have emerged in global practices of infrastructure development in general and PPP in particular.

Trend 1. Infrastructure planning.

The practice of infrastructure planning is common in many countries around the world with considerable experience in attracting private investment. A marked increase in the number of countries that use some form of infrastructure planning is a notable trend of recent years.

Trend 2. State support for infrastructure investments.

Against the background of growing interest of global investors to infrastructure assets, many countries, faced with serious underfunding of national infrastructure, introduce additional tools to support relevant projects and increase infrastructure financing. One of the most important areas of support for infrastructure projects is creation of specialized national financial institutions that provide financial support for PPP projects. In particular, creation of specialized infrastructure funds is a significant practice.

Another important tool of state support for infrastructure investment is an increase of budget infrastructure spending. It is noteworthy that many countries use the external debt instrument to increase relevant expenditures.

Trend 3. Further institutionalization of PPP

Institutionalization is an important aspect of public policy in infrastructure and PPP development. In most countries, certain specialized institutions already exist, but vary considerably in terms of organizational structure, autonomy and authority. However, with development of national markets, some countries are revising existing government bodies in favor of greater specialization and empowerment, as well as creating new organizations.

The recent trend is creation of national interdepartmental PPP bodies responsible for one or another aspect of PPP development. The trend is remarkable in the most developed infrastructure markets—as countries accumulate competencies, they shift the focus of infrastructure development governance from the national to the regional level. Such shifts are taking place in Canada and Australia.

Trend 4. Revision of PPP legal support

Another trend over the past year has been the revision of legal framework for public–private partnerships in a number of developing countries. PPP markets in such counties tend to be in their infancy, and legislators and regulators do not yet have the necessary experience. This leads to significant shortcomings in legal security.

Trend 5. Availability fee remains the main mechanism for reimbursement of private investment

Although the possibility of commercializing the demand for infrastructure in PPP is often perceived as a tool to improve budget efficiency, in world practices availability payment is still a key mechanism for reimbursement of private investment. According to a Moody's study published last fall, in terms of the risk of project default, availability payments are significantly safer than direct tolls. Thus, according to the Agency's calculations, on the 10-year horizon after the launch, the probability of default in projects in which the key payment mechanism is a direct toll or so-called "shadow payments" is 13.7%. At the same time, for projects where the main payment mechanism is the availability payment, this probability is only 2.1%.

Trend 6. Infrastructure exports

Against the background of the growing global construction market, including the sphere of public infrastructure, some countries are beginning to actively support "infrastructure exports" of their companies entering foreign tenders.

Some countries are trying to enhance their competitiveness by coordinating and concentrating competencies at the governmental level. Another way is signing of special bilateral agreements, the subject of which may vary from exchange of information to provision to foreign companies from a certain jurisdiction priority an access to infrastructure.

Trend 7. Digitalization of the PPP

Special attention to digitalization of infrastructure market and increasing availability of information is an important trend of recent times. In this regard, for example, many countries launch public electronic portals for disclosure of information on PPP projects, create unified information systems on national infrastructure, etc. Various pre-project support initiatives are being launched at the supranational level through the creation of electronic platforms.

Russia is actively working and has already taken concrete steps to strengthen legal support for PPP, as well as state support for infrastructure investments in the form of funding from the budget. With regard to infrastructure planning, additional institutionalization of PPP, prioritization of availability payment as the main mechanism for reimbursement of private investment and digitalization of PPP in Russia, active work is underway, but specific steps are only being developed. There is no work at all in Russia on infrastructure exports and state support for infrastructure investments through special financial institutions.

Trends	Is Russia in a trend?
Trend 1 Infrastructure planning	
Trend 2 State support for infrastructure investment	
Special financial institutes	
Additional budgetary spending	
Trend 3 Further PPP institutualization	
Trend 4 Strengthening of PPP legal framework	
Trend 5 Availability payment as a key mechanism of reimbursement of private investment	
Trend 6 Infrastructure exports	
Trend 7 Digitalization of PPP	

(continued)

(continued)

Trends	Is Russia in a trend?
Note:	**green color** indicates trends, according to which Russia is actively working and has already taken concrete steps **yellow color** indicates trends, according to which Russia is actively working, but specific steps are only being developed **red color** indicates trends that Russia does not meet

Conclusion

In general, there are reasons to make a conclusion that by the end of 2010-s PPP market in Russia has formed. It operates according to relatively stable rules, steady combinations of players with developed core competencies have taken shape, and implementation of PPP projects has become a widespread and routine practice. In addition, the market coverage has reached a significant scale and continues to expand in different dimensions, including increment of new industry segments, increase of the pool of participants (authorities, investors, operators, financiers, consultants, experts), and growing complexity of contract mechanisms. In terms of project preparation, the PPP market has made a huge breakthrough for the better, as evidenced by the increase in the number of projects and their capital intensity.

At the same time, a number of issues impeding development of the PPP sector remain and therefore require their solution:

- *General problems of "state-business relationship"*

There is still a high level of administrative pressure on business from various state and regulatory bodies, property rights are not sufficiently guaranteed, the practice of merging power with friendly companies and entrepreneurs, giving them a privileged position in the market and creating most favorable conditions to the detriment of other players and in violation of the rules of fair competition is widespread, the judicial system is still far from complete independence in its decisions, widespread corruption in relations between companies and entrepreneurs and officials, low efficiency and opacity of law enforcement agencies continue to be the "birthmarks" of the model of relations between the state and business (Administrativnyj klimat v RF 2017; Biznes pod ugolovnym pressom 2017; Kniga zhalob i predlozhenij 2018; etc.).

- *Systemic problems in the sphere of PPP (disclosed further by category)*

• Further improvement of the regulatory environment

- imperfection of payment mechanisms for financing implementation of concession projects;
- challenging inclusion of the mechanism of minimum guaranteed yield in concession projects;

- challenging inclusion in concession agreements of obligations that depend on the occurrence of certain events, conditions;
- inability to guarantee procurement of services carried out using the object of concession;
- inability to enter into agreements with a plurality of public parties;
- challenging inclusion of certain requirements to the participants of the tender in the framework of prequalification and establishing the ability to confirm such claims by third parties;
- the risk of inability to change the target destination of the object to be transferred to the concessionaire for reconstruction;
- challenging inclusion in a private concession initiative provisions about the payment of the grantor;
- impossibility of compensation to a private initiator who lost concession competition of the costs of developing the initiative;
- imperfection of the norms of Law 224-FZ on security of the object;
- complexity and too long duration of the procedures for assessing effectiveness and determining comparative advantage of PPP project under Law 224-FZ;
- impossibility to use deferred payment mechanism for the launch and implementation of infrastructure projects (TIF);
- need for "liberalization" of the structure of obligatory medical insurance (OMI) tariff and the order of its establishment for PPP projects, the inability to guarantee the volume of medical care provided within PPP projects (Osnovnye tendencii v sfere 2017; Obzor naibolee znachimyh 2019).

• Further institutionalization of PPP

- lack of a single authority at the Federal level, responsible for the development of the PPP,
- lack of a specialized or interagency body responsible for infrastructure development, absence of the Federal project office for PPP development (Gosudarstvenno-chastnoe partnerstvo 2019).

• Establishment of a system of forecasting and planning of infrastructure development

- fragmentation of the infrastructure, and the lack of transparent long-term plans of integrated development of territories, the lack of unified statistics and assessment of infrastructure (Eganyan 2018);

• Launch of special financial support mechanisms for PPP projects (debt financing, project development financing, support measures) (Ivanov 2016; Tkachenko and Ivanov 2018).

In general, in the coming years, we can expect further development of PPP in Russia—both in terms of improving the market conditions and in terms of intensive launch of projects. These trends will be supported by the state's remaining high attention to PPP and the large volume of infrastructure projects being prepared, many of which can be implemented with minimal financial support from the budget (Poslanie Prezidenta 2018; Ob utverzhdenii Kompleksnogo plana 2018; Ob utverzhdenii Strategii 2019).

References

Administrativnyj klimat v RF. Prilozhenie k Dokladu Prezidenta RF. (2017). Upolnomochennyj pri Prezidente Rossijskoj Federacii po zashchite prav predprinimatelej (Administrative climate in Russia. Annex to the Report of the President. Commissioner under the President of the Russian Federation for the protection of the rights of entrepreneurs). Retrieved May 10, 2019, from https://doklad.ombudsmanbiz.ru/2017/pdf/7.pdf.

Biznes pod ugolovnym pressom. Resheniya. Analiticheskij doklad. Doklad Prezidentu RF (2017) Upolnomochennyj pri Prezidente Rossijskoj Federacii po zashchite prav predprinimatelej (Business under criminal pressure. Decisions. Analytical report. Report to the President of the Russian Federation. Commissioner under the President of the Russian Federation for the protection of the rights of entrepreneurs (2017). Retrieved May 11, 2019, from https://doklad.ombudsmanbiz.ru/2017/pdf/4.pdf.

Eganyan A. (2018) Trilliony na razvitie: kak budet rabotat' novyj fond dlya «majskih ukazov» (Trillions on development: how the new Fund for "May decrees" will work: Forbes). Retrieved from May10, 2019, from https://www.forbes.ru/biznes/364095-trilliony-na-razvitie-kak-budet-rabotat-novyy-fond-dlya-mayskih-ukazov.

Federal'nii Zakon № 486-FZ «O sindicirovannom kredite (zajme) i vnesenii izmenenij v otdel'nye zakonodatel'nye akty RF» ot 31.12.2017 (Federal law No. 486-FZ "On syndicated loan" of 31.12.2017). Consultant Plus. Retrieved May 11, 2019, from https://www.consultant.ru/document/cons_doc_LAW_286745/.

Federal'nii zakon ot 13.07.2015 № 224-FZ "O gosudarstvenno-chastnom partnyorstve, munitsipalno-chastnom partnyorstve v Rossiyskoy Federatsii i vnesenii izmenenii v otdelnie zakonodatelnie akti Rossiyskoy Federatsii" (Federal Law no. 224-FZ of July 13, 2015 "On Public-Private Partnership, Municipal-Private Partnership in the Russian Federation and Amendments to Certain Legislative Acts of the Russian Federation"). Retrieved May 10, 2019, from https://www.consultant.ru/document/cons_doc_LAW_182660/.

Federal'nii Zakon ot 21.07.2005. No.115-FZ "O kontsessionnikh soglasheniyakh" (Federal law No. 115-FZ of July 21, 2005 "On Concession agreements"). Retrieved May 10, 2019, from https://www.consultant.ru/document/cons_doc_LAW_54572/.

Gosudarstvenno-chastnoe partnyorstvo (Public-private partnership). Ministry of Economic Development of the Russian Federation. Retrieved May 09, 2019, from https://economy.gov.ru/minec/activity/sections/privgovpartnerdev/index.

InfraONE. (2018). Infrastruktura Rossii: indeks razvitiya (The infrastructure of Russia: development index).

InfraONE. (2019). Investicii v infrastrukturu. Analiticheskij obzor (2019) (Investment in infrastructure. Analytical review).

Ivanov, O. V. (2016). *Teoriya i mirovaya praktika gosudarstvenno-chastnogo partnerstva (Theory and world practice of public-private partnership)* (p. 299). Moscow: MGIMO-University.

Ivanov O.V. Gosudartsvenno-chastnoe partnerstvo kak instrument razvitiya infrastruktury I modernizatsii ekonomiki. Opyt stran Aziatsko-tikhookeanskogo regiona (Public-private partnership as an instrument of development of infrastructure and modernization of economy. Experience of Asia-Pacific countries). Moscow, MGIMO-University, 2019. 300 p.

Kniga zhalob i predlozhenij rossijskogo biznesa. Doklad Prezidentu RF. (2018). (Book of complaints and suggestions of Russian business. Report to the President of the Russian Federation (2018)). Upolnomochennyj pri Prezidente Rossijskoj Federacii po zashchite prav predprinimatelej

(Commissioner under the President of the Russian Federation for the protection of the rights of entrepreneurs). Retrieved May 10, 2019, from https://doklad.ombudsmanbiz.ru/2018/pdf/3.pdf.

Mekhanizmy gosudarstvenno-chastnogo partnyorstva v ekonomicheskoi politike Rossii (Mechanisms of public-private partnership in the economic policy of Russia). (2018). O.V. Ivanov (Ed.). Moscow: MGIMO-University.

Ob utverzhdenii Strategii prostranstvennogo razvitiya do 2025 goda ot 14.02.2019 (2019) (About the approval of the Strategy of spatial development till 2025 of 14.02.2019). Ministry of Economic Development of the Russian Federation. Retrieved May 09, 2019, from https://economy.gov.ru/minec/activity/sections/planning/sd.

Ob utverzhdenii Kompleksnogo plana modernizacii i rasshireniya magistral'noj infrastruktury na period do 2024. (2018). (About the approval of the Comprehensive plan of modernization and expansion of the core infrastructure for the period till 2024 (2018)). Official website of the Government of Russia. Retrieved May 10, 2019, from https://government.ru/docs/34297/.

Obzor naibolee znachimyh sudebnyh sporov v sfere gosudarstvenno-chastnogo partnerstva v 2018 godu.. (2019). (Review of the most significant court disputes in the field of public-private partnership in 2018 (2019)). Law office "Kachkin and partners", Moscow.

Osnovnye tendencii v sfere koncessionnyh soglashenij. Analiz sudebnoj i antimonopol'noj praktiki (2017) (The main trends in the field of concession agreements. Analysis of judicial and antitrust practice (2017)). Law office "Kachkin and partners", Moscow.

Poslanie Prezidenta V.V. Putina Federal'nomu Sobraniyu 01.03.2018 (2018) (Message from President Vladimir Putin to the Federal Assembly of 01.03.2018 (2018)). Official website of the President of Russia. Retrieved May 09, 2019, from https://www.kremlin.ru/events/president/news/56957.

Proekt nacional'nogo doklada o privlechenii chastnyh investicij v razvitie infrastruktury i primenenie mekhanizmov GCHP v RF. Rejting regionov po urovnyu razvitiya GCHP 2017–2018 (2018) (Draft national report on attracting private investment in infrastructure development and application of Public-Private Partnership mechanisms in the Russian Federation). PPP National Development Center.

Prosto i chestno ob investiciyah v infrastrukturu i gosudarstvenno-chastnom partnerstve v Rossii. Analiticheskii obzor. Reiting regionov 2018–19. (Simply and honestly about investments in infrastructure and PPP in Russia. Analytical review. Rating of regions 2018–2019). ROSINFRA. PPP Development Center, 2019.

Sberbank zapustit pervyj v Rossii fond posevnyh investicij v infrastrukturu (2018) (Sberbank will launch Russia's first seed investment Fund in infrastructure (2018)). Economy/state Investments and projects, Vedomosti. Retrieved May 09, 2019, from https://www.vedomosti.ru/economics/articles/2018/11/27/787550-sberbank-fond-posevnih-investitsii.

Tkachenko, M. V., & Ivanov, O. V. (2018). O nekotoryh instrumentah finansovoj podderzhki GCHP-proektov v mirovoj praktike: rekomendacii dlya Rossii (About some instruments of financial support of PPP projects in the world practice: recommendations for Russia) // Ekonomika i upravlenie: problemy, resheniya (Economics and management: problems, solutions), 5: 74–84.

Ukaz Prezidenta Rossiiskoi Federatsii "O nacional'nyh celyah i strategicheskih zadachah razvitiya Rossijskoj Federacii na period do 2024 goda" (2018) (The decree "On the national goals and strategic objectives of development of the Russian Federation for the period up to 2024" of 07.05.2018). Official website of the President of Russia. Retrieved May 09, 2019, from https://kremlin.ru/events/president/news/57425.

World Economic Forum. (2018). The Global Competitiveness Report 2017–2018.

Part II
Regulatory and Legal Framework of PPP in Russia. Forms of PPP in Russian Practices

Chapter 3
Common and Special Legislation on PPP. Comparative Analysis of Federal Law on Concessions (Law-115) and Federal Law on Public-Private and Municipal-Private Partnerships (Law-224)

Elena B. Zavyalova, Agnessa O. Inshakova, and Evgeny Y. Moiseichev

Abstract Basic legal acts of common and special legislation on public-private partnership in Russia and specific features of common and special legislation on public-private partnership are introduced. General schemes of implementation of PPP projects under the Federal law on concession agreements (115-FZ) and the Federal law on PPP (224-FZ) are presented. Based on a comparative analysis of the rules and provisions of 115-FZ and 224-FZ, distinctive features and most important differences of concession agreement and PPP agreement are identified and systematized. On the basis of analysis of the legal framework, specific recommendations on improvement of the federal and regional PPP legal framework are proposed.

Keywords Public-private partnership · PPP governance · PPP policy · Federal law "on concession agreements" (115-FZ) · Federal law "on public-private partnership municipal-private partnership" (224-FZ) · Legislative and regulatory framework

JEL-Codes H44 · K12 · K15 · O21 · R58

E. B. Zavyalova (✉)
Department of Economic Policy and Public-Private Partnership, MGIMO University, Vernadsky Ave., 76, 119454 Moscow, Russia
e-mail: e.zavyalova@inno.mgimo.ru

A. O. Inshakova
Doctor of Law, Department of Civil and Private International Law (the Basic Department of the Southern Scientific Center of the Russian Academy of Sciences), Volgograd State University, Prospekt Universitetskij, 100, 400062 Volgograd, Russia
e-mail: gimchp@volsu.ru; ainshakova@list.ru

E. Y. Moiseichev
Strategic Development, Analytical and Information Support for PPPs, Center for PPP Projects, JSC "Avtodor-invest", Malaya Dmitrovka str., 16/6, 127006 Moscow, Russia
e-mail: moiseichev@pppcenter.ru

O. V. Ivanov and A. O. Inshakova (eds.), *Public-Private Partnerships in Russia*, Competitive Government: Public Private Partnerships,
https://doi.org/10.1007/978-3-030-56352-3_3

Introduction

Federal law No. 115-FZ of July 21, 2005, "On concession agreements" and Federal law No. 224-FZ of July 13, 2015, "On public-private partnership, municipal-private partnership in the Russian Federation" created legal conditions for attracting private investment in infrastructure projects and defined basic provisions of the state policy of Russia in the field of PPP.

At the same time, it is premature to talk about the complete formation of all the necessary institutional and regulatory legal environment at the Federal, regional, and local levels, as well as an effective PPP project management system. PPP Legislation today provides the legal basis for the development of public infrastructure in Russia through the implementation of PPP projects, but there is a sufficient number of "gaps in the law" and law enforcement practice is often characterized by inconsistency and inconsistency. In addition, the problem of administrative, financial, and technical barriers in the implementation of PPP projects has not yet been solved.

Results

PPP Legislative Framework in Russia

The institute of public-private partnership is regulated in the Russian Federation by common and special legislation. Structural composition of the system of common legal acts defining principles and rules of interaction between the state and regulating PPP issues outside of special legislation is presented in the following Chart 3.1.

PPP Special Legal Framework

Specific legislation on PPP in the Russian Federation includes the following:

Federal laws

- The Federal law of July 21, 2005, N 115-FZ "On concession agreements" (115-FZ);
- Federal law No. 224-FZ of July 13, 2015, "On public-private partnership, municipal-private partnership in the Russian Federation and amendments to certain legislative acts of the Russian Federation" (224-FZ);
- Federal law of April 5, 2013, N 44-FZ "On the contract system in the procurement of goods, works and services for state and municipal needs" (44-FZ);
- The Federal law of July 18, 2011, N 223-FZ "About purchases of goods, works, services by separate types of legal entities" (223-FZ).

Legislation/Regulation	Scope of application
The Constitution of the Russian Federation as an act of direct action, containing the following important provisions:	- principles of equality before the law, non-discrimination (art. 19); - prevention of economic activities aimed at monopolization and unfair competition (art. 34); - the possibility of concluding agreements between the Executive authorities of the Federal and regional levels in order to transfer powers from one level to another (article 78), etc.
Administrative legislation (the Code of administrative offences of the Russian Federation)	- regulating activities of public authorities in PPPs the implementation of state policy in the field of public-private partnership, - determining status and competence of RF Executive authorities in relations with a private partner
Civil legislation (Civil code of the Russian Federation, Federal law No. 39-FZ of 25.02.1999 "On investment activities in the Russian Federation carried out in the form of capital investments").	- regulating relations between partners in PPP agreements
Tax legislation - Tax Code	– calculation and payment of VAT, corporate income tax and property tax under concession agreements
Budget legislation - Budget Code	Federal laws on approval of the budget for the
	relevant planning period
Land legislation - Land Code	Land Code, Federal law of 21.12.2004 №172-FZ "On the transfer of land and land plots from one category to another", etc.
Town-planning legislation - Town-planning code	- Town-planning code - establishing requirements for design and construction/reconstruction of the project object
Legislation on public procurement	- regulating procedure for placing public orders for supply of goods, works and services for state (municipal) needs
Legislation on protection of competition - Federal law No. 135-FZ of 26 July 2006 "On protection of competition"	- any alienation of state property shall be carried out by means of tendering (Art. 17.1)
Legislation on tariffs - Federal law of 30.12.2004 №210-FZ "On regulation of tariffs of public utilities»;	- regulation of tariffs of public utilities
Regulatory legal acts regulating the legal regime of certain types of infrastructure	- Federal law of 10.01.2003 17-FZ "On railway transport in RF" - Air code - Federal law No. 257-FZ of 19 July 2011 "On roads and road activities in RF" - Federal law of 08.11.2007 №261-FZ "On sea ports in RF"
Regulatory legal acts establishing requirements for operation of facilities	for example, safety, environmental protection, use of cultural and natural heritage sites, land

Chart 3.1 System of common legal acts regulating PPP

Regional legislation

Prior to the adoption of Federal law No. 224-FZ "On public-private partnership, municipal-private partnership in the Russian Federation" (hereinafter—224-FZ), the subjects of the Russian Federation independently adopted and developed regional laws[1]. In total, about 70 regional PPP laws had been adopted.

On July 13, 2015, Law 224-FZ, which established a unified regulation of PPP at the Federal level, was adopted. 224-FZ obliged all subjects of the Russian Federation to put regional PPP legislation in full compliance with provisions of 224-FZ by January 1, 2025 *(Law on public-private partnership: the application's manual./PPP development center. M., 2015).*

Federal Law No. 115-FZ "On Concession Agreements". Basic Provisions and Key Features

In accordance with Law 115-FZ, under concession agreement a private partner (concessionaire) undertakes to construct/reconstruct at his own expense property the ownership of which belongs to a public partner (Concedent), to carry out activities with the use (operation) of the object, and the Concedent undertakes to grant the concessionaire for the period established under agreement, the right of possession, and use of the object for the performance of these activities (Federal law 115-FZ "On concession agreements" of July 21, 2005).

The specifics of this form of public-private partnership are to preserve the title of the object under agreement with the public party (Practice of using concession agreements for the development of regional infrastructure in Russia./PPP development center. Moscow, 2014).

The distinctive features of concession as a tool to attract investment in infrastructure include the following:

- contractual basis of partnership and long-term character of interaction regulated by the Federal legislation;
- object of concession is Federal, regional, or municipal property;
- possibility of payments of the concessionaire to the state for possession and use of the object (so-called "concession fee") or structuring concession transactions with the Concedent's fee;
- financial participation of the private partner in capital expenditures, that is, in construction/reconstruction of the object under agreement;

[1]In particular, the Law "On the participation of St. Petersburg in public-private partnerships" was adopted in 2006. It gives the following definition of PPP (item 1.1 of Art. 4): "Public-private partnership is a mutually beneficial cooperation of St. Petersburg with the Russian or foreign legal entity or natural person, or acting without formation of legal entity under the agreement of simple partnership (the agreement on joint activity) Association of legal entities in implementation of socially significant projects which is performed by the conclusion and execution of agreements, including concession".

- transfer of possession and use rights only to the private partner, while retaining ownership with the public partner;
- guarantees of the rights of the concessionaire provided by the state.

115-FZ defines participants (parties) of the concession agreement:

(1) the Concedent—the Russian Federation (on behalf of which the Government of the Russian Federation or the Federal Executive authority authorized by it acts), or the subject of the Federation, or municipality;
(2) concessionaire—an individual entrepreneur, Russian, or foreign legal entity or acting without a legal entity under a partnership agreement (joint venture agreement) two or more of these legal entities (№115-FZ, Art. 5P.1).

In accordance with Article 8 of 115-FZ, the Concedent bears certain rights and obligations, presented in Table 3.1.

Under the agreement, the Concedent may also be subject to some other obligations, including

- payment of the Concedent's fees (amendments to 115-FZ of July 21, 2014);
- approval of the maximum fare of toll roads (amendments to 115-FZ of February 28, 2014);
- to provide guarantees to financing organizations.

According to part 2 of Art. 8, the concessionaire in the performance of the concession agreement is obliged to

Table 3.1 Rights and obligations of the Concedent under Law 115-FZ

Rights	Obligations
To provide to the concessionaire rights of possession and use of the property owned by the Concedent	To grant to the concessionaire, for the period specified in the agreement, the rights of possession and use of the object under agreement to carry out activities under agreement
To assume part of the costs for construction/reconstruction of the object under concession agreement, as well as the use (operation) of the object	To perform other obligations under agreement (based on the freedom of contract), not contrary to the law
To provide budget guarantees	
To assume obligations on preparation of the territory necessary for construction/reconstruction of object under agreement for the implementation of activities under agreement	
To control the concessionaire's compliance with the terms of the agreement in accordance with the Federal law	

(1) carry out construction/reconstruction of the under agreement and start its operation in the terms established under agreement;
(2) use (operate) the object under agreement for the purposes and in the manner established by the concession agreement;
(3) ensure, when implementing activities under agreement, possibility of obtaining of relevant goods, work, services by consumers;
(4) provide to consumers privileges established by Federal laws, laws of the subject of the Russian Federation, regulatory legal acts of local government, including privileges on payment of goods, works, and services in cases and in the order which are established under the concession agreement;
(5) maintain the object under agreement in good condition, carry out at his own expense current and major repair, and bear maintenance costs of the object.

General features concession agreement is presented under Russian PPP legislation are presented in Chart 3.2.

Federal Law No. 224-FZ "On Public-Private Partnership, Municipal-Private Partnership in the Russian Federation…". Basic Provisions and Key Features

Prior to January 1, 2016, PPP agreements were concluded in the subjects of the Russian Federation on the basis of regional laws. As of December 31, 2015, more than 70 regional PPP laws were adopted in the regions and about 100 projects based on these legal acts were implemented. Basically, these were projects in which the private partner assumes obligations to construct and maintain an infrastructure object, and the public partner transfers to him land plots and subsequently gradually buys out the created object or rents it for the purpose of performing certain public functions. This model of implementation of PPP projects had a number of restrictions at the level of Federal legislation, which significantly reduced possibility and attractiveness of its application.

To eliminate existing restrictions related to the implementation of PPP projects under regional laws, 224-FZ was developed and adopted. The law established at the Federal level unified PPP legal regulation, single conceptual device, universal terminology, including the term "public-private partnership", unified rights and obligations of the parties under agreement, fixed mechanisms of protection of interests of private partners, widened possibilities for project structuring by expanding a range of contractual models, and legitimization of alternative forms of PPP project implementation ("quasi-PPP") in the Russian Federation (the Federal law 224-FZ of July 13, 2015) (Inshakova Agnessa et al. 2019).

The PPP agreement is a civil law agreement between a public partner and a private partner, concluded for a period of not less than 3 years in the manner and on the terms established by 224-FZ.

General scheme of realization

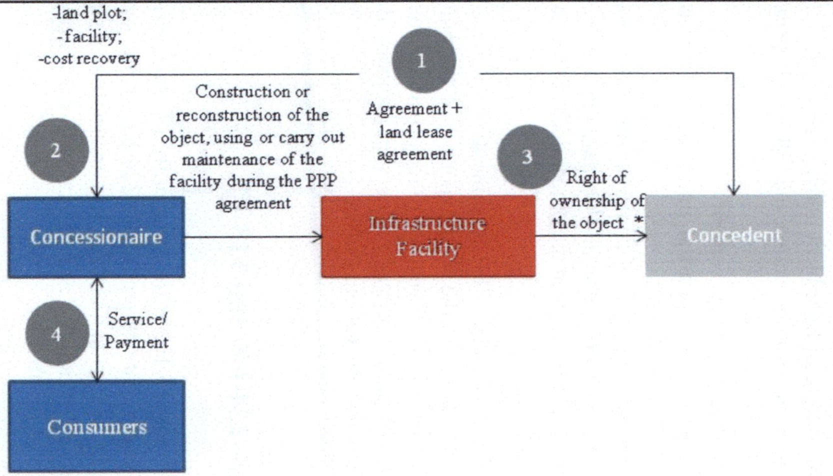

Eligible infrastructure

- heat and water supply, sanitation
- facilities for production, transmission and distribution of electricity and heat;
- roads
- subway and other public transport;
- railway transport;
- pipeline transport;
- sea and river ports; hydraulic structures;
- airports and related infrastructure;
- health, education, culture, sports, tourism, sanatorium and resort health treatment;
- solid waste treatment facilities;
- objects of improvement of territories;
- objects of social service;
- objects of production, processing and storage of agricultural products;
- buildings and constructions for warehousing, storage and repair of property of the Armed Forces of the Russian Federation
- ICT infrastructure (including software, databases, information systems); data center

Specifics of application

- ownership of infrastructure in question remains with Concedent (right of priority redemption in case of privatization is possible)
- guarantees of minimum income and compensation of the investor's costs in case of various events;
- compensation of expenses incurred by Concedent, to construct and/or maintain infrastructure including payment of expected returns and debt servicing fees
- no risks of Concedent's default on expenditure commitments;
- obligatory use of infrastructure by Concessionaire

Chart 3.2 General features of concession agreement under Federal law 115-FZ

According to part 1 of Article. 12 of 224-FZ, under the PPP agreement, the private partner undertakes to create, in whole or in part, at the expense of its own or borrowed funds, real estate or real estate and movable property that is technologically related to each other[2] and intended to carry out activities under the agreement, and to carry out operation/maintenance of such property; a public partner undertakes to provide the private partner with the right to own and use the object for implementation of the activities specified in the agreement and to ensure the emergence of the private partner's ownership of the object under agreement, subject to the requirements provided for under 224-FZ and the agreement (Inshakova Agnessa et al. 2019).

General scheme of implementation, features of application, as well as eligible infrastructure facilities for which a PPP agreement can be concluded are presented in Chart 3.3.

The Law 224-FZ

- construction and/or reconstruction by a private partner;
- full or partial financing of the construction of the facility;
- operation and/or maintenance;
- emergence of a private partner's ownership of the object under agreement.
- Also, by the will of the parties, the agreement may include the following optional elements:
- design by the private partner of the object of the agreement;
- implementation by the private partner of full or partial financing of operation and/or maintenance of the facility under agreement;
- provision by the public partner of partial financing of construction of the object under agreement, as well as financing of its operation and/or maintenance;
- private partner's obligations on subsequent transfer of the object under agreement to the ownership of the public partner.

formulated the following mandatory elements of the PPP agreement:

The last of the above elements is mandatory if the total expenses of the public partner for construction of the facility will be higher than those of the private partner's (Recommendations for implementation of public-private partnership projects. Best practices/Ministry of economic development of Russia, 2016).

Comparative Analysis of Laws 224-FZ and 115-FZ

The key difference between 224-FZ and 115-FZ is the possibility of transferring ownership of an infrastructure object to a private partner under 224-FZ. At the same time, the investor is obliged to provide full or partial financing for construction of such infrastructure and operation of the facility strictly in accordance with the purpose, which is registered as an encumbrance of the facility.

---

[2]With the exception of ICT facilities.

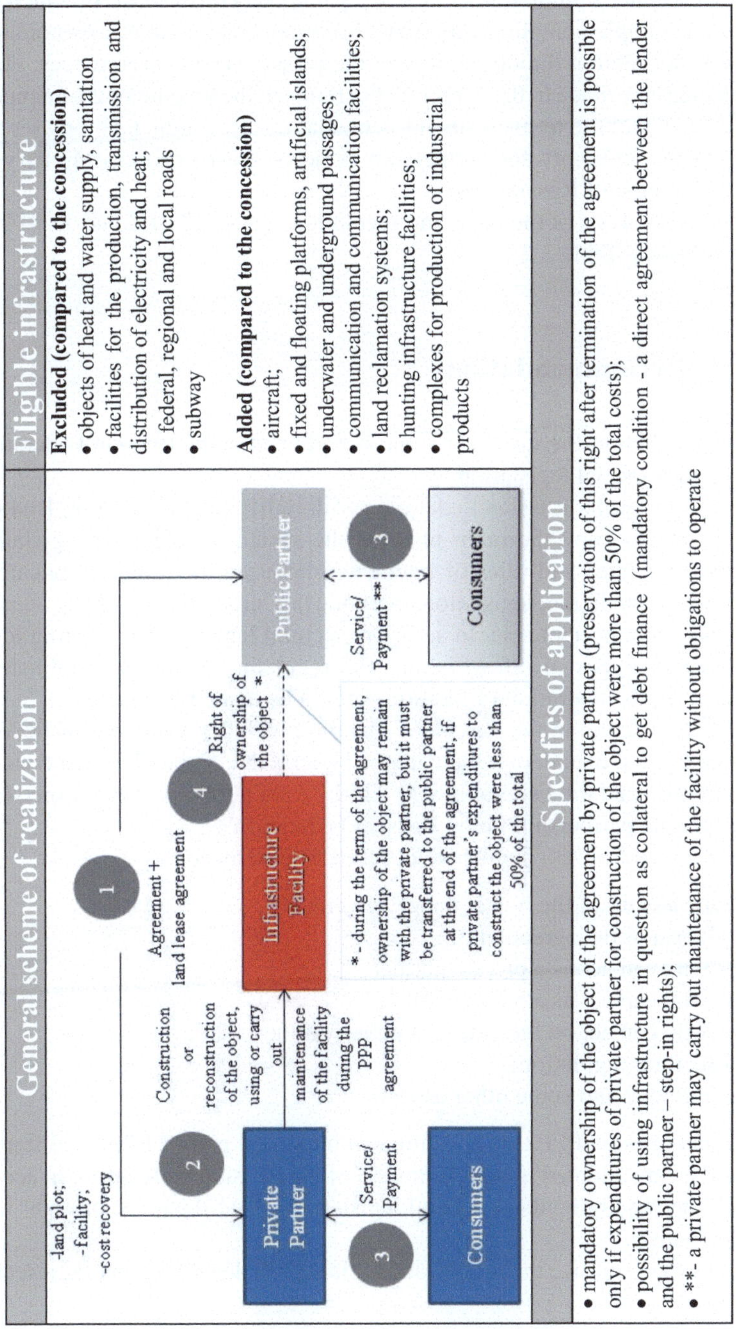

Chart 3.3 General features of PPP/MPP agreements under Federal law 224-FZ

In the interests of the investors, the PPP Law and the Law on concessions provide a mechanism to guarantee immutability of the key parameters on the basis of which the decision on project implementation was made. In case of changes in macroeconomic conditions or in legislation directly affecting the project (taxes, preferences, etc.), reasonable changes are made to the agreement in terms of the amount of co-financing by the public party and the terms of its implementation (Recommendations for the implementation of public-private partnership projects. Best practices/Ministry of economic development of Russia, 2016).

A comparative analysis of the rules and regulations under 224-FZ and 115-FZ is given in the following Table 3.2.

Conclusions/Recommendations

- The institute of Public-Private Partnership is regulated in the Russian Federation by common and special legislation.
- The Constitution of the Russian Federation, Administrative, Civil, Tax, Budget, and Land Codes occupy the main place in the system of common legislation defining the principles and rules of interaction between the state and business. Urban planning legislation, legislation on public procurement, and tariffs legislation also play an important role. In addition, sectoral legislation regulating legal regime of certain types of infrastructure and regulatory legal acts establishing requirements for the operation of facilities should be taken into account.
- Special PPP legislation in the Russian Federation includes a number of Federal and regional laws, the main of which are the Federal law № 115-FZ "On concession agreements" and the Federal law № 224-FZ "On public-private partnership, municipal-private partnership in the Russian Federation".
- 224-FZ and 115-FZ have a number of differences in terms of
  - private ownership of the object under agreement;
  - minimal term of the agreement;
  - persons who can act as a private partner;
  - persons who can act as a public partner;
  - persons who can act on the side of a public partner;
  - special sectoral regulation;
  - private initiative and some other aspects.
- Also, regional laws on PPP that constitute an important part of PPP legal framework in Russia are adopted in all 85 subjects of the Russian Federation. In accordance with the requirements of federal legislation, all of them are brought into compliance with it.
- In order to further improve the federal and regional PPP legal framework, it seems desirable to

Table 3.2 Comparative analysis of the rules and regulations under 224-FZ and 115-FZ

Comparison parameter	Concession Law (115-FZ)	Law on PPP (224-FZ)
Private ownership of the object under agreement	Possible solely on the side of the Concedent (public partner). The object under agreement can be purchased by the concessionaire in case of inclusion in the priority privatization program after the expiration of the agreement	Possible on the side of a private partner. The object should be transferred to the ownership of the public partner if capital investments of the public party in its construction exceed 50% of the total cost of the object
Minimum duration of the agreement	Not set	3 years
Objects of the agreement	Close-end list of objects is established	
Private partner	Russian or foreign legal entity or a group of persons (consortium) acting without formation of a legal entity under a partnership agreement	Russian or foreign legal entity, in which the share of state control cannot be more than 50%
Public partner	– The Russian Federation, the subject of the Russian Federation or the municipality, on behalf of which the Government of the Russian Federation, the Federal Executive authority, public authority of the subject of the Russian Federation, local government act respectively	The Russian Federation, the subject of the Russian Federation or municipality on behalf of which – the Government of the Russian Federation, Federal Executive authority; – executive body of the subject of the Russian Federation, – the head of the municipality or other authorized local self-government body act respectively
Possible actors on the side of the public partner	Bodies and legal entities, including the state company "Russian roads", as well as state budgetary institutions, state, or municipal unitary enterprises (for certain types of objects)	Bodies and legal entities specified in the 224-FZ, including budgetary institutions and unitary enterprises (on all types of objects; on separate rights and duties the list of which is established by the Government of the Russian Federation)
Sectoral regulation	With regard to heat supply facilities, centralized hot water supply, cold water supply, or sanitation	Not set

(continued)

Table 3.2 (continued)

Comparison parameter	Concession Law (115-FZ)	Law on PPP (224-FZ)
Private initiative (unsolicited proposal)	Provided (duration of the consideration ~ up to 150 days)	Provided (duration of the consideration ~ up to 400 days)
Authorized bodies under the law	Not directly provided	Directly provided at the Federal, regional, and local levels
Evaluating effectiveness and comparative advantage of project implementation	Not provided	Provided and carried out by the authorized body (in case of the project of the municipal level—the regional authorized body) within a period not exceeding 90 days
Tender	Two-stage (preliminary selection and evaluation of bids) regulated in detail	
Standard or model forms of agreements	Approximate forms of the agreement are established	Absent

- collect and compile information on positions of participants of the PPP market on the problematic issues of PPP regulation;
- develop proposals on further improvement of PPP legal framework and to send them to the relevant authorized bodies of state power;
- participate in the activities of advisory and other working bodies established under the Federal bodies of state power on the improvement of PPP legal framework;
- organize and hold workshops, round tables, and other events involving representatives of Federal and regional authorities as well as of expert community;
- develop draft legal and regulatory acts, conduct anti-corruption expertise of draft legal acts.

References

Belitskaia, A. V. (2012). *Pravovoe regulirovanie gosudarstvenno-chastnogo partnyorstva (Legal regulation of public-private partnership)* (p. 2012). Moscow: Statut.

Blashentsev, B. O. (2017). *Problemy pravovogo regulirovaniya gosudarstvenno-chastnogo partnyorstva. (Problems of legal regulation of public-private partnership).* Territory of science. №4

Conclusion and use of concession agreements. Center for Development of PPP. (2017). http://pppcenter.ru/assets/files/relegal_broshure_final_pages.pdf. Accessed 10 March 2019.

Decree of the Government of the Russian Federation of December 19, 2013 No. 1188 "On approval of requirements for a bank guarantee provided in the event that the object of a concession agreement is heat supply facilities, centralized hot water supply systems, cold water supply and (or) water disposal, certain objects of such systems" (with and additions). GUARANTOR (no date). http://base.garant.ru/70543348/. Accessed 7 June 2019.

Decree of the Government of the Russian Federation of December 19, 2015 No. 1386 "On approving the form of a proposal for implementing a public-private partnership project or a municipal-private partnership project, as well as information requirements contained in a proposal for implementing a public-private partnership project or a municipal-private partnership project". GUARANTOR (no date). http://base.garant.ru/71288558/. (Accessed 7 June 2019)

Delmom, J., & Delmon, V. R. (Eds.) (2013). *International project finance and public-private partnerships*. A Legal Guide to Key Growth Markets.

Diaz, G. R. (2017). The contractual and administrative regulation of public-private partnership. *Utilities Policy 48*, 109–121. https://doi.org/10.1016/j.jup.2016.04.011

Eberhard, A. (2007). Infrastructure regulation in developing countries: an exploration of hybrid and transitional models. 41733. *The World Bank*, pp. 1–47. http://documents.worldbank.org/curated/en/528801468176332574/Infrastructure-regulation-in-developing-countries-an-exploration-of-hybrid-and-transitional-models. (Accessed 7 June 2019).

EBRD. (2007). *Law in Transition 2007: Public-private partnerships and legal reform in Russia (2007)*. https://www.ebrd.com/documents/legal-reform/law-in-transition-2007-publicprivate-partnerships.pdf (Accessed: 7 June 2019).

EBRD. (2012). *Concession. PPP Laws Assessment 2011: Cover Analysis Report*. https://www.ebrd.com/downloads/legal/concessions/pppreport.pdf. (Accessed 7 June 2019).

Egorov, E. V., & Minina, I. S. (2018). Pravovoe regulirovanie gosudarstvenno-chastnogo partnyorstva (Legal regulation of public- private partnerships)/ Gosudarstvennnoe upravlenie. Elektonniy vestnik. June № 68.

Evaluating the environment for public- private partnerships in Eastern Europe and the Commonwealth of Independent States (EECIS). Public private partnership (no date). https://ppp.worldbank.org/public-private-partnership/library/evaluating-environment-publicprivate-partnerships-eastern-europe-and-commonwealth-independe. (Accessed 7 June 2019).

Farquharson, E., et al. (2011). *How to engage with the private sector in public-private partnerships in emerging markets*. Washington, DC: World Bank Publications.

Federal'nyj zakon "O gosudarstvenno-chastnom partnerstve, municipal'no-chastnom partnerstve v Rossijskoj Federacii i vnesenii izmenenij v otdel'nye zakonodatel'nye akty Rossijskoj Federacii" ot 13.07.2015 N 224-FZ. (Federal Law No. 224-FZ of July 13, 2015 "On Public-Private Partnership, Municipal-Private Partnership in the Russian Federation and Amendments to Certain Legislative Acts of the Russian Federation"). https://base.garant.ru/71129190/. Accessed 10 March 2019.

Federal'nyj zakon "O koncessionnyh soglasheniyah" ot 21.07.2005 N 115-FZ (Federal law No. 115-FZ of July 21, 2005 "On Concession agreements"). https://base.garant.ru/12141176/. (Accessed 10 March 2019).

Fostering investment in infrastructure – OECD. (no date). http://www.oecd.org/investment/investment-policy/fostering-infrastructure-investment.htm. (Accessed 7 June 2019)

Gosudarstvenno-chastnoe partnerstvo: ponyatie i perspektivy sovershenstvovaniya zakonodatel'nogo regulirovaniya, Aktual'nye problemy social'no-ekonomicheskogo razvitiya Rossii (2010) (Public-Private Partnership: Understanding and Prospects for Improving Legislative Regulation, Actual Problems of Russia's Socio-Economic Development (2010)). http://pppcenter.ru/29/novosti/smi-o-centre/19032010.html. Accessed 7 June 2019.

Government Decree of 03.12.2015 N 1309 "On approval of the Rules for the authorized body to conduct negotiations related to the consideration of the proposal to implement a public-private partnership project, a municipal-private partnership project to assess the project's effectiveness and determine its comparative advantage". GUARANTOR (no date). http://base.garant.ru/71267332/. (Accessed 7 June 2019).

Government Decree of 04.12.2015 N 1322 "On approval of the Rules for the preliminary selection of bidders for the right to conclude an agreement on public-private partnership, an agreement on municipal-private partnership". GUARANTOR (no date). http://base.garant.ru/71270104/. (Accessed 7 June 2019).

Government Decree of 12.12.2015 N 1366 "On approval of a list of individual rights and obligations of a public partner that can be exercised by its authorized bodies and (or) legal entities in accordance with federal laws, other regulatory legal acts of the Russian Federation, regulatory legal acts of constituent entities of the Russian Federation, municipal legal acts".

GUARANTOR (no date). http://base.garant.ru/71280918/. (Accessed 7 June 2019)

Government Decree of 30.12.2015 N 1514 "On the procedure for the authorized body to assess the effectiveness of a public-private partnership project, a municipal-private partnership project and determine their comparative advantage" (with amendments and additions). GUARANTOR (no date). Available at: http://base.garant.ru/71296434/. (Accessed 7 June 2019).

Guidebook on PPP Frameworks in the APEC Region. (2015). https://apec.org:443/Publications/2015/07/Guidebook-on-PPP-Frameworks-in-the-APEC-Region. (Accessed 7 June 2019).

Guasch, J. L., Laffont, J.-J., & Straub S. (2006). Renegotiation of concession contracts: A theoretical approach. In: *Review of Industrial Organization 29*(1–2), 55–73. https://doi.org/10.1007/s11151-006-9109-5

Inshakova Agnessa, O., & Goncharov Alexander, I. (2019). Innovation as an integral condition for the development of modern foreign trade turnover of energy resources and its legal regulation. In: O. V. Inshakov, A. O. Inshakova, E. G. Popkova (Eds.*), Energy sector: A systemic analysis of economy, foreign trade and legal regulations* (pp. 67–78). Cham: Springer Science + Business Media.

Inshakova Agnessa, Alexander Goncharov, Vladimira Dolinskaya, & Alla Kalinina. (2019). Corporate conflicts in the system of public relations, law, and legislation of the russian federation. In: E. G. Popkova (Ed.) *«Conflict-Free» socio-economic systems* (pp. 75–88). Emerald Publishing Limited.

Ivanov, O. V. (2016). *Teoriya i mirovaya praktika gosudarstvenno-chastnogo partnerstva (Theory and world practice of public-private partnership).* Moscow: MGIMO-University.

Ivanov, O. V., & Ivanova, A. O. (2019). *Gosudarstvenno-chastnoe patnerstvo v stranakh Aziatsko-tikhookeanskogo regiona (Public-private partnership in the countries of Asia-Pacific region)* (p. 270). Moscow: MGIMO-University.

Law on public-private partnership: the application's manual (2015). PPP development center. Moscow.

Marques, R. C., & Berg, S. (2010). Revisiting the strengths and limitations of regulatory contracts in infrastructure industries. *Journal of Infrastructure Systems, 16*(4), 334–342. https://doi.org/10.1061/(asce)is.1943-555x.0000029.

Marique Y. (2014). *Public-private partnerships and the law: Regulation, institutions and community* (p. 305). Edward Elgar Publishing Ltd. https://doi.org/10.4337/9781781004555.

Mekhanizmy gosudarstvenno-chastnogo partnyorstva v ekonomicheskoi politike Rossii (Mechanisms of public-private partnership in the economic policy of Russia). Ed. by O.V.Ivanov. MGIMO-University, Moscow. 2018. 409 p.

Postanovlenie Pravitel'stva RF ot 3 dekabrya 2015 g. N 1309 "Ob utverzhdenii Pravil provedeniya upolnomochennym organom peregovorov, svyazannyh s rassmotreniem predlozheniya o realizacii proekta gosudarstvenno-chastnogo partnerstva, proekta municipal'no-chastnogo partnerstva na predmet ocenki effektivnosti proekta i opredeleniya ego sravnitel'nogo preimushchestva" (Government Decree of 03.12.2015 N 1309 "On approval of the Rules for the authorized body to conduct negotiations related to the consideration of the proposal to implement a public-private partnership project, a municipal-private partnership project to assess the project's effectiveness and determine its comparative advantage"). GUARANTOR (no date). http://base.garant.ru/71267332/. (Accessed 7 June 2019).

Postanovlenie Pravitel'stva RF ot 4 dekabrya 2015 g. N 1322 "Ob utverzhdenii Pravil provedeniya predvaritel'nogo otbora uchastnikov konkursa na pravo zaklyucheniya soglasheniya o gosudarstvenno-chastnom partnerstve, soglasheniya o municipal'no-chastnom partnerstve" (Government Decree of 04.12.2015 N 1322 "On approval of the Rules for the preliminary selection of bidders for the right to conclude an agreement on public-private partnership, an agreement on municipal-private partnership"). GUARANTOR (no date). http://base.garant.ru/71270104/. (Accessed 7 June 2019).

Postanovlenie Pravitel'stva RF ot 12 dekabrya 2015 g. N 1366 "Ob utverzhdenii perechnya otdel'nyh prav i obyazannostej publichnogo partnera, kotorye mogut osushchestvlyat'sya upolnomochennymi im organami i (ili) yuridicheskimi licami v sootvetstvii s federal'nymi zakonami, inymi normativnymi pravovymi aktami Rossijskoj Federacii, normativnymi pravovymi aktami sub"ektov Rossijskoj Federacii, municipal'nymi pravovymi aktami" (Government Decree of 12.12.2015 N 1366 "On approval of a list of individual rights and obligations of a public partner that can be exercised by its authorized bodies and (or) legal entities in accordance with federal laws, other regulatory legal acts of the Russian Federation, regulatory legal acts of constituent entities of the Russian Federation Federation, municipal legal acts"). GUARANTOR (no date). http://base.garant.ru/71280918/. (Accessed 7 June 2019).

Postanovlenie Pravitel'stva RF ot 30 dekabrya 2015 g. N 1514 "O poryadke provedeniya upolnomochennym organom ocenki effektivnosti proekta gosudarstvenno-chastnogo partnerstva, proekta municipal'no-chastnogo partnerstva i opredeleniya ih sravnitel'nogo preimushchestva" (s izmeneniyami i dopolneniyami) (Government Decree of 30.12.2015 N 1514 "On the procedure for the authorized body to assess the effectiveness of a public-private partnership project, a municipal-private partnership project and determine their comparative advantage" (with amendments and additions)). GUARANTOR (no date). Available at: http://base.garant.ru/71296434/. (Accessed 7 June 2019).

Postanovlenie Pravitel'stva RF ot 11 maya 2017 g. N 558 "Ob osobennostyah provedeniya sovmestnogo konkursa na pravo zaklyucheniya koncessionnogo soglasheniya, ob"ektom kotorogo yavlyayutsya ob"ekty teplosnabzheniya, centralizovannye sistemy goryachego vodosnabzheniya, holodnogo vodosnabzheniya i (ili) vodootvedeniya, otdel'nye ob"ekty takih sistem" (s izmeneniyami i dopolneniyami) (Resolution of the Government of the Russian Federation of 05/11/2017 N 558 "On the peculiarities of holding a joint competition for the right to enter into a concession agreement, the object of which are heating facilities, centralized hot water systems, cold water supply and (or) water disposal, certain objects of such systems")). GUARANTOR (no date). http://base.garant.ru/71674534/. (Accessed: 7 June 2019).

Postanovlenie Pravitel'stva RF ot 19 dekabrya 2015 g. N 1387 "O poryadke napravleniya publichnomu partneru zayavleniya o namerenii uchastvovat' v konkurse na pravo zaklyucheniya soglasheniya o gosudarstvenno-chastnom partnerstve, soglasheniya o municipal'no-chastnom partnerstve" (Resolution of the Government of the Russian Federation of 12.19.2015 N 1387 "On the procedure for sending to the public partner a statement of intent to participate in the competition for the right to conclude an agreement on public-private partnership, an agreement on municipal-private partnership"). GUARANTOR (no date). http://base.garant.ru/71287608/. (Accessed 7 June 2019).

Postanovlenie Pravitel'stva RF ot 19 dekabrya 2015 g. N 1388 "Ob utverzhdenii Pravil rassmotreniya publichnym partnerom predlozheniya o realizacii proekta gosudarstvenno-chastnogo partnerstva ili proekta municipal'no-chastnogo partnerstva" (Resolution of the Government of the Russian Federation of December 19, 2015 N 1388 "On approval of the Rules for consideration by a public partner of a proposal to implement a public-private partnership project or a municipal-private partnership project"). GUARANTOR (no date). http://base.garant.ru/71287612/. (Accessed 7 June 2019).

Postanovlenie Pravitel'stva RF ot 24 aprelya 2014 g. N 368 "Ob utverzhdenii Pravil predostavleniya antimonopol'nym organom soglasiya na izmenenie uslovij koncessionnogo soglasheniya" (s izmeneniyami i dopolneniyami) (Resolution of the Government of the Russian Federation of April 24, 2014 N 368 "On Approval of the Rules by the Antimonopoly Authority to Consent to Amendment of the Terms of the Concession Agreement" (with amendments and additions)). GUARANTOR (no date). http://base.garant.ru/70645088/. (Accessed 7 June 2019).

Postanovlenie Pravitel'stva RF ot 31 marta 2015 g. N 300 "Ob utverzhdenii formy predlozheniya o zaklyuchenii koncessionnogo soglasheniya s licom, vystupayushchim s iniciativoj zaklyucheniya koncessionnogo soglasheniya" (Resolution of the Government of the Russian Federation of March 31, 2015 N 300 "On approval of the form of a proposal to conclude a concession agreement with a person initiating a concession agreement") GUARANTOR (no date). http://base.garant.ru/709 41052/. (Accessed 7 June 2019).

PPP Reference Guide 3.0. Public private partnership (2017). https://ppp.worldbank.org/public-pri vate-partnership/library/ppp-reference-guide-3-0. (Accessed 7 June 2019).

Praktika primeneniya koncessionnyh soglashenij dlya razvitiya regional'noj infrastruktury v Rossii (2014). (Practice of using concession agreements for the development of regional infrastructure in Russia. PPP development center. Moscow. 2014.). http://pppcenter.ru/assets/docs/ppp+.pdf. (Accessed 10 March 2019).

Prikaz Ministerstva ekonomicheskogo razvitiya RF ot 20 noyabrya 2015 g. № 863 "Ob utverzhdenii poryadka provedeniya peregovorov, svyazannyh s rassmotreniem predlozheniya o realizacii proekta gosudarstvenno-chastnogo partnerstva, proekta municipal'no-chastnogo partnerstva, mezhdu publichnym partnerom i iniciatorom proekta" (Order of the Ministry of Economic Development of the Russian Federation of November 20, 2015 No. 863 "On approval of the procedure for conducting negotiations related to the consideration of a proposal on the implementation of a public-private partnership project, a municipal-private partnership project between a public partner and a project initiator" (no date)). http://www.garant.ru/products/ipo/prime/doc/ 71182664/. (Accessed 7 June 2019).

Prikaz Ministerstva ekonomicheskogo razvitiya ot 30 noyabrya 2015 goda N 894 "Ob utverzhdenii Metodiki ocenki effektivnosti proekta gosudarstvenno-chastnogo partnerstva, proekta municipal'no-chastnogo partnerstva i opredeleniya ih sravnitel'nogo preimushchestva" (Order of the Ministry of Economic Development of Russia of November 30, 2015 No. 884 "On approval of the Methodology for evaluating the effectiveness of a public-private partnership project, a municipal-private partnership project and determining their comparative advantage". (no date)). http://docs.cntd.ru/document/420321343. (Accessed 7 June 2019).

Prikaz Ministerstva ekonomicheskogo razvitiya RF ot 27 noyabrya 2015 g. N 888 "Ob utverzhdenii poryadka monitoringa realizacii soglashenij o gosudarstvenno-chastnom partnerstve, soglashenij o municipal'no-chastnom partnerstve" (Order of the Ministry of Economic Development of the Russian Federation of November 27, 2015 N 888 "On approval of the procedure for monitoring the implementation of agreements on public-private partnership, agreements on municipal-private partnership"). GUARANTOR (no date). http://base.garant.ru/71282688/. (Accessed 7 June 2019).

Prikaz Minekonomrazvitiya Rossii ot 01.10.2013 N 563 (red. ot 30.09.2015) "O trebovaniyah k forme i soderzhaniyu vychislitel'noj programmy po opredeleniyu diskontirovannoj vyruchki uchastnika konkursa na pravo zaklyucheniya koncessionnogo soglasheniya ili dogovora arendy v otnoshenii ob"ektov teplosnabzheniya, centralizovannyh sistem goryachego vodosnabzheniya, holodnogo vodosnabzheniya i (ili) vodootvedeniya, otdel'nyh ob"ektov takih sistem, nahodyashchihsya v gosudarstvennoj ili municipal'noj sobstvennosti" (Order of the Ministry of Economic Development of Russia of 01.10.2013 N 563 (no date)). https://legala cts.ru/doc/prikaz-minekonomrazvitija-rossii-ot-01102013-n-563/. (Accessed 7 June 2019).

Public-Private Partnership: Civil, Administrative, Financial and Legal Aspects/ Department of Administrative and Financial Law, Peoples' Friendship University of Russia/ Preface. d.yu.n., prof. A.B. Zelencova (2012). Available at: http://dereksiz.org/v-e-sazonov-gosudarstvenno-cha stnoe-partnerstvo-grajdansko-pra.html (Accessed 10 March 2019).

Public-Private Partnership: Understanding and Prospects for Improving Legislative Regulation, Actual Problems of Russia's Socio-Economic Development (2010). http://pppcenter.ru/29/nov osti/smi-o-centre/19032010.html. (Accessed 7 June 2019).

Rekomendacii po realizacii proektov gosudarstvenno-chastnogo partnerstva. Luchshie praktiki (2016). Ministerstvo ekonomicheskogo razvitiya Rossijskoj Federacii (Recommendations for the public-private partnership projects implementation. Best practices (2016). Ministry of Economic Development of the Russian Federation). http://economy.gov.ru/minec/activity/sections/privgo vpartnerdev/support/ 20160829. Accessed 10 March 2019.

Resolution of the Government of the Russian Federation of 05/11/2017 N 558 "On the peculiarities of holding a joint competition for the right to enter into a concession agreement, the object of which are heating facilities, centralized hot water systems, cold water supply and (or) water disposal, certain objects of such systems"). GUARANTOR (no date). http://base.garant.ru/71674534/. (Accessed: 7 June 2019).
Resolution of the Government of the Russian Federation of 12.19.2015 N 1387 "On the procedure for sending to the public partner a statement of intent to participate in the competition for the right to conclude an agreement on public-private partnership, an agreement on municipal-private partnership". GUARANTOR (no date). http://base.garant.ru/71287608/. (Accessed 7 June 2019).
Resolution of the Government of the Russian Federation of December 19, 2015 N 1388 "On approval of the Rules for consideration by a public partner of a proposal to implement a public-private partnership project or a municipal-private partnership project". GUARANTOR (no date). http://base.garant.ru/71287612/. (Accessed 7 June 2019).
Resolution of the Government of the Russian Federation of April 24, 2014 N 368 "On Approval of the Rules by the Antimonopoly Authority to Consent to Amendment of the Terms of the Concession Agreement" (with amendments and additions). GUARANTOR (no date). http://base.garant.ru/70645088/. (Accessed 7 June 2019).
Resolution of the Government of the Russian Federation of March 31, 2015 N 300 "On approval of the form of a proposal to conclude a concession agreement with a person initiating a concession agreement"| GUARANTOR (no date). http://base.garant.ru/70941052/. (Accessed 7 June 2019)
Seungwoo Son. (2012). Legal Analysis on Public-Private Partnerships regarding Model PPP Rules (2012). Available at: https://uncitral.un.org/sites/uncitral.un.org/files/media-documents/uncitral/en/20120704_report_on_ppp_legal_issuesson_seungwoover.11.pdf (Accessed: 7 June 2019).
Shadrina, E. V., Vinogradov, D. V. (2013). Zakonodatel'stvo o GCHP: ekonomicheskoe obosnovanie i mirovaya praktika. (PPP legislation: economic rationale and world practice). Voprosy gosudarstvennogo i municipal'nogo upravleniya (State and municipal governance issues), (2013. 4: 164–188.
Tuktarov Yu. E., Dubinchina, S. V. (2016). Koncessionnoe soglashenie: pravovaya priroda, sfera primeneniya, poryadok zaklyucheniya i ispolneniya: Rukovodstvo dlya praktikuyushchih yuristov, gosudarstvennyh i municipal'nyh sluzhashchih (Concession agreement: legal nature, scope of application, procedure for conclusion and execution. A guide for lawyers, civil servants and local government employees). Statut, Moscow, 2016.
Zakon o gosudarstvenno-chastnom partnerstve: rukovodstvo po primeneniyu 2015. (Public-private partnerships law: guidelines 2015). Centr razvitiya GCHP (PPP Development Center). Moscow. http://p3institute.ru/netcat_files/23/25/Zakon_Block_28_09_2015_v01__2__003_pdf. (Accessed 10 March 2019)
Zverev, A. A. et al. (2009). Public private partnership. Ways to improve the legislative framework (2009). Available at: https://www.ebrd.com/downloads/legal/concessions/framewk.pdf (Accessed: 10 March 2019).

Chapter 4
Organizational and Legal Forms of PPP. Concessions, PPP Agreements, Alternative or "Quasi"-PPPs

Maxim V. Tkachenko and Elena B. Zavyalova

Abstract Various organizational and legal forms of implementation of infrastructure projects in the Russian Federation are investigated and systematized. The main characteristics of regulatory documents, advantages, and disadvantages of individual legal forms, major factors behind the choice of a PPP form as well as the key rights and obligations of the parties are identified and defined. The statistical data and examples characterizing the practice of use of different organizational and legal forms for the implementation of infrastructure projects in Russia are introduced.

Keywords Public-private partnership · Concession agreements · PPP agreements · Quasi-PPP · Organizational and legal forms

JEL-Codes H11 · H41 · H44

Introduction

The participation of the state, its subjects, and municipalities in the property turnover is regulated mainly by civil law norms with the involvement of private law mechanisms for regulating relations (*Civil liability of public subjects. Theory and practice. Monograph, 2018*). The General principles of state participation in civil law relations are enshrined in Chap. 5 of part one of the Civil Code of the Russian Federation (*Agreement as a General legal value: Monograph, 2018*). Thus, it is possible to implement an infrastructure project in the Russian Federation with the participation

M. V. Tkachenko (✉)
Executive Director of the National PPP Center, Potapovskaya Roshcha str. 7, building 1, 119454 Moscow, Russia
e-mail: tkachenkomv.mos@gmail.com

E. B. Zavyalova
Department of economic policy and public-private partnership, MGIMO University, Vernadsky Ave., 76, 119454 Moscow, Russia
e-mail: e.zavyalova@inno.mgimo.ru

O. V. Ivanov and A. O. Inshakova (eds.), *Public-Private Partnerships in Russia*, Competitive Government: Public Private Partnerships,
https://doi.org/10.1007/978-3-030-56352-3_4

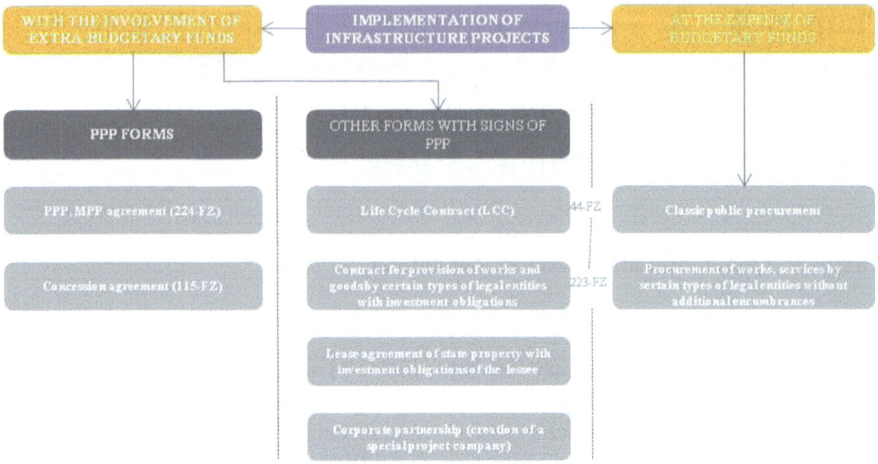

Chart 4.1 Organizational and legal forms of implementation of infrastructure projects in the Russian Federation

of budgetary funds using various organizational and legal forms. All of them are presented in Chart 4.1.

Without attracting extra-budgetary funds, it is possible to implement an infrastructure project in the form of a classical public procurement,[1] or in the form of procurement of works and services by certain types of legal entities with state participation.[2]

With the involvement of extra-budgetary funds, infrastructure projects are implemented either in the "classical" forms of PPP, including concession agreements[3] or PPP/MCHP agreements,[4] or in other contractual forms that have the characteristics of PPP—in the form of so-called quasi-PPP.

In any case, to classify a particular project as a PPP, it must meet the following criteria:

- the parties to the agreement are the public partner and the private partner;
- contractual relations have arisen with respect to the infrastructure object;
- the relationship of the parties is legally fixed;
- the equal nature of these relationships is observed;
- the social orientation of these relations is observed;
- distribution of risks, revenues, and costs between the parties.

[1]Federal law No. 44-FZ "On the contract system in the procurement of goods, works and services…".

[2]Federal law No. 223-FZ "On procurement of goods, works and services by certain types of legal entities" and regulations on procurement of relevant legal entities.

[3]Federal law No. 115-FZ "On concession agreements".

[4]Federal law No. 224-FZ "On public-private partnership, municipal-private partnership".

Table 4.1 Classification of PPPforms of PPP and major quasi-PPP forms in Russia

Organizational and Legal forms	Legal framework
Forms of public-private partnership (according to the normative definition)	
Concession agreement	Federal law No. 115-FZ "On concession agreements"
Agreement on public-private partnership, municipal-private partnership (PPP/MPP)	Federal law No. 224-FZ "On public-private partnership, municipal-private partnership…" (regional legislation was applied until 01.01.2016)
Contractual forms of attraction of extra-budgetary funds into the development of public infrastructure, having signs of PPP (alternative, or "quasi-PPP")	
Life cycle contract	Federal law No. 44-FZ "On the contract system in the procurement of goods, works and services…"
Lease agreement (gratuitous use) of state property with investment obligations of the lessee	Civil Code of the Russian Federation, Federal law No. 135-FZ "On protection of competition", regional legal acts
Long-term contract for the provision of works and services to certain types of legal entities (companies with state participation) with the investment obligations of the contractor (contract within the corporate procurement system)	Federal law No. 223-FZ "On procurement of goods, works and services by certain types of legal entities" and regulations on procurement of relevant legal entities
Corporate partnership (creation of a special project company)	Budget Code of the Russian Federation

The main forms of quasi-PPP, regulated by the legislation of the Russian Federation, include a life cycle contract, a lease agreement with investment and (or) preferential terms, and an investment agreement. Thus, the classification of contractual forms of PPP and the main forms of quasi-PPP (discussed in detail below) in the Russian Federation is as follows (Table 4.1):

The choice of a specific form of implementation of the infrastructure project, as a rule, is due, but not limited to the influence of the following factors:

- property type: ready-made or newly created (greenfield);
- industry specifics;
- payment mechanisms;
- structure and nature of risks, etc.

In Russian practice, infrastructure projects implemented in the utilities and energy sector are, in the vast majority of cases, classical concessions (2,653 out of 2,731 projects). This is due to the fact that in accordance with the Federal law of July 27, 2010 № 190-FZ "On heat supply" (Federal law "On heat supply" of 27.07.2010N 190-FZ 2010) and the Federal law of December 7, 2011N 416-FZ "On water supply and sanitation" (Federal law 'On water supply and sanitation' of 07.12.2011N 416-FZ 2011) from January 1, 2015 the rights of ownership and use of objects in the municipal property must be to be transferred only under concession agreements, providing for the creation or reconstruction of the property (Inshakova et al. 2019).

In the social sphere, where there are no strict legislative requirements, the ratio of classical forms of PPP and quasi-PPP is approximately the same: 266 projects against 186.

Large-scale projects that require significant investment in newly created facilities, such as in the transport sector, are also mainly implemented with the use of classical forms of PPP. Such projects include the following:

- Elegest—Kyzyl—Kuragino railway for 127 billion rubles of private investment-concession agreement;
- Northern latitudinal railway on the Ob–Salekhard–Nadym section for 100 billion rubles of private investment—concession agreement;
- The Western high-speed diameter highway for 69 billion rubles of private investments—PPP agreement;
- Creation of water supply and sanitation system in Volgograd on 58 billion rubles of private investments—concession agreement.

At the same time, regional preferences cannot be excluded. For example, the richest "region" of Russia—a city of Federal importance, Moscow prefers to implement its largest projects in the form of a life cycle contract or a long-term state contract with an investment component: projects for the purchase of metro vagons and low-floor trams with a total volume of private investment of 150 billion rubles.

In General, concessions occupy the lion's share in the market both in terms of volume and number of projects. In Russia, 2,815 projects are implemented under concession agreements (85% of the total number of projects), with a total volume of private investment of 1 trillion rubles (47% of the total). Quasi-PPP accounts for 12% of projects and 38% of investments. But the PPP/MPP, including in the framework of regional legislation—the youngest and so far only gaining popularity forms (3% by number and 15% by investment).

The table below shows the main statistics on the use of various forms of PPP in Russia at present (Table 4.2).

Results

Concession Agreement

Concession is one of the oldest PPP mechanisms in Russia. The formation of the railway industry in Russia in the nineteenth century actually took place on the basis of concession agreements. Even the Soviet Union used concessions for economic development until 1937.

Nowadays, concession is the most popular PPP form in Russia which accounts for more than 80% of all PPP projects. Most of the investment under concession

Table 4.2 Scale of application of different PPP forms in Russia

PPP form	Number of projects	Private investment (billion RUB)
Concession agreement	2815	1021
Agreement on public-private partnership, municipal-private partnership (PPP/MPP)	95	329
Quasi-PPP, including	388	833
Lease with investment obligations	245	218
Long-term contracts under 223-FZ	11	64
Investment agreement/contract	27	63
Life cycle contract, LCC	27	318
Corporate PPP	42	165
Energy service contract	35	2
Offset contract	1	3

Source Simply and honestly about infrastructure investment and public-private partnership in Russia. National PPP Center, 2019

agreements goes to the transport industry: 574 billion rubles of private investment. According to the number of concessions in the absolute separation of the utility and energy industry—2653 project.

As in Tsarist times, now there are large concessions in railway construction. For example, the Elegest–Kyzyl–Kuragino railway worth 126.6 billion rubles (fully private investment) will be built under concession.

Concession agreements provide that the concessionaire (private partner) carries out construction and (or) reconstruction of the object of the agreement, owned by the Concedent (public partner) or to be transferred to the ownership of the Concedent after construction, with the subsequent operation of the object by the concessionaire on the right of possession and use.

The concessionaire under concession agreement undertakes construction and (or) operation of the object at the expense of his own or borrowed funds, taking into account the possibility of co-financing by the Concedent, and carries out activities defined in the agreement using the object of the concession agreement.

The concessionaire may also be subject to additional obligations:

- payment of the concession fee to the Concedent;
- preparation of project documentation of the object of the agreement;
- preparation of the territory;
- sales of manufactured goods, performance of works,
- providing services during the term of the agreement.

The expenditure obligations of the public partner stipulated by concession agreement are binding and cannot be reduced due to the budgetary situation in contrast to the expenditure obligations of the budget under a public procurement contract, thus, concession agreement increases the degree of protection of the concessionaire.

For concession agreements in the municipal sphere, separate requirements for tender procedure, essential conditions, order of pricing for services, as well as a number of other significant conditions for preparation, conclusion, and execution of such agreements are established (they are determined by a special chapter of the Law on concession agreements).

Public-Private Partnership Agreement

Prior to January 1, 2016, public-private partnership agreements were concluded in the subjects of the Russian Federation on the basis of regional laws. As of December 31, 2015, more than 70 regional laws on PPP were adopted in the constituent entities of the Russian Federation and more than 100 projects were implemented. As a rule, these were projects in which the private partner assumed obligations for the construction and maintenance of an infrastructure object, and the public partner transferred to him land plots for these purposes and subsequently gradually bought out the created object or rented it for the purpose of performing certain public functions. This model of implementation had a number of restrictions at the level of Federal legislation, which significantly limited the possibility and attractiveness of its application.

To eliminate the existing restrictions related to the implementation of PPP projects under regional laws and also in order to unify the conceptual framework, rights, and obligations of PPP partners, etc., the Federal law No. 224-FZ "On public-private partnership, municipal-private partnership in the Russian Federation and amendments to certain legislative acts" was developed and adopted on July 13, 2015. Among other things, the law was also intended to legitimize as much as possible the use of mixed civil law contracts that have the signs of PPP in the Russian Federation. 224-FZ introduces a special concept of public-private partnership. Under traditional, accepted in many countries, understanding of the term "public-private partnership" refers to those special projects of public-private interaction, in which reimbursement of investment is carried out at the expense of the public partner, unlike concessions, in which return of investment is conducted by the private partner by collecting fees from consumers. In the interpretation of 224-FZ, public-private and municipal-private partnerships are understood as projects implemented exclusively under the model of private ownership of an infrastructure object, and everything else is called concessions, which fall under both traditional concessions and traditional PPP projects based on public property (*Actual problems and trends in the practice of dispute resolution in the field of public-private partnership in Russia, 2018*).

The key features of PPP under the PPP law are: mandatory emergence of the right of private ownership of the PPP agreement object and the possibility of preserving this right following the implementation of the project under certain conditions, as well as the possibility of a private partner to carry out maintenance of the agreement object without its operation (provision of the final service to consumers), which is not possible under concession form of PPP projects. Thus, PPP agreements as a form of implementation of infrastructure projects are potentially more interesting to such private investors who:

- plan to use the object of the agreement as collateral to reduce the cost of debt financing in the project;
- are interested in keeping ownership of the facility after completion of the PPP project;
- are not ready to assume risks and obligations on rendering final service to consumers with the use of the object of the agreement, carrying out exclusively maintenance of object of the agreement after its commissioning;
- plan to implement the PPP project in respect of objects that are not covered by the 115-FZ "On concession agreementsConcession agreements".

All PPP concluded after January 1, 2016, should be in accordance with the requirements of the Federal law on PPP and regional PPP laws are to be brought into compliance with the Federal law by January 1, 2025 (Federal law 'On amendments to certain legislative acts of the Russian Federation' of 03.07.2016N 360-FZ 2016).

Unlike the concession form of PPP, which is already settled, tools of PPP/MPP agreement continue to shape. Previously, PPP/MPP agreements were implemented within the framework of regional legislation. However, since 2018, they began to be concluded under Federal law 224-FZ. In 2018, 4 projects of this form at once passed commercial closing, all of them belong to the social sphere: in Volgograd, it was agreed to create a sports complex and a center of additional education worth 40 million rubles, in Naberezhnye Chelny of the Republic of Tatarstan–a sports complex worth 395 million rubles, in Voronezh—a sports cluster worth 203 million rubles, in Izhevsk—automatic gas stations worth 148 million rubles.

In order not to give the impression that only multimillion or billion-ruble contracts are concluded under the concession and the PPP/MPP, an example of very small transactions can be given. it is a concession agreement on water supply facilities on the territory of the Shafranovsky village council in the Republic of Bashkortostan. The volume of private investment is just 62 thousand rubles (about $1,000).

Diagrams below illustrate current practices of using classical forms of PPP in the implementation of infrastructure projects in various industries.

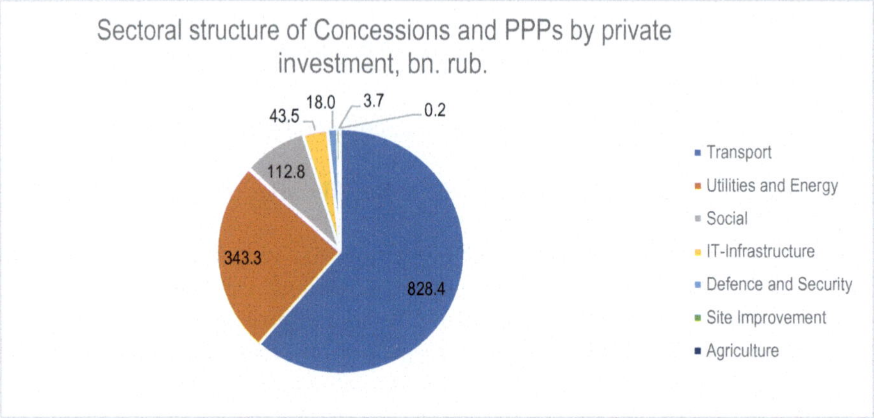
Sectoral structure of Concessions and PPPs by private investment, bn. rub.
43.5
18.0
3.7
0.2
112.8
343.3
828.4
Transport
Utilities and Energy
Social
IT-Infrastructure
Defence and Security
Site Improvement
Agriculture

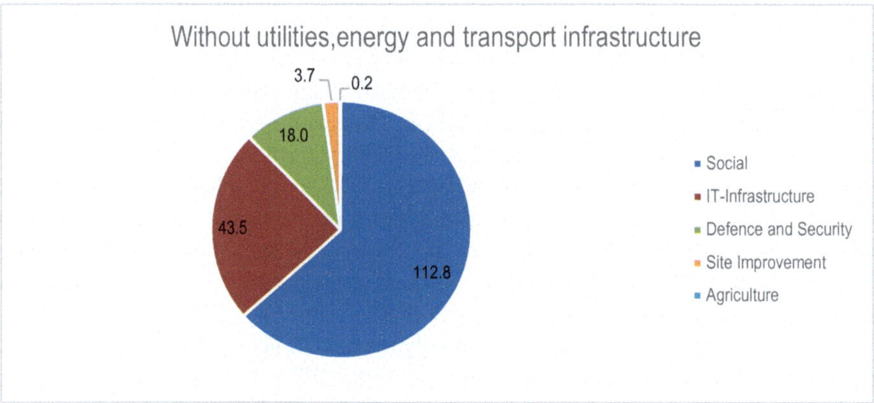
Without utilities,energy and transport infrastructure
3.7
0.2
18.0
43.5
112.8
Social
IT-Infrastructure
Defence and Security
Site Improvement
Agriculture

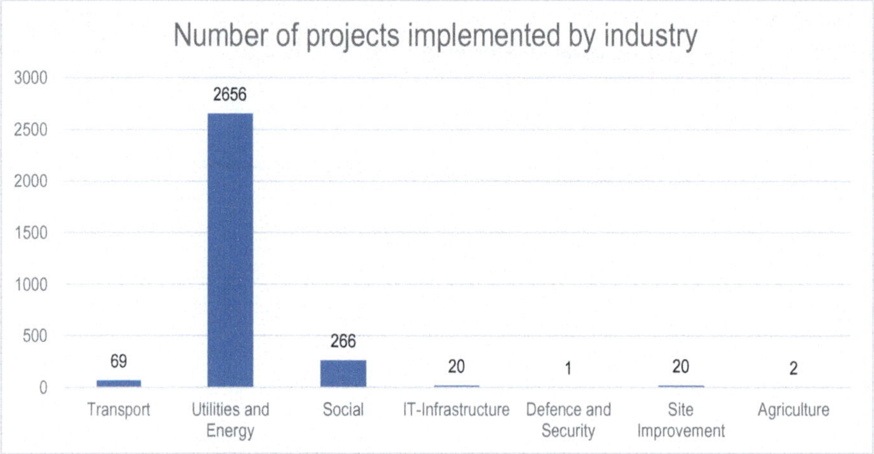
Number of projects implemented by industry
3000
2500
2000
1500
1000
500
0
69
2656
266
20
1
20
2
Transport
Utilities and Energy
Social
IT-Infrastructure
Defence and Security
Site Improvement
Agriculture

Forms of Alternative, or Quasi-PPP

Along with classical forms of PPP, such as concessions and PPP/MPP agreements, alternative formats, also known as quasi-PPP, are quite popular. Currently, among 3422 PPP projects implemented in Russia in different formats, about 400 infrastructure projects are implemented in the form of quasi-PPP. If we exclude 2653 concessions in the communal utilities sector, whose conclusion is due to the legislative framework, in comparison with the remaining 162 concessions quasi-PPP can be even considered the most popular format of PPP.

This is not surprising, since quasi-PPP projects are more flexibly structured, they can be customized to the specific needs of the parties, as well as to bypass some of the limitations of the classical forms of PPP, which will be discussed in more detail below.

Anyway, private investors are eager to choose the quasi-PPP format in their work with the state. So what is quasi-PPP?

We identify seven forms of such partnerships:

1. life cycle contract;
2. lease with investment obligations;
3. corporate partnership;
4. long-term contract with investment obligations;
5. investment agreement with PPP features;
6. offset contract;
7. energy service contract with signs of PPP.

The biggest in cost, the most expensive are life cycle contracts (LCC). Under this mechanism, for example, Moscow city procures buses, trams, and subway cars. These are large long-term contracts for tens of billions of rubles. Along with LCC, investors also often use the lease with investment obligations contracts and corporate partnerships. They account for 218 billion rubles and 165 billion rubles, respectively.

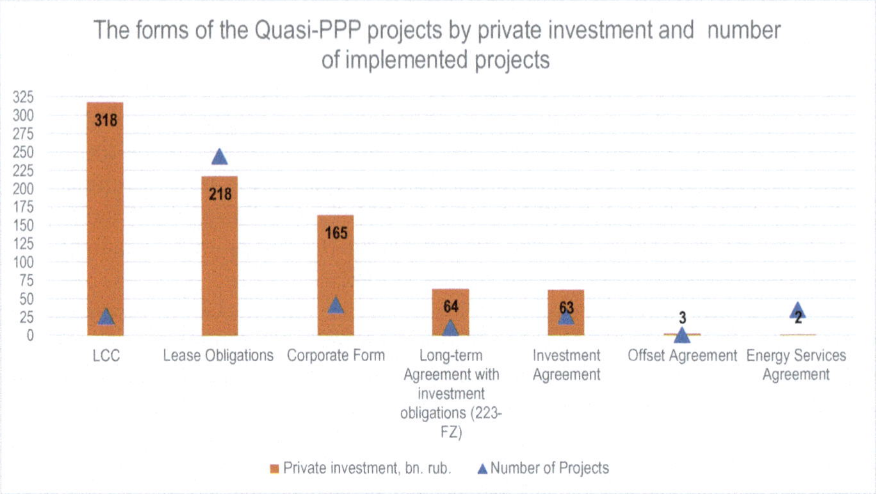

Source Simply and honestly about infrastructure investment and public-private partnership in Russia. National PPP Center, 2019

If we explore quasi-PPP by industry, the largest share of private investment is in transport (56% of the total, or 464 billion rubles). Communal utilities and energy sector is in the second place (26%), and the social sector holds the third place (16%). All other industries account for 2%.

The diagrams below illustrate current practices in the use of various forms of quasi-PPP in selected industries.

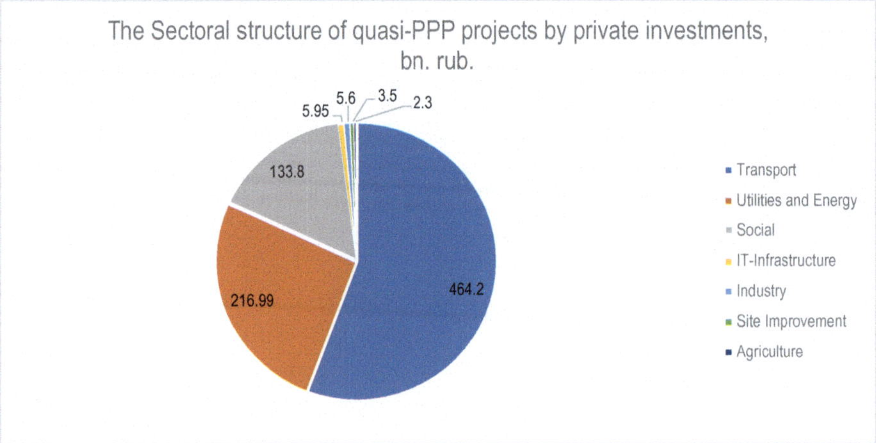

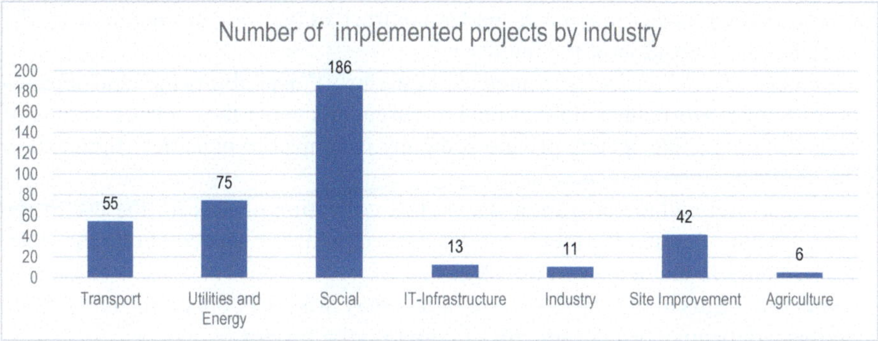

The main types of infrastructure projects implemented in the quasi-PPP format are explored in more detail below.

Life Cycle Contract

As mentioned above, life cycle contracts (LCC) are particularly popular in the transport infrastructure sector, especially in Moscow city and the Moscow region. Under LCC trams, subway cars, buses are procured and garbage disposal and many other works on infrastructure development are carried out.

The conclusion of life cycle contracts (LCC) between the state and private investors is regulated by Part 16 of Article 34 of the Federal law № 44-FZ "On the contract system in the procurement of goods, works and services for state and municipal needs" of April 5, 2013. This contract provides for the purchase of goods or work (including, if necessary, design and construction of the object), subsequent maintenance, repair, and if necessary, operation and (or) disposal of the goods delivered or created as a result of the work of the object. The conclusion of such a contract is possible only in certain cases defined by the decree of the government of the Russian Federation dated 28.11.2013 № 1087 "On determining the cases of concluding life cycle contracts" (*the Decree of the Government of the Russian Federation "On the determination of a life cycle contract's cases" of 28.11.2013 No. 1087; ed. of 29.10.2018*).

Key characteristics of LCC are

- this contract covers all stages of the facility lifecycle —design, construction, operation;
- private partner under LCC independently makes all design and technical decisions necessary for the implementation of the project, and bears all technical risks and risks of design decisions;
- initially, the project is financed by a private partner represented by a special project company (SPV);

- public partner makes payments under contract only from the moment of the beginning of operation of the facility;
- payment under the project is an annual (or quarterly) "availability fee" and depends only on the performance of functional requirements under the contract. In case of noncompliance, the special private company is subject to penalties stipulated in the contract;
- LCC does not include operating issues, i.e., collection of fees for the use of the infrastructure facility. Payments for the service, which is carried out by the state, are tied only to the quality of the object;
- ownership rights to the infrastructure object may arise for both public and private parties—depending on the specifics of a particular project;
- payments for services from the public partner must be guaranteed for the entire duration of the contract.

Given that LCC contracts are subject to the general requirements of the Federal law "On the contract system in the procurement of goods, works, services for state and municipal needs" of April 5, 2013 № 44-FZ in terms of determining the initial (maximum) price of the contract, as well as the immutability of the contract terms throughout the life cycle and the possibility of termination of the contract by the public partner without additional compensation to the private partner, this form of implementation of infrastructure projects has not yet been widely used (*Life cycle Contracts—what will the future bring?* 2013) (Chart 4.2).

Lease Contract with Investment Obligations

Lease agreement with investment obligations is difficult to describe by one example, because projects implemented in this format are very diverse. These include, for example, the project for reconstruction of the Olympic complex "Luzhniki" in Moscow with total private investment of 46 billion rubles, construction of a solar power in Novokuibyshevsk (10 billion rubles of private investment) and at the same time the project for the construction of the passenger seaport of St. Petersburg "Sea facade" with 23 billion rubles of private investment.

Lease agreement with investment and/or preferential terms is concluded in accordance with Chap. 34 of the Civil code of the Russian Federation. The terms of the contract provide for investment by the tenant at the expense of own or borrowed funds in development (reconstruction) of the leased property. In this case, the tenant only uses the leased property for a fee and is responsible for its proper operation and maintenance. The legal regulation of the procedure for holding tenders or auctions for the right to conclude lease agreements for state or municipal property is carried out in accordance with regional legislation and separate regulatory legal acts of the Federal Antimonopoly service.

The general scheme of realization

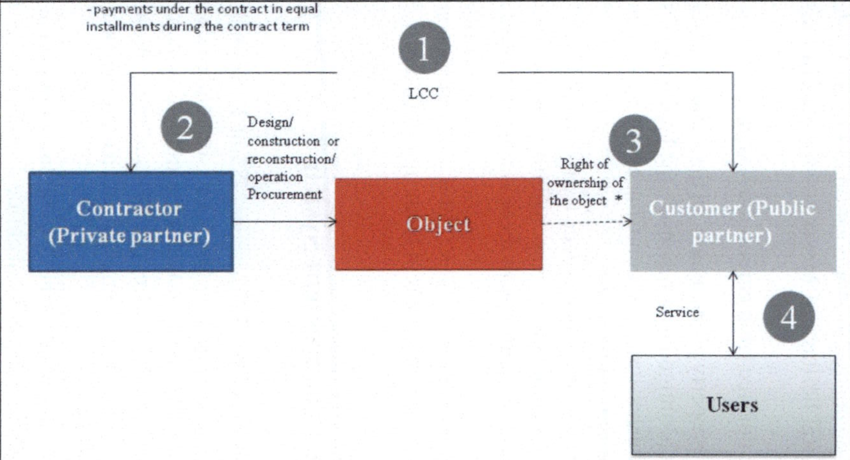

Possible infrastructure

Design and construction of
- roads
- sea and river ports infrastructure
- airports
- objects of communal utilities system
- objects of solid waste treatment
- subway and city street transport infrastructure
- railway transport infrastructure

Design, construction and reconstruction
- objects of sanatorium and health resort
- culture objects

Design, construction and operation
- objects of social service

Design and reconstruction (restoration)
- objects of cultural heritage

Procurement
- railway rolling stock
- metro and urban land transport vehicles
- aircraft ships, river and sea ships

Specifics of application

- integration under one government contract of services (works) for design and construction of the infrastructure facility
- payment for services (works) in equal installments during the term of the contract
- contractor (private partner)'s risk of public partner's unilateral failure to fulfill spending obligations under the contract
- impossibility of including inflation and other external risks into the price of the contract
- impossibility to solve property-related issues (lease, transfer of the object for use, etc).

Chart 4.2 General scheme of implementation and specifics of the application of the life cycle contracts (LCC)

This form of attracting private business to the development of public infrastructure is actively used by the Moscow city Government within the framework of the so-called "ruble per square meter" program in relation to preschool education, health care, as well as cultural heritage objects (*"1 ruble per 1 square meter" program* 2019). The program provides for open auctions, under the results of which the winning investor receives a rental object, during the regulatory period carries out repair and restoration work and after the start of medical or educational activities receives the preferential rental rate. In health care, the lease term is 20 years, in education—49 years. The objects for the programs are selected taking into account the demand for medical and educational services, which ensures the demand from the population. There are serious requirements for applicants: for example, schools and kindergartens must comply with the standard for loading, and at least 80% of children in kindergartens and 50% of students in schools must be registered at the place of residence in Moscow. Since the start of the program, 108 buildings and premises have been transferred to investors, 55 of them are already operating at a reduced rental rate. At the same time, 60 objects were transferred to investors for the creation of mini-clinics within walking distance, 29—for creation of private kindergartens and schools, 19 objects of cultural heritage of Moscow—for restoration in accordance with security obligations.

The model of the lease agreement is not free from certain drawbacks:

- separable improvements become the property of the tenant. In the event of a break in the relationship, the public partner is obliged to compensate the lessee the costs separable improvements (under the concession agreementConcession agreements it remains in the ownership of the state/municipality);
- the intended use of the land and object by the tenant needs tight control;
- it is impossible to lay down all the mechanisms of responsibility for the social component of the project (in the concession agreement there is a strict control of the Concedent);
- the lessee can "squeeze" separable improvements, collect debts, go bankrupt, and leave the market (the concessionaire is not interested in bankruptcy) (Chart 4.3).

Contract Within the Corporate Procurement System

Projects such as the construction of the highway M-11 "Moscow—Saint-Petersburg", the Central ring road in the Moscow region, the highway M4 "Don" are implemented in the form of agreements in the framework of the corporate procurement system.

Such agreements are concluded between a private investor and a state corporation, a state (municipal) unitary enterprise or a joint-stock company with a total state share in the authorized capital of more than 50%.

Features of these contractual relations are fixed in the Federal law "On procurement of goods, works and services by certain types of legal entities" of July 18, 2011 № 223-FZ. The organizations specified in the law are obliged to adopt provisions regulating their procurement activities. Such a provision contains requirements for

The general scheme of realization

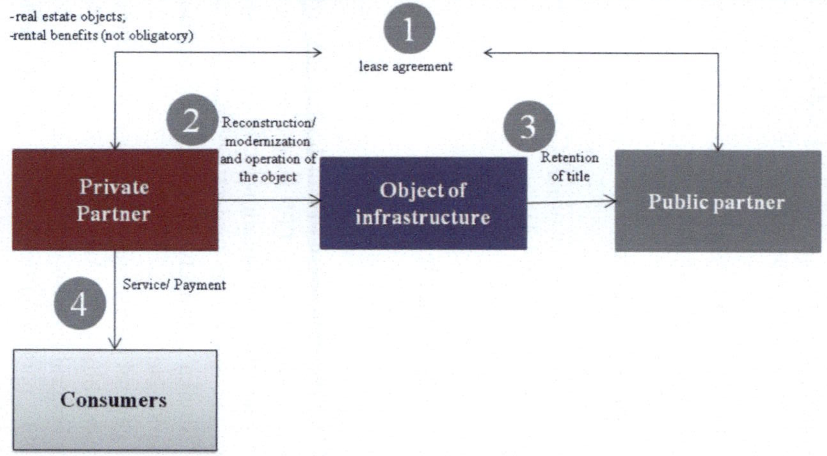

Possible infrastructure

Open-end list of objects - any real estate objects which are in the state/municipal property which can be transferred for lease

Perspective areas

Any type of public infrastructure that is cost-effective without additional financial involvement from the budget during the operational phase, for example:

- primary link of health care system in settlements with a high rate of compulsory medicine insurance and solvent population
- pre-school education facilities in settlements with solvent population and a high need for these types of services are not covered by the state municipality
- objects of cultural heritage, cost of restoration and maintenance of which are offset by benefits of their use for various purposes (restaurants, shops, etc.).) a
- airports and airport infrastructure with high passenger traffic

Specifics of application

- possibility to flexibly establish investment obligations of the tenant
- possibility to establish for certain types of objects a preferential rental rate after implementation of investment obligations (example: "ruble per square meter")
- impossibility to provide in the contract neither full nor partial budget financing of the cost of reconstruction/ restoration or modernization and operation of the object (maintenance, targeted use, etc.)
- lessee 's risks of the lessor (public partner)'s unilateral change of rent fee

Chart 4.3 General scheme of implementation and specifics of the application of Lease contract with investment obligations procurement, including the procedure for the preparation and conduct of the procurement procedure and the terms of their application, the procedure for the conclusion and execution of contracts, as well as other provisions related to procurement (Inshakova et al. 2017).

The legal entity, which is subject to the said law, has the right to establish its own forms of contractual relations, including those with the signs of PPP. For example, the Order of procurement activities of the state company "Russian roads" defines such types of agreements as the operator agreement, the agreement on joint implementation of the investment project (on cooperation with the financing organization in the implementation of the investment project), a comprehensive long-term investment agreement (for trust management), and others.

Long-term contracts with investment obligations have a number of specific features:

- maximum flexibility in structuring the project and in terms of selection of the private partner in view of full regulation of these issues within the framework of the procurement regulations of the legal entity acting on the customer's side;
- risks for the investor associated with the insufficient financial stability of the customer and the lack of direct regression of the customer's obligations to the federal, regional, and local budget;
- impossibility of direct participation of budgets of the budget system of the Russian Federation in the execution of expenditure obligations of the customer to the contractor (if such obligations are provided);
- inability to use other state or municipal property, except for the property under the jurisdiction of the customer;
- the customer (public partner) under the contract can be any JSC with a share of the state, including development corporations (Chart 4.4).

Investment Agreement with Socially Significant Encumbrances

One of the most common non-concessionary legal forms of PPP in the Russian Federation is an investment agreement. Examples of such quasi-PPP are the project for the construction and reconstruction of water supply and sanitation facilities in Rostov-on-Don and the South-West of the Rostov region, the project to create a system of noncash payment for passengers "Strelka", projects to create multifunctional hospitals, health centers, amusement parks, etc.

The grounds for the conclusion and general provisions of investment agreements between public and private partners are established by Article 421 of the Civil Code ("on freedom of contracts") and by the Federal Law on investment activity.

The following standard forms of public partner participation are possible within the framework of the investment agreement:

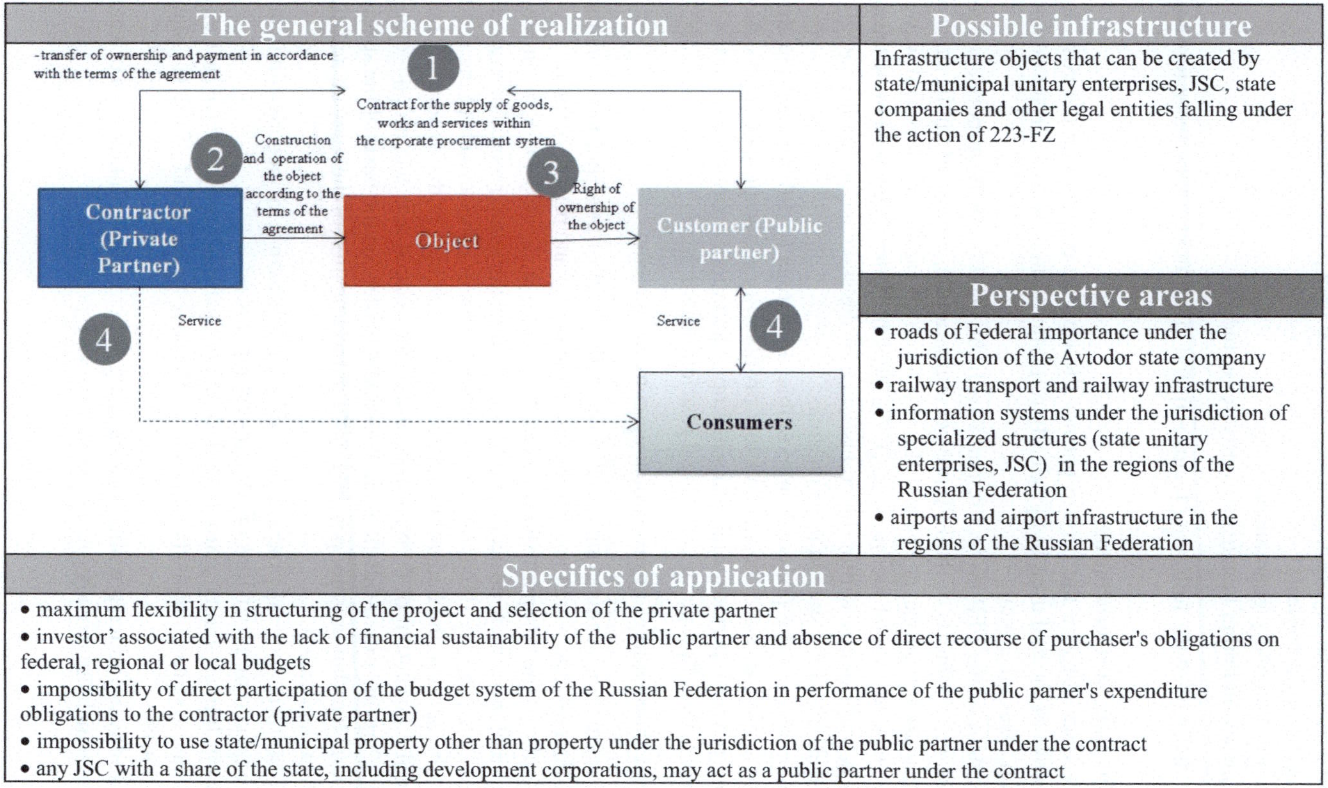

Chart 4.4 General scheme of implementation and specifics of the application of contracts within the corporate procurement system

- provision of property for temporary possession and use, as well as ownership (including by alienation of shares/interests owned by a public partner);
- co-financing of the project;
- provision of budgetary guarantees;
- providing tax and other benefits to a private partner.

We can distinguish the following features of the investment contract as a form of PPP:

- flexibility in project structuring;
- the state does not give the private partner the right to compensate the costs at the expense of the end user, but gradually reimburses them with a certain rate of return on invested capital;
- management of the PPP project remains with the state (railway, airports, social facilities, etc.). Objects of the PPP project are, as a rule, objects of public infrastructure used for public needs and the provision of public services (railways, airports, utilities, social facilities, etc.). At the same time, management of these objects is traditionally within the competence of the state and is conditioned by the obligations of the state in relevant areas;
- implementation of the project is impossible or extremely difficult without the participation of the state (because of low profitability of the project, high costs and long payback periods, high risks of implementation, restriction of turnover of certain types of property, other legal restrictions, etc.).

The main shortcomings of investment agreements include:

- lack of regulation of this contractual form at the level of the Civil Code and/or special Federal law, which leads to risks for the public and private partner.
- absence of a single competitive procedure fixed at the Federal level for the implementation of investment projects, as a result of which the winner would be granted rights to state property (land, other real estates). This drawback leads to the need to take into account the Federal mandatory rules enshrined in the Land code, the Law on the protection of competition, and other Federal acts when conducting tenders. Carrying out of full-fledged investment tenders on the basis of the specified federal legislation is not possible without modification of the relevant acts of the federal legislation;
- lack of uniform judicial practice, as well as the presence of negative judicial practice on certain provisions of investment agreements;
- inability or limited ability to use certain financial instruments of PPP (infrastructure bonds, co-financing at the expense of the Investment Fund of the Russian Federation);
- impossibility or limited possibility of securing individual guarantees for a private investor, which are already quite common for PPP projects.

Special Investment Contract

A special investment contract (SPIC) is an agreement between an industrial investor and the state, which sets out obligations of the investor to create and master the production of industrial products, as well as guarantees of the stability of tax and regulatory conditions and provision of state support measures.

Within the framework of SPIC, the public entity undertakes to implement measures to stimulate activities in the industry during the term of the agreement, defined by federal, regional, and municipal legislation. The investor undertakes to create/modernize and (or) to master production of industrial products in the Russian Federation during the term provided by the agreement, including agreed volume of investments; agreed financial indicators; manufacturing products of agreed quality, and quantity.

The advantages of SPIC include

- guarantees of tax measures to support the investor;
- guarantees of nonincrease of tax burden during the term of SPIC;
- guarantees of non-deterioration of business conditions during the term of SPIC;
- possibility of obtaining information and consulting support, support for scientific, technical and innovation activities, support for the development of human resources;
- possibility to choose a set of preferences provided;
- accelerated and simplified procedure for obtaining the status of a Russian manufacturer;
- lack of competitive procedures for the conclusion of the contract;
- a wide range of industries for use of the contract.

Operator Agreement/Operation and Maintenance (O&M)

The types of the above contractual forms of PPP include the operator agreement used for the implementation of investment infrastructure projects. Its nature is similar to so-called "service contracts", common in world practice. However, the operator agreement is not regulated in Russian federal law as an independent contract and is a mixed contract within the meaning of Article 421 of the Civil Code).

Operator agreement is an agreement under which there is no construction and/or reconstruction, but only maintenance, repair, and operation of the existing infrastructure. It is a long-term contract for works and services related to the operation of the facility. For example, in the case of road maintenance, the contract includes:

- execution of works on maintenance of road sections;
- performance of works on repair of road sections;
- performance of works (services) on the operation of toll collection systems at toll sites, including the maintenance and maintenance of the system and the collection of user fees for the passage of vehicles on toll sites.

The most well-known example of the use of the operator agreement in Russia is the long-term operator agreement for maintenance, repair, and operation on a fee basis of the Federal highway M4-Don (Section "Results"), concluded in 2011 between the state company "Russian roads" and a private operator. The subject of this contract is a set of works and services, including the creation of an automated traffic management system and organization of charging. As a rule, such agreements are concluded in the form of mixed contracts.

Corporate (Institutional) PPP in Russia

In international practice, corporate or institutional PPP is a PPP form under which public and private partners create a joint legal entity (business company), that carries out reconstruction (rarely the creation) and subsequent operation of the infrastructure. In the Russian Federation, this form of interaction between the state and business is used in the management of airport infrastructure, as well as in the health sector.

In the Russian Federation, some corporate forms of public-private partnership are enshrined in regional legislation. In particular,

- share participation of the subject of the Russian Federation in the authorized (share) capitals of legal entities;
- provision of budget investments to a private partner with the emergence of state ownership of the equivalent part of the authorized (share) capital of the relevant legal entity;
- creation of an organization with a mixed form of ownership, for which the authorized bodies conduct a competitive selection of the investor.

The public partner in this case can be represented by the following organizations:

- state corporations (Vneshekonombank State Corporation, Russian Technologies State Corporation, Deposit Insurance Agency, etc.);
- state-owned companies ("Avtodor" state company);
- joint-stock companies with a total share of public legal entities in the authorized capital of more than 50% (RUSNANO, Russian Venture Company, etc.);
- state and municipal unitary enterprises;

Special project company (or special project vehicle, SPV) can be established only in the form of JSC. The main reasons for choosing a corporate form of cooperation are as follows:

- no need for competitive procedures;
- establishing a balance of interests depending on the share of participation;
- possibility to conclude a corporate agreement providing for detailed terms of cooperation, including mechanisms of withdrawal from the project and liability of the parties for breach of obligations;

- direct participation of each partner in SPV activities, joint decision-making on key issues.

Examples of PPP projects with the use of the corporate mechanism mainly relate to projects for airport development, however, for example, the Government of Moscow city is actively using SPV for the implementation of PPP projects. In particular, with the use of this form has been created and successfully operating JSC "Urban transportation system of light rail" (public transportation), JSC "Medsi II" (health care), etc.

Conclusions

- Organizational and legal forms of interaction between the state and business in the field of infrastructure in Russia include both "classic" forms—such as concession agreements and PPP agreements—and forms of "quasi-PPP"—life cycle contract; lease agreement with investment obligations; agreement within the corporate procurement system; investment agreement; etc.
- The above organizational and legal forms are unified by the presence of PPP features, according to which
  - the parties of the agreement are public and private partners;
  - contractual relations have arisen with respect to the infrastructure object;
  - relationship of the parties is legally fixed;
  - these relations have equal nature;
  - these relations have social orientation;
  - risks, distribution of revenues and costs are allocated between the parties.
- In addition, implementation of PPP infrastructure projects in the Russian Federation is also possible in the form of a corporate partnership that provides creation of a special project company regulated by the Budget Code of the Russian Federation.
- The choice of a specific form of implementation of infrastructure project, as a rule, is due to a range of factors such as type of object (brownfield or greenfield), sectoral specifics, payment mechanisms; structure of risk allocation, nature of risks, etc.
- The most popular form of PPP projects are concession agreements mainly due to the fact that the legislation establishes mandatory requirements for the transfer of objects of the communal utility sector exclusively under concession agreements.
- Quasi-PPP is also popular due to the high flexibility in structuring these projects. At the same time, these projects are extremely diverse in terms of industry.
- PPP/MPP projects emerged only a few years ago, so they have not yet gained high popularity.

References

Aktual'nye problemy i tendencii v praktike razresheniya sporov v sfere publichno-chastnogo partnerstva v Rossii. (2018). (Actual problems and trends in the practice of dispute resolution in the field of public-private partnership in Russia). http://pravoprim.spbu.ru/yurisprudentsiya/administrativnoe-regulirovanie/item/418-aktualnye-problemy-i-tendentsii-v-praktike-razresheniya-sporov-v-sfere-publichno-chastnogo-partnerstva-v-rossii. Accessed 10 Mar 2019.

Avhadeev, V. R., Astashova, V. S., & Andrichenko, L. V., et al. (Eds.). (2018). Dogovor kak obshchepravovaya cennost': Monografiya (Contract as a General legal value: Monograph). Institut zakonodatel'stva i sravnitel'nogo pravovedeniya pri Pravitel'stve Rossijskoj Federacii (The Institute of Legislation and Comparative Law under the Government of the Russian Federation). Statut, Moscow. http://www.izak.ru/upload/iblock/4b5/4b54f3c75eb79b053fe2629361daa44c.pdf. Accessed 10 Mar 2019.

Federal'nyj zakon 'O vnesenii izmenenij v otdel'nye zakonodatel'nye akty Rossijskoj Federacii' ot 03.07.2016N 360-FZ. (2016). (Federal law 'On amendments to certain legislative acts of the Russian Federation' of 03.07.2016N 360-FZ). http://www.consultant.ru/document/cons_doc_LAW_200729/. Accessed 10 Mar 2019.

Federal'nyj zakon 'O vodosnabzhenii i vodootvedenii' ot 07.12.2011N 416-FZ. (2011). (Federal law 'On water supply and sanitation' of 07.12.2011N 416-FZ (2011)). http://www.consultant.ru/document/cons_doc_LAW_122867/. Accessed 10 Mar 2019.

Federal'nyj zakon "O teplosnabzhenii" ot 27.07.2010N 190-FZ. (2010). (Federal law 'On heat supply' of 27.07.2010N 190-FZ (2010)). https://www.consultant.ru/document/cons_doc_LAW_102975/. Accessed 10 Mar 2019.

Federal'nyj zakon "O zakupkah tovarov, rabot, uslug otdel'nymi vidami yuridicheskih lic" ot 18.07.2011N 223-FZ. (2011). (Federal law "On procurement of goods, works and services by certain types of legal entities" (2011)). http://www.consultant.ru/document/cons_doc_LAW_116964/. Accessed 10 Mar 2019.

Grazhdansko-pravovaya otvetstvennost' publichnyh sub'ektov. Voprosy teorii i praktiki. Monografiya. (2018). (Civil liability of public entities. Theory and practice. Monograph). https://www.chitai-gorod.ru/catalog/book/1051101/. Accessed 10 Mar 2019.

Inshakova, A. O., Goncharov, A. I., Mineev, O. A., & Sevostyanov, M. V. (2017). Amendments to the civil code of the Russian Federation: Contradictions of theory and practice, contributions to economics, In *Russia and the European Union: Development and Perspectives Number XIII* (pp. 147–153).

Inshakova, A. O., Goncharov, A. I., & Marchukov, I. P. (2019). Common energy policy and development paths legal regulation of foreign trade turnover of energy resources in the CIS and in the EEU. In O. V., Inshakova, A. O., Popkova, E. G. (Eds.), *Energy sector: A systemic analysis of economy, foreign trade and legal regulations* (pp. 207–225). Cham: Springer Science + Business Media.

Ivanov, O.V. (2019). Gosudartsvenno-chastnoe partnerstvo kak instrument razvitiya infrastruktury i modernizatsii ekonomiki. Opyt stran Aziatsko-tikhookeanskogo regiona (Public-private partnership as an instrument of development of infrastructure and modernization of economy. *Experience of Asia-Pacific countries)* (300 p). Moscow: MGIMO-University.

Ivanov, O.V., & Ivanova, A.O. (2019). Gosudarstvenno-chastnoe patnerstvo v stranakh Aziatsko-tikhookeanskogo regiona (Public-private partnership in the countries of Asia-Pacific region) (270 p). Moscow: MGIMO-University.

Jooste, S. F., Scott, W. R. (2012) The public-private partnership enabling field: Evidence from three cases. *Administration and Society*, *44*(2), 149–182. https://doi.org/10.1177/0095399711413868.

Kontrakty zhiznennogo cikla – chto den' gryadushchij nam gotovit? (2013). (Life cycle contracts—What does the future hold for us?). https://www.vegaslex.ru/data/2013/06/25/1234630764/report.pdf. Accessed 10 Mar 2019.

Mekhanizmy gosudarstvenno-chastnogo partnyorstva v ekonomicheskoi politike Rossii (Mechanisms of public-private partnership in the economic policy of Russia). (2018). In Ivanov, O. V. (409 p). Moscow: MGIMO-University.

Pakhomova, E. O., Goosen, E. V., & Nikitenko, S. M. (2017). New forms of public-private partnership for sustainable development of the fuel and energy sector. In *International Scientific and Research Conference on Knowledge-Based Technologies in Development and Utilization of Mineral Resources*, , Vol. 84, No. 1, KTDMUR 2017; Novokuznetsk; Russian Federation.

Postanovlenie Pravitel'stva RF ot 28.11.2013 N 1087 (red. ot 29.10.2018) "Ob opredelenii sluchaev zaklyucheniya kontrakta zhiznennogo cikla". (2013). (The RF Government decree of 28.11.2013 No. 1087 (ed. by 29.10.2018) "On determination of a contract's life cycle" (2013)). http://www.consultant.ru/document/cons_doc_LAW_155054/. Accessed 10 Mar 2019.

Programma "1 rubl' za 1 kv. metr". (2019). (The program "1 ruble per 1 square meter"). https://stroi.mos.ru/infographics/proghramma-1-rubl-za-1-kv-mietr. Accessed 10 Mar 2019.

Prosto i chestno ob investiciyah v infrastrukturu i gosudarstvenno-chastnom partnerstve v Rossii. (2019). (Simply and honestly about investments in infrastructure and public-private partnership in Russia (2019)). PPP Development Center.http://pppcenter.ru/assets/docs/reit240419.pdf. Accessed 10 Mar 2019.

Part III
PPP Governance in Russia

Chapter 5
Strategic Planning in Russia. Transition to Formation of Long-Term Infrastructure Plans

Oleg V. Ivanov and Vladimir V. Piskunov

Abstract The concept of infrastructure strategic planning and its immanent characteristics are explored. Current world practices of state infrastructure planning are introduced and generalized. The paper analyzes and illustrates the existing system of strategic planning of infrastructure in Russia both at the Federal and regional levels, and provides concrete practical examples of relevant government documents. Based on the study of relevant international experience and current situation in Russian economy, key problems of Russia's approach to the governance of infrastructure development are identified, and specific recommendations on possible ways to improve efficiency of the infrastructure planning system are proposed.

Keywords Infrastructure development · Public administration · Infrastructure planning · Strategic planning · Infrastructure plan

JEL-Codes H44 · O18 · O20 · O29

Introduction

Given the long-term and complex nature of the infrastructure development challenge, without a clear understanding of the needs and opportunities, as well as an appropriate target setting, it is unlikely to be effective. These aspects can only be achieved through a systemic approach (Howes and Robinson 2006).

The need for "consistency" in the development of national infrastructure is due to several factors. First, it is the nature of infrastructure itself. In most cases, some infrastructure facilities are more or less dependent on others: for example, the development

---

O. V. Ivanov (✉)
Department of economic policy and public–private partnership, MGIMO University, Vernadsky Ave. 76, 119454 Moscow, Russia
e-mail: ivanov_ov@mail.ru

V. V. Piskunov
Consultant, the National PPP Center, Malaya Dmitrovka str. 16-6, 127006 Moscow, Russia
e-mail: vvpiskunov@outlook.com

O. V. Ivanov and A. O. Inshakova (eds.), *Public-Private Partnerships in Russia*, Competitive Government: Public Private Partnerships,
https://doi.org/10.1007/978-3-030-56352-3_5

of industrial zones will be impractical without the accompanying logistics infrastructure, and energy sales networks will be useless without production capacity—and vice versa. In this regard, even at the microlevel, they should be considered at least in conjunction with each other, and at the macrolevel, with the entire infrastructure network. Second, the approach to infrastructure development must be sound and sustainable over time—if priorities are changed too often, the economic efficiency of investment will decline. Thirdly, the “coordination” component of the decision-making process is also important, whether it is the interaction of the two agencies responsible for different aspects, or the movement along the administrative vertical. For successful infrastructure development, all stakeholders must have a synchronized agenda (National PPP Center 2018).

At the same time, the systemic approach not only improves the efficiency of planning as such, but can also play the role of a communication tool between the state and the private sector, the demand for which in the development of public infrastructure is steadily growing. Having an understanding of the strategic contours of the country’s future infrastructure development and the wide availability of information about specific opportunities is the key to efficiency in attracting private capital and competencies (Inshakova et al. 2019).

Today, in Russia, infrastructure planning is rather fragmented. Although certain elements of infrastructure planning can be found in various forms and at various levels-from economic development strategies and state programs to regional and municipal list of objects for which it is planned to conclude concession agreements-all of them are used separately, and it is impossible to speak about any "system" formed yet. Given the acuteness of infrastructure problems, the significant potential of the private sector in their solution, comprehensive measures to introduce the practice of infrastructure planning and ensure its consistency can give a significant impetus to the infrastructure development of Russia.

Results

What International Experience Says

In recent years, the number of countries in the world where long-term infrastructure planning has become an important function of the state in the field of infrastructure development has been growing (Ivanov 2019). Based on the conceptual study of the future development of the economy, such planning makes it possible to determine the vector of development, to predict the target quantitative and qualitative parameters, to build guidelines for sources of financing.

International experience suggests that the value of long-term planning can be particularly useful when the number of infrastructure projects on the horizon for implementation in 20–30 years starts to be measured in the hundreds, and their sectoral coverage extends to a broad range of areas of infrastructure (Mekhanizmy

2018). Indeed, in many countries around the world, individual infrastructure sectors tend to be managed by different government authorities, and such "departmental disunity" has often been an obstacle to the development of a unified approach to the infrastructure complex and to the cross-sectoral balancing of infrastructure development. The global financial and economic crisis has revealed such shortcomings in the implementation of infrastructure projects as the imbalance of resources in the long term and the lack of cross-sectoral coordination of investment decisions. Strategic infrastructure planning is also intended to address these problems.

In today's foreign practice, "systemic" infrastructure planning is provided mainly by two tools—institutionalization, including the creation of specialized coordination bodies, and the development of infrastructure plans (Box 2017). The relevant institutions and documents may be of different nature and have different status (World Bank 2017). As an example, we can take several countries that occupy higher positions compared to Russia on the integrated indicator of "infrastructure quality" in the latest ranking of the World Economic Forum (World Economic Forum 2018) and at the same time actively applying public–private partnership mechanisms—Australia, the UK, the Netherlands, Singapore, Japan, and Spain (see Table 5.1).

Analysis of approaches of different countries to strategic infrastructure planning (Ivanov 2016a, b) leads to the conclusion that it should primarily be aimed at harmonization of infrastructure policy: both vertical (i.e., ensure continuity of planning documents at different levels) and horizontal (synchronize documents on related industries and ensure effective interaction of complementary authorities). At the same time, it should result in documents prioritizing individual projects and at the same time effectively serving as a tool for communication with the private sector interested in infrastructure investments (PwC 2017).

Table 5.1 Infrastructure development strategic planning documents in the leading countries of the world

Country	Planning document	Date of adoption
Singapore *First place*	Concept plans Master plans	Every 40–50 years Every 10–15 years
Holland *Fourth place*	National Strategy for infrastructure and spatial development	2012
Japan *Fifth place*	Action plan for fundamental reform of PPP for 2013–2024 Program of accelerated infrastructure development based on PPP for 2014–2016	2013 2014
Spain *Tenth place*	PPP program for the development of roads	2017
Britain *Eleventh place*	National infrastructure plan (list of priority infrastructure projects)	2012
Australia *Thirty-first place*	Infrastructure development plan (list of priority infrastructure projects + strategic structural reforms) Regional infrastructure plans	2013

Strategic Planning in the Russian Federation

A clear system of state planning documents, which should determine the vector and specific steps for the further development of the country, including infrastructure, was formed after the adoption of the Federal law of 28.06.2014 № 172-FZ "On strategic planning in the Russian Federation" (hereinafter—172-FZ). The new system has streamlined the planning process "vertically," providing three integrated phases: forecasting, goal setting, and programming. For infrastructure, each phase should perform the following functions:

- Forecasting involves the analysis of the current state of infrastructure development based on the assessment of the current and projected demand for public infrastructure, correlating with the main trends of socio-economic development (fertility, traffic flows, purchasing power, etc.)
- Goal setting involves the inclusion of infrastructure development in the Strategy of socio-economic development (SIR) of the Federal level for subsequent continuity in the documents of goal setting of the Russian Federation subjects and sectors of the economy. At this stage, goals and targets are defined to reflect the desired level of infrastructure availability.
- Programming solves the problem of an integrated assessment of the possibility and feasibility of the implementation of certain projects for their inclusion in state and municipal programs, for the subsequent display of these projects and the form of their implementation in the planning/programming documents.

This logic is quite clearly maintained in practice. For example, at the Federal level, the key document of goal setting is the *Strategy of socio-economic development of Russia,* developed by the Ministry of economic development of Russia. The forecast basis for the Strategy is several documents: "*Forecast of scientific and technological development of the Russian Federation for the period up to 2030*," the Budget forecast of the Russian Federation, as well as the long-term forecast of socio-economic development of the Russian Federation. At the same time, the Annual address of the President of the Russian Federation to the Federal Assembly of the Russian Federation and the decrees adopted in its execution have begun to play an increasingly important role in planning in recent years, including in the infrastructure part.

Strategy of socio-economic development of Russia is decomposed by a variety of strategies at a lower level, including sectoral strategies and strategies of socio-economic development of macro-regions. Strategic plans are specified in the State Programs of the Russian Federation, as well as in territorial planning schemes (Chart 5.1).

According to the Federal law No. 172-FZ "On strategic planning in the Russian Federation" dated June 28, 2014, the system of strategic planning at the regional level is in general identical to the Federal one (see Chart 5.2).

Thus, from a formal point of view, Russia already has a system of strategic planning. At the same time, the infrastructure component does not yet provide for any

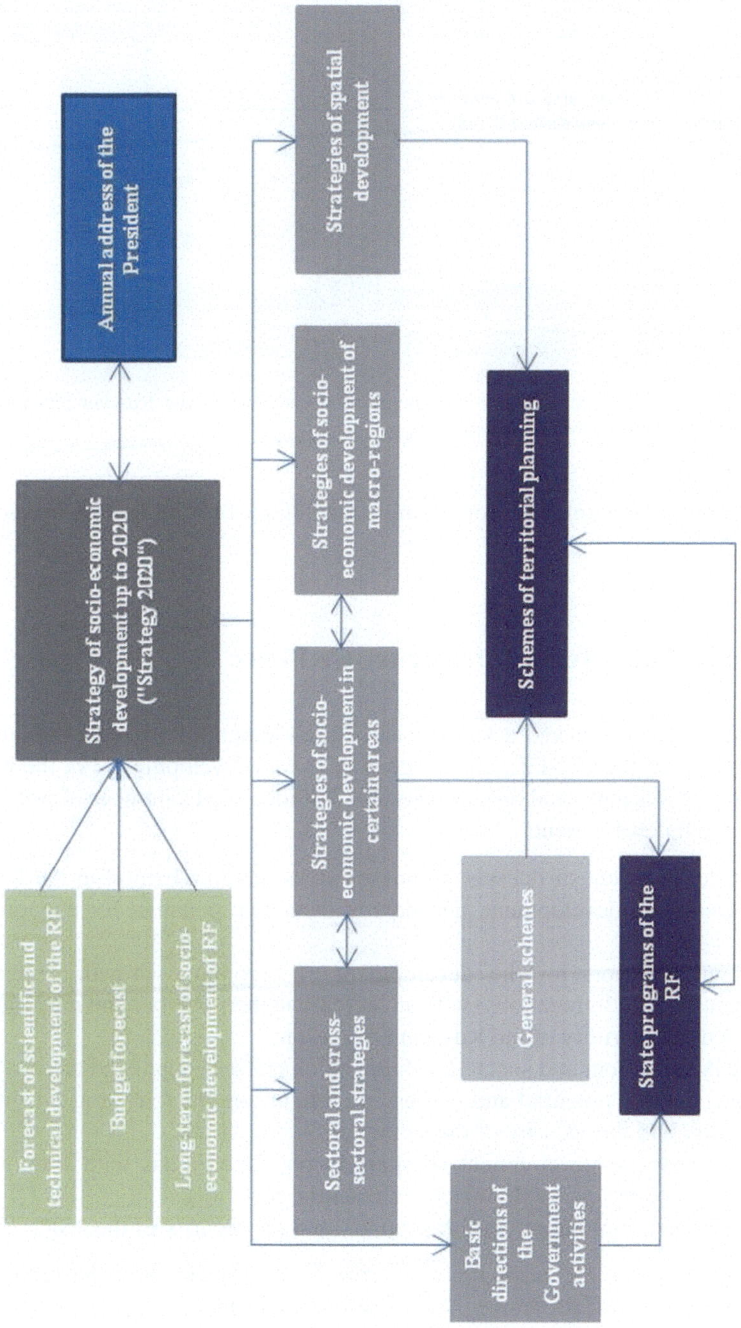

Chart 5.1 System of strategic planning documents at the Federal level in Russia

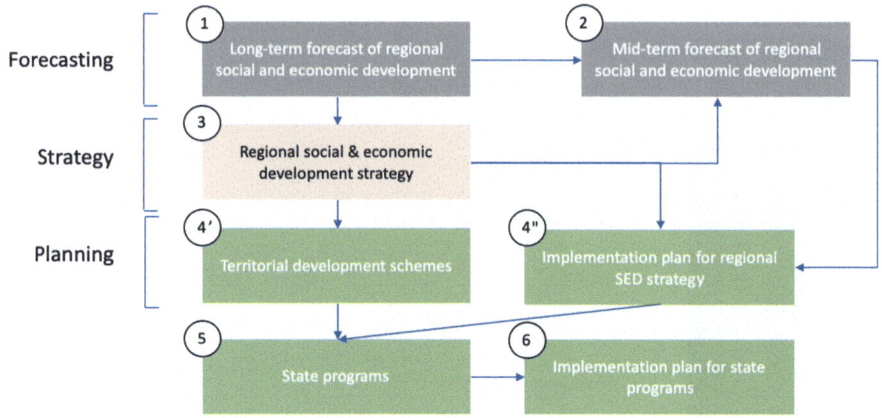

Chart 5.2 System of strategic planning documents of the subject of the Russian Federation (regional level)

specialized program documents—for example, analogues of foreign infrastructure plans.

Transition to Long-Term Infrastructure Plans

For a long time, Russia lacked a key infrastructure element of strategic planning system envisaged by the 172-FZ—the Strategy of spatial development. For the first time, its Concept was approved only in May 2017. It identified a number of priority areas for regional development:

- advanced development of densely populated areas, lagging behind in the level of socio-economic development, and having their own potential for economic growth;
- infrastructural support for the development of "economic growth centers" (including urban agglomerations) with an increase in their number and maximum dispersion in the territory of the Russian Federation;
- economic development and social development of sparsely populated areas with their own economic potential and (or) essential to ensure the territorial integrity of the country and the security of the state;
- the necessary social development of sparsely populated areas with low own potential for economic growth, which are essential for
- ensuring the territorial integrity of the country and the security of the state.

It also set the task of preparing for each territory an assessment of the need for transport and energy infrastructure, human resources in the context of the main professions, and a corresponding assessment of the need for a profiling social infrastructure, especially in the areas of education and health.

A new impetus to the development of the Strategy was given in the Message of the President of the Russian Federation to the Federal Assembly for 2018, in which Vladimir Putin called "to deploy a large-scale program of spatial development of Russia, including the development of cities and other settlements, and at least double the costs for these purposes in the next six years" (Putin 2018). The final text of the document was approved by the Government of the Russian Federation in February 2019 by Order No. 207-R.

The new Strategy defines the tasks, principles, priorities, and main directions of Russia's spatial development, spatial development scenarios, including the priority (target) scenario, perspective centers of economic growth, macro-regions, perspective economic specializations of the subjects of the Federation, target indicators of Russia's spatial development.

Within the framework of the Strategy implementation, it is envisaged to increase the availability and quality of the main transport, energy, information, and telecommunication infrastructure, reduce the level of interregional differentiation in the socio-economic development of the subjects of the Federation, reduce intraregional socio-economic differences, expand the geography and accelerate economic growth, scientific, technological, and innovative development of Russia due to the socio-economic development of promising centers of economic growth, the social and economic development of the Far East, which is ahead of the average Russian rates, and the provision of sustainable growth of the permanent population in this macro-region.

The list of promising centers of economic growth includes cities that form large urban agglomerations and the largest urban agglomerations that will contribute to economic growth more than 1% annually (20 centers); promising centers of economic growth of the subjects of the Federation, which will contribute to economic growth from 0.2 to 1% annually (44 centers); promising centers of economic growth of the subjects of the Federation, which will contribute to economic growth up to 0.2% annually (31 centers); promising mineral and agro-industrial centers (27 centers); and promising centers of economic growth, which have the conditions for the formation of world-class scientific and educational centers (20 centers).

The Strategy also formed 12 macro-regions: Central, Central black earth, North-West, North, South, North Caucasus, Volga-Kama, Volga-Ural, Ural-Siberian, South Siberian, Angara-Yenisei, far East.

The Strategy provides for the creation of a new mechanism for the development of territories (investment sites) with a special regime for doing business, taking into account the promising specialization of the subjects of the Federation and other features of the territories. In order to avoid duplication of state support measures, the Federal authorities, with the state support of the economic sectors of each particular subject of the Federation, will take into account the prospective economic specializations of the bordering subjects of the Federation and its members in one macro-region.

It is noteworthy, however, that the infrastructure support for the socio-economic development of the territories, according to the Strategy, will be implemented within the framework of the Comprehensive plan for the modernization and expansion of the main infrastructure until 2024 (approved by Government decree No. 2101-p of September 30, 2018, hereinafter—the Comprehensive Plan) and national projects—that is, a document that was adopted almost six months before the approval of the Strategy. Moreover, the action plan for the implementation of specific objectives of the Strategy will be prepared only by the second half of 2019. It will be applied as a tool that will specify the necessary changes of legal acts and build a relationship with the other strategically important documents.

The Comprehensive Plan includes 11 Federal projects. Nine of them are aimed at modernization and expansion of transport infrastructure. These Federal projects envisage the development of the West–East and North–South transport corridors for transportation of goods and the improvement of the level of economic connectivity of the territory of Russia through the expansion and modernization of railway, aviation, road, sea, and river infrastructure. Two more projects—"Guaranteed provision of affordable electricity," "Guaranteed provision of transportation of oil, oil products, gas, and gas condensate"—are aimed at modernization and expansion of energy infrastructure (energy part of the comprehensive plan). Still, despite their fundamental importance for the country's infrastructure framework, the document can hardly be considered comprehensive and is only a partial implementation of a full-fledged infrastructure plan.

Thus, on the one hand, the first "impulse" steps have already been taken at the Federal level to ensure the "systemic" infrastructure planning; on the other hand, they are obviously not enough in themselves, and many years of work, including at the regional level, are still to be done to build the entire system.

In terms of infrastructure planning, great hopes were placed on the so-called "infrastructure mortgage"—a plan of measures to improve existing and develop new mechanisms for infrastructure development, approved in March 2018. According to the published plan, until June 2018, it was planned to implement 16 measures aimed at developing mechanisms for the construction and reconstruction of infrastructure in Russia, improving legislation in the field of PPP for implementation. However, most of them were never fulfilled.

Among the activities of the plan, it is worth mentioning the "infrastructure map"—a consolidated long-term plan for the infrastructure development of the Russian Federation, the procedure for the development of which, according to the approved action Plan ("road map") for the development of public–private partnership tools, was to be developed by the Ministry of economic development of Russia, together with interested authorities, in may 2018.

Taking into account foreign experience and the existing system of state strategic planning documents (which does not provide for such a document directly), the "infrastructure map" could become part of the Plan for the implementation of Russia's spatial development Strategy, reflecting the key long-term targets for infrastructure development, approaches to the formation of sectoral infrastructure frameworks within the macro-regions, as well as a set of key infrastructure projects planned for implementation in the country. In particular, such a "map" can become one of the elements of the action plan for the implementation of specific tasks of the spatial development Strategy (Tarakanov et al. 2019).

Regional Aspect

At the regional level, the approach to infrastructure planning is also vertical and therefore conceptually similar to the Federal approach.

Different kinds of strategies, for example, socio-economic strategies, investment strategies, etc., may be considered as upper-level regional documents. Such documents lay down the framework approach of the region to the development of its infrastructure, may contain consolidated targets and prioritize individual instruments (for example, public–private partnership). For example, the new draft Strategy of socio-economic development for the period up to 2030 of the Republic of Bashkortostan—one of the leaders of the National rating of regions on the level of PPP development on planning parameters—contains a separate section on infrastructure: it presents a fairly detailed description of the status quo in the sectoral context and defines the target development metrics to be achieved by the end of the period. In the Strategy of socio-economic development of the Smolensk region, public–private partnership is singled out.

The implementation of the strategies is ensured through regional development programs and similar documents, which define the basic list of activities required for this purpose. Such documents can be both sectoral and general—in most regions, they can operate in parallel. For example, in the Novosibirsk region, there are at least ten sectoral state programs in which the theme of regional infrastructure development is decomposed and developed. In some cases, the regions reinforce the need to implement specific high-priority infrastructure projects in their programs.

Further detailing of infrastructure planning is carried out within the framework of specific plans and lists of priority projects. For example, in the field of public–private partnership, it is mandatory for the regions to update and publish annually lists of infrastructure facilities preparing for transfer to concession agreements.

Current Issues and Recommendations

Unfortunately, current strategic planning of infrastructure development at both the Federal and regional levels in Russia is not free from a number of shortcomings, the main of which are the following:

- lack of inter-sectoral synchronization;
- poor forecasting (assessment of current and future infrastructure gaps), including due to lack of competencies;

- lack of an effective priority management system (when deciding on the implementation of an infrastructure project, no truly comprehensive assessment of multiplicative effects and budgetary efficiency is carried out);
- development of goal setting and programming documents does not take into account the specifics and feasibility of public–private partnership (PPP) mechanisms to eliminate certain "infrastructure gaps" (OECD 2014).

These shortcomings not only hinder the effective management of budget expenditures of investment nature, but also are a negative factor for attracting private investment in the development of public infrastructure. The "reset" of the system of strategic planning for the development of public infrastructure, in our opinion, should be carried out in the following main areas (Ivanov et al. 2018):

- formation of an effective system of forecasting the need for public infrastructure facilities ("infrastructure gaps") in the territory of the Russian Federation for the long term;
- integration of PPP as one of the tools of socio-economic development of the territory in the documents of target setting of the subject of the Russian Federation, including the investment Strategy (if applicable);
- improvement of the procedure for the formation of state programs and other documents of the planning/programming of subject of the Russian Federation in regard to the feasibility of application of PPP mechanisms at the stage of their formation (the introduction of a "filter" on the possibility of using PPP).

At the same time, the above measures do not solve the most important problem—the lack of inter-sectoral synchronization in the development of infrastructure, as well as the medium-term nature of most planning documents in the field of infrastructure (Konovalov 2017).

As noted above, the so called "infrastructure plans" are developed and implemented in many countries (UK, Australia, Singapore, etc.) to solve this problem. (Chart 5.3).

In Russian domestic practice, such a plan could perform the tasks of intersectoral and interregional balancing of the development of public infrastructure for subsequent adjustment and synchronization of strategic planning documents (state programs, territorial planning schemes, targeted investment programs, investment programs of natural monopolies, action plans for the implementation of socio-economic development strategies, etc.).

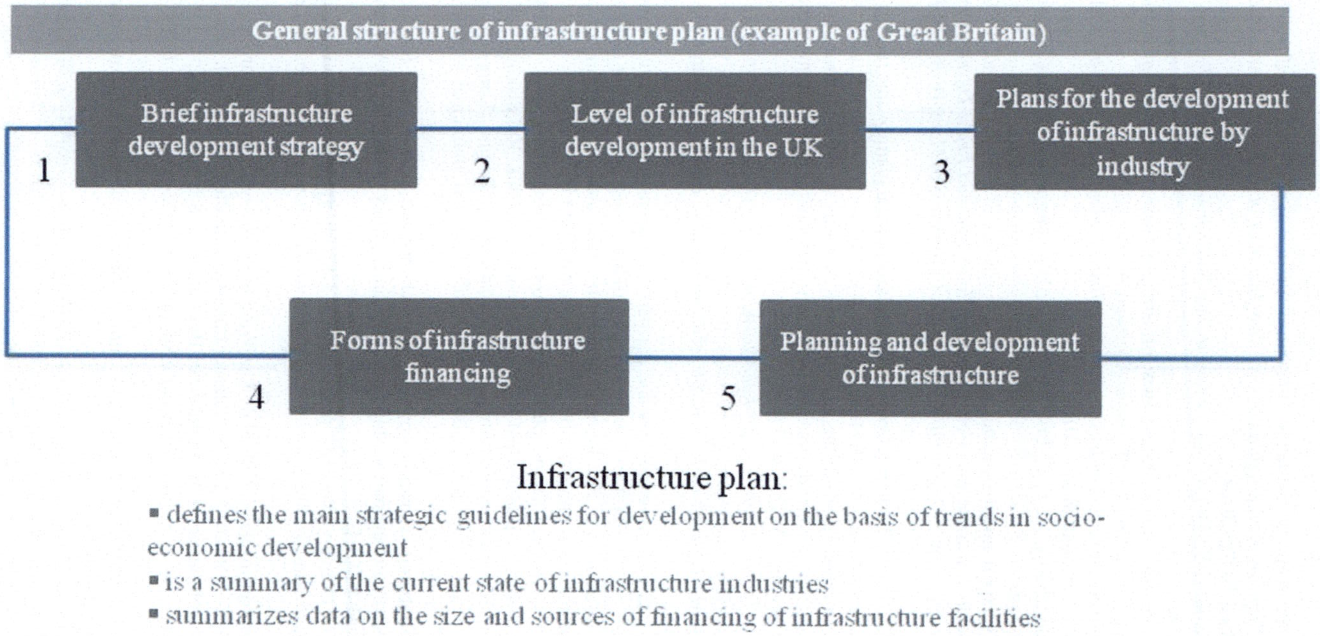

Chart 5.3 Major aspects of the formation of the "infrastructure plan" as an element of the strategic planning system

References

Box, A. (2017). Rethinking infrastructure planning—Preparing for an unpredictable future. KPMG Australia. https://home.kpmg/au/en/home/insights/2017/06/rethinking-infrastructure-planning.html. Accessed 10 Apr 2019.

Howes, R., & Robinson, H. (2006). *Infrastructure for the built environment: Global procurement strategies*, Routledge.

Infrastructure New South Wales. http://www.infrastructure.nsw.gov.au/state-infrastructure-strategy/state-infrastructure-strategy-2012.aspx. Accessed 20 Apr 2019.

Infrastructure SA. Government of South Australia. http://www.infrastructure.sa.gov.au/strategic_infrastructure_plan. Accessed 20 Apr 2018.

Inshakova, A. O., Goncharov, A. I., & Ershova, I. V. (2019). Digital blockchain registration of legally significant stages
of complex good's export-import supplies by business entities of the EAEU and BRICS jurisdictions. In *Competitive Russia: Foresight Model of Economic and Legal Development in the Digital Age: Proceedings of the International Scientific Conference in Memory of Oleg Inshakov (1952–2018)* (pp. 328–336). Cham: Springer Nature.

Ivanov, O. V. (2016a). Strategicheskoe celepolaganie i dolgosrochnoe planirovanie razvitiya infrastruktury kak faktory povysheniya effektivnosti gosudarstvenno-chastnogo partnerstva (mezhdunarodnyj opyt). (Strategic goal-setting and long-term planning of infrastructure development as factors of increase in effectiveness of public-private partnership (international experience). Public-Private Partnerships, Vol. 3. №. 3 (pp. 173–188).

Ivanov, O. V. (2016b). *Teoriya i mirovaya praktika gosudarstvenno-chastnogo partnerstva (Theory and world practice of public-private partnership)* (p. 299). Moscow: MGIMO-University.

Ivanov et al. (2018). *Mechanisms of PPP in the economic policy of Russia.* Ivanov, O.V. (Ed). MGIMO-University.

Ivanov, O. V. (2019). Gosudartsvenno-chastnoe partnerstvo kak instrument razvitiya infrastruktury i modernizatsii ekonomiki. Opyt stran Aziatsko-tikhookeanskogo regiona (Public-private partnership as an instrument of development of infrastructure and modernization of economy. Experience of Asia-Pacific countries) (300 p). Moscow, MGIMO-University.

Konovalov, A. (2017). Dolgosrochnoe planirovanie razvitiya obshchestvennoj infrastruktury-prioritet gosudarstvennogo i municipal'nogo upravleniya. Vestnik Rossijskogo universiteta druzhby narodov. Seriya: Gosudarstvennoe i municipal'noe upravlenie (Long-term planning of public infrastructure development is a priority of state and municipal administration). *RUDN-Journal of Public Administration, 4*(1).

Mekhanizmy gosudarstvenno-chastnogo partnerstva v ekonomicheskoj politike Rossii. (2018). (Mechanisms of public-private partnership in the economic policy of Russia). O.V. Ivanov (Ed.) (409 p). Moscow: MGIMO-University.

National Infrastructure Delivery Plan and Pipeline. (2018). UK Government. http://www.gov.uk/government/collections/national-infrastructure-plan#national-infrastructure-pipeline. Accessed 10 Apr 2019.

Natsionalnii infrastrukturnii plan 2016–2030. Osnovnie napravleniya infrastrukturnogo razvitiya Respubliki Belarus v 2016-2013 godah (National Infrastructure Plan 2016–2030. Key directions of infrastructure development of the Republic of Belarus in 2016–2030). Minsk.

OECD. (2014). Overview of public governance of public-private partnerships in the Russian Federation.

PPP Reference Guide 3.0. (2017). World Bank. https://library.pppknowledgelab.org/documents/4699. Accessed 07 May 2019.

PPP/PFIの抜本改革に向けたアクションプラン。平成25年6月6日。民間資金等活用事業推進会議決定 (Action plan for drastic reform of PPP/PFI. June 6, 2015—*in Japanese*).

PPP/PFI推進アクションプラン。平成28年5月18日 民間資金等活用事業推進会議 (PPP/PFI action plan. May 18, 2016 – *in Japanese*).

Proekt Nacional'nogo doklada o privlechenii chastnyh investicij v razvitie infrastruktury i primenenii mekhanizmov gosudarstvenno-chastnogo partnerstva v Rossijskoj Federacii. (2018). (Draft national report on attracting private investment in infrastructure development and application of Public-Private Partnership mechanisms in the Russian Federatio). National PPP Center.

Putin, V. (2018). Poslanie Prezidenta Rossijskoj Federacii Federal'nomu Sobraniyu Rossijskoj Federacii (Message From The President Of The Russian Federation To The Federal Assembly Of The Russian Federation).

Second Global Infrastructure Investment Index. (2014). Competing for private finance. ARCADIS.

Strategiya prostranstvennogo razvitiya Rossiskoi Federatsii na period do 2025 goda. (2019). (Strategy of spatial development of the Russian Federation). Ministry of Economic Development of the Russian Federation (2019). http://os.economy.gov.ru/documents/11006/.

Tarakanov, V. V., Inshakova, A. O., & Goncharov, A. I. (2019). Interactive demo on-line maintenance foreign trade deals of business entities of BRICS jurisdictions. In *Competitive Russia: Foresight Model of Economic and Legal Development in the Digital Age: Proceedings of the International Scientific Conference in Memory of Oleg Inshakov (1952–2018)* (pp. 319–327). Cham: Springer Nature.

Understanding infrastructure opportunities in ASEAN. Infrastructure Series Report 1. (2017). PwC. https://www.pwc.com/sg/en/publications/assets/cpi-mas-1-infrastructure-opporuntities-in-asean-201709.pdf. Accessed 11 May 2019.

Urban Development Authority. A Singapore Government Agency Website. http://www.ura.gov.sg/uol/master-plan/vision-and-principles/Our-Planning-Process. Accessed 10 Apr 2019.

Valverde, M., & Moore, A. (2019). The performance of transparency in public–private infrastructure project governance: The politics of documentary practices. *Urban Studies, 56*(4), 689–704.

World Bank. (2017). PPP Reference Guide 3.0. https://library.pppknowledgelab.org/documents/4699. Accessed 07 May 2019.

World Economic Forum. (2015). The global competitiveness report 2014–2015. http://www3.weforum.org/docs/WEF_GlobalCompetitivenessReport_2014-15.pdf. Accessed 11 May 2019.

World Economic Forum. (2018). The global competitiveness report 2017–2018. World Economic Forum. http://www3.weforum.org/docs/GCR2017-2018/05FullReport/TheGlobalCompetitivenessReport2017%E2%80%932018.pdf. Accessed 11 May 2019.

民間資金等の活用による公共施設等の整備等に関する事業の実施に関する基本方針。平成25年9月20日閣議決定 (Basic policy on implementation of projects related to the improvement of public facilities by the use of private funds. September 20, 2015—*in Japanese*).

Chapter 6
PPP Governance at the Federal and Regional Level

Oleg V. Ivanov, Agnessa O. Inshakova, and Alexander V. Poroshin

Abstract The system of public-private partnership governance at the Federal level in Russia is investigated. Focus of analysis is concentrated on the major PPP units, its core functions, and interaction. Especially, important role of the National PPP Center and key directions of its activities are explored. Emerging instruments of public support for PPP projects are systemized and studied. In regard to PPP governance at the regional level, results of PPP rating of regions are introduced. PPP activities of the regions through the prism of achievement of the integral indicator of PPP development are analyzed. Methodology of calculation of the indicator and its component factors are introduced. Major trends in PPP development in the regions are identified. The analysis of regional PPP institutional environment and legal framework brings light on key areas of success and main weaknesses that still remain but can transform into important points of growth in the coming years.

Keywords Public-private partnership · Management system · PPP bodies · Rating of russian regions · Institutional environment · Regulatory framework

JEL-Codes H11 · H44 · L88 · L 97 · R11 · R12

O. V. Ivanov (✉)
Department of economic policy and public-private partnership, MGIMO University, prospect Vernadskogo 76, 119454 Moscow, Russia
e-mail: ivanov_ov@mail.ru

A. O. Inshakova
Department of Civil and Private International Law (the Basic department of the Southern Scientific Center of the Russian Academy of Sciences), Volgograd State University, Prospekt Universitetskij, 100, 400062 Volgograd, Russia
e-mail: gimchp@volsu.ru; ainshakova@list.ru

A. V. Poroshin
Strategic development, analytics and information support of PPP, Center of PPP projects, JSC "Avtodor-invest", Malaya Dmitrovka str. 16-6, 127006 Moscow, Russia
e-mail: caunte@gmail.com

O. V. Ivanov and A. O. Inshakova (eds.), *Public-Private Partnerships in Russia*, Competitive Government: Public Private Partnerships,
https://doi.org/10.1007/978-3-030-56352-3_6

Introduction

Analysis of the major trends in development of public-private partnership in the world over the past decade shows that despite the variety of specific institutional, legal, organizational, managerial, mental, psychological, and other factors that influence PPP governance in various countries, centralization of public administration, significant strengthening of its organizational and institutional foundations as well as an integrated approach to PPP governance are most common and dominant features.

This approach is reflected in elaboration of conceptual and doctrinal foundations of PPP policy, transition to a long-term planning of infrastructure development, further strengthening of legislative and regulatory framework of PPP, creation of PPP units of different types with different functions, and establishment of system of public support of PPP. In general, we can say that governance is becoming an increasingly important factor influencing PPP development in the country and its transformation into an effective tool for improvement of infrastructure.

Results

PPP Governance. Types of PPP Units at the Federal Level, Its Main Functions

According to the UNECE indicative model of PPPs development, Russian Federation moved from "emerging" stage of PPP development to the stage of "formation," which involves

- strengthening of PPP legal and regulatory framework;
- establishment of PPP units and development institutions;
- development of PPP practical guidelines;
- creation of conditions for attraction of new sources of financing (pension savings, insurance savings, etc.);
- introduction of various elements of government support for PPP;
- implementation of budget and other incentives to develop PPP operators market.

Also, the specifics of the PPP market in the Russian Federation is the gradual accumulation of PPP practices in various sectors of infrastructure and expansion of the range of industries in which PPP mechanisms are applied.

There is no integral system of PPP governance in Russia yet. Nevertheless, progress in establishment of such a system has begun, and quite a number of important institutional elements can now be seen as emerged and functioning.

Ministry of economic development plays an important role in PPP governance in Russia. The Department of investment policy and development of entrepreneurship in the Ministry carries out functions to ensure development of PPP state policy and legal regulation in this field.

The Department:

- develops proposals for improvement and extension of forms of PPP in the investment sphere, including development of PPP normative and legal acts;
- prepares, selects, and monitors projects based on PPP arrangements;
- participates in negotiations with international organizations and institutions to ensure signing of international agreements on implementation of joint projects;
- prepares conclusions on the compliance of investment projects, PPP, and concession projects of national importance aimed at socioeconomic development of the Russian Federation and corresponded with sectoral development strategies approved by the Government of the Russian Federation.

A decision on establishment of PPP Coordination Council under the Ministry is under consideration. It is presumed that the body will ensure effective cooperation of Federal Executive bodies, subjects of the Russian Federation, financial institution, and experts to develop joint proposals to improve the efficiency of PPP projects, improve legislation, and simplify access to PPP tools.

The composition of the Council is still under discussion. It is assumed that it will be headed by the Minister of economic development and will include heads or Deputy heads of Federal authorities—line ministries, which are directly responsible for the implementation of projects in relevant sectors: health, education, transport, etc. The Council will also include representatives of legislative bodies, in particular the state Duma. To accumulate the best practices, it is planned to invite representatives of the TOP ten of the PPP development rating of regions. Interaction with business is very important, so the Council is planned to include leading public entrepreneurship organizations—Chamber of Commerce and Industry, "Business Russia," etc. When an agenda will include sectoral issues (transport projects, healthcare projects, etc.), it is planned to invite industry business to the working groups. Representatives of nongovernment and scientific organizations are also expected to take part in the Council, because without them it will not be quite correct to make system-forming decisions and discuss development issues.

The Ministry of economic development is the initiator and chief developer of relevant PPP legislation, including the Federal law on public-private and municipal-private partnerships. Among other systemic issues the Ministry deals with, preparation of methodological normative documents including methodology for assessing effectiveness of PPP projects should be noted.

The Ministry has also prepared so-called "PPP-standard," which is de facto an institutional scheme for development of PPP in the regions: where to start, what institutions to create, and how to accompany projects.

PPP units have also been established in a number of other Russian ministries and agencies.

Since 2006, the *Ministry of transport* of the Russian Federation has an Expert Council on public-private partnership.

The Ministry of healthcare of the Russian Federation has a Department of infrastructure development and public-private partnership. A few years ago, Coordination Council of the Ministry for development of public-private partnership in the field of healthcare was established. The Council headed by the Minister includes representatives of Federal ministries and departments (industry and trade, finance, Federal service for supervision in the sphere of healthcare), members of the Federation Council, deputies of the State Duma of the Russian Federation, heads of public and scientific organizations, etc. Representing interests of business community, Chairman of the Committee on public-private partnership of the Chamber of Commerce and Industry, Chairman of the National PPP center, etc., are taking part in the Coordination Council's work.

According to the Regulation on the Council, its main functions are

- consideration of proposals for application of PPP mechanisms in healthcare, aimed at development of infrastructure and improving the quality and availability of medical care;
- consideration of proposals to improve PPP regulatory framework in healthcare;
- consideration of proposals to remove restrictions on attracting private investment in healthcare;
- consideration of proposals for preparation of investment projects in healthcare;
- monitoring of implementation of PPP projects in healthcare.

In 2014, PPP Center under *the Ministry of construction, housing, and communal utilities* of the Russian Federation began its work. This center was established to promote PPP in the sector and provide administrative support to PPP projects. The center is headed by the Deputy Minister of construction and housing.

In recent years, *the National PPP Center* (hereinafter referred to as the Center), the first and only nongovernmental nonprofit organization in Russia, formed to coordinate public authorities, local governments, and business and expert community in implementation of activities related to PPP mechanisms, has been playing an increasingly important role in PPP matters in the country.

The purpose of the Center is to unite resources of the state and business, to consolidate expert community in the field of public-private partnership to attract investment and competence into development of public infrastructure. The initiators of the Center were large entrepreneurship structures, state authorities, public organizations, and expert and scientific community.

The Center's activities are carried out in the following key areas:

- *support of PPP projects*

The Center developed the concept of "Qualified customer," on the basis of which the following range of services is provided to public authorities in the regions:

- development of draft legal acts regulating the activities of the state authorities of the subject in the field of PPP;
- provision of standard organizational documents for the activities of regional branches of development centers;
- consulting on the application of PPP project management methodology;
- creation of "Qualified customer" office—the specialized organization for management of PPP projects.

"Qualified customer" office can be created within an institutional framework of the subject of the Russian Federation or on a contractual basis by giving the Center the powers of the Qualified customer.

The National PPP Center is officially recognized by the World Bank as the National PPP unit in Russia and the single coordinator of methodological support to the RF subjects in the implementation of PPP projects.

- *research activity*

The Center prepares information and analytical materials, as well as conducts applied research for the benefit of government agencies and private companies.

- *examination of legislation*

The Center participates in preparation of normative legal acts of Federal and regional importance, conducts examination of the legislation.

- *personnel training*

The Center established PPP Institute (www.p3institute.ru), which operates educational events, conducts educational programs for professional development and retraining of personnel in the sphere of PPP. Educational programs are conducted in cooperation with leading universities of Russia with involvement of prominent Russian and foreign PPP experts on the basis of

- the Department of Economic policy and public-private partnership of MGIMO University. Training courses are designed to train masters and bachelors specializing in public-private partnership, relations with public authorities and public organizations. Short-term professional development programs are also implemented for government and business representatives;
- "Scientific and educational PPP center" of the Russian Academy of national economy and public administration under the President of the Russian Federation. Priority activities of the center include carrying out fundamental, applied research and works in the field of methodology of management of PPP projects, training, and advanced training of specialists and scientific and pedagogical personnel, and development of international cooperation in the field of PPP;
- "North-Western scientific and educational PPP center" on the basis of St. Petersburg State Polytechnic University. The research center carries out research in the field of project management, implementation of research results in the project activities of organizations engaged in public-private partnership, retraining of personnel of public and municipal administration, public corporations, as well as commercial structures working in the field of public-private partnership.

- *information support*

As part of the information cooperation between the National PPP center and the Ministry of economic development of the Russian Federation, Platform for supporting of infrastructure projects (ROSINFRA) was created (pppi.ru). ROSINFRA is a portal providing market participants with up-to-date information on development of PPP mechanisms and PPP projects implemented in the subjects of the Russian Federation. With the support of the Center and the Russian Chamber of Commerce and Industry, the only PPP-specialized Federal media in Russia—PPP Journal (www.pppjounal.ru)—was established. The Center also created a PPP communication agency "PPP-INFO" (www.p3info.ru) to implement complex information projects and public events.

In 2019, the Center concluded the work on the digital platform "ROSINFRA," which is a comprehensive digital solution to assist the launch of infrastructure and investment projects with state participation. Creation of the Platform is aimed at facilitating communication between market participants of investment projects with state participation by launching a set of services that allows

- to share—fast and convenient—experience, successful practices and involve experts for preparation and implementation of PPP projects;
- to select optimal parameters of PPP projects (structurator) and evaluate its effectiveness (efficiency calculator) in online mode;
- to receive full, up-to-date, reliable, and personalized information about the market and investment initiatives;
- to organize convenient interaction of project team members, stakeholders, experts, and authorities with each other;
- to find and select a partner to prepare, launch, and implement PPP projects;
- to train personnel and to attract third-party under the project (out-staffing);
- to select and justify public participation (form and amount of support) for PPP projects.

The Committee on public-private partnership of the Chamber of Commerce and Industry of the Russian Federation (RF CCI) plays an important role in promoting development of PPP in the country. The main purpose of its establishment is to consolidate efforts of business and scientific community, regional chambers of commerce, and Federal and regional authorities to create favorable environment for implementation of PPP in various spheres and sectors of the economy.

The key tasks assigned to the Committee are

- improvement of PPP legal and regulative base in the Russian Federation;
- establishment of close and sustainable relations with business and expert community in implementation of PPP projects;
- provision of methodological and information assistance to development of PPP in Russia.

Since its establishment, the PPP Committee has become a professional platform for interested representatives of government and business, banking, and scientific communities. Today, it is one of the few competent authorities that allows to develop joint decisions of business and the state in the field of PPP. The Committee has developed a number of systemic documents, such as Guidelines for implementation of PPP projects in the subjects of the Russian Federation, Methods for assessing comparative advantage of PPP Versus. public procurement, etc. Experts of the Committee participated in the preparation of the Federal law "On public-private, municipal-private partnership in the Russian Federation" and amendments to the Federal law "On concession agreements."

Together with the National PPP center, the PPP Committee of the RF CCI implemented a number of significant projects. In particular, the rating of Russian regions on the level of PPP development is prepared annually, and the Department of Economic policy and PPP has been opened in MGIMO. The CCI site is planned to be used for development and promotion of new promising projects, in implementation of which PPP mechanisms can be applied. The task is to turn CCI into a leading expert platform in the field of PPP in Russia, bringing together representatives of leading business associations, business structures, financial institutions, companies specializing in support of investment and infrastructure projects, state corporations, and scientific and expert organizations. The key partners on the part of the state are the Ministry of economic development, the Ministry of transport, the Ministry of defense, the State Duma, etc.

Joint-stock company *"VEB Infrastructure" (JSC "InfraVEB")*—a subsidiary of the State Corporation "Vneshekonombank"—is actively working on PPPs. JSC "InfraVEB" deals with formation and structuring of projects, optimizing allocation of risks, choice of optimal financial models for projects. The company helps to prepare projects of regional and urban development with involvement of extra-budgetary investments. This is an intellectually capacious and capital-intensive business, and risky. Therefore, we can say that in fact JSC "InfraVEB" engaged in venture investing.

JSC "InfraVEB" also plays one of the central roles in implementation of the so-called "Project financing factory," a new mechanism of financial support for infrastructure projects in Russia, launched in 2018.

Given the long-term and complex nature of the task of the country's infrastructure development, its implementation is unlikely to be effective without a clear understanding of the existing needs and opportunities, as well as appropriate goal-setting. These aspects can be ensured only through a systematic approach.

The need for "systemic approach" is due to several factors. First, it is desirable due to the nature of infrastructure itself. In most cases, some infrastructure facilities are more or less dependent on others: for example, development of industrial zones will be impractical without accompanying logistics infrastructure, and energy sales networks will be useless without production capacity—and vice versa. In this regard, even at the microlevel, they should be considered at least in conjunction with each other, and at the macrolevel, with the entire infrastructure network. Second, the approach to infrastructure development must be sound and sustainable over time—if priorities are changed too often, economic efficiency of investment will decline. Thirdly, the "coordination" component of the decision-making process is also important, whether it is an interaction of two agencies responsible for different aspects, or a movement along the administrative vertical. For successful infrastructure development, all stakeholders must have a synchronized agenda.

At the same time, "systemic approach" not only improves efficiency of planning as such, but can also play the role of a communication tool between the state and the private sectors, the demand for which in development of public infrastructure is steadily growing. Having an understanding of strategic contours of the country's future infrastructure development and availability of information about specific opportunities is the key to efficiency in attracting private capital and competencies.

In Russia, today, infrastructure planning is extremely fragmented. Although certain elements of infrastructure planning can be found in different forms and at different levels—from state programs and economic development strategies to regional and municipal lists of facilities for which concession agreements or PPP agreements are planned—they are all used in a piecemeal manner and there is no consistency. Given the acuteness of infrastructure problems, the significant potential of the private sector in their solution, comprehensive measures to introduce the practice of infrastructure planning and ensure its consistency can give a significant impetus to the infrastructure development of Russia (Tarakanov et al. 2019).

As part of the improvement of existing and development of new mechanisms for infrastructure development, the Russian Government plans to implement a system of measures, including

- establishment of the Governmental Commission on development of infrastructure;
- creation of infrastructure map (long-term infrastructure development plan);
- maintaining an open register of infrastructure projects;
- development of conceptual methods of evaluation of economic effects from implementation of projects with "budget leverage";
- extension of quasi-TIF (Tax Increase Financing) mechanisms to infrastructure projects.

In addition, creation of a single infrastructure management center (including the principles of public-private partnership) on the basis of VEB State Corporation under discussion.

Ranking of Regions by PPP Development Level. PPP Governance at the Regional Level

In 2014, the Government of the Russian Federation by the Order of April 10, 2014 № 570-p approved the indicator "Level of development of public-private partnership in the subject of the Russian Federation," by which the leaders of the regions should be guided in their work. The indicator is calculated by methodology applied in the Rating of Russian regions "PPP-START"—a comprehensive assessment of the readiness of the RF subject to the construction of public infrastructure with involvement of private investors on PPP principles. The "readiness of the subject of Federation to implement PPP projects" means fulfillment of a number of conditions that provide a favorable climate for implementation of PPP investment projects.

This study is conducted by the Center annually to determine the level of PPP development in the subjects of the Russian Federation. The research aims to systematize accumulated regional experience in implementation of PPP projects and to demonstrate an objective picture of PPP development in the country.

Method of Calculating the PPP Rating of Regions

The PPP rating of the regions is calculated on the basis of three groups of indicators:

institutional environment—creation of conditions for successful launch and implementation of PPP projects (availability of qualified specialists, authorized PPP units, PPP development institutes, PPP information resource on the Internet, etc.);
regulatory framework—regulatory and legal acts regulating interaction of authorities in the launch and implementation of PPP projects;
implementation of PPP projects—experience in implementation of projects in the form of PPP agreements and concession agreements, and in the form of quasi-PPP.

Calculation of the complex indicator "Level of development of the sphere of public-private partnership in the subject of the Russian Federation" is made according to the following formula:

$$\boldsymbol{Rj} = \boldsymbol{\alpha} \times \boldsymbol{Lj} + \boldsymbol{\beta} \times \boldsymbol{Nj} + \boldsymbol{\gamma} \times \boldsymbol{Ej},$$

where

j	serial number of the subject of the Russian Federation;
α, β, γ	values that determine the significance of the constituent factors, while $\alpha = 0{,}03$, $\boldsymbol{\beta} = 0{,}03$, and $\gamma = 0{,}04$;
Lj	importance of the factor "Development of institutional environment of the Russian Federation in the field of public-private partnership";
Nj	the importance of the factor "Legal support of public-private partnership";
Ej	value of the factor "Experience of implementation of public-private partnership projects."

Calculation of the value of the factor "Development of the institutional environment of the subject of the Russian Federation in the field of public-private partnership" is made according to the following formula:

$$\begin{cases} Ij = \sum Li \\ Ii = ai \times ki \end{cases}$$

where

Ii value of the *i*-th criterion (in points); ai—binary evaluation of the i-th criterion (ai = 0; 1);
ki coefficient determined by expert method characterizing the quality of the *i*-th criterion;
ki [0–100], percent;
n number of criteria;
Ij [0–10].

Calculation of the value of the factor "Development of institutional environment" is made on the basis of estimates on the following set of criteria:

(a) availability of an authorized body in the field of public-private partnership.

K1 coefficient, determined by expert means, characterizes existence of a relevant act approving the authority's powers and a regulation on the relevant unit of the authority. Decreasing expert coefficient (from 0.5 to 1) is applied on the basis of evaluation of the effectiveness of this body;

(b) availability of a specialized structure responsible for support of PPP projects.

K2 coefficient, determined by expert means, characterizes existence of a structure responsible for supporting PPP projects from initiation stage to direct implementation. Decreasing expert coefficient (from 0.5 to 1) is applied on the basis of evaluation of the effectiveness of this structure;

(c) availability of specialists with appropriate qualifications in the field of PPP.

K3 coefficient, determined by expert means, characterizes the presence of more than five specialists who have undergone specialized training in PPP projects management. Decreasing expert coefficient (from 0.5 to 1) is applied on the basis of assessment of the quality of relevant training programs;

(d) availability of an interdepartmental body responsible for consideration of initiated PPP projects and development of PPP policies.

K4 coefficient, determined by expert means, characterizes existence of a regulation on the relevant body and rules of its work. Decreasing expert coefficient (from 0.5 to 1) is applied on the basis of assessment of the effectiveness of the relevant body;

(e) availability of a single body responsible selection of a private partner (concessionaire).

K5 coefficient, determined by expert means, characterizes existence of an act defining the relevant powers of the body. Decreasing expert coefficient (from 0.5 to 1) is applied on the basis of evaluation of the effectiveness of the relevant body (quality of the preparation of tender documentation, use of effective tools to inform potential bidders, and the openness of tender procedure);

(f) consideration of PPP mechanisms in the target setting documents of the subject of the Russian Federation, including strategy of social and economic development, plan of implementation of strategy of social and economic development, etc.

K6 coefficient, determined by expert means, characterizes inclusion of PPP mechanisms in strategic goal-setting documents of the subject of the Russian Federation. Decreasing expert coefficient (from 0.5 to 1) is applied on the basis of assessment of the quality of implementation of PPP mechanisms in strategic planning documents;

(g) consideration of PPP mechanisms in development and approval of planning and programming documents of the subject of the Russian Federation.

K7 coefficient, determined by expert means, characterizes presence of an integrated assessment of the possibility and feasibility of PPP mechanisms application for implementation of planning and programming documents of the subject of the Russian Federation. Decreasing expert coefficient (from 0.5 to 1) is applied on the basis of assessment of the quality of the implementation of PPP mechanisms in planning and programming documents;

(h) availability of the specialized PPP information resource in the Internet or a section on official website of the subject of the Russian Federation.

K8 coefficient, determined by expert means, characterizes availability of an appropriate information resource. Decreasing expert coefficient (from 0.5 to 1) is applied on the basis of assessment of completeness and frequency of information updates;

(i) availability in open access of the list of objects in regard to which conclusion of PPP agreements and concession agreements is planned.

K9 coefficient, determined by expert means, characterizes the fact that such a list has been formally approved and/or is publicly available. Expert step-down ratio (0.5–1) is applied on the basis of evaluation of the completeness of presented information (information about planned projects, information about objects in respect of which private initiative is appropriate, etc.);

(j) availability of tax preferences and other measures to support private partners.

K10 coefficient, determined by expert means, characterizes existence of regulatory legal acts providing for measures to stimulate the use of PPP mechanisms through tax incentives and other mechanisms to support private investors. Decreasing expert coefficient (from 0.5 to 1) is applied on the basis of evaluation of effectiveness of implemented measures.

The calculation of the value of the factor "Legal support of the sphere of public-private partnership in the subject of the Russian Federation" is made according to the following formula:

$$\begin{cases} Nj = \Sigma N_i; \\ Ni = ai \times ki \end{cases}$$

where

Ni value of the i-th criterion (in points);
ai binary evaluation of the i-th criterion (**ai** = 0; 1);
ki the coefficient defined by expert way, characterizing quality of the i-th criterion, **ki** = [0–100], percentage;
n number of criteria; **Nj** = [0–5].

The calculation of the value of the factor "Legal support of PPP" in the subject of the Russian Federation is made on the basis of assessments of the following set of criteria:

(a) existence of the order of interdepartmental interaction of executive authorities at the stage of development and consideration of PPP projects.

Coefficient K1, determined by expert means, characterizes disclosure of this order in the relevant regulatory (normative) legal (legal) act (acts). Decreasing expert coefficient (from 0.5 to 1) is applied on the basis of assessment of completeness of the relevant act (coverage of all stages and cases of interaction: in case of private initiative, with local governments, in regulated sectors, etc.);

(b) availability of the order of decision-making on implementation of PPP projects in the subject of the Russian Federation.

K2 coefficient, determined by expert means, characterizes disclosure of this order in relevant regulatory legal acts and regulation of interaction of executive authorities when deciding on implementation of PPP projects. Decreasing expert coefficient (from 0.5 to 1) is assigned on the basis of assessment of detail and quality of relevant regulatory legal act;

(c) availability of the order of interdepartmental interaction at control, supervision of monitoring, and maintaining the register of PPP projects.

K3 coefficient, determined by expert means, characterizes the disclosure in relevant regulatory legal acts of the order of interdepartmental interaction in monitoring of PPP agreements and concession agreements, as well as the maintenance of the register of PPP projects.

Lowering expert coefficient (from 0.5 to 1) is applied on the basis of assessment of efficiency of application of the corresponding act;

(d) availability of rules of decision-making on conclusion of PPP agreements and concession agreements for the term exceeding validity period of approved limits of budgetary obligations.

K4 coefficient, determined by expert means, characterizes the disclosure in relevant regulatory legal acts of this order. Decreasing expert coefficient (from 0.5 to 1) is applied on the basis of assessment of the relevant act;

(e) compliance of PPP regulatory framework with the norms of Federal legislation.

K5 coefficient, determined by expert means, characterizes introduction of changes in PPP regulatory legal acts in order to bring these normative legal acts in accordance with the norms of Federal legislation. Decreasing expert coefficient (from 0.5 to 1) is applied on the basis of a qualitative assessment of normative legal acts, taking into account the changes made.

Expert coefficients in calculation of the factors "Development of PPP institutional environment" and "Legal support of PPP" are assigned on the basis of estimates of the staff of the National PPP center and are agreed with members of the Expert Council of the National PPP center by sending a summary of the regions with comments.

Calculation of the value of the factor "Experience in implementing PPP projects" is made according to the following formula:

$$\mathbf{Ej} = \boldsymbol{\Sigma}(\varepsilon\mathbf{jlk} \times \ldots \times \varepsilon\mathbf{jnm}),$$

where

- ***n*** total number of criteria;
- ***m*** total number of projects;
- ***εjk*** value of the i-th criterion "Experience in implementing public-private partnership projects" for the k-th public-private partnership project, ejlk = [0–1];
- ***kj*** coefficient of sectoral differentiation of projects, taking into account the fact of implementation of projects in two or more industries;
- ***Ej*** [0–13, 75].

The value of the coefficient of sectoral differentiation of projects is determined as follows:

- for projects implemented in two industries, $k = 1$;
- for projects implemented in three or more industries, $k = 1, 2$.

Calculation of the value of the factor "Experience in implementing public-private partnership projects" is made on the basis of assessments on the following set of criteria:

Criteria	Description	Value (score)
Compliance of the project with PPP features	The project is implemented on the basis of Federal laws No. 224-FZ of 13 July 2015 "On public-private partnership, municipal-private partnership in the Russian Federation and amendments to certain legislative acts of the Russian Federation" or No. 115-FZ of 21 July 2005 "On concession agreements"	1

(continued)

(continued)

Criteria	Description	Value (score)
	The project is implemented on the basis of other normative legal acts regulating relations in the sphere of public-private partnership, in any of the possible organizational and legal forms that meet the criteria of PPP	0.5

The reduction factors used in the calculation of the criterion for each project separately include.

Criteria	Description	Value of the reduction factor (score)
Status (stage) of the project	Operational stage (including if the project is successfully completed)	1
	Investment stage (creation, construction and (or) reconstruction)	0.9
	Pre-investment stage (design, preparation for construction, attraction of financing)	0.8
	Stage of selection of the private partner and the signing of the agreement	0.7
Volume of private investment	More than 500 million rubles	1
	From 200 million to 500 million rubles	0.9
	From 50 million to 200 million rubles	0.7
	From 10 million to 50 million rubles	0.5
	From 1 million to 10 million rubles	0.2
	Less than 1 million rubles	0
Duration of the project (validity of the agreement)	More than 15 years	1
	From 10 to 15 years	0.85
	From 5 to 10 years	0.6
	From 3 to 5 years	0.3
	Less than 3 years	0.1
Administrative level of the project	Regional	1
	Inter-municipal	0.8
	Municipal	0.5

(continued)

(continued)

Criteria	Description	Value of the reduction factor (score)
The complexity of the project is	Determined on the basis of expert assessments. It takes into account the number of property objects that are involved in the project, problems with the title, intergovernmental participation, availability of debt financing, etc.	1–1.5

Rating of Regions in Terms of PPP Development: 2018–2019

The following table shows the rating of regions by PPP development level for 2018–2019 in descending order of the integral indicator of PPP development (Table 6.1).

Assessment of PPP institutional environment and PPP regulatory framework showed that, by 2018, all regions received positive estimates for the two indicators, which thus reflects the full or partial implementation of the relevant mechanisms. In particular, PPP units (authorized bodies) were established and PPP regulatory framework was brought into compliance with Federal legislation in all regions.

In terms of improving the institutional environment and regulatory framework, the main efforts of regional authorities in 2018 were focused on the following aspects of PPP development:

- establishment of PPP authorized bodies, including bodies authorized to consider private concession initiative;
- systematic training of specialists in the field of PPP;
- formation and development of PPP-specialized regional information resources in the Internet;
- approval and publication of lists of objects for which it is planned to conclude PPP/MPP agreements and concession agreements;
- development of interagency cooperation procedures at the stage of preparation and consideration of PPP projects;
- updating of provisions of municipal and regional legal acts contradicting the Federal legislation;
- determination of rules of decision-making on the conclusion of PPP agreements, concession agreements for a period exceeding the period of validity of the approved limits of budget commitments.

As a result, in terms of these indicators, the regions achieved the greatest and even maximum results. In turn, the minimum indicators of PPP development were demonstrated in regard to such aspects as

Table 6.1 Rating of subjects of the Russian Federation on the level of PPP development (2018–2019)

Place	Region	Integral indicator
1–6	Moscow city	90,0%+
1–6	Saint Petersburg	90,0%+
1–6	Moscow region	90,0%+
1–6	Republic of Bashkortostan	90,0%+
1–6	Samara region	90,0%+
1–6	Khanty-Mansiysk Autonomous District–Ugra	90,0%+
7	Novosibirsk region	85,3%
8	Perm region	84,1%
9	Tambov region	84,1%
10	Nizhny Novgorod region	83,2%
11	Khabarovsk territory	82,9%
12	Irkutsk region	82,6%
13	Krasnoyarsk region	80,2%
14	Sverdlovsk region	79,6%
15	Yamalo-Nenets Autonomous district	79,1%
16	Leningrad region	79,0%
17	Chelyabinsk region	78,7%
18	Vladimir region	77,3%
19	Udmurt Republic	76,4%
20	Kaluga region	72,8%
21	Ulyanovsk region	72,8%
22	Republic of Tatarstan	72,6%
23	Tyumen region	72,5%
24	Republic of Buryatia	72,2%
25	Republic of Sakha (Yakutia)	72,1%
26	Amur region	71,9%
27	Rostov region	67,4%
28	Tula region	66,7%
29	Vologda region	63,1%
30	Kamchatka region	61,9%
31	Arkhangelsk region	57,6%
32	Volgograd region	55,0%
33	Voronezh region	52,7%
34	Altai Republic	52,0%
35	Belgorod region	51,5%

(continued)

Table 6.1 (continued)

Place	Region	Integral indicator
36	Kemerovo region	51,0%
37	Kaliningrad region	50,9%
38	Astrakhan region	50,5%
39	Lipetsk region	50,1%
40	Smolensk region	49,2%
41	Penza region	48,7%
42	Republic of Mordovia	46,0%
43	Saratov region	45,8%
44	Murmansk region	45,7%
45	Stavropol territory	45,4%
46	Orenburg region	44,2%
47	Primorsky region	41,0%
48	Chuvash Republic	40,7%
49	Krasnodar region	39,8%
50	Omsk region	39,5%
51	Yaroslavl region	39,0%
52	Sakhalin region	38,3%
53	Ryazan region	38,0%
54	Republic of Dagestan	37,7%
55	Altai region	37,6%
56	Ivanovo region	37,1%
57	Magadan region	36,1%
58	Chukotka Autonomous District	35,6%
59	Republic of Komi	34,5%
60	Novgorod region	34,4%
61	Kirov region	33,6%
62	Kabardino-Balkar Republic	33,1%
63	Tomsk region	32,5%
64	Kursk region	31,9%
65	Republic of Crimea	30,7%
66	Zabaikalsky region	29,5%
67	Republic of Khakassia	29,1%
68	Kostroma region	27,8%
69	Pskov region	27,1%
70	Karachay-Cherkess Republic	26,7%

(continued)

Table 6.1 (continued)

Place	Region	Integral indicator
71	Republic of Karelia	25,0%
72	Republic of Mari El	24,8%
73	Republic of Chechnya	23,7%
74	Sevastopol city	23,1%
75	Adygeya republic	22,8%
76	Jewish Autonomous region	21,6%
77	Kurgan area	20,4%
78	Nenets Autonomous District	19,5%
79	Tver region	18,4%
80	Orel region	18,3%
81	Bryansk region	17,8%
82	Republic of Tuva	17,7%
83	Ingush republic	14,9%
84	Republic of North Ossetia–Alania	13,4%
85	Republic of Kalmykia	12,0%

Source Data of the National PPP center

- regulation of control, supervision, and monitoring procedures as well as maintenance of registers of PPP projects (absent in 49 regions);
- regulation of decision-making procedure on conclusion and implementation of PPP agreement, concession agreement (not in 31 regions);
- establishment of a single body responsible for selection of the private partner (concessionaire) (absent in 57 regions).

In general, we can note a significant increase in the average level of development of PPP institutional environment and PPP regulatory framework in the regions in 2017 (+12.5%). If this integral indicator of the "average" subject of the Russian Federation in 2015 was 5.4 points out of 15 possible, in 2018 it increased to 8.7 points. The reasons that influenced the growth of the average level of development of PPP institutional environment and PPP regulatory framework include

- general increase of interest to the PPP institute on the part of regional authorities (caused, first of all, by the entry into force on January 1, 2016 224-FZ, which directly defines the powers of regional and municipal authorities in the field of PPP);
- emergence on the PPP market of new subjects of the Russian Federation, which previously held a wait-and-see position, and now ousted the former leaders whose positions seemed unshakable.

Among the general conclusions of the rating for 2018–2019, the following points should be specially noted.

- In the calculation of the rating, 2445 PPP projects of more than 5000 presented by the subjects of the Russian Federation were taken into account;
- 375 of the considered PPP projects are implemented in the subjects of the Russian Federation at the regional level;
- 2070 of the PPP projects are being implemented in the subjects of the Russian Federation at the municipal level;
- in 82 regions, at least one project PPP is implemented;
- 1685.0 billion rubles is the amount of contracted private investment in PPP projects in the subjects of the Russian Federation;
- 15.4 years is an average duration of PPP projects in the Russian Federation; in regional projects, it increased to 19.3 years, in municipal, to 14.7 years;
- 8.7 points (out of possible 15) is an average regional indicator of development of PPP institutional environment and PPP regulatory framework of PPP;
- all 85 regions have established an authorized body in the field of PPP (PPP unit);
- in all 85 regions, PPP regulatory framework is brought into compliance with the norms of Federal legislation;
- 13 regions achieved the highest possible score for experience of implementation of PPP projects.

In General, according to the results of the rating, it is possible to identify two key trends that emerged in 2017:

- a number of regions have already reached the maximum indicators in these aspects of the level of PPP development, which means that the current indicators of the PPP rating are no longer relevant for them and require their further development;
- the share of the values of the factors of the level of institutional environment and regulatory support (in their current version) in the overall integrated indicator of PPP development in the region has significantly decreased.

If earlier—in order for a particular subject of the Russian Federation to be among the leaders in public-private partnership—it was enough to create an effective institutional environment and adopt a sufficient number of legal acts on PPP topics, now even the maximum values for the relevant factors do not guarantee the region's entry even into the TOP 30 in terms of PPP development. The factor of "project implementation experience" began to play the priority value for the Rating of regions in terms of PPP development.

Thus, it can be concluded that an effective institutional environment in the field of PPP has ceased to be a competitive advantage of the regions and has become a mandatory (but insufficient) condition for attracting the desired infrastructure investor.

PPP Governance at the Regional Level

At the regional level, it has become common practice to divide PPP powers among several bodies. The system of these bodies usually includes

- authorized body (regional executive authority), responsible for interdepartmental coordination in the field of PPP, for monitoring PPP projects and consideration of private concession initiatives;
- specialized structure (joint-stock company with state participation or budgetary institution—development corporation, investment agency, etc.) responsible for launching and supporting PPP projects;
- interagency body (investment council, commission for PPP, etc.) responsible for PPP policy-making and consideration of initiated PPP projects.

Results of monitoring of PPP institutional environment in the regions of Russia reveal that under Law 224-FZ, an authorized body is defined in all regions, under Law115-FZ (concession law), an authorized body is established in less than half of the regions, and in the rest, relevant powers are divided between sectoral authorities.

In a number of regions with the most developed PPP governance system, other specialized institutions such as project offices and other project management tools used in consideration, launch, and implementation of PPP projects have been established in recent years. Let us review some of them.

- *Case No. 1. Project office "PPP Center" under the Ministry of investment and innovation of the Moscow region*

Since 2015, a project office "PPP Center" has been operating under the Ministry of investment and innovation of the Moscow region. At the moment, priority sectors for investment have been identified, standardization of processes has been implemented, and automation of procedures and transfer of work with investors' applications to electronic form has been started. Measures to improve investment climate of the Moscow region, quality of the environment for business and residence are taken on a regular basis. The PPP center conducts analysis of project feasibility, calculation of effectiveness of draft agreements, including financial, budgetary, evaluation of the socioeconomic effect of projects, and assessment of comparative advantages of PPP projects in comparison with conventional procurement.

- *Case No. 2. Project offices of state budgetary institution "City Agency for investment management" in Moscow*

In Moscow, in 2011, in order to effectively solve problems in the field of investment activity, the state budgetary institution of Moscow—the City investment management agency—was created. In the investment departments of the government of Moscow a system of quality management of training of the administrative personnel (ISO 9001:2015) is implemented.

Project offices directly concerned with support of sectoral PPP projects (ranging from receiving complaints from investors, verification of legal and economic models, and ending with the signing of the PPP agreements) are established and operated in the structure of the Agency.

1. *Project office "Legal support of investment activity and PPP"*

Provides legal support for investment activities and PPP projects. Within the framework of PPP projects, it prepares draft decisions of Moscow city authorities, draft normative and non-normative acts, draft tender documents, and draft contracts and agreements. Project office develops conclusions, analytical materials, methods, and recommendations on investment activities and PPP.

2. *Project office "Economic expertise"*

Conducts economic analysis of effectiveness of proposed investment projects and develops supporting materials for decision-making on their possible financing from budgetary or extra-budgetary sources. Considers projects of production, investment programs of organizations and programs of energy saving of municipal complex, and subjects of electric power industry. Analyzes the investment objects involved in the economic turnover for further tendering procedures. Develops proposals to improve economic mechanisms related to investment activities.

3. *Project office of "Industrial production and social infrastructure"*

Analyzes effectiveness of proposed investment projects and develops supporting materials for decision-making on their possible financing from budgetary and/or extra-budgetary sources. Carries out preliminary study, analysis, and preparation of supporting materials on implementation of investment projects. Coordinates and supports investment projects received by the project office in various forms at different stages of implementation of investment projects, interaction with executive authorities, participants of investment projects on implementation of investment projects, PPP projects. Develops proposals for formation and evaluation of investment opportunities, including the forms of implementation of investment projects, PPP projects.

4. *Project office "Strategy and analysis of investment activity"*

Prepares materials on development of investment activities, analytical materials on investment needs, and possibility of their implementation.

5. *Project office "Single investment portal. Line of direct appeals"*

It is engaged in optimization of investment process, ensuring openness of investment activity of executive authorities, increase of level of awareness of participants of investment activity, and consideration of addresses of citizens and legal entities concerning implementation of investment projects. It implements the functionality for operational provision of complete and accurate information about the objects planned to be involved in the investment process. Provides monitoring, information support, and maintenance of the state information system designed to ensure the implementation of investment policy.

6. *Project office "urban Planning and land Commission"*

Prepares materials for implementation of investment contracts, defines and changes economic conditions for their implementation, and takes measures for completion of investment projects. Develops proposals to improve legal mechanisms and legislation on issues related to investment activities, methodological materials on the evaluation, and monitoring of investment projects. Monitors the performance of obligations under investment contracts.

7. *Project office "Promotion of investment opportunities"*

Promotes investment opportunities, achievements, and benefits, including presentation of investment projects with involvement of Russian and international investors. Promotes development of investment culture and inter-investment communication, and informs potential investors about investment opportunities.

8. *Project office "Preparation of legal opinions on investors' costs and examination of price indicators"*

Performs collection, processing, and analysis of information on prices for goods, works, and services of Russian and foreign organizations with the aim of providing information, analytical and administrative support for control of investment programs in the city.

In 2018, in order to organize project activities in Moscow, a working group was established to coordinate activities aimed at the implementation of Moscow city projects, and regulations on the organization of project activities were approved. The regulation on the organization of project activities in Moscow establishes procedure for implementation by Moscow authorities of activities related to initiation, preparation, and implementation of Moscow city projects, ensuring achievement of goals, indicators, and results of Federal projects.

Conclusion

The lack of a unified system of PPP governance is one of the main reasons hindering development of PPP in Russia. One of the most important factors in the successful development of PPP is the coordinated action of state bodies in development and implementation of projects. The lack of such coherence will increasingly affect qualitative characteristics of PPP development in the country. Outwardly, impressive quantitative indicators of growth in number of PPP projects in the country should not divert attention from existing serious substantive problems that are noted by domestic experts (poor preparation and elaboration of the majority of PPP projects, lack of sufficient competencies and deficit of professional staff on the side of the public partner, dominance of projects with small investment, long terms of coordination with the authorities of different levels of issues related to implementation of projects, etc.) and which can be solved only on the basis of improvement of the PPP governance system.

To date, almost all regions have formed basic foundations of PPP institutional environment and regulatory framework. First of all, it is necessary to note the presence in all regions of PPP units (authorized body in the field of PPP) and bringing PPP regulatory framework in accordance with Federal legislation. In addition, most regions have established specialized structures to support PPP projects and interdepartmental bodies for PPP policy-making and consideration of initiated PPP projects. A significant number of regions employ qualified teams of specialists with competencies in the field of PPP. Among the problem areas, there is lack of regulatory consolidation of interdepartmental cooperation procedures in the preparation and implementation of PPP projects, the lack of a system of support measures for private investors, as well as the lack of unified bodies for competitive selection of private partners and concessionaires.

References

Draft National report on attracting private investment in infrastructure development and application of public-private partnership mechanisms in the Russian Federation. (2018). ANO "national PPP Center". Moscow: ANO "national PPP Center". http://pppcenter.ru/assets/files/260418-rait.pdf.

Mekhanizmy gosudarstvenno-chastnogo partnyorstva v ekonomicheskoi politike Rossii (Mechanisms of public-private partnership in the economic policy of Russia). (2018). Mechanisms of public-private partnership in the economic policy of Russia: textbook. O. V., Ivanov (Ed.). Moscow: MGIMO University.

Ob utverzhdenii Kompleksnogo plana modernizacii i rasshireniya magistral'noj infrastruktury na period do 2024. (2018). (About the approval of the Comprehensive plan of modernization and expansion of the core infrastructure for the period till 2024 (2018)). Official website of the Government of Russia. http://government.ru/docs/34297/. Accessed 10 May 2019.

Ob utverzhdenii plana meropriyatij po razvitiyu instrumentariya gosudarstvenno-chastnogo partnyorstva ("infrastrukturnaya ipoteka") ot 12.03.2018 (About the approval of the plan of actions for development of tools of public-private partnership ("infrastructure mortgage") of 12.03.2018). Official website of the Government of Russia. http://m.government.ru/all/31625/. Accessed 9 May 2019.

Ob utverzhdenii Strategii prostranstvennogo razvitiya do 2025 goda ot 14.02.2019. (2019). (About the approval of the Strategy of spatial development till 2025 of 14.02.2019). Ministry of Economic Development of the Russian Federation. http://economy.gov.ru/minec/activity/sections/planning/sd. Accessed 9 May 2019.

Proekt nacional'nogo doklada o privlechenii chastnyh investicij v razvitie infrastruktury i primenenie mekhanizmov GCHP v RF. Rejting regionov po urovnyu razvitiya GCHP 2017–2018. (2018). (Draft national report on attracting private investment in infrastructure development and application of Public-Private Partnership mechanisms in the Russian Federation). PPP National Development Center.

Prosto i chestno ob investiciyah v infrastrukturu i gosudarstvenno-chastnom partnerstve v Rossii. Analiticheskii obzor. Reiting regionov 2018–19. (Simply and honestly about investments in infrastructure and PPP in Russia. Analytical review. Rating of regions 2018–2019). ROSINFRA. PPP Development Center, 2019.

Research "Public-private partnership in Russia 2016–2017: Current state and trends, rating of regions" Association PPP development Center. Moscow: Association "PPP development Center", 2017. http://pppcenter.ru/assets/docs/raytingREG2017_B5_Block_31-03-2017-web.pdf.

Tarakanov, V. V., Inshakova, A. O., & Goncharov, A. I. (2019). Interactive demo on-line maintenance foreign trade deals of business entities of BRICS jurisdictions. In *Competitive Russia: Foresight Model of Economic and Legal Development in the Digital Age: Proceedings of the International Scientific Conference in Memory of Oleg Inshakov (1952–2018)* (pp. 319–327). Cham: Springer Nature.

Tseli i zadachi Nacional'nogo centra gosudarstvenno-chastnogo partnyorstva. Oficial'nyj portal ANO "Nacional'nyj centr gosudarstvenno-chastnogo partnyorstva". http://pppcenter.ru/about/mission.html (Goals and objectives of the National center of public-private partnership. Official portal of ANO national center of public-private partnership.

Ukaz Prezidenta Rossiiskoi Federatsii "O nacional'nyh celyah i strategicheskih zadachah razvitiya Rossijskoj Federacii na period do 2024 goda". (2018). (The decree "On the national goals and strategic objectives of development of the Russian Federation for the period up to 2024" of 07.05.2018). Official website of the President of Russia. http://kremlin.ru/events/president/news/57425. Accessed 9 May 2019.

Chapter 7
Instruments of Government Support for PPP Projects

Vladimir V. Piskunov and Evgenia A. Starikova

Abstract The issues of government support for infrastructure projects implemented on the principles of public-private partnership are studied. General classification of public support instruments is offered. Financial and non-financial instruments used in world practices and in the Russian Federation, including direct and indirect financing of projects, state guarantees and benefits, administrative and methodological support of market participants are classified and analyzed. Based on the study of relevant international experience and current situation in Russia, major existing problems are identified, and recommendations are made on possible ways to improve the effectiveness of the system of support for public-private partnership projects in Russia, including the creation of separate specialized financial institutions.

Keywords Support measures · Public-private partnership · Support of PPP projects · Subsidies · Government guarantees · Capital grant · Infrastructure

JEL-Codes H44 · K12 · O21 · R58

Introduction

According to many authoritative experts, implementation of PPP projects is basically impossible without appropriate support from the state (Farquharson et al. 2011; Cuttaree et al. 2011; US Department of Transportation. Federal Highway Administration 2010). As the name "Public–Private Partnerships" indicates, PPP is a partnership arrangement where active support from public authorities to private sector development of infrastructure projects is required. There is no general recipe for effective

V. V. Piskunov (✉)
National PPP Center, Malaya Dmitrovka str. 16-6, 127006 Moscow, Russia
e-mail: vvpiskunov@outlook.com

E. A. Starikova
MGIMO University, Vernadsky Ave., 76, 119454 Moscow, Russia
e-mail: evan3132@gmail.com

O. V. Ivanov and A. O. Inshakova (eds.), *Public-Private Partnerships in Russia*, Competitive Government: Public Private Partnerships,
https://doi.org/10.1007/978-3-030-56352-3_7

public support to PPP projects. Each government has to assess the country's attraction to domestic and foreign private investment and to decide which steps will effectively encourage private sector investment and development of infrastructure projects.

Instruments of such support applied in the world practices can be divided into two enlarged groups: financial and non-financial. This division is based on the nature of impact of support measures on the cash flow of the private partner within the project. Thus, financial measures directly reduce project costs of the private partner, for example, through budget co-financing or tax savings derived from the action of public benefits. Measures of non-financial support have an indirect impact on costs of the private partner, for example, by increasing efficiency of the private partner's actions as a result of methodological support and advice from the state (Table 7.1).

In the Russian Federation, such tools are also in great demand: given the critical importance of public infrastructure and in the context of budgetary constraints, certain mechanisms must be used. In conditions when the state is not ready to increase direct budget expenditures, indirect support measures are gaining particular popularity (InfraONE 2019, p. 30).

At the same time, the country still does not have an effective system of government support for PPP projects, primarily in terms of financial assistance, as there are no some key financial institutions. In this regard, it is advisable to analyze the existing support tools in Russia and, taking into account foreign experience, to give recommendations on their expansion.

Results

Direct Co-financing of PPP Projects

In the world practice, direct budget co-financing of public-private partnership is one of the most widely used support tools. It involves covering part of the capital or operating costs for the implementation of specific projects undertaken by the public party under the PPP agreement, through direct financial participation in the project.

The mechanism of national investment funds is widely used for this purpose in the world. India, for example, has Viability Gap Funding (VGF), Infrastructure Development Finance Company (IDFC), and India Infrastructure Finance Company (IIFC) (ADB 2011). In Canada, Canadian PPP Fund (PPP Canada Fund), which became the country's first specialized financial instrument for the implementation of PPP projects, successfully operated for more than a decade. Co-investment by this Fund in the amount of almost 1 billion dollars US allowed to draw into PPP projects nearly 5 billion USD of private investment (Ivanov 2016; Ivanov and Ivanova 2019).

In the Russian legislation according to the Law on concession agreements (115-FZ), expenses of the public partner include expenses for the construction/reconstruction and/or use of the facility under concession agreement, as well as the Concedent's payment (part 13, article 3), according to the Law on PPP/MPP

Table 7.1 Classification of government support measures for PPP projects

Financial measures	Non-financial support
Co-financing – Costs for construction/reconstruction and operation of the facility **Equity investment** – Investments in exchange for the right to influence development of the company **Preferential lending** – Provision of loans at a reduced or zero interest rate **Project development financing** – Financing of pre-project preparation (legal and financial structuring, marketing, etc.)	**Administrative and legislative support** – Promotion of strategic initiatives; – Accelerated procedure of approval of permits and other documentation, "one window" system » ; – Connection of infrastructure object to technological networks; – Adoption of necessary regulations in order to stimulate the market and to ensure stability of legal regulation
Subsidization – Federal subsidies to lower budgets; – Subsidizing the interest rate on loans; – Subsidizing payment of rent or lease	**Methodological support and market research** – Study of PPP projects market, its volume and opportunities, calculation of infrastructure gaps – Development of guidelines
Government guarantees – Guarantee security in the form of guarantees to expand companies' access to credit resources; – Reducing investors' risks by insuring financial liabilities of the private partner	**Legal and financial advice** – Compensation for the lack of legal and economic competences of private partner's employees; – Structuring of PPP project and assistance in resolving issues arising in the process of project implementation
Government benefits – Tariff regulation, establishment of tariffs favorable for the industry and/or private companies; – Tax benefits at the Federal, regional, and municipal levels; – Privileges for rent of premises, land, equipment leasing	**Information and educational support** – Coverage of PPP projects and provision of necessary data; – Formation of project database; – Carrying out "road-show" and search for possible sources of investment; – Improving skills of all PPP participants and attracting new stakeholders

Source compiled on the basis of World Bank (2017). PPP Reference Guide 3.0; ESCAP (2008). Government support for PPPs; etc.

in the Russian Federation (224-FZ) expenses of the public partner, include partial funding for creation of the object of the agreement (clause 3 of part 3 of article 6); expenses on construction of object of the agreement (paragraph 5 of article 12); financing operation and/or maintenance of the facility under agreement (clause 3 of part 3 of article 6); and bearing part of the costs of operation and/or maintenance of the facility (part 5, article 12).

Theoretically, financing of such expenses is possible due to two financial mechanisms: subsidies in favor of legal entities (under article 78 of the Budget Code of the Russian Federation) and budget investments (under article 79 of the RF Budget Code) (Chart 7.1).

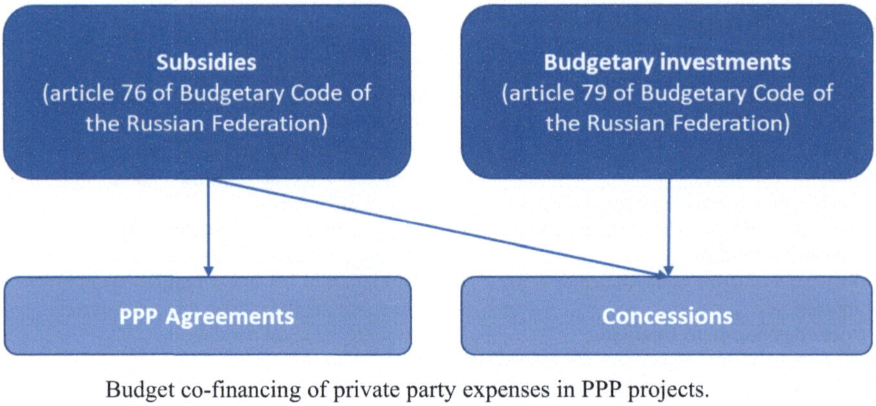

Chart 7.1 Budget co-financing of private party expenses in PPP projects

Mechanism of budget investments in Russia has significant limitations. First, a prerequisite for obtaining it is the state (municipal) ownership of the object of investment. In this regard, the mechanism is not actually applicable to implementation of projects under the 224-FZ. Secondly, budget investments can only be capital investments. By contrast, subsidies to a legal entity are a more flexible mechanism. So, the subsidy can be used also for payment of works (services) of the concessionaire on maintenance and operation of object of the agreement, to compensate any expenses of the concessionaire that he was not able to recoup at the expense of profit (Inshakova et al. 2019).

In practice, direct participation of the higher budget for a long time focused on activities of the Investment Fund of the Russian Federation and was limited to the mechanism of budget investments and provision of budget allocations to the authorized capitals of open joint-stock companies, including through participation in their establishment (article 10 of the Rules for the formation and use of budget allocations of the Investment Fund of the Russian Federation). However, over time, the work of the Fund was recognized as ineffective, and in 2017 it was abolished by the Decree of the President of the Russian Federation.

Investment funds still remain at the regional level—the subjects of the Russian Federation have an opportunity to use this mechanism. However, many of the existing regional funds were originally created for transfers from the Federal Investment Fund, and the format of their further use is not yet clear. One option is to transform them into specialized funds for financing project development training.

In 2018, Russia introduced an analogue of Investment Fund—the budget Fund for Infrastructure development created as one of the tools for the implementation of the May 2018 decrees of the President of the Russian Federation. From 2019 to 2024, the Fund can finance more than 170 projects. It will be filled by additional state borrowings in the amount of up to 0.5% of GDP per year. It is planned that the volume of these loans for 6 years will be about 3.5 trillion rubles. At the same time, the order of distribution of funds has not yet been determined (Starostina 2018).

Recent launch of the so-called "Project financing factory" on the basis of Vnesheconombank (VEB) was a positive step in institutionalization of financial support for infrastructure projects. This is a new tool of support for business that involves allocation of large concessional loans for construction of industrial enterprises. Several market participants act as creditors within the Factory: a number of Russian banks and state corporation VEB itself. They provide a borrower with a "syndicated" loan, which is accompanied by additional support from the Ministry of Finance. Thus, the state is also ready to provide borrowers with state guarantees: 294 billion rubles have been allocated in the budget until 2020. The total amount of funding that selected projects will receive in the first years under the "factory" mechanism is estimated at a trillion rubles (Tolstoukhova 2019).

The first three projects for the Factory have already been selected: a project for the construction of a plant for the production of sulfuric acid and oleum at the site of the company "KuibyshevAzot" in the Samara region, a project for the construction of the third stage of methanol production in the Tula region, and construction of a mining and metallurgical plant on the basis of the Udokan deposit in the TRANS-Baikal region.

Currently, the Ministry of economic development proposes to expand the list of industries that are covered by the financing of the factory—in the future, projects in the field of education, ecology, and health will be eligible for loans. The lists of infrastructure and manufacturing industries can also be expanded (Adamchuk and Bazanova 2019).

It is also worth noting such an instrument of state participation in the implementation of PPP projects as project preparation financing—in the world practice it draws significant attention. It allows a public initiator to provide necessary resources for preparation of significant projects, qualitative structuring of which by a public partner is not possible. Although the importance of project preparation financing in Russia has been recognized long ago, there are not so many relevant instruments still: only the financial company VEB Infrastructure can be named.

A new "seed" fund of Sberbank and infrastructure company InfraONE promises to become an interesting tool of financial support. It is planned that the Fund will be established from 2019 for 6 years. The size of the Fund will be more than 10 billion rubles. The Fund is to support about 150 projects for $210 million, and with reinvestment their number will increase to 200. The Fund plans to prepare 50–60 projects annually, expanding their number in the market by a third. The preparation costs of documents would amount to 60–150 million rubles for one project. After commercial closure, the Fund will exit the project with compensation from the private investor. It should be noted, however, that the Fund is more a commercial tool than a tool of government support.

Subsidization

Another tool for direct financial support of PPP projects from higher budgets is subsidies in the form of inter-budget transfers. At the same time, in this case, the money is only transferred in favor of lower budgets, and the actual costs of a particular project are carried out by the region/municipality itself.

In the world practices, Australia is a vivid example of subsidizing regional budgets for the implementation of PPP projects. The tool is used in the framework of the Australian construction fund, which was founded in 2008 to finance strategically important public infrastructure in transport, telecommunications, water, and energy. In 2009–2010, for example, 90% of all Federal assistance in favor of the States was provided by Australian government through the Fund in the form of grants (Bounds 2012, p. 8).

In Russian practice, subsidies to lower budgets are provided through two main mechanisms—with the help of investment funds and within the framework of state programs (Solntsev 2017).

Until recently, subsidies to lower budgets were carried out, in particular, within the framework of the Investment Fund of the Russian Federation and the Fund for promotion of housing and communal services reform. However, the first, as already mentioned, has been abolished, and the latter has recently changed the rules for provision of funding. Thus, in August 2017, subsidies to the budgets of the subjects in terms of capital and operating costs for municipal projects were excluded from the list of eligible forms of support provided by the Fund for promotion of housing and communal services reform.

The second channel of subsidies is government programs. As an example, we can cite the Federal target program "Development of physical culture and sports in the Russian Federation for 2016–2020", which provides for the possibility of co-financing of state programs of the Russian Federation. In particular, subsidies are provided for the construction and reconstruction of low-budget (up to 25 million rubles) sports facilities. In 2018, PPP in sports was subsidized by the Ministry of Sports of the Russian Federation by 150 million rubles, and in 2019 the amount of assistance is expected to double

One more example is the state program of the Russian Federation "Development of the transport system". "Promoting the development of roads of regional, inter-municipal and local importance", involving the provision of budget transfers to the relevant projects, is one of its main goals. In particular, the rules for providing funding under the category "other budget transfers" mean the possibility of allocating money for projects implemented in the format of public-private partnership. Methodology of the selection of such projects is fixed by the order of the Ministry of transport of August 1, 2016, №221.

Another option of subsidizing, common in the world practice, is interest rate subsidies on loans. This mechanism is also used in Russia. In particular, such a mechanism is used in activities of the Fund for development of housing utilities—at the expense of the Fund it is possible to subsidize part of the loan rate in excess of 5% per annum.

State Guarantee

In international practice, there is a common approach in which the state does not directly participate in the financing of infrastructure projects (for example, through direct budget investments), but assumes a number of contingent obligations of a guarantee nature. In many cases, however, direct and guarantee financial support is used in conjunction. Among the guarantee mechanisms are guarantees on debt obligations, exchange rates, deferred payments, tariffs, the level of demand for services, payments at the end of the project, etc.

The Republic of Korea is one of the many foreign examples. The country has a special Fund of credit guarantees, specializing exclusively in support of PPP projects (Ivanov 2016). Another example is the infrastructure guarantee Fund of Argentina announced in September 2017. The Fund was established by the inter-American development Bank and the World Bank; the first will contribute $ 600 million to the Fund, the second—$ 300 million (Pagano 2017).

The possibility of providing investors with state guarantees is directly fixed in both 115-FZ and 224-FZ. However, in practice, state guarantees (both Federal and regional) in PPP projects are used in a very limited number of projects—in the context of the economic crisis, the mechanism is mainly used to support individual backbone enterprises, rather than infrastructure projects. By the end of 2016, the accumulated amount of public debt under the guarantee obligations of the Russian Federation reached 2.6 trillion rubles, while the share of project financing in it was only 3%. In recent years, the bulk of state guarantees—in 2016, for example, 175.3 billion rubles were allocated for them in the Federal budget—are used as part of anti-crisis support. Anti-crisis guarantees of 2012–2016 occupy almost 52% in the structure of accumulated guarantee obligations.

Government Benefits

Tax benefits are an important tool to improve the economy of PPP projects and stimulate interest from private investors. In world practice, as a rule, PPP projects are subject to only General tax benefits, but in some countries there are also specialized benefits. In South Korea, for example, for projects implemented under the BOT (build-operate-transfer) scheme, the rates of value-added taxes and real estate registration are reset, and for long-term projects (more than 15 years), the tax on interest on concession bonds is reduced (up to 15%). Also, Korean public partners in most cases establish benefits for PPP projects for obtaining a land plot (Ivanov 2016).

Another example is the Philippines. Thus, in July 2017 in the country in 14 regions came into force the rule of 10-year zero income tax for PPP projects.

In Russian practice, the provision of benefits for income, property, land, and transport taxes is widespread at the regional and municipal levels. For example, certain preferences are established for the property that is the object of the concession agreement under the law of the Leningrad region of November 25, 2003, № 98-oz "On the property tax of organizations". Similar examples can be found today in many other Russian regions, as such measures are effective and at the same time easily replicated. Below is a brief overview of the regional measures of assistance to private investors applied in the Moscow region (Table 7.2).

Since 2017 in many regions of Russia specialized tax benefits for PPP projects began to be actively implemented. For example, in Bashkiria, the expert council of the State Assembly considered the development of public-private partnership in housing and communal sector of the Republic and concluded that investors in the sector need tax incentives. According to the council's assumption, short-term tax losses of the budget will be more than compensated by the benefits from the implementation of projects. Two amendments to the legislation were proposed: one of them provides for the exemption of investors who have concluded an agreement on PPP from paying property tax from 1 to 10 years. The other provides a discount on income tax up to 30%. Similar changes were proposed in the Murmansk region by the Ministry of industry and entrepreneurship development. They provide for the introduction of tax benefits on profits and property of enterprises for investors implementing PPP projects into the Law "On state support of investment activities in the Murmansk region".

Administrative Support

Due to the complexity of PPP mechanism as a form of implementation of investment projects, administrative support from the state is highly desirable. The main objective of such support is to simplify and accelerate the procedures for involving a private investor in the development of public infrastructure. A common tool for such support is the "one window" principle, which is used to some extent in almost all PPP countries. A vivid example is the UK: - at the local level there are special organizations for development of PPP, established by the Treasury and local authorities.

Among examples of administrative support in Russia is the experience of the Department of competition policy of Moscow city administration, which works on the principle of "one window" and simplifies the entire process of submitting necessary documentation and bringing pre-investment stage of the project to its logical closure.

The role of information exchange between the authorities and the market is also important. In Russian practice, major infrastructure forums organized by the National PPP Centre, for example, can be identified as one of the instruments of such exchange. Among the main ones is the annual infrastructure Congress "Russian PPP week". The Congress serves as a platform for all market participants to discuss issues related to the

Table 7.2 Key measures to support private investment in the Moscow region

	Type	Incentives	Legal basis for granting
General fiscal measures			
1	Property tax	**With the conclusion of the agreement** 0-1,5% (for 5 or 8 years) Investments of more than 1 or 3 billion rubles. **Article of direct action** 0% (for 4 years) Investments in the construction of buildings for 50 million rubles	Law of the Moscow region No. 151/2004-OZ "On preferential taxation in the Moscow region" (articles 26.15-26.18)
2	Profit tax	**With the conclusion of the agreement** 12.5% (for 5 or 7 years) Investments of more than 1 or 3 billion rubles. **Article of direct action** 13.5% (for 4 years) Investments more than 1 or 3 billion ruble	Law of the Moscow region No. 151/2004-OZ "On preferential taxation in the Moscow region" (articles 26.15-26.18)
Incentives for residents of special economic zones			
1	Property tax	0% (for 8 years)	Law of the Moscow region No. 151/2004-OZ "On preferential taxation in the Moscow region" (article 26.10)
2	Profit tax	0% (for 8 years) 5% (for 6 years) 13.5% (more) Subject to the conditions (resident status, direction of the released funds for development)	Law of the Moscow region No. 151/2004-OZ "On preferential taxation in the Moscow region" (article 26.10)
3	Land and transport tax	0% (for 5 years)	Law of the Moscow region No. 151/2004-OZ "On preferential taxation in the Moscow region" (article 26.10) RF Tax Code
Measures to support industrial investment			
1	The reimbursement of expenses for engineering infrastructure	Up to 80 million rubles	Resolution of the Government of the Moscow region of August 23, 2013, №662/37

(continued)

Table 7.2 (continued)

	Type	Incentives	Legal basis for granting
2	Industry development Fund	Loans from 50 to 300 million rubles	Agreement with the Fund of January 26, 2017
Provision of land plots			
1	Land for rent without bidding)	In case of compliance with the criteria (see text)	Law of the Moscow region No. 27/2015-OZ of March 18, 2015

strategic planning of PPP development in Russia, removing of barriers, replication of best practices, etc. It is worth noting sectoral and regional forums held by the National PPP Center—for example, the annual strategic forum "Transport systems of Russia" and events held in various Federal districts of the country, in particular, the forum of the Central Federal district on PPP. Such events help, among other things, to form the law-making agenda of the state.

Methodological Support and Market Research

One of the important elements of non-financial support of PPP projects is methodological and analytical support of the market.

A widespread international practice is the development and dissemination of methodological recommendations on the use of PPP mechanisms by public authorities or national centers of public-private partnership. In most countries with developed PPP markets—for example, in the UK, Canada, and Australia—a comprehensive methodological framework for supporting PPP projects has already been established. In some countries—for example, in South Africa—methodological guidelines essentially replace PPP legislation.

The role of methodological support is also recognized in Russia. However, today it is difficult to talk about the presence of its broad base. Work in this direction has just begun. Thus, at the end of 2016, the Ministry of economic development of Russia issued official Recommendations for the implementation of public-private partnership projects. More developed practice of preparing sectoral guidelines, for example, the relevant ministries, together with the AVTODOR group of companies and the development housing Association, have developed tools to provide methodological support for PPP projects in the road and housing sectors. Such recommendations were developed by the Ministry of Health and the Ministry of Sports of the Russian Federation for the industries under their jurisdiction. The national PPP center is also actively working in this direction. In particular, the relevant publications were devoted to the social sphere, housing, and communal services. Since September 2017, the national PPP center has been publishing monthly expert releases on topical issues of the Russian PPP.

Information and Educational Support

An important factor for successful application of PPP is information support, since all market participants wish to have full information to make quality decisions. In world practice, functions of information support are often transferred to national PPP centers.

This practice exists in Russia too. Thus, the Russian National PPP center with support of the Ministry of economic development created the Platform for supporting infrastructure projects "ROSINFRA" (pppi.ru) which maintains a comprehensive database of PPP projects implemented in Russia.

In fact, the ROSINFRA Platform is designed to become an accelerator of design solutions, expertise, and financial instruments to assist in the preparation and launch of infrastructure projects, as well as to assist in obtaining state support and attracting private investment in infrastructure projects.

Within the framework of the ROSINFRA Platform, a number of services have been implemented to help market participants of infrastructure investments accelerate the process of preparation and launch of projects, as well as improve their quality. In particular, the Platform has already launched:

- *database of implemented projects*—the full base of successful cases, which will allow market participants to structure their projects faster and better.
- *"stock exchange" of planned projects*—aggregated investment proposals of regional and municipal authorities in the field of infrastructure, as well as information on support measures, authorized bodies, and investment strategy of public legal entities in the field of infrastructure.
- *analysis of the PPP market*—a set of interactive modules containing information about the infrastructure component of national projects; rating of regions by the level of PPP development; judicial practice and practice of Federal Antimonopoly Agency; analytical information on development of infrastructure and PPP in Russia and the world, as well as other useful analytical materials.
- *infrastructure marketplace*—a convenient platform for the selection of qualified suppliers and performers for any of the stages of preparation and implementation of infrastructure projects.
- *expert assistance*—a convenient service for the selection of qualified experts for online consultations in the preparation and launch of projects, as well as search for specialists for registration in the project team or staff.

The following services will also be launched by the end of 2019:

- *Project office*—a convenient service for communication of project teams in the preparation of projects, as well as interdepartmental coordination of municipal and regional authorities in the initiation of PPP projects
- *Online Academy*—a platform for distance education on implementation of PPP projects

Investment portals of relevant Federal and regional ministries are also an important element of information support. In particular, the information portal on investments in housing and communal services is conducted by the Ministry of construction. The majority of Russian regions have similar portals of general profile.

An important long-term tool to support PPP is educational support. Institute of PPP development established by the National PPP center makes a significant contribution in this respect. The Institute conducts a variety of training programs for both representatives of the public side and employees of private companies. In total, the PPP Institute trained more than 5500 market participants both on the public and private sides and implemented comprehensive training programs in 22 regions of the Russian Federation. However, a multiplier effect will be achieved only when the relevant programs, educational and professional standards for the public side are unified and approved at the Federal level, and competencies will be transferred on a network basis from specialist to specialist, from the level of power to the level of power.

At the level of fundamental University education, young specialists in PPP are trained in such universities as MGIMO, Higher school of Economy, Financial University, Russian Academy of national economy and state service, and St. Petersburg University of Economics. Training programs are being improved every year, the interdisciplinary nature of training is developing—from economic and legal knowledge to understanding the system of PPP public governance.

Conclusions/Recommendations

To date, the world has accumulated a wealth of experience in supporting PPP projects. Through the use of a variety of tools for such support, it is possible to implement PPP projects across a wide spectrum of industries in many countries of the world, especially in developing countries.

The increasing use of relatively new instruments—in particular, special financial institutions—targeted infrastructure funds draws attention. High organizational and institutional variability of funds allows to use different approaches, tools, and methods of financial support of projects, to offer a wide range of financial products (Schur 2016).

Unfortunately, today these instruments actually fall out of the Russian practice of PPP projects—in Russia there are no yet infrastructure funds that provide low-cost credit resources or issuing guarantees for the implementation of long-term infrastructure projects. There are no such tools as guarantee funds in Russian PPP arsenal, although the need for their creation has long been spoken of by domestic business. The role and practice of participation of regional investment funds in the implementation of infrastructure projects on the principles of public-private partnership has not been defined.

One of the main risks that constrain domestic investors in deciding to implement projects in the regions (especially in small towns and rural settlements) is the lack of stability of local budgets (Tkachenko and Ivanov 2018). That is why many investors are not ready to implement long-term PPP projects, in which the municipality acts as a public party, fearing that due to various events in the long term, the local budget will not be able to fulfill its obligations to the investor to co-finance part of the cost of creating an object or to pay the so-called "accessibility fee". It is obvious that in order to solve this problem and to stimulate private investment in the development of public infrastructure, it would be useful to adapt to the Russian conditions the concept of a "safety cushion" successfully used in many countries of the world in the form of special trust funds that would guarantee fulfillment of obligations of the public side to a private partner (concessionaire) in the event of economic crisis and other events.

It is also important to create a mechanism of preferential lending to investors in PPP infrastructure projects. The creation of such a mechanism will ensure variability of financial measures to support projects, take into account individual characteristics of projects when choosing the optimal form of support (capital grant and/or concessional lending), ensure the best budgetary efficiency, and increase the success of relevant projects. Such a mechanism in Russia could be launched on the basis of one of the development institutions, for example, Vnesheconombank (VEB), by analogy with the Project financing Factory, but taking into account specifics of PPP projects (Inshakova et al. 2017).

The simultaneous implementation in Russia of the concept of preferential lending and the capital grant Fund for PPP projects will require the creation of a single center for the examination of socio-economic effects of the implementation of infrastructure projects, one of the key functions of which will be to justify the choice of an optimal form (provision of direct financing and/or concessional loan) and amount of state support (Table 7.3).

Table 7.3 Recommendations for establishing financial institutions in Russia to support infrastructure projects

Problem of equity leverage	Problem of budgetary leverage	Problem of project preparation financing
Creation of a factory of private equity funds in infrastructure with partial budget and quasi-budget participation	Establishment of a special financial institution to provide capital grants and project guarantees	Creation of project development financing mechanisms (funds and assistance programs)
– Will help to solve the problem of access to regional PPP projects to equity investors – Will allow construction companies and operators with limited investment opportunities to participate in PPP projects	– Capitalization through placement of bonds under state guarantees – May be an alternative mechanism of tax-increment financing	– Budget and quasi-budget funds can be provided for preparation of priority projects for national economy in the form of grants; – For other projects financing can be carried out on a returnable basis (credit, installments, share in the company, etc.)

References

Adamchuk, O., & Bazanova, E. (2019). Vlasti reshili uprostit' rabotu fabriki proektnogo finansirovaniya «VEB.RF» (The authorities decided to simplify the work of the VEB.RF project financing factory). Economy/Investments and projects, Vedomosti. https://www.vedomosti.ru/economics/articles/2019/03/28/797711-fabriki-proektnogo-finansirovaniya. (Accessed 28 March 2019).

Inshakova, A. O., Goncharov, A. I., Inshakova E. I. (2019). Innovative technologies of oil production: Tasks of legal regulation of management and taxation. In Ivanov, O. V., Inshakova, A. O., & Popkova, E. G. (Eds.), *Energy sector: A systemic analysis of economy, foreign trade and legal regulations* (pp. 79–94). Cham: Springer Science + Business Media.

Bounds, G. (2012). Public investment across levels of government: The case of Victoria, Australia. Report for the 28th OECD Territorial Development Policy Committee: 4–5.

Cuttaree, V., & Mandri-Perrott C. (Eds.). (2011). Mechanisms available to government to support PPP projects. In Cuttaree, V. (ed.) *Public-private partnerships in Europe and central Asia* (pp. 57–68), World Bank. https://doi.org/10.1596/9780821387030_CH07.

ESCAP. (2008). Government support for PPPs. https://www.unescap.org/ttdw/ppp/ppp_primer/35_government_support_for_ppps.html. (Accessed 10 March 2019).

Farquharson, E., Torres de Mästle, C., Yescombe, E. R., Encinas, J. (Eds.). (2011). *How to engage with the private sector in public-private partnerships in emerging market.* World Bank.

InfraONE. (2019). Investitsii v infrastukturu, Analiticheskii obzor (Investment in infrastructure. Analytical review), Moscow. https://infraone.ru/analitika/investitsii_v_infrastrukturu_2019_infraone_research.pdf?12. (Accessed 10 May 2019).

Inshakova, A. O., Goncharov, A. I., Kazachenok O. P., Kochetkova S. Y. (2017) Syndicated lending: intensification of transactions and development of legal regulation in modern Russia. *Journal of advanced research in law and economics, VIII*, № 3(25), pp. 838–842.

Ivanov, O. V. (2016). *Teoriya i mirovaya praktika gosudarstvenno-chastnogo partnerstva (Theory and world practice of public-private partnership)* (p. 300). Moscow: MGIMO-University.

Ivanov, O. V., & Ivanova, A. O. (2019). *Gosudarstvenno-chastnoe patnerstvo v stranakh Aziatsko-tikhookeanskogo regiona (Public-private partnership in the countries of Asia-Pacific region)* (p. 270). Moscow: MGIMO-University.

Pagano, M. (2017). Anuncian un fondo de US$ 900 millones para financiar obra pública. Clarin Economia. https://www.clarin.com/economia/crean-fondo-junto-bid-bm-financiar-obra-publica_0_rkpCO8Vc-.html. (Accessed 10 April 2019).

World Bank. (2017). PPP Reference Guide 3.0. https://library.pppknowledgelab.org/documents/4699. (Accessed 15 April 2019).

US Department of Transportation Federal Highway Administration. Project Finance Primer. (2010). Washington, DC.

Schur, M. (2016). *Public–private partnership funds observations from international experience.* ADB East Asia Working paper series, No.6.

Solntsev, K. (2017). *Proekty gosudarstvenno-chastnogo partnerstva i mery ikh podderzhki v mirovoy praktike (Public-private partnership projects and measures of their support in the world practice).* Public-Private Partnership. №4 (1).

Starostina, Y. (2018). *Rossijskaya infrastruktura do Suehtsa dovedyot (Russian infrastructure will bring to the Suez Canal).* Economy, RBK. https://www.rbc.ru/newspaper/2018/09/20/5ba1419f9a79477da774546e. (Accessed 18 September 2018).

Tkachenko, M., & Ivanov, O. (2018). O nekotorikh instrumentakh finansovoi podderzhki GCHP-proektov v mezhdunarodnoi praktike: rekommendatsii dlya Rossii (On some tools of financial support of PPP projects in international practice: recommendations for Russia)/ Ekonomika I Upravlenie: Problemy, Resheniya (Economy and Governance: problems, decisions). 2018, №5, pp.74–84.

Tolstoukhova, N. (2019). *Zavodnoj klyuch: Bol'she otraslej poluchat podderzhku ot "Fabriki proektnogo finansirovaniya (More industries will get support from Project Finance Factory)*

Economy, RG.ru. https://rg.ru/2019/04/03/fabrika-proektnogo-finansirovaniia-okazhet-podderzhku-mnogim-otrasliam.html. (Accessed 03 April 2019).
World Bank. (2017). PPP Reference Guide 3.0 https://library.pppknowledgelab.org/documents/4699. (Accessed 15 April 2019).

Part IV
Project Management. Life Cycle of a PPP Project. Key Stages and Tasks

Chapter 8
Preparation and Assessment of PPP Projects

Vasily A. Marinin and Nikolai V. Studenikin

Abstract This paper details the stage of preparation and approval of the PPP project, including an assessment of the effectiveness and justification of the comparative advantage of the chosen form of implementation, taking into account the requirements of legislation and current market practice in the Russian Federation. The authors formulated major national specifics and basic approaches to key sub-phases of preparation of a PPP project: concept development of a PPP project, the analysis of the conditions of its realization, the legal and financial structuring, evaluation of the effectiveness and substantiation of comparative advantages.

Keywords Project management · Life cycle · Feasibility analysis · Efficiency assessment · Comparative advantage · Feasibility study · PPP project structuring · Risk matrix · Financial model of the project

JEL-codes H44 · H43 · K12 · K15

Introduction

According to the National PPP Center analyses, on average, only every third of initiated PPP projects in the Russian Federation enters the stage of competitive selection of a private partner and only 70% of them manage to find private investors and pass the stage of commercial and financial closure (conclusion of a loan or other agreement to attract financing). Thus, an average of 20–30% of project PPP initiatives reach from the idea to the financial closure The quality of some of the PPP and

V. A. Marinin (✉)
Strategic Development, Analytical and Information Support for PPPs', Center for PPP Projects, JSC "Avtodor-invest", Malaya Dmitrovka str., 16-6, Moscow, Russia
e-mail: marininvas@gmail.com

N. V. Studenikin
MGIMO University, Vernadsky Ave., 76, 119454 Moscow, Russia
e-mail: n.studenikin@gmail.com

O. V. Ivanov and A. O. Inshakova (eds.), *Public-Private Partnerships in Russia*, Competitive Government: Public Private Partnerships,
https://doi.org/10.1007/978-3-030-56352-3_8

concession agreements that have been concluded leaves much to be desired, which may further affect the success of their implementation.

The reason for such a low percentage of successfully launched PPP projects in Russia is primarily the lack of competence of market participants and inefficient project management at the stage of preparation and approval of the project.

At the same time, the introduction of effective models and best foreign practices of PPP project management, including the unification and digitalization of processes, allows:

- to provide a higher quality of development of PPP projects;
- to increase the degree of controllability and verifiability of the results of the implementation of PPP projects;
- reduce existing and potential administrative and other barriers to the successful implementation of PPP projects;
- to provide maximum information openness of the whole process management of PPP projects, with the aim of attracting the widest range of participants.

Effective management of PPP projects is based on a clear understanding of their life cycle and the role of each participant at each stage.

Based on the PMBoK methodology, the National PPP Center identifies five key stages of the life cycle of any PPP project (given for the case of launching the project under the classical competitive procedure and from the position of a public partner):

- initiation of the project (initial assessment of the feasibility and concept development);
- project planning (development of feasibility study, financial and legal model, implementation schedule, etc.))
- selection and conclusion of an agreement with a private partner
- support of pre-investment stage;
- organization of control and monitoring of the project implementation by the private partner.

Connection of these stages with the main phases of PPP project, provided by the legislation on PPP in Russia, is shown in Chart 8.1.

In turn, within the framework of preparation and approval of the PPP project, the initiators usually follow the following sequence of steps:

- Step 1: Development and coordination of the project concept, formation of the working (project) group.
- Step 2: Technical, legal, and marketing analysis of project implementation conditions.
- Step 3: Technical, legal, and financial structuring of the project (preparation of necessary documentation).
- Step 4: Evaluation of the effectiveness and substantiation of comparative advantagesComparative advantage of selected forms and model of PPP project.
- Step 5: Decide on the implementation of the PPP project and launch a tender procedure for the selection of a private partner (if applicable).

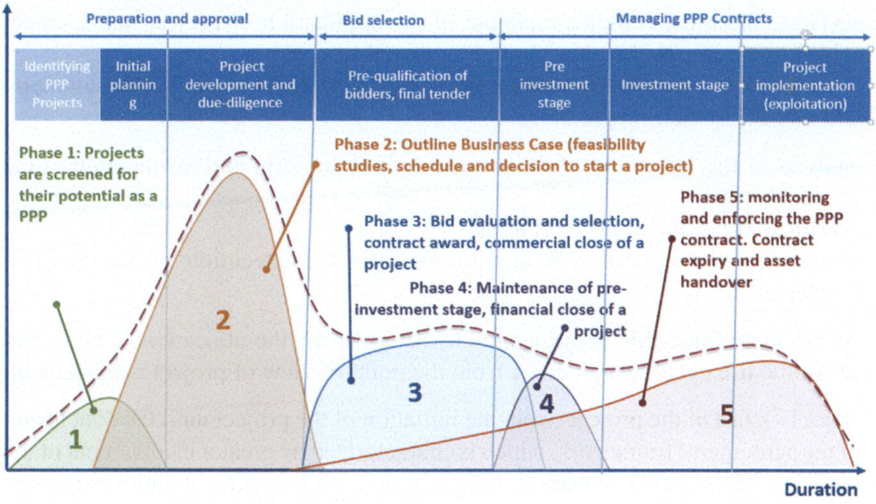

Chart 8.1 Key stages of PPP project life cycle

This sequence of steps is universal, but some nuances may differ depending on the chosen form of PPP project implementation. For example, performance evaluation and justification of comparative advantage is a mandatory requirement for the launch of PPP projects implemented only within the framework of the Federal law № 224-FZ "On public-private partnership, municipal-private partnership in the Russian Federation…", for projects implemented within the framework of the concession model, the procedure for assessing the effectiveness and justification of comparative advantage is not mandatory and applies only if the public partner himself considers it necessary to conduct it.

Results

The project is a unique set of coordinated actions with specific deadlines, undertaken to achieve certain goals in terms of compliance with the requirements for cost and quality. Given this definition, we can say that the relations arising from the public and private parties in the framework of public-private partnership, clearly have a project nature, as: strictly limited by the term of the agreement, have a clear goal—to achieve certain socially significant results and involve fixing in the agreement (contract) the amount of financial participation of each party.

At the same time, PPP project management has its own peculiarities.

First, the sectoral specificity of PPP mechanisms and the need to strike a balance between the interests of business, society, and the state, significantly complicates the process of development and coordination of such projects. It can be said that PPP projects are the most complex example of the application of project management principles that can only be encountered in the public sector.

Secondly, PPP projects are more long-term and complex, and more attention should be paid to their preparation:

- analysis of the feasibility of the project in the long-term and justification of the chosen form;
- careful stydy of the terms of contract;
- organization of control and monitoring over the execution of the contract (agreement).

At the same time, PPP projects are characterized by the allocation of two main stages of the life cycle, which differ from the point of view of project management:

- stage 1—start of the project (from the initiation of the project until the conclusion of the agreement) framework, which is characterized by greater involvement of the public and application of methods of forecasting and modeling of future processes;
- stage 2—project implementation (from agreement to completion of the project), where the role of the public sector is practically reduced to monitoring the actions of the private party, and the methods of project management by the private partner are similar to the approaches used in construction projects or life cycle contracts.

Given this feature, it can be said that at the stage of implementation, PPP projects are almost completely managed on the basis of parameters and in accordance with the plans developed at the launch stage, that is, the life cycle of the PPP project is predictive. Therefore, the effectiveness of project management at the stage of launching a PPP project is even more important than at the stage of direct implementation, especially for the public side (Inshakova et al. 2019).

In turn, the launch stage can also be divided into two sub-stages:

(1) project preparation and approval;
(2) selection of a private partner for the project.

Step 1: Development and approval of the project concept

In the Russian Federation, there are no uniform requirements for the PPP project concept or unified forms of such a document. In practice, as the concepts of PPP projects, there are both short presentations with the most significant parameters, and detailed, several hundred pages, analytical documents with a detailed analysis of the advantages and disadvantages of using a particular form of project implementation, as well as the legal and technical conditions in which the project is implemented.

Despite the differences in approaches, it is possible to identify the main issues that are usually answered by the concept, regardless of the format of its provision:

- What problem is the project aimed at and what is its relevance?
- What are the objectives of the project and how are they correlated with the objectives and targets of the relevant strategic planning documents?

- Who are the main participants of the project? Who should be part of the project team during the project launch phase?
- What are the main technical and economic indicators of the object planned to be created?
- What services are planned to be provided using the object of the agreement?
- What are the expected deadlines for the main stages of the project?
- What is the estimated total cost of creating an object of agreement?
- Is a public partner ready to provide financing and in what amount?
- What is the expected distribution of the parties' obligations in the project?
- What risks is a public partner ready to carry?
- What risks—in the public partner's view—shall bear a private partner?
- What are the advantages of using PPP mechanisms for project implementation?

An important task before the project is formally launched and directed in the prescribed manner for approval and evaluation, is to conduct preliminary discussions of the concept of the project with the main potential stakeholders: the authorities, the public, and potential private partners, population (users). Such a discussion allows to understand at the earliest stage whether the project is viable and under what conditions it can attract potential investors.

To organize such a discussion, interdepartmental bodies (councils or commissions on investments and (or) PPP) or special online platforms that are constantly operating or being formed for the project are most often used.

Nota Bene

Especially for the purpose of identifying potential interested parties and partners for the launch and implementation of PPP projects in the subjects of the Russian Federation National PPP Center and the Ministry of economic development of the Russian Federation has launched the official online Platform of support for infrastructure projects "ROSINFRA" (rosinfra.ru). With the help of this platform, any public legal entity can find for its "PPP initiative", which is at the stage of the concept, potential investors, private partners (including those ready to come out with a private initiative), experienced consultants, and other possible partners interested in the project.

Either as part of the concept development or after its approval, a project team can be formed to prepare and launch the project. As a rule, the formalization of such a team consisted of state (municipal) employees occurs through the creation of a permanent or temporary working group. Given the cross-sectoral nature of PPP projects, their complexity and capital intensity, such a working group, as a rule, is headed by a representative of the Supreme Executive authority in the rank of not less than Deputy senior official (Governor, head of the municipality). Often the authorities formalize the beginning of work on the project through the adoption of a special order, which defines the deadlines for the preparation of the project and the responsible persons, can also be determined by the composition of the working (project) group.

The hierarchical structure of works on preparation of the concept of a PPP project is introduced in Chart 8.2.

Step 2: Marketing, technical, and legal analysis

If the concept of the project is approved in principle by all potential participants, a marketing, technical, and legal analysis of the project implementation conditions is carried out (there are often cases when these works are carried out within the framework of the development of the project concept).

Such analysis can be carried out either by potential public partner (initiator) on its own, or with the involvement of consulting companies or specialized development institutions (agencies, development corporations, foundations, international financial organizations, etc.).

Marketing analysis is understood as the activity of search, collection, and preliminary analytical processing of information that is important for the successful launch and implementation of the project in the future.

The need for marketing analysis in relation to PPP projects is determined by the following factors:

- presence of a large number of participants with multidirectional interests (as a rule, the initiator of the PPP project is the state, and the main executor are private investors, who need to be interested and involved in the project);
- capital intensity of PPP projects, which determines the need to attract large amounts of private investment and debt, using a variety of debt financing instruments;
- political and social sensitivity of the population to the introduction of fees for the use of public-private partnership, which determines the need for appropriate research, and also outreach to the population;
- long period of project implementation, determining the complexity of the forecast of the main financial and economic indicators of the project;
- high risks of implementation of PPP projects, complexity of forecasting their size and impact on the long-term;
- the need to analyze the demand for goods/services provided using the PPP facility;
- the need to assess the possibility and feasibility of attracting state support.
- As part of the marketing analysis, as a rule, the following aspects of the implementation of the infrastructure project are clarified:
- will the infrastructure facility or the services provided with its use be in demand;
- what is the market of demand for the object/services in terms of geography, target groups of consumers and their number, including taking into account development trends;
- what is the level of competitive supply, whether competing projects are planned and their impact is taken into account;

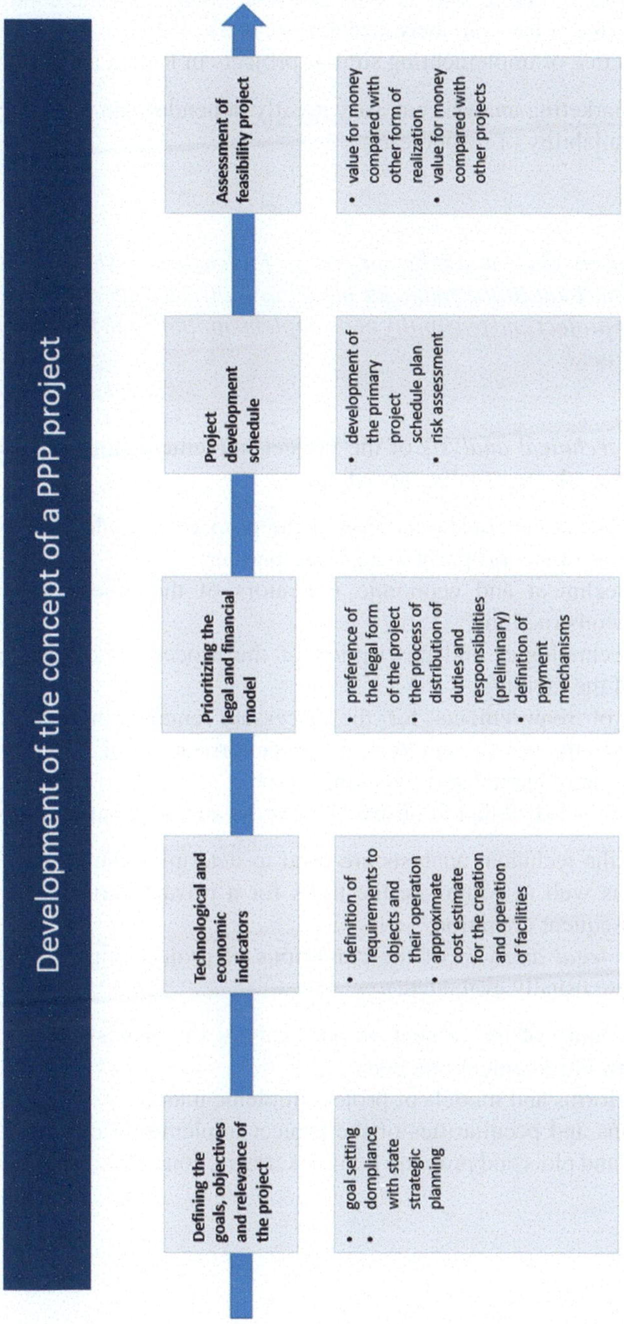

Chart 8.2 Hierarchical structure and order of works on preparation of the concept of a PPP project

- what backs up the confidence in the availability of demand for services in the long-term, including taking into account possible changes in the conditions of their provision (fee collection, increased access, etc.);
- what is the practice of implementing similar projects in Russia and abroad?

The depth of marketing analysis can vary greatly depending on the objectives of the project and availability of resources.

Nota Bene

Marketing analysis plays a significant role in forecasting cash flows, which are taken into account in the financial model and directly affect commercial efficiency of the project and feasibility of its implementation both for the private and public partners.

As part of the *technical analysis* of the project implementation conditions, the following types of work are usually carried out:

- estimation of current technical condition of the property complex, if the project presumes transfer of any property to a private partner;
- definition of technical and economic indicators of the objects planned for construction/reconstructions;
- definition of technologies and description of the process of operation and/or maintenance of the facility;
- determination of requirements for the necessary engineering infrastructure (supply of electricity, water, sanitation, gas, access roads, etc.);
- general estimation of capital and operating costs;
- development of the schedule of construction works and necessary repairs.

The results of the technical analysis are used to determine the costs of project implementation, as well to formulate the tasks for a private partner to create an object and its subsequent operation.

As part of the *legal analysis* of the conditions of project implementation the following issues are usually evaluated:

- fundamental legality of the project on the basis of the analysis of legislation, judicial, and law enforcement practice;
- available legal forms and models of project implementation;
- legal restrictions and peculiarities of the project implementation, including the legal status of land plots and property complex, restrictions of sectoral legislation, etc.;

- regulatory risks of project implementation: budget legislation, competition law, environmental legislation, tariff regulation, etc.;
- tax aspects of project implementation.

The results of the legal analysis are used to determine the possibility and conditions for the use of PPP mechanisms in the implementation of the project, as well as the limitations of the legal environment in which it will be implemented,

Step 3: Technical, legal, and financial structuring of the project (preparation of feasibility study, risk matrix, and legal documentation)

As in the case of the project concept, there are no unified requirements for the feasibility study of the PPP project in the Russian Federation. As a rule, a PPP project feasibility study is understood as a comprehensive document that justifies the feasibility of the PPP project and contains both analysis of the initial conditions of the project (legal, technical, economic), and analysis of costs and revenues in implementation of the project, as well as an assessment of the project effectiveness.

Subject to the use of this approach to the understanding of the feasibility study of the project, such a document should include:

- results of marketing, legal, and technical analysis;
- description of the chosen legal model of project implementation;
- description of the technological process;
- requirements to the created object and necessary engineering infrastructure;
- description of main equipment, fixtures, and accessories;
- integrated calculation of the consolidated cost of products/services;
- duration of a project;
- description of the payment mechanism and payment schedule;
- financial model of project implementation;
- calculation of efficiency criteria (financial/commercial, budgetary, socioeconomic, etc.).

The hierarchical structure of works on preparation of feasibility study of PPP project is shown in Chart 8.3.

Financial model is the main component of the project feasibility study.

Financial model is a method of calculation of financial and economic indicators of the project, which can be implemented, for example, in the form of a spreadsheet file (MS Excel) or configured in a specialized software product.

The purpose of the financial model is:

- evaluation of income and expenses for the project;
- determination of the parameters of project payback;
- calculation of key project performance indicators;
- evaluation of budget participation in the project: the amount of budget payments, tax revenues, net present value (NPV) of the project for the budget;
- evaluation of comparative advantage of the project implementation using PPP mechanisms;
- quantitative assessment of project risks for both private and public partners;

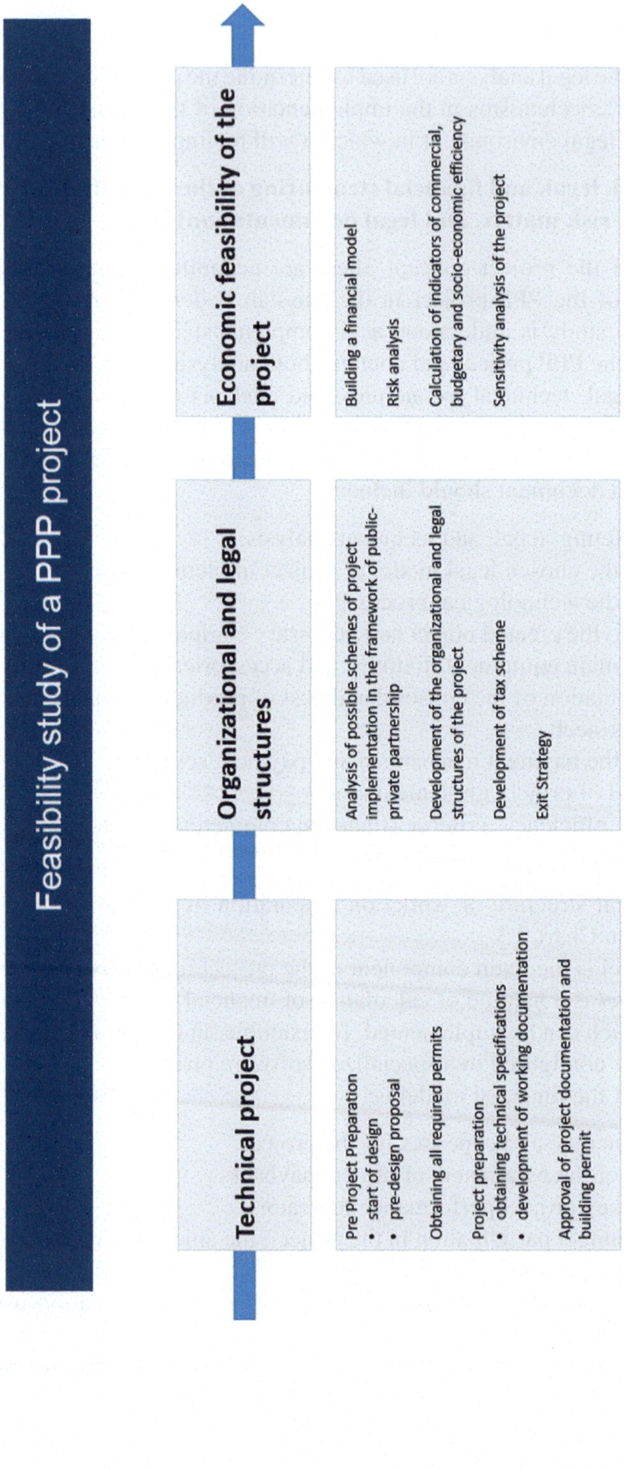

Chart 8.3 Hierarchical structure of works on preparation of feasibility study (FS) of a PPP project

The initial data for the financial model are

- capital expenditures for creation (reconstruction) of the agreement object;
- operating costs for operation and/or maintenance of the facility of the agreement, including taking into account the investment costs of the private partner compensated at the stage of operation;
- volume of goods produced, works performed, services provided;
- the forecast of tariffs;
- potential cost and volume of borrowed financing;
- macroeconomic assumptions;
- volume and procedure of financial participation of budgets of the budget system of the Russian Federation;
- tax assumptions.

The output of the financial model should include:

- cash flow forecast;
- profit and loss forecast;
- financial balance of the project;
- quantitative risk assessment;
- evaluation of the commercial effectiveness of the project, including net present value (NPV) of the project, internal rate of return (IRR), payback period (PB), profitability for the private partner and for financing organizations;
- calculation of the comparative advantage of the project implementation using PPP mechanisms.

Before developing a financial model, the initiator must determine the payment mechanism in the project, for which it is necessary:

- to determine the sources and structure of project financing during the construction phase;
- to determine the required level of participation of the public partner in the financing of the project;
- to determine the order and conditions for the allocation of excess revenue in the project (if applicable);
- to determine the system of fines for the implementation of the project;
- to assess the expected tax burden on the private partner and possible tax and other revenues to the budgets of the budget system of the Russian Federation as a result of the project implementation;
- to determine the optimal model of risk distribution between the parties.

One of the key factors in the success of a PPP project along with the allocation of risks is to determine the optimal level of participation of the public partner in financing the project.

Financial participation can be carried out at different stages (design, construction, operation, and/or maintenance) and in different forms (fixed payment or payments tied to certain conditions: loading, profitability, etc.). From the legal point of view, possible mechanisms of budget participation in the implementation of PPP projects in the Russian Federation, depending on the form of implementation are presented in Table 8.1.

There are three main types of payment mechanisms (mechanisms of compensation to the private partner of investments) used in the world practice of PPP projects:

- direct fee collection by concessionaire (*direct toll* or *user-pay*);
- minimum guaranteed income (*MGI, minimal revenue guarantee*)
- availability payment.

These payment mechanisms have a set of features that make it possible to determine their appropriateness, taking into account the specifics of the project.

Table 8.1 Eligible mechanisms of budget participation in PPP projects in the Russian Federation

International definition	Purpose	Transfer of funds	Budget code of Russia	Federal law (224, PPP)	Federal law (115, Concession)
Capital grant	Co-financing costs during the creation of the object	Fixed payments at the stage of creation	Budget subsidies (article 78.2)	Public partner partially finances the facility at the stage of operation and (or) maintenance (part 2 of article 6)	Concedent partially compensates the expenses for the creation and (or) reconstruction of the facility (article 3, paragraph 13)
Operation Grant	Co-financing of operation and (or) maintenance costs, as well as return on investment	Fixed payments during operation and (or) maintenance ("availability fee »)			Concedent's payment (article 13, paragraph 3)
		Compensation payment paid in case the project does not achieve any indicators (minimum revenue guarantee, or MRG)			

In general, we can say that the success of a PPP project depends on the optimal ratio of the following important parameters obtained during its structuring:

- expected profitability of the project for the private partner and, as a consequence, duration of the project;
- form and possible level of budget participation in the financing of the PPP project, including the ratio of "operational grant" and "capital grant";
- allocation of risks between the parties;
- guarantees to be provided to financing organizations;
- correctness of calculations of capital and operating costs, as well as of demand and revenues in the project.

Each of these parameters, both during the development of the project and in its subsequent coordination and discussion with potential stakeholders, can be changed in order to achieve the optimal combination. That is why for any PPP project it is advisable to develop a financial model that allows sensitivity analysis and can automatically recalculate output when input values change.

Risk assessment in a PPP project is an important point in its structuring and development of financial and legal documentation. As part of this assessment, a complete list of risks associated with the implementation of the project for all participants and stakeholders should be made. Risks are generally understood as probable changes in the project indicators, primarily related to income and expenses. The composition and significance of risks in a PPP project depend on its specifics.

The distribution of risks in a PPP project plays a significant role in the success of its launch and implementation. Accounting and risk assessment should be carried out from the moment of concept development (qualitative) to the immediate implementation of the project (quantitative). It is also recommended to maintain a "register" of realized risks, which indicates not only the list of risks, but the degree of their impact on the project as well (Inshakova Agnessa and Goncharov Alexander 2017).

The risk matrix is usually presented in the form of a table that contains the following information:

- list of risks (risk events) to which the project is exposed at various stages (approval, tender procedure, commercial and financial closure, direct implementation);
- risk qualification according to the probability of occurrence and consequences for project implementation;
- quantitative and/or qualitative risk assessment;
- distribution of risks among project participants, including indication of who will bear additional costs during their implementation;
- measures to be implemented to reduce the impact of risks.

Usually, risks are carried by the party that can manage it better.

General model of qualitative risk assessment when launching a PPP project is presented in Chart 8.4.

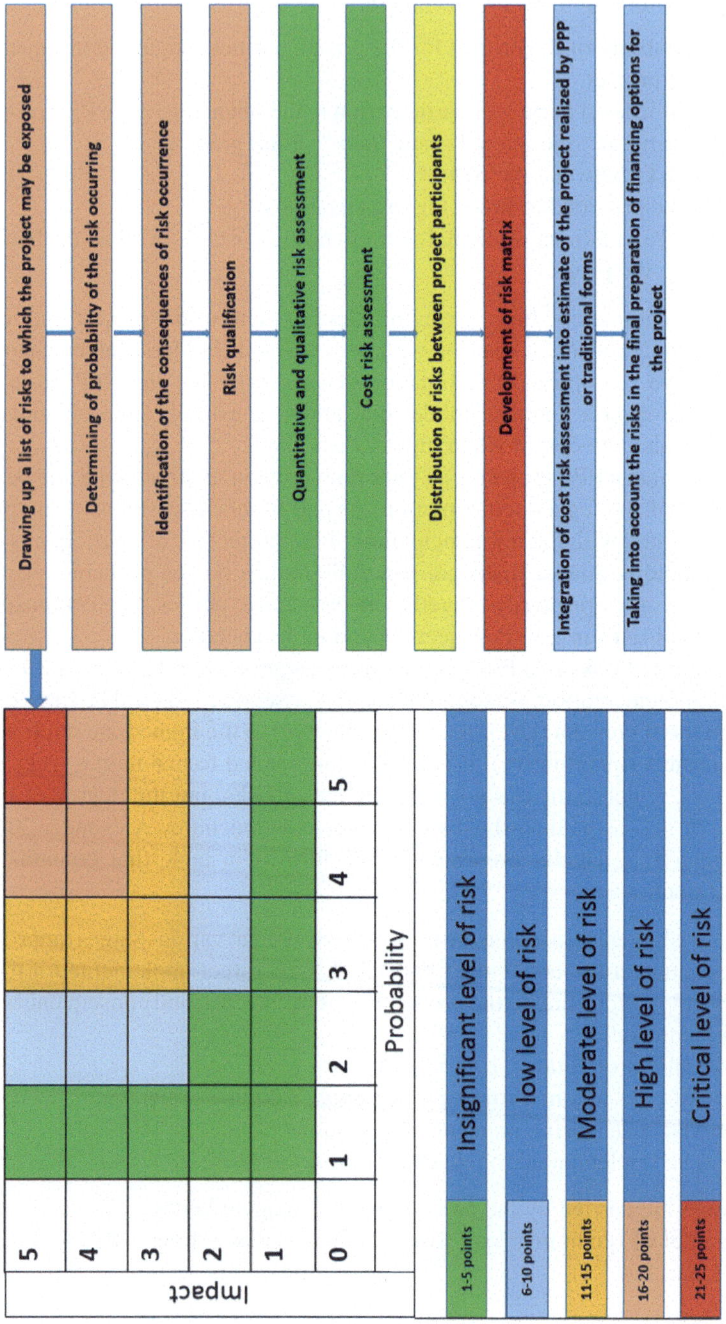

Chart 8.4 General model of qualitative risk assessment in PPP projects in Russia

Nota Bene

Risks that can be realized after commercial closure of the project (signing of the agreement) should be clearly described in the agreement text, indicating which party and to what extent is responsible for their management.

Drawing up a risk matrix is a mandatory stage of preparation only for projects implemented within the framework of the 224-FZ "On public-private partnership, municipal-private partnership in the Russian Federation…". Still, for large concession projects, participants also use this approach for better legal structuring and future project management.

The final stage of PPP project structuring is the development of the draft agreement. The availability of the draft agreement before the launch of the tender procedure is a prerequisite only for projects implemented within the framework of the 224-FZ "On public-private partnership, municipal-private partnership in the Russian Federation…", as well as for concession projects in certain industries (water supply and sanitation). This requirement was established by the legislator based on the need for a comprehensive accounting and quantitative assessment of the risks of the public partner, which can be carried out only based on the wording of the conditional obligations of the public partner prescribed in the agreement. At the same time, the final text of the agreement, both in the case of concession projects (except for the cases mentioned above) and projects within the framework of the 224-FZ, as a rule, is developed only after the tender procedure and negotiations on commercial closure, since the private investor may be interested in adjusting those provisions of the agreement that are not significant and were not the criteria of the tender.

However, despite the fact that in most cases the agreement in the final form is developed only at the time of commercial closure (signing), it is important to determine essential and other significant terms of the agreement before sending it for approval, in order to comprehensively assess the conditional and unconditional obligations of the public partner and make a balanced decision on the implementation of the project.

At the stage of development and initiation of the project, it is advisable to define and formulate the following terms of the agreement:

- associated with object agreement:
  - provisions defining conditions and procedure for the emergence of a private partner's (concessionaire) ownership of the object of the agreement,
  - provisions defining the legal basis for the transfer of the property complex, including the land plot to a private partner (concessionaire) for implementation of the agreement (lease or other rights),
  - provisions relating to the possibility and conditions of the pledge of the object of the agreement,
  - provisions relating to the possibility and conditions of the pledge of rights under the agreement;

- related to the subject of the agreement:
  - provisions describing obligations of the private partner to create and/or reconstruct the object of the agreement,
  - provisions describing conditions and features of implementation by the parties of operation and/or maintenance of object of the agreement;
- related to the financial participation of the public partner in the project:
  - provisions describing the mechanism of payments from the project budget,
  - provisions describing conditions and amount of compensation for loss of income and performance of other conditional expenditure obligations of the public party,
  - provisions describing special compensation for the project by the public partner;
- related to the further fate of the object of the agreement after the termination of the agreement;
- related to project risk allocation.

Step 4: Performance evaluation and justification of the comparative advantage of the chosen form and model of PPP project implementation

Stage of consideration (approval and evaluation) of a PPP project implemented under the Law on concession agreements (115-FZ) in the Russian Federation is not regulated.

For PPP projects implemented within the framework of the PPP/MPP law (224-FZ), a special procedure for consideration of the project by the PPP authorized body is established (RF Government resolution No.1514 of December 30, 2015, "On procedure for the authorized body to assess the effectiveness of the public-private, the municipal-private partnership project, and to determine their comparative advantage").

The general order of procedure of evaluating effectiveness and comparative advantages of PPP project by a competent authority in accordance with the requirements of the Law on PPP/MPP of the Russian Federation is presented in Chart 8.5.

As you can see from the Chart 8.5, the procedure includes the following main steps:

- evaluation of financial efficiency of the project;
- evaluation of socioeconomic effects of the project;
- determining comparative advantage of the project.

The purpose of the *financial efficiency assessment* in Russia is to determine the commercial feasibility of the project (payback of the project for the private partner).

The project is considered to meet the financial performance criterion if the net present value of the project for the private partner $NPV_{pp} \geq 0$.

Net present value of the project for the private partner is calculated as follows:

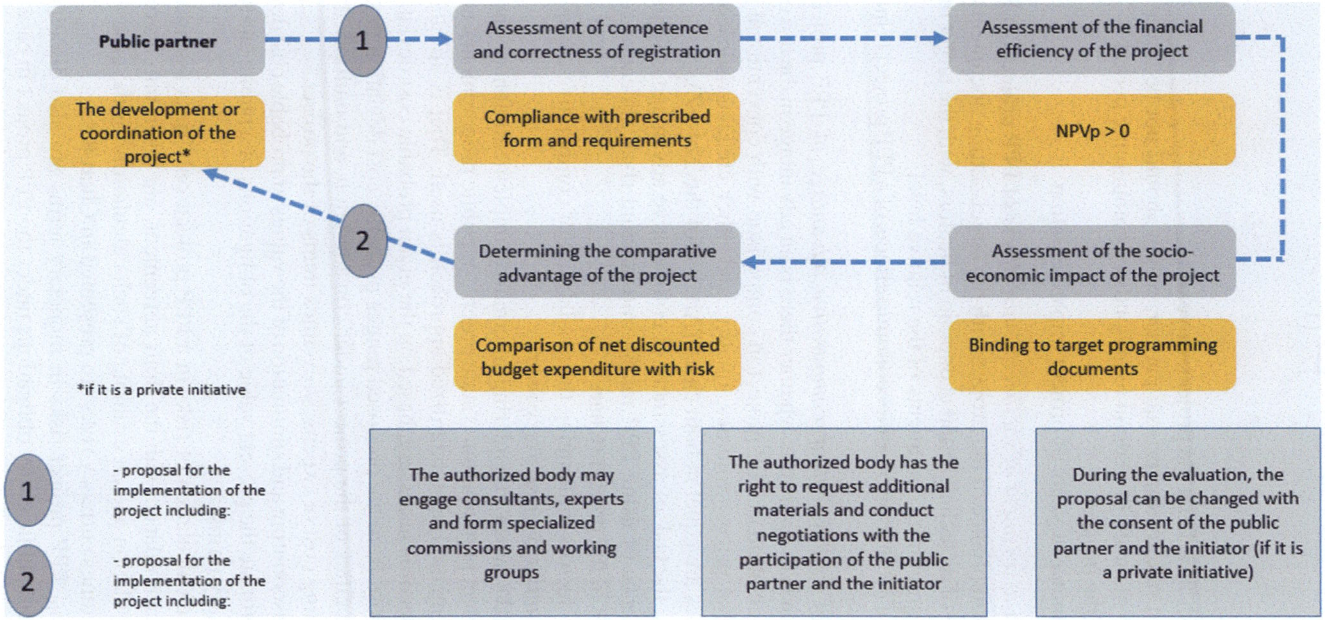

Chart 8.5 General procedure of PPP project efficiency assessment in the Russian Federation

$$NPV_{pp} = \sum_{t=1}^{T} \frac{FCF_{pp_t}}{(1 + r_{pp})^t}$$

where:

FCF_{pp_t} free cash flow from the project, in year t;
r_{pp} discount rate for the private partner, which should not be lower than the yield to maturity of Federal loan bonds of comparable period + 2.5%;
t year of the project;
T total number of years of project implementation

The purpose of *assessment of socioeconomic effects* of PPP projects in Russia is to determine the compliance of the project with the target-setting documents, as well as the compliance of its technical and economic indicators, with the target indicators of the current programming documents of the relative level.

General logic of evaluation of socioeconomic effects of a PPP project is introduced in Chart 8.6.

The purpose of *assessment of comparative advantage* of PPP project in the Russian Federation is to determine whether there is an advantage in the use of budget funds for implementation of PPP project in comparison with conventional procurement, provided that prices, volumes, quality, and other characteristics of goods, works, and services are equal in both cases (Art.3–6 of the 224-FZ).

In other words, the task of assessment of comparative advantage is to justify the budgetary expedience of using PPP, taking into account risks allocation and other assumptions made in the project (Chart 8.7).

One of the key factors influencing the availability of comparative advantage in a PPP project is *quantitative risk assessment*.

To quantify risks when considering alternative implementation of the project through direct budget participation ("state order", or public procurement), according to the evaluation method, a standardized approach is used. That is, in quantitative assessment of risks, it is necessary, based on the given probable cost deviations (see Table 8.2), to choose from the proposed ranges probable cost deviation that is most relevant to the specifics of the project under consideration, and multiply this value by the corresponding cost or expenses/revenues items of the project.

As a result of discounting and summation of the values of probable cost deviations, it is possible to estimate the present value of the obligations of a public entity in case of risks (in monetary terms).

For quantitative calculation of risks in a PPP project, only risks assumed by the public partner in accordance with the draft agreement, are taken into account. The model of risk calculation and an example of such calculation for the case when the public partner assumes currency risks are presented in Chart 8.8.

Along with this, PPP project risks in monetary terms are also discounted and summed to estimate public entity obligations under the PPP project in case of risks.

If criteria of financial efficiency or socioeconomic effects of PPP project are not met, and if the coefficient of comparative advantage (k_{vfm}) < 0, the authorized body

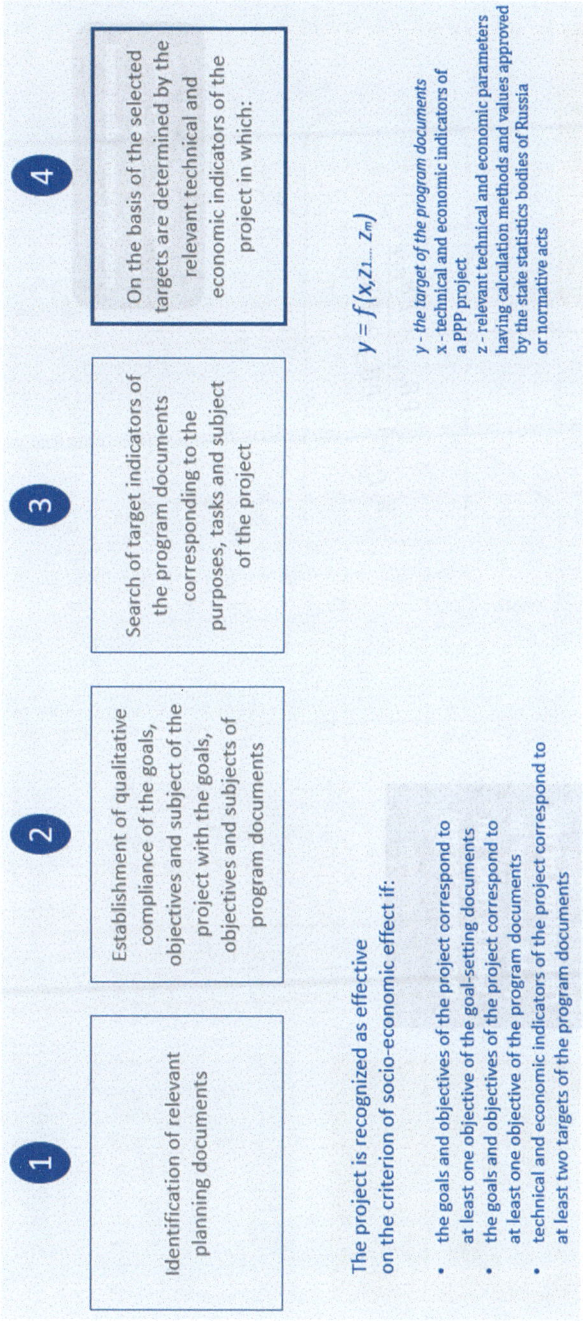

Chart 8.6 General logic of evaluation of socioeconomic effects of PPP projects under the Law on PPP/MPP (224-FZ)

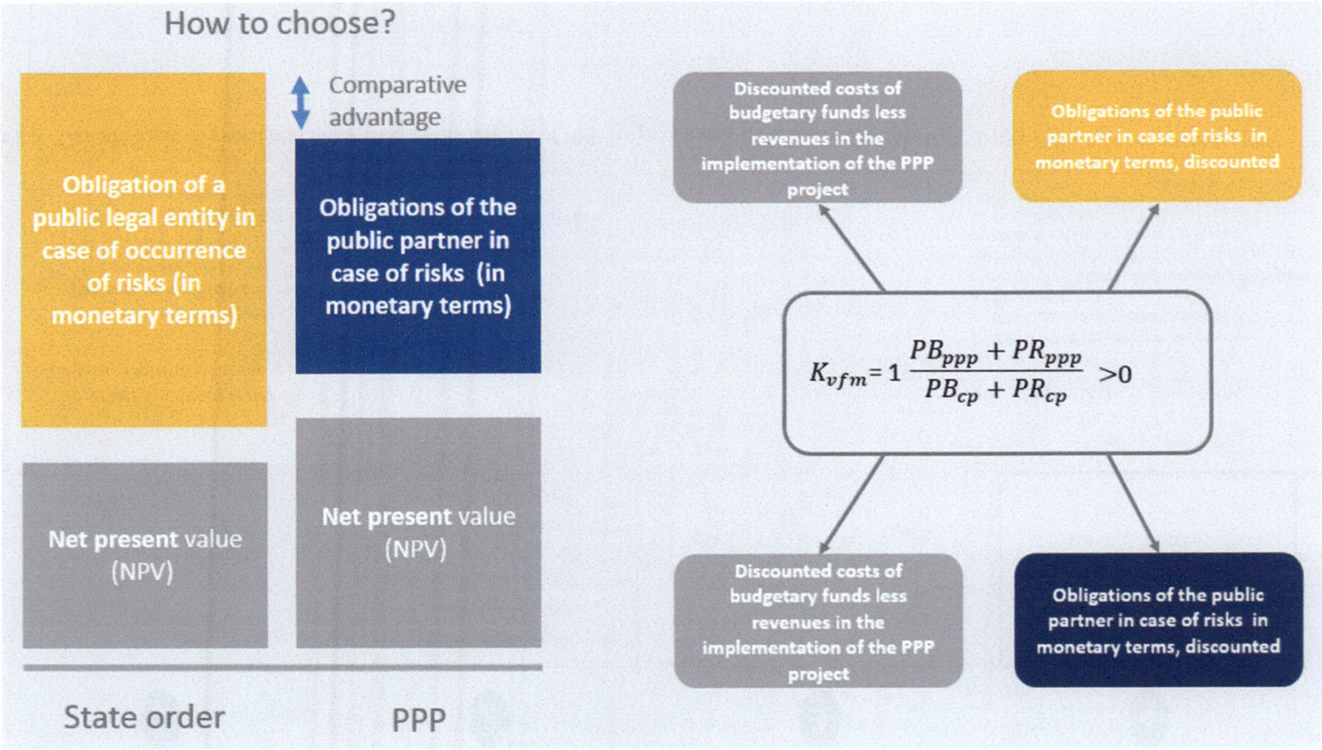

Chart 8.7 General approach to assessing comparative advantage of a PPP project under the Law on PPP/MPP

Table 8.2 Types of risks evaluated in the Russian practice

No.	Type of risks	Project cost items	Probable deviations
1	Risks of design and preparatory activities	Expenses at the pre-investment stage of the project, including: costs of preparation, purchase of land for the placement of the object, etc.	(7%; 15%)
2	Risks of creation of the object	Expenses for construction, reconstruction, technical re-equipment of the facility, etc.	(5%; 12%)
3	Risks of the object operation	Expenses of operation, maintenance of the facility, etc.	(15%; 25%)
4	Risks of income from the use of the object	Revenue from the provision of paid services to the population	(20%; 40%)
5	Other risks	Other risks, including the loss of the object, political events, not taken into account above	(5%; 10%)

gives a negative opinion on the effectiveness of the project, which automatically blocks its further implementation (it is applicable only for projects implemented under the PPP/MPP law in the Russian Federation).

Step 5: Decision on PPP project implementation and launch of tender procedure for selection of private partner

As a result of the project structuring and its evaluation, the public partner decides on the project implementation. According to the requirements of the legislation, such a decision should be taken

- for federal projects—by the Government of the Russian Federation,
- for regional projects—by the Supreme executive authority of the subject of the Russian Federation,
- for municipal projects—by the head of the municipality.

According to requirements of the legislation the following parameteres are approved by such a decision:

- goals and objectives of the project implementation;
- public partner, as well as the list of bodies and legal entities, acting on the side of the public partner in the event of the transfer of certain rights and obligations of the public partner to such bodies and legal entities;
- significant terms of the agreement;
- the values of the project efficiency criteria and the values of its comparative advantage indicators, on the basis of which a positive conclusion of the authorized body is obtained;
- type of tender (open or closed), as well as a list of persons who are invited to participate in the tender (in case of a closed tender);

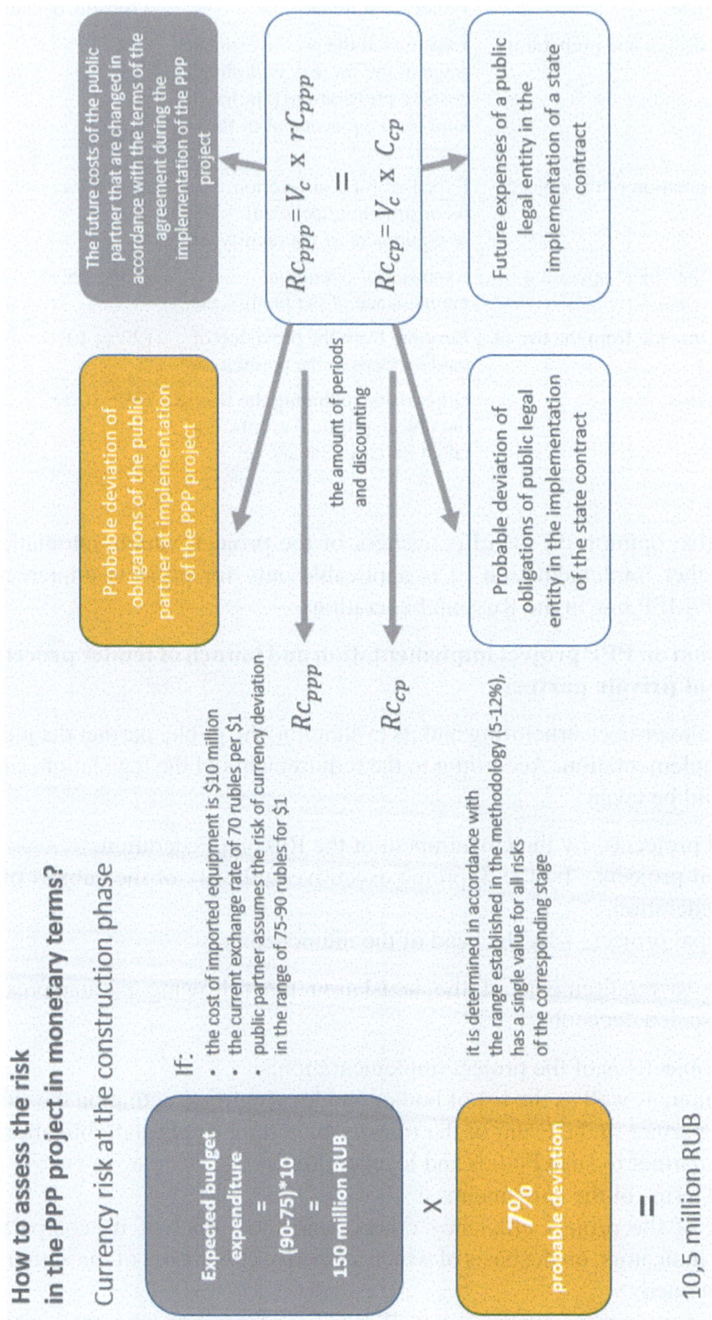

Chart 8.8 Example of currency risks assessment in a PPP project

- criteria and parameters of tender criteria;
- tender documentation or procedure and terms of its approval;
- terms of the tender for the right to conclude an agreement;
- terms and order of placement of the information on tendering on the official site of the Russian Federation in "Internet";
- procedure and terms of conclusion of the agreement;
- composition of the tender Commission and procedure for its approval.

Thus, it can be stated that the decision to implement the PPP project launches a competitive procedure for the selection of a private partner and establishes the general conditions for the implementation of the project.

Conclusions

When preparing and coordinating PPP projects, both public authorities and private investors in the Russian Federation face the same problems as most countries using PPP mechanisms:

- insufficient level of competence of public specialists in PPP;
- poor inter-agency coordination;
- lack of an integrated approach to project management.

All these problems lead to delays in the launch of PPP projects, and—not seldom—to complete abandonment of the project at an early stage or following the results of tenders, due to poor structuring or not taking into account a number of critical risks.

To solve this problem, the Russian Federation, like other countries, is trying to implement and improve approaches to PPP project management. Taking into account specifics of legislative regulation and peculiarities of the public administration system in Russia, when building a PPP project management system, the methodological approaches of PMBOK rather than PRINCE are used, which is expressed in the division of the project life cycle into separate sub-stages with their results (approval of the concept, decision on the project implementation, selection of a private partner, and conclusion of an agreement with him, etc.) and the composition of project teams.

At the same time, it is worth noting some features of the PPP project management system in the Russian Federation:

- as a rule, project management is used for large PPP projects with investments of more than 1 billion rubles, which is less than 5% of the total, which does not allow the mass dissemination of the principles of project management in the sphere of PPP in the Russian Federation;
- strict legislative regulation of certain stages in the life cycle of projects with a simultaneous lack of any regulation of other phases leads to the unsystematic development of a methodological framework;

- insufficient integration of project management principles into the public administration system as a whole hinders the development of these approaches to PPP projects.

References

Federal'nyj zakon "O koncessionnyh soglasheniyah" ot 21.07.2005 N 115-FZ (Federal law No. 115-FZ of July 21, 2005 "On Concession agreements"). https://base.garant.ru/12141176/. Retrieved March 10, 2019.

Guidebook on Promoting Good Governance in Public-Private Partnerships (2008). United Nations Economic Commission for Europe.

Inshakova Agnessa, O., & Goncharov Alexander, I. (2017). Securities as a subject of financial and economic interest and object of civil law relations. *Pravo–Zhurnal vysshei shkoly ekonomiki 4*, 97–110.

Inshakova, A., Goncharov, A., & Kazachenok, O. (2019). Legal regulation of the syndicated lending: Banking innovations in contemporary Russia. *Revista Espacios 39*(28), 7.

Ivanov, O.V. (2019). Gosudartsvenno-chastnoe partnerstvo kak instrument razvitiya infrastruktury i modernizatsii ekonomiki. Opyt stran Aziatsko-tikhookeanskogo regiona (Public-private partnership as an instrument of development of infrastructure and modernization of economy. Experience of Asia-Pacific countries) (p. 300) Moscow: MGIMO-University.

Kommentarij k Federal'nomu zakonu ot 13 iyulya 2015 g. N 224-FZ "O gosudarstvenno-chastnom partnerstve, municipal'no-chastnom partnerstve v Rossijskoj Federacii i vnesenii izmenenij v otdel'nye zakonodatel'nye akty Rossijskoj Federacii" (2016) (Comment to the Federal Law of July 13, 2015 N 224-FZ "On Public-Private Partnership, Municipal-Private Partnership in the Russian Federation and Amendments to Certain Legislative Acts of the Russian Federation"(2016) (Batrova T. A., Antropceva I. O., Vorob'ev N. I., Shapkina E. A., Pushkin A. V., Artem'ev E. V., Ruzanov I. V., Kandelaki G. G., Bogatyreva N. V., Kotuhov S. A.). SPS Konsul'tant Plyus (Consultant).

Kwak, Y. H., Chin, Y. Y., & Ibbs, C. W. (2009). Towards a comprehensive understanding of public private partnerships for infrastructure development. *California Management Review, 51*(2), 51–78.

Leigland, J. Is the public sector comparator right for developing countries? URL: http://info.worldbankorg/etools/docs/library/240066/ISTHEP~1.PDF.

Luchshie praktiki realizacii proektov gosudarstvenno-chastnogo partnerstva v social'noj sfere. (2016). (Best PPP practices in social sphere (2016)). PPP National Development Center. http://pppcenter.ru/assets/docs/pppcenter_a4_2016_v2_web.pdf. Retrieved March 11, 2019.

Mekhanizmy gosudarstvenno-chastnogo partnyorstva v ekonomicheskoi politike Rossii (Mechanisms of public-private partnership in the economic policy of Russia). (2018). In O. V. Ivanov (ed) (p. 409). Moscow: MGIMO-University.

O pervoocherednyh merah po sovershenstvovaniju koncessionnogo zakonodatel'stva. (2017). (On priority measures for concession legislation development (2017)). PPP National Development Center. http://pppcenter.ru/assets/files/reliz_21092017.pdf. Retrieved March 11, 2019.

Otcenka effektivnosti proektov GCHP po sravneniyu s inymi formami realizacii infrastrukturnyh proektov v stranah-uchastnicah EAES. (2018). (PPP projects effectiveness assessment compared to other forms of infrastructure projects in the countries participating in the EAEU (2018)). PPP National Development Center.

Federal'nyj zakon "O gosudarstvenno-chastnom partnerstve, municipal'no-chastnom partnerstve v Rossijskoj Federacii i vnesenii izmenenij v otdel'nye zakonodatel'nye akty Rossijskoj Federacii" ot 13.07.2015 N 224-FZ. (Federal Law No. 224-FZ of July 13, 2015 "On Public-Private Partnership, Municipal-Private Partnership in the Russian Federation and Amendments to Certain Legislative Acts of the Russian Federation"). https://base.garant.ru/71129190/. Retrieved March 10, 2019.

Popondopulo, V. F., & Shevelevoj, N. A. (Eds.). (2015). *Publichno-chastnoe partnerstvo v Rossii i zarubezhnyh stranah: pravovye aspekty (Public-Private Partnership in Russia and Foreign Countries: Legal Matters).* Moscow: Infotropik Media.

Rekomendacii po realizacii proektov gosudarstvenno-chastnogo partnerstva. Luchshie praktiki. (2016). (Recommendations for the public private partnership projects implementation. Best practices (2016)). Ministry of Economic Development of the Russian Federation. http://economy.gov.ru/minec/activity/sections/privgovpartnerdev/support/20160829. Retrieved March 10, 2019.

Rekomendacii po realizacii proektov gosudarstvenno-chastnogo partnerstva v sub"ektah Rossijskoj Federacii. (2013). (Recommendations for the public-private partnership projects implementation in the subjects of the Russian Federation). PPP Development Center. www.pppi.ru/sites/all/themes/pppi/img/pppsphere_managment1.pdf. Retrieved March 10, 2019.

Rukovodstvo k Svodu znanij po upravleniyu proektami (Rukovodstvo PMBOK). (2017). (A guide to the project management body of knowledge (PMBOK guide) (2017)). Project Management Institute, PMI.

World Bank. (2017). PPP Reference Guide 3.0 www.library.pppknowledgelab.org/documents/4699. Retrieved March 12, 2019.

Chapter 9
Selection of a Private Partner for PPP Project Implementation. Launch of PPP Projects Under "Unsolicited Proposal" (Private Initiative)

Evgeny Y. Moiseichev and Nikolai V. Studenikin

Abstract A detailed analytical review of the legislative regulation of the procedures for the preparation and conduct of the competition for the selection of a private partner in public-private partnership projects used in the Russian Federation is provided. Research of the launch of PPP projects under a private initiative is conducted. Systematized features and advantages of unsolicited proposals' system are analyzed and compared with international practices.

Keywords Public-private partnership · Competition · Competitive procedures · Selection of a private partner · Direct negotiations · Competition criteria · Private initiative

JEL-codes H44 · H43 · K12 · K15

Introduction

Selection of a private partner is one of the key stages of the public-private partnership project implementation process. The main task of this stage for the public partner is to identify and attract to the project the most suitable investor, who would ensure effective implementation of the infrastructure project on most favorable for the public party contractual terms.

International experience shows that the most effective way to select a private partner is competitive tendering. Efficient regulation of the tender procedure, as well as the resources and time that will be spent on its preparation and implementation,

E. Y. Moiseichev (✉)
Strategic Development, Analytical and Information Support for PPPs', Center for PPP Projects, AVTODOR-Invest, Malaya Dmitrovka str., 16/6, 127006 Moscow, Russia
e-mail: moiseichev@pppcenter.ru

N. V. Studenikin
MGIMO University, Vernadsky Ave., 76, 119454 Moscow, Russia
e-mail: n.studenikin@gmail.com

O. V. Ivanov and A. O. Inshakova (eds.), *Public-Private Partnerships in Russia*, Competitive Government: Public Private Partnerships,
https://doi.org/10.1007/978-3-030-56352-3_9

will make it possible to reduce the risk of failure in the selection process and increase the chances of productive implementation of the project (National PPP Center 2018).

The process of competitive procedures does not always follow a unified format. Due to country characteristics, specific regulations, specific nature of the project or the number of participants, the mechanisms of the competition may vary. At the same time, in most foreign jurisdictions, approaches to their regulation remain as flexible as possible, assuming several options at once (World Bank 2017).

In the Russian Federation, the selection of the private partner within PPP projects is regulated by the Federal law of July 13, 2015, N 224-FZ "On public-private, municipal-private partnership in the Russian Federation" (hereinafter—the Law on PPP/MPP) and a number of decrees, including the Decree of the Government of the Russian Federation of December 4, 2015, N 1322 "About the approval of Rules of carrying out the preliminary selection of participants of competition on the right of the conclusion of the agreement on public-private partnership, the agreement on municipal-private partnership".

For concession agreements rules of carrying out tender are established by the Federal law of July 21, 2005, N 115-FZ "On concession agreements".

In both "classic" forms of PPP used in Russia, the regulation of competitive procedures is generally identical, but there are differences in certain aspects (see Table 9.1).

Table 9.1 Key normative legal acts of the Russian Federation regulating competitive tender procedures in PPP projects

Normative legal act	Subject of regulation
PPP/MPP agreements	
Federal law of July 13, 2015, N 224-FZ "On public-private partnership, municipal-private partnership..."	Chapter 5. Identification of a private partner for the implementation of public-private partnership project, municipal-private partnership project • Procedural order of selection of the private partner
The Decree of the Government of the Russian Federation of December 4, 2015, N 1322 "About the approval of Rules of carrying out the preliminary selection of participants of competition on the right of the conclusion of the agreement on public-private partnership, the agreement on municipal-private partnership"	• Additional regulation of the preliminary selection procedure
Concession agreements	
Federal law of 21 July, 2005, N 115-FZ "On concession agreements"	Chapter 3. Procedure for concluding a concession agreement • Procedural order of selection of the private partner

Also, in the Russian Federation, for both concession models and PPP agreements, a simplified procedure for concluding an agreement with a private partner in accordance with the procedure of unsolicited proposal ("private initiative") may be applied. In international practices, the mechanism of the unsolicited proposal is, in fact, an alternative to the classical competition method of choosing a private partner for the implementation of a PPP project.

The advantages of such a mechanism for the public partner are that it reduces both time for the development of the project and time of tender procedures, as well as saves budget funds for the preparation of tender documentation and the tender. For potential investors, introduction of such a mechanism provides opportunities for concluding a PPP agreement without holding a tender and implementing the project on their own terms.

It is obvious that in the Russian context, significance of a private initiative mechanism especially increases for regional and municipal projects, since many regions and municipalities do not always have necessary competencies, funding, and experience for independent development and structuring of complex PPP projects. Thus, by shifting the costs of pre-investment project development to interested private partners, efficiency of budget spending increases.

In world practices, different approaches are used to provide preferences to private initiators of PPP projects within the framework of unsolicited proposal (private initiative) procedure. The most popular are:

- *bonus system*—proposal of an initiator receives a bonus (usually up to 5% of the value) and is considered to be the preferred bid if its value exceeds the value of the best offer by no more than this amount;
- *Swiss system*—an initiator of the proposal is entitled to conclude an agreement on the terms of the best offer from a third party;
- *mixed system*—an initiator is recognized as the preferred bidder (winner) if the value of his offer exceeds the value of the best offer by no more than 5%. If the difference between the two is greater (5–20%), an additional contest is held between them, during which the initiator's bonus is no longer taken into account.

In international practices, an unsolicited proposal (private initiative) mechanism also uses schemes in which an initiator either does not receive any preferences, or is recognized as a winner without competitive procedures.

Results

General Typology of Competitive Procedures

The legislation of the Russian Federation provides for two-stage competitive procedures for the selection of a private partner in PPP projects, including pre-selection and evaluation of bids. In this case, the law on PPP/MPP of the Russian Federation—in contrast to the Law on concessions of the Russian Federation—established the possibility to exclude pre-selection from the procedure (Revzina and Shamirzayeva 2019).

The legislation defines two types of competition:

- open: applications for participation may be submitted by an unlimited number of persons;
- closed: applications for participation may represent only those persons who are invited to participate in the contest.

Closed procedures are used only for projects that are classified as a state secret.

Selection of a private partner may also be conducted without competition, in particular, in cases where only one successful participant has entered the competition or no alternative proposals have been received under the private initiative mechanism. The conclusion of a concession agreement without competition is also possible with a person who's right to own and use the property that can be used as the object of the concession agreement and is necessary for activities under the concession agreement, arose on the basis of the lease agreement, subject to the following conditions simultaneously:

1. the object of the concession agreement is the property that was transferred to the lessee in accordance with the lease agreement, created and/or reconstructed by the lessee under such agreement and in accordance with this Federal law may be the object of the concession agreement;
2. the lease agreement, according to which the lessee has the right to own and use the property that is the object of the concession agreement, was concluded before July 1, 2010.

In the Russian Federation, it is also allowed to hold a joint tender if it is necessary to conclude a PPP agreement or a concession agreement with two or more public partners, for example, when it is planned to build several identical or related infrastructure facilities, while these facilities belong to and are located on the territory of different public legal entities. In such a case, the public partners are obliged to conclude an agreement on holding a joint tender, within the framework of which they determine mutual rights and obligations, responsibility, as well as one public partner who will act as the organizer of the joint tender. According to the results of the joint competition, one winner is determined, with whom each public partner enters into a separate agreement (Inshakova Agnessa et al. 2017).

Preparation of Tender Documentation

The formal start for the launch of competitive procedures is the decision on implementation of the PPP project, which, among other things, determines the criteria of the competition and the parameters of the competition criteria, timing of publication of the notice about the competition, the type of competition (open or closed), as well as the list of persons invited to participate in the competition (in case of a closed competition). Taking into account these data, the public partner develops tender documentation and agrees with the relevant authorized body, depending on the level of project implementation.

The tender documentation should first of all contain:

1. conditions of competition;
2. pre-qualification requirements;
3. criteria of the contest;
4. order of the competition;
5. timing of signing of the agreement;
6. information about the Deposit to be made.

To conduct the competition, the public partner creates a competition Commission. The number of members of the Commission may not be less than five. The Commission is entitled to make decisions if no less than fifty percent of the total number of its members are present at its meeting, and each member of the Commission has one vote. Among its key functions are the following:

1. notice of the launch of the contest;
2. acceptance of bids;
3. pre-selection and evaluation of bids

Tender Procedures

Competitive Invitation

The announcement of the competition is published by the competition Commission in the official publication determined by the public partner and posted on the official website in the information and telecommunications network "Internet" (in case of an open competition) or sent to persons in accordance with the decision to conclude a concession agreement or PPP agreement simultaneously with the invitation to participate in the competition (in case of a closed competition) within the period established by the tender documentation, but not less than thirty working days before the deadline for submission of applications for participation in the competition.

Submission of Applications for Participation in the Competition

At the first stage, the contestants submit applications for participation in it. Applications must meet requirements established by the tender documentation and contain the documents and materials provided by the tender documentation and confirming the applicants' compliance with requirements for the participants of the competition. The deadline for submission of applications for participation in the competition shall be not less than thirty working days from the date of publication of the notice of the competition or from the date of sending such a message to persons in accordance with the decision to conclude a concession agreement at the same time with an invitation to participate in the competition.

Envelopes with applications for participation in the competition are opened at the meeting of the competition Commission in the manner, on the day, in time and place established by the tender documentation.

Preliminary Selection

Preliminary selection of participants is carried out by the competition Commission in accordance with the procedure established by the tender documentation. The task of pre-selection is to determine:

- compliance of the application for participation in the competition with the requirements contained in the tender documentation;
- the applicant's compliance with the requirements to the participants of the competition;
- the applicant's compliance with requirements for a private partner in accordance with the Federal law, under which the PPP project is implemented.

The competition Commission has the right to demand from the applicant an explanation of the provisions submitted by him and confirming the applicant's compliance with the specified requirements of documents and materials.

Based on the results of the preliminary selection of participants, the competition Commission shall decide on the admission of the applicant to participate in the competition or on the refusal to admit the applicant to participate in the competition and draw up this decision by the Protocol of the preliminary selection of participants.

Pre-selection Criteria

During the pre-selection the compliance with the "formal" criteria established by the laws is verified in the first place, namely:

- absence of decisions on liquidation or termination of the participant's activity;
- absence of decisions about recognition of the applicant as bankrupt and about opening of bankruptcy proceedings against him.

For agreements within the framework of the PPP/MPP law of the Russian Federation additional basic requirements are also established, namely:

- non-application of administrative punishment in the form of administrative suspension of activity of legal entity in the order, established by the Code of the Russian Federation about administrative offenses, on the date of submission of the application for participation in competition;
- no arrears on taxes, fees and arrears on other mandatory payments, as well as arrears on the payment of interest for the use of budgetary funds, penalties, fines, no other financial sanctions not earlier than one month before the date of submission of the application for participation in the competition;
- availability of licenses necessary in accordance with the legislation of the Russian Federation for certain types of activities, certificates of admission of self-regulatory organizations to perform the work provided for in the agreement and other permits necessary for the implementation of the agreement.

In addition to the above-mentioned "formal" criteria, pre-selection may also require qualification, professional and business qualities of the participants. In fact, the list of such criteria in both laws is open.

An important feature of the PPP/MPP Law of the Russian Federation is provided under them the possibility to confirm the above qualification, professional and business criteria not only by applicant himself but also by the third parties, namely:

- a person who directly or indirectly owns at least ten percent of the authorized capital of the person who submitted an application for participation in the competition;
- a person, not less than ten percent of whose authorized capital is in direct or indirect possession of the above-mentioned person;
- a person with whom the applicant for participation in the competition entered into an agreement of intent providing for the performance of certain obligations of the private partner.

The law on concessions of the Russian Federation does not provide for the possibility of confirming qualifications by the third parties but in practice, for a long time, provisions on the possibility of confirming qualifications in this way were actively included in the tender documentation for concession projects (National PPP Center 2017)

Preferred Bidder

The tender Commission within three working days from the date of signing by its members of the Protocol of preliminary selection of participants, but not later than sixty working days before the expiration of the deadline for submission of bids to the Commission sends a notification to the participants of the competition with a proposal to submit bids.

Envelopes with tender proposals are opened at the meeting of the tender Commission in the order, on the day, in time and place established by the tender documentation. All envelopes with bids submitted by the participants to the tender Commission before the deadline for submission of bids are subject to opening, except for envelopes with bids submitted by the participants of the tender, who did not comply with the procedural requirements established by the tender documentation with regard to the order, the size and/or the deadline for making deposits.

Based on the results of consideration of bids, the tender Commission makes a decision on compliance or non-compliance of bids with the requirements of the tender documentation.

Evaluation of bids is carried out in the following order:

1. in case the competition criterion is set to increase its initial value, the value calculated by the condition contained in the proposal and such criterion is determined by multiplying the coefficient of such criterion by the ratio of the difference between the values contained in the proposal and the smallest of the values contained in all proposals to the difference between the largest of the values contained in all proposals and the smallest of the values contained in all proposals;
2. in case the criterion of the competition is set to reduce its initial value, the value calculated by the condition contained in the proposal and such criterion is determined by multiplying the coefficient of such criterion by the ratio of the difference between the largest of the values contained in all proposals and the value contained in the proposal to the difference between the largest of the values contained in all proposals conditions and the smallest of the values contained in all proposals;
3. for each proposal, the values calculated according to all the criteria of the competition in accordance with the provisions of paragraphs 1 and 2 shall be summed up and the final value shall be determined.

The preferred bidder (winner of the tender) is the participant who offered the best conditions. If only one tender bid was made, the tender shall be deemed invalid. In this case, the public partner has the right to consider it—subject to compliance with the requirements of the tender documentation, including the criteria of the competition—and to make a decision on concluding the agreement with a sole participant in accordance with the terms and conditions contained in the submitted tender offer, within thirty days from the date of adoption of the decision on recognizing the tender void.

In case two or more bids contain equal best conditions, the participant of the tender, who submitted the tender offer to the tender Commission earlier than the other participants is declared the winner of the tender.

Decision on the determination of the winner of the tender is formalized by the Protocol of consideration and assessment of bids in which the following are specified:

- criteria of the contest;
- terms and conditions contained in the bids;

- results of bids review with indication of competition proposals in relation to which a decision on their inconformity with requirements of the tender documentation was made;
- results of bids evaluation;
- name and location (for a legal entity), surname, name, patronymic and place of residence (for an individual entrepreneur) of the winner, justification of the decision made by the competition Commission to recognize the participant as the winner of the competition.

The results of the competition are reported within 15 working days from the date of signing the Protocol.

Evaluation Criteria of Bids

The competition criteria are established by the decision to enter into a concession agreement or PPP/MPP agreement and are used to evaluate bids in accordance with the established procedure.

The following criteria can be used for concession projects:

1. terms of creation and/or reconstruction of the object of concession agreement;
2. period from the date of signing the concession agreement to the day when the created and/or reconstructed object of the concession agreement will meet the technical and economic indicators established by the concession agreement;
3. technical and economic indicators of the object of the concession agreement;
4. volume of production of goods, works, services in the implementation of activities under the concession agreement;
5. period from the date of signing the concession agreement to the day when the production of goods, performance of works, provision of services in the implementation of activities provided for by the concession agreement will be carried out in the amount established by the concession agreement;
6. size of the concession fee;
7. upper limit prices (tariffs) for goods produced, works performed, services rendered, surcharges to such prices (tariffs) in the implementation of the activities provided for by the concession agreement, and (or) long-term parameters for the regulation of the concessionaire;
8. obligations assumed by the concessionaire in case of failure to receive the planned income from the use (operation) of the object of the concession agreement, the occurrence of additional costs in the creation and/or reconstruction of the object of the concession agreement, the use (operation) of the object of the concession agreement.
9. size of the budget co-financing of the project (capital expenditures, operation costs, payment of the Concedent);
10. qualitative characteristics of project documentation (in case the private partner carries out the development of such documentation under agreement).

To calculate the evaluation of criteria 1–9, the following parameters are set:

- initial condition as a numeric value;
- decrease or increase of the initial value of the competition criterion in the tender offer;
- coefficient that takes into account the importance (weight in the overall assessment) of the competition criterion.

For projects in the framework of the Law on PPP/MPP of the Russian Federation may apply the following criteria:

1. technical criteria;
2. financial and economic criteria;
3. legal criteria (duration of the agreement, risks assumed by the public partner and the private partner, including the obligations assumed by the private partner in cases of failure to receive the planned revenues from the operation and/or maintenance of the object of the agreement, the occurrence of additional costs when creating the object of the agreement, its operation and/or its maintenance).
4. size of budget co-financing of the project;

For the calculation of these criteria, parameters similar to those provided for by the law on concessions of the Russian Federation are established, while limiting weight coefficients (weight in the overall assessment) for criteria 1–3 are established: technical criteria—up to 0.5; financial and economic criteria—up to 0.8; legal criteria—up to 0.5.

In the Russian Federation, the mechanism of private initiative is used, but no special bonuses are provided to the initiator when evaluating his bid (Chart 9.1).

It should be noted that concession legislation provides additional criteria for the spheres of heat supply, water supply and sanitation.

The PPP legislation in Russia provides that the development of a proposal for the implementation of a PPP project can be provided by both a public party and a private investor.

The basic mandatory requirements to the private initiator, the discrepancy of which excludes the possibility of the investor's participation in the PPP project, are also established:

- absence of administrative suspension of the activities of a legal entity;
- failure to liquidate a legal entity, the absence of a decision of the arbitration court to initiate bankruptcy proceedings;
- absence of debts on taxes and levies, debts on other obligatory payments.

The form of the proposal for the conclusion of the concession agreement is approved by the Government of the Russian Federation. This form includes general information on the applicant's compliance with the established requirements, as well as on the compliance of the initiative with the programs of development of municipal infrastructure systems of settlements, urban districts, state programs of the Russian Federation, subjects of the Russian Federation, municipal programs (Tuktarov and Dubinchin 2016).

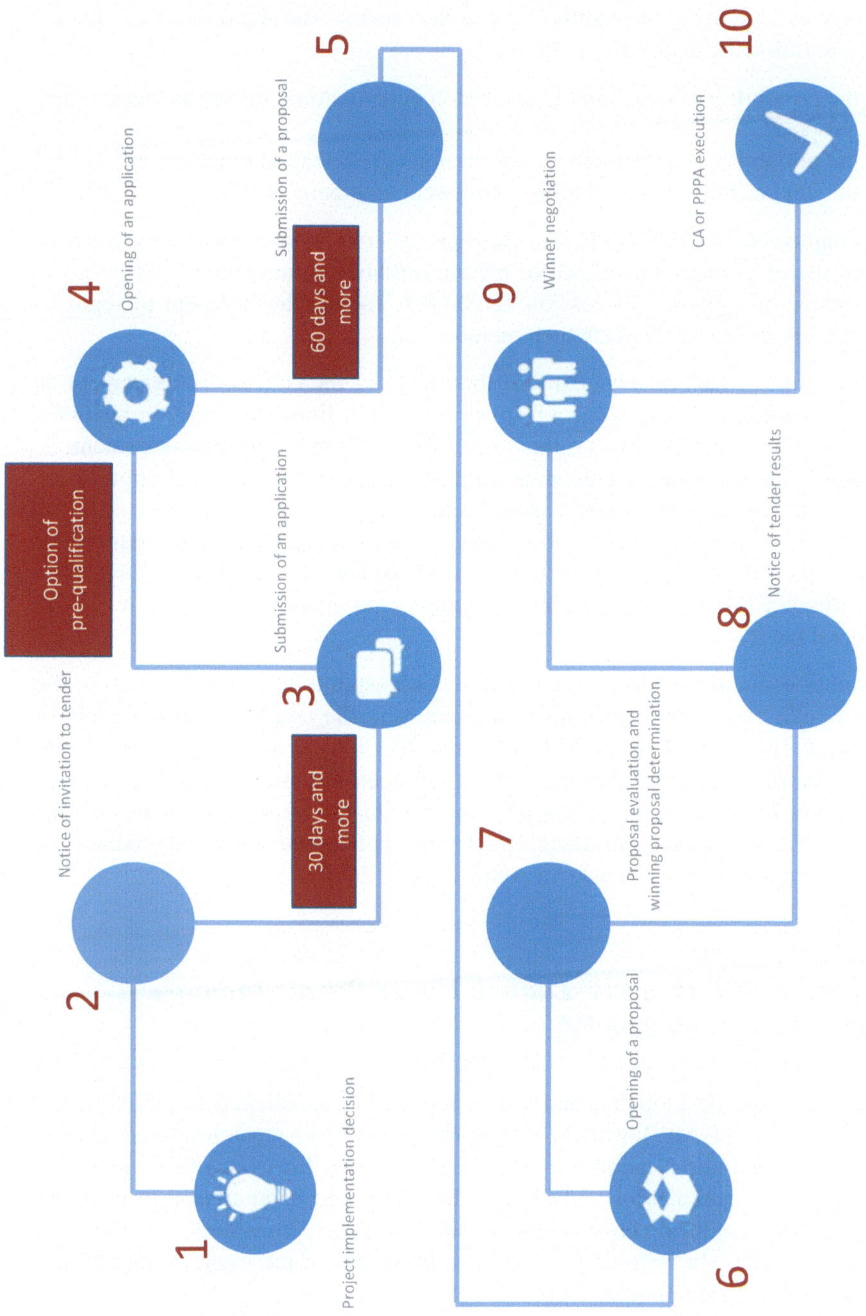

Chart 9.1 Tender procedure for selection of a private partner in PPP agreements and concession agreements in the Russian Federation

Consideration of the concession project by the authorized body does not include an assessment of the effectiveness of the project and determination of its comparative advantage. According to the results of the project review, the authorized body makes one of the following decisions:

- on the possibility of concluding concession agreement on the terms presented in the proposal;
- on the possibility of concluding a concession agreement on other terms;
- on the impossibility of concluding a concession agreement.

In contrast to the PPP/MPP law, the law on concession agreements contains an open list of grounds for refusal of private initiative to implement PPP projects (the Practice of applying concession agreements for the development of regional infrastructure in Russia 2014), which include:

- public entity's lack of ownership of the object of the concession agreement as well as withdrawal of the object from circulation or limitation of its circulation;
- existence of the third party's rights to the object of the concession agreement;
- public law entity's lack of resource support for conclusion and execution of the concession agreement on the proposed terms;
- creation/reconstruction of the object of concession agreement is not required or does not correspond to the state programs of the Russian Federation, subjects of the Russian Federation, municipal programs, and also other cases provided by Federal laws.

Another distinctive feature of the private concession initiative is the place of the stage of collecting applications for participation in the tender in the life cycle of the project. Under the Law on PPP/MPP, the decision on implementation of PPP project is carried out before the collection of statements of intent to participate in the competition. In contrast, the decision on the conclusion of concession agreements (Law 115-FZ) is adopted after the collection of applications about the readiness to participate in the contest (Inshakova Agnessa et al. 2017).

Specifics of PPP Projects' Launch Under Private Initiative in Accordance with 224-FZ

The mechanism of development and consideration of an unsolicited proposal (private initiative) under PPP/MPP law (224-FZ) is not regulated by a separate article, relevant rules are included into General provisions governing the life cycle of PPP project.

A significant specifics of 224-FZ is a limited range of eligible private initiators—only Russian legal entities (Law on public-private partnership: guidelines for application, 2015). In contrast to 115-FZ, a proposal for the implementation of a PPP/MPP project cannot be made by:

- foreign legal entities;
- associations of legal entities;
- individual entrepreneur;
- state and municipal unitary enterprises;
- state and municipal institutions;
- public law companies, state corporations;
- business partnerships and companies, as well as non-profit organizations, controlled by the state (50%+).

224-FZ also makes for a potential private partner necessary:

- to have appropriate licenses, permits, and memberships in self-regulating organizations;
- to provide the public partner at the initial stage with a Bank guarantee issued to the initiator in the amount of not less than 5% of the estimated financing of the project.

It should be noted that the requirements for the proposal to implement the project are identical both for projects initiated by the public party and for projects developed by a potential private partner. The corresponding fairly detailed form of the proposal for the implementation of a PPP project was approved by the Russian Government resolution № 1386 of December 19, 2015, and contains 54 points allowing to present the project comprehensively. Thus, it can be concluded that structuring of a PPP project under 224-FZ requires much more serious preparation and deep elaboration of the proposal by the initiator compared to 115-FZ (Recommendations for implementation of PPP projects. Best practices/Ministry of Economic Development, 2016).

Another distinctive feature of the 224-FZ is the existence of the special stage of consideration by a public partner of the project prepared by a private initiator (before sending it for evaluation to the appropriate authorized body) (Chart 9.2).

Based on the results of the project review, the public partner may make a negative decision if (close-end list of grounds):

- the proposal does not comply with the principles of PPP or the approved form of such a proposal (the content of the project does not meet the requirements of 224-FZ);
- operation, technical use, and/or transfer to private property of the object of the agreement, as well as the conclusion of the agreement concerning the specified object is not allowed;
- the public partner has no ownership right to the specified object;
- the object is not free from the rights of the third parties or there are already concluded agreements with respect to the object;
- there are no budget funds for the project;
- the object does not require reconstruction or creation;
- the initiator of the project refused to negotiate.

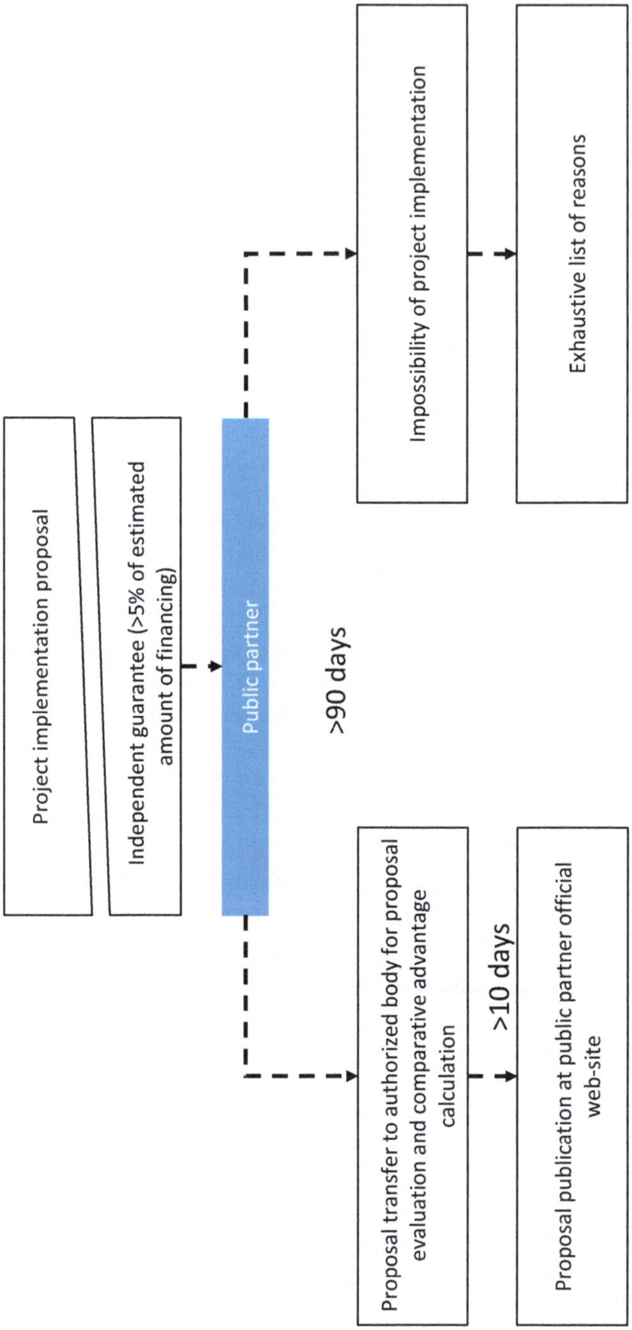

Chart 9.2 First stage of unsolicited proposal review—review by the public partner

The existence of a closed list of grounds for rejection of the project is certainly an undeniable advantage of 224-FZ in the eyes of potential private investors. It is worth noting, however, that in practice there is a fairly broad interpretation of the above grounds for rejection of a PPP project.

In case of negotiations at any stage of consideration of the proposal, the initiator of the project—a private partner—is their mandatory participant. It should be noted that if during the negotiations the parties do not come to a consensus and some disagreements remain, it is also the basis for a negative decision on the project.

Another distinctive feature of the private initiative under 224-FZ is that if the decision on implementation of the project is made on the basis of the proposal of a private party, such decision approves a limited list of information, namely:

- goals and objectives of the PPP project;
- public partner, as well as a list of bodies and legal entities acting on the side of the public partner;
- essential terms of agreement.

At the same time, if the decision to implement the project is made on the basis of the proposal of the public party, it approves the expanded list of information (including the value of the project performance criteria and the value of indicators of its comparative advantage, on the basis of which a positive conclusion of the authorized body was received).

The procedure for evaluating the effectiveness of the project by the authorized body and determining its comparative advantage in accordance with the 224-FZ is identical for projects prepared as a private or public initiative.

In case a decision to implement the project (under 224-FZ) is made on the basis of a proposal developed by a private partner, the public partner within 45 days shall accept from other person's statements of intent to participate in the tender for the right to conclude a PPP/MPP agreement. In the absence of relevant statements PPP/MPP agreement is concluded with the initiator of the project without tender (Chart 9.3).

An important specifics of unsolicited proposal procedure under 224-FZ is the possibility of compensation of the costs incurred to the project initiator, if as a result of the tender a third party becomes a preferred bidder. However, unfortunately, at present this provision is actually only declarative, the mechanism of its implementation is not regulated in the legal framework, and this aspect is another "point of improvement" for PPP legislation in Russia.

Conclusions

To date, the Russian Federation has already developed a thorough approach to the regulation of competitive procedures for selection of a private partner in public-private partnership projects, corresponding to the best international and regional practices.

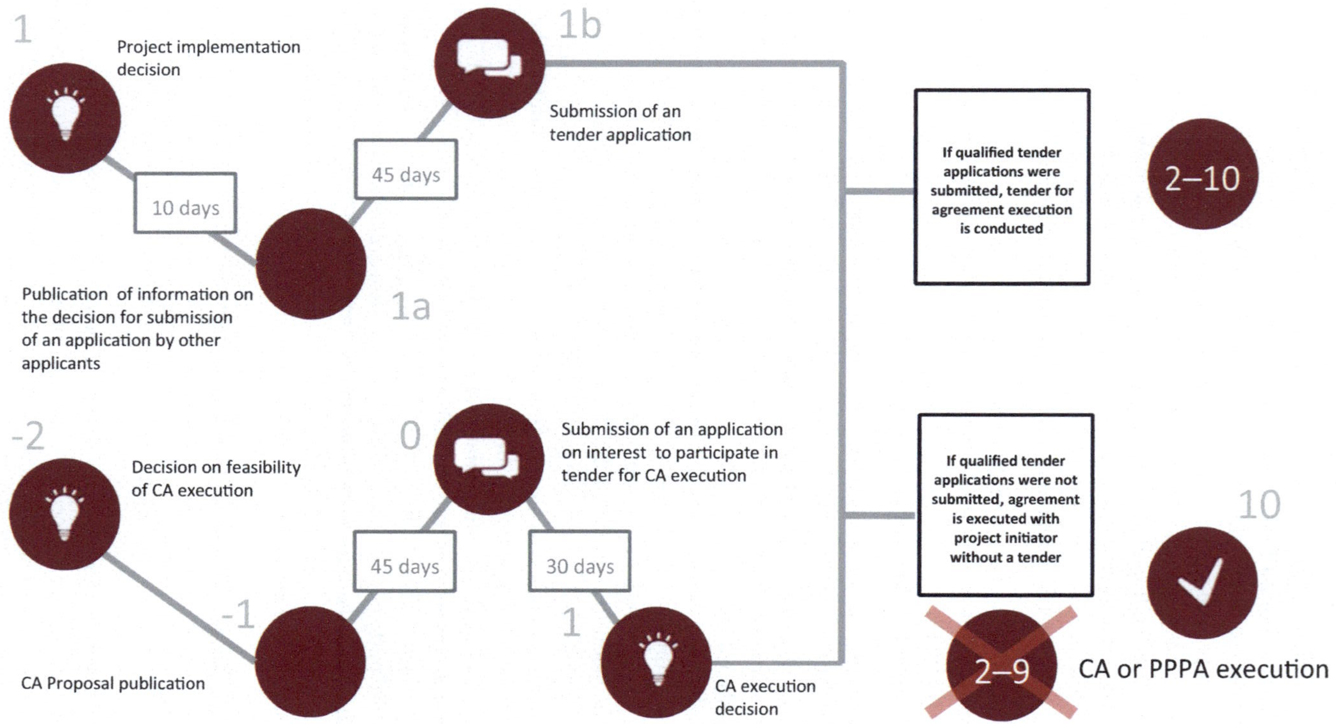

Chart 9.3 Specific features of a private partner's selection in case of unsolicited proposal ("private initiative")

Although there are still gaps in the regulation of tenders, the main potential for legislative development seems to lie in its harmonization between the two major laws—the concession Law and the PPP/MPP Law.

Another important direction in the coming years may be the harmonization of supranational nature—in the Eurasia Economic Union (EAEU) region, there is an increasing demand for the cooperation of the member States of the Union in implementation of integration infrastructure projects, in connection with which there is a need for standardization of legal support tools for PPP (PPP projects effectiveness assessment in the countries of the EAEU 2018) (Table 9.2).

Just as it is accepted in international practices, in Russia there is a possibility of submission of a private initiative ("unsolicited proposal") within "classical" forms of implementation of PPP projects: concession agreements (115-FZ) and agreements on public-private, municipal-private partnership (224-FZ).

The procedures for private initiative under the 115-FZ and 224-FZ are similar in many respects, but also have their differences, advantages, and disadvantages. The main differences are the openness/closeness of the range of possible applicants for

Table 9.2 Key parameters of a private partner's selection regulation in PPP projects in the Russian Federation

Russian Federation		
	Law on concessions	Law on PPP/MPP
Regulation mode	Law + sub-legislative acts	Law + sub-legislative acts
Selection options	(1) Tender (2) Direct negotiations**	(1) Tender (2) Direct negotiations**
Types of tender	(1) Open (2) Closed (state secrets)	(1) Open (2) Close (state secrets)
Stages of tender*	Two-stage	(1) One-stage (2) Two-stage
Preliminary selection (pre-qualification)	Yes	Possible
Preliminary selection (pre-qualification) criteria	Formal + qualification (open-end list)	Formal + qualification (open-end list)
Bids evaluation (stages)	One-stage	One-stage
Bids evaluation (type of criteria list)	Close-end	Open-end
Negotiations with preferred bidder (winner)	Provided	Not provided
Bonuses/guarantees to the private initiator (in case of tender)	Not provided	Not provided

*When calculating the number of stages of the tender, the presence of the pre-selection stage is taken into account. In this regard, the description may differ from the official terminology used in the legislation

**Direct negotiations are used in case of unsolicited proposal (private initiative)

private initiative and the lists of grounds for rejection of private initiative, as well as the presence/absence of the possibility of compensation to the initiator of the project for the costs of structuring and initiation.

References

Federal'nyj zakon "O gosudarstvenno-chastnom partnerstve, municipal'no-chastnom partnerstve v Rossijskoj Federacii i vnesenii izmenenij v otdel'nye zakonodatel'nye akty Rossijskoj Federacii" ot 13.07.2015 N 224-FZ. (Federal Law No. 224-FZ of July 13, 2015 "On Public-Private Partnership, Municipal-Private Partnership in the Russian Federation and Amendments to Certain Legislative Acts of the Russian Federation". https://base.garant.ru/71129190/. Retrieved March 10, 2019.

Federal'nyj zakon "O koncessionnyh soglasheniyah" ot 21.07.2005 N 115-FZ (Federal law No. 115-FZ of July 21, 2005 "On Concession agreements"). https://base.garant.ru/12141176/. Retrieved March 10, 2019.

Guidebook on PPP Frameworks in APEC Region: Investment Experts' Group-May (2015). Jakarta: APEC.

Guidebook on Promoting Good Governance in Public-Private Partnerships. (2008). United Nations Economic Commission for Europe.

Guidelines for Successful Public–Private Partnerships. (2003). European Commission, Brussels. www.ec.europa.eu/regional_policy/sources/docgener/guides/ppp_en.pdf. Retrieved March 12, 2019.

Inshakova Agnessa, O., Goncharov Alexander, I., Mineev Oleg, A., & Sevostyanov Maxim, V. (2017). Amendments to the civil code of the Russian Federation: Contradictions of theory and practice. In *Contributions to economics. Russia and the European Union: development and perspectives number XIII* (147–153).

Kommentarij k Federal'nomu zakonu ot 13 iyulya 2015 g. N 224-FZ "O gosudarstvenno-chastnom partnerstve, municipal'no-chastnom partnerstve v Rossijskoj Federacii i vnesenii izmenenij v otdel'nye zakonodatel'nye akty Rossijskoj Federacii" (2016) (Comment to the Federal Law of July 13, 2015 N 224-FZ "On Public-Private Partnership, Municipal-Private Partnership in the Russian Federation and Amendments to Certain Legislative Acts of the Russian Federation"(2016)) (Batrova T. A., Antropceva I. O., Vorob'ev N. I., Shapkina E. A., Pushkin A. V., Artem'ev E. V., Ruzanov I. V., Kandelaki G. G., Bogatyreva N. V., Kotuhov S. A.). SPS Konsul'tant Plyus (Consultant).

Luchshie praktiki realizacii proektov gosudarstvenno-chastnogo partnerstva v social'noj sfere. (2016). (Best PPP practices in social sphere (2016)). PPP National Development Center. http://pppcenter.ru/assets/docs/pppcenter_a4_2016_v2_web.pdf. Retrieved March 11, 2019.

Mekhanizmy gosudarstvenno-chastnogo partnyorstva v ekonomicheskoi politike Rossii (Mechanisms of public-private partnership in the economic policy of Russia). (2018). In O. V. Ivanov (Ed.) (p. 409). Moscow: MGIMO-University.

O pervoocherednyh merah po sovershenstvovaniju koncessionnogo zakonodatel'stva. (2017). (On priority measures for concession legislation development (2017)). PPP National Development Center. http://pppcenter.ru/assets/files/reliz_21092017.pdf. Retrieved March 11, 2019.

Ocenka effektivnosti proektov GCHP po sravneniyu s inymi formami realizacii infrastrukturnyh proektov v stranah-uchastnicah EAES. (2018). (PPP projects effectiveness assessment compared to other forms of infrastructure projects in the countries participating in the EAEU (2018)). PPP National Development Center. http://pppcenter.ru/assets/files/issledovanie_100118.pdf. Retrieved March 11, 2019.

Osobennosti otbora chastnogo partnera v GChP-proektah v stranah EAJeS. (2018). (Characteristics of the private partner selection process in PPP projects in the EAEU countries (2018)) PPP

National Development Center. http://pppcenter.ru/assets/files/18062018analitika.pdf. Retrieved March 11, 2019.
Praktika primeneniya koncessionnyh soglashenij dlya razvitiya regional'noj infrastruktury v Rossii (2014) (The practice in the application of concession agreements for the development of regional infrastructure in Russia) http://pppcenter.ru/assets/docs/ppp+.pdf. Retrieved March 10, 2019.
Private Sector Participation in Municipal and Environmental Infrastructure Projects: Review and Evaluation. (2014). EBRD. www.ebrd.com/evaluation-overview/special-studies-by-sector.html. Retrieved March 12, 2019.
Rekomendacii po realizacii proektov gosudarstvenno-chastnogo partnerstva. Luchshie praktiki. (2016). (Recommendations for implementation of public private partnership projects. Best practices). Ministry of Economic Development of the Russian Federation. http://economy.gov.ru/minec/activity/sections/privgovpartnerdev/support/20160829. Retrieved March 10, 2019.
Rekomendacii po realizacii proektov gosudarstvenno-chastnogo partnerstva v sub"ektah Rossijskoj Federacii (2013) (Recommendations for implementation of public-private partnership projects in the subjects of the Russian Federation (2013)). PPP Development Center. www.pppi.ru/sites/all/themes/pppi/img/pppsphere_managment1.pdf. Retrieved March 10, 2019.
Revzina, O., Churakov, R., Shamirzayeva, L. (2019). Russia. In: Werneck, B., Saadi, M. (Eds.), The Public-Private Partnership Law Review (pp. 175–186). Edition 5. Law Business Research Ltd. https://thelawreviews.co.uk//digital_assets/d82c190d-27e5-4f50-beec-1851fe0c70ea/The-Public-Private-Partnership-Law-Review-Edition-5.pdf. Retrieved March 12, 2019.
Shaoul, J. (2005b). A critical financial analysis of the private finance initiative: Selecting a financing method or allocating economic wealth? *Critical Perspectives on Accounting, 16*(4), 441–471. https://doi.org/10.1016/j.cpa.2003.06.001.
Tuktarov Yu. E., Dubinchina, S. V. (2016). Koncessionnoe soglashenie: pravovaya priroda, sfera primeneniya, poryadok zaklyucheniya i ispolneniya: Rukovodstvo dlya praktikuyushchih yuristov, gosudarstvennyh i municipal'nyh sluzhashchih (Concession agreement: legal nature, scope of application, procedure for conclusion and execution. A guide for lawyers, civil servants and local government employees). Statut, Moscow.
Zakon o gosudarstvenno-chastnom partnerstve: rukovodstvo po primeneniyu (2015) (Public-private partnerships law: guidelines. (2015). Centr razvitiya GCHP (PPP Development Center). Moscow. http://p3institute.ru/netcat_files/23/25/Zakon_Block_28_09_2015_v01__2__003_pdf. Retrieved March, 10 2019.

Chapter 10
Commercial and Financial Closure. Monitoring and Control of PPP Projects Implementation

Alexander V. Poroshin and Nikolai V. Studenikin

Abstract The paper analyzes the features of the project life cycle at the stages of commercial and financial closure, control and monitoring of implementation. Among these features, the procedures provided for by the legislation and their sequence, conditions, and mechanisms for successful movement of the project from the moment of signing the agreement to the signing of the financing documentation and further to the organization of effective control and monitoring of its implementation are explored. The composition of procedures and documents at key points of appropriate stages of the project life cycle, factors, and conditions for the qualitative finalization of specific processes, as well as the main risks and ways to minimize them are considered.

Keywords Public-private partnership · Concession agreement · Public-private partnership agreement · Public partner · Private partner · Commercial closure · Financial closure · Project implementation control · Project implementation monitoring

JEL-Codes H43 · H44 · K12 · K15

Introduction

In international practices, many countries have developed standard procedures for managing PPP projects. This makes it more likely that PPP projects will be implemented in accordance with long-term strategic documents of state policy and also

---

A. V. Poroshin (✉)
Strategic development, analytics and information support of PPP, Center of PPP projects, JSC "Avtodor-invest", Malaya Dmitrovka str. 16-6, 127006 Moscow, Russia
e-mail: caunte@gmail.com

N. V. Studenikin
MGIMO University, Vernadsky Ave., 76, 119454 Moscow, Russia
e-mail: n.studenikin@gmail.com

O. V. Ivanov and A. O. Inshakova (eds.), *Public-Private Partnerships in Russia*, Competitive Government: Public Private Partnerships,
https://doi.org/10.1007/978-3-030-56352-3_10

helps to coordinate effectively between project participants, as well as between them and the authorities.

The process of PPP project management is divided into a number of stages, the transition to the next stage is possible upon completion of the previous work.

This approach is applied because, firstly, it enables the timely participation of oversight bodies in the management of PPP projects, and secondly, it allows to filter PPP projects at the pre-preparation stage and thus to avoid the loss of time and resources. As a rule, evaluation of the project at an early stage of development increases its prospects both in terms of socioeconomic effect and return on investment.

At the stage of commercial and financial closure, the "driver" of the project on the public side—the participant most interested in the successful achievement of the goals of the stage—is the PPP authority.

During the control and monitoring of the project implementation, such a "driver" of the project on the public side is the authority authorized in the field in which the project is implemented—the industry (sector) authority, with the involvement of other authorities that can assist in monitoring the quality of execution of the terms of the agreement by the private partner, depending on the stage of project implementation (design, construction, operation, and/or maintenance).

Results

Commercial and Financial Closure (Negotiations with the Winner, Signing of the Project Agreement and Loan Agreement)

Negotiations with the winner of the competition, commercial and financial closing are three consecutive parts of the general closing stage of the project, after which the implementation stage begins. In this case, the financial closure of the project can occur both simultaneously with the commercial closure and after a certain (in many cases—significant) period of time.

Negotiations with the winner of the competition precede commercial and financial closure. Such negotiations take place in the form of scheduled and unscheduled meetings with the preferred bidder. As part of the negotiations, the final terms on which the agreement will be signed are formed. Discussion at this stage may be subject to any conditions other than the invariant conditions—that is, the essential terms and conditions included in the tender documentation, as well as other conditions that in the framework of the decision on the implementation of the project were defined as immutable. At the stage of commercial closure, different parameters can be discussed, for example

- status and conditions of creation and operation of the object of the agreement, as well as other property technologically related to the object of the agreement;

- provision of land;
- special circumstance;
- payment mechanism;
- conditions and amount of compensation upon termination;
- fines and penalties.

The main points for discussion at this stage are, as a rule, special circumstances and compensation in case of termination. Special circumstances are essentially an additional tool for risk management and risk allocation between the private and public partner (concessionaire and Concedent).

The two starting points for commercial closure are:

- pre-selection of applicants;
- identification of a private partner based on the results of a competition or any other procedure.

Negotiations are held in the form of open consultations, bilateral meetings with all applicants within road shows and negotiations in the form of scheduled and unscheduled meetings with the winner of the competition.

Additional special circumstances and compensation, as a rule, suggest the emergence of new conditional expenditure commitments of the public side, which can affect the comparative advantage of the project and make it ineffective from the point of view of budget participation. It is, therefore, recommended that the comparative advantage of the project be re-evaluated at the stage of commercial closure prior to the signing of the agreement, taking into account the new conditions to be included in the text of the agreement.

It should also be noted that part of the position of potential private partners/concessionaires can be taken into account even before the tender, as the public party has the right to hold open consultations and bilateral meetings with all applicants within road shows.

What Is Commercial Closure?

Commercial closure has no strict legal definition. Commercial closure is a procedure of legal registration of all obligations of the parties involved in a PPP project: public partner (Concedent), private partner (concessionaire), contractors, suppliers, landlords, etc. These obligations are usually formalized in an agreement between public and private partners. Accordingly, the date of signing the agreement is the date of commercial closure.

The minimum legal requirements for commercial closure in Russia are as follows:

- the agreement is concluded after the signing of the Protocol on the results of the competition/decision on the conclusion of an agreement with the only participant (the draft agreement is sent to the winner of the competition/the only participant with the terms included in it in accordance with the received proposal) and after negotiations;

- the agreement is signed on the terms approved by the tender documentation, taking into account the changes agreed by the parties at the stage of negotiations (the terms that were determined on the basis of the tender offer, as well as the terms that are fixed in the tender documentation as unchangeable);
- the private partner should not be in a state of liquidation or bankruptcy;
- the notice on signing of the agreement shall be published.

Commercial closure implies that by the time of signing the agreement the terms of signing determined by tender documents are met. These terms include:

- concurrence on the text of the agreement;
- submission of key project documents—contract, operation contract, insurance contracts, financial documentation, and others;
- agreement on the financial model with the public partner;
- provision of documents confirming the private investor's performance of all internal procedures and obtaining all necessary permits in accordance with the current legislation.

Additional requirements for commercial closure may be set out in the tender documents.

Documents as Part of Commercial Closure

Tender documents may require a private partner to provide a number of documents for commercial closure, including:

- bank guarantees or other security documents provided by the documentation;
- documents confirming contribution to the authorized capital;
- documents confirming the authority to sign and perform all necessary competitive procedures.

As a rule, the public partner is not required to provide any special documents (on confirmation of the powers of the signatories, etc.) during the commercial closure.

During commercial closure, the Act of commercial closure (and/or the Act of financial closure if financial close occurs simultaneously), confirming fulfillment of the closing conditions, can be composed.

Documents related to the execution of the agreement on PPP (contracts with experts, auditors, construction plans, etc.) are usually signed after the commercial closure.

The general structure of the documents that can be signed by the project participants at the stage of commercial closure is shown in the Chart 10.1.

Documents to be signed can be divided into three groups:

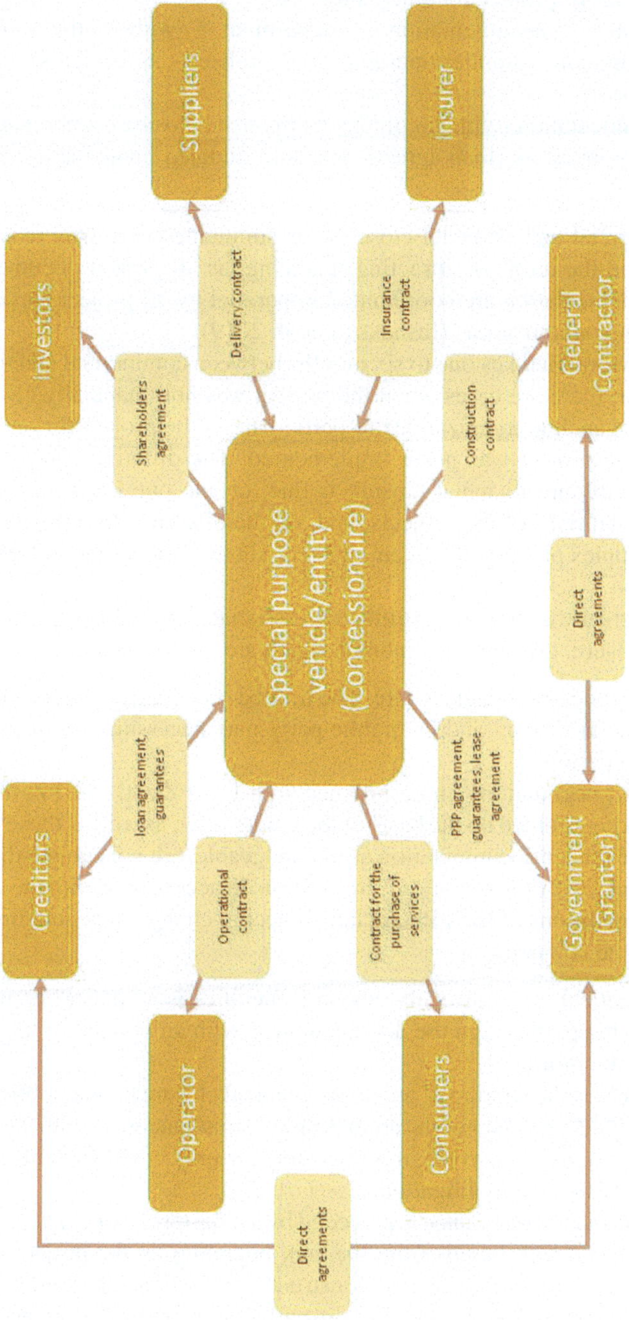

Chart 10.1 General structure of documents signed by project participants at the stage of commercial closure

- PPP/concession documentation: PPP agreement, lease agreements, acts of acceptance and transfer of project documentation, etc.
- Contract/operator documentation: agreement with the General contractor/equipment supplier/operator and related agreements (security documentation).
- Financial documentation (with simultaneous financial closure): agreements with debt and equity investors (loan agreements, subordinated financing agreements, etc.).

Ideally commercial and financial close occur simultaneously. This reduces the risks of changes in the terms of attracting financing, as all project documentation and terms of implementation are coordinated in parallel by all project participants, including financing organizations (Inshakova et al. 2019).

In practice, however, it takes one to six months between commercial and financial closure. Moreover, there are cases when the project was not financially closed due to the refusal of financing organizations to participate in the project for one reason or another, and the project was never implemented. The difference in the timing between commercial and financial closure is due, on the one hand, to the scale, specific features and risks of the projects, and, on the other hand, to the volume of financing, the complex process of agreeing final credit terms together with changing market conditions.

In practice, there are a number of difficulties associated with the implementation of commercial closure, the most common of which are the following:

- tight deadlines for commercial closure. The limited time for negotiations between the winner/sole participant and the public party may necessitate an extension of the negotiation period.
- limited scope of negotiations. In accordance with 115-FZ and 224-FZ, the terms and conditions determined on the basis of the tender offer, as well as those directly specified in the tender documentation as unchangeable, are not subject to change within the framework of negotiations. In addition, in accordance with the 224-FZ, the essential conditions of the PPP are not subject to change in negotiations with the winner of the competition.

A possible practical way out of the above difficulties is a "paper" commercial closure, in which the parties sign the documentation with an obligation to agree on detailed terms in the future.

Financial closure is the signing of an act on financial closure by the public partner and the proffered bidder (winner of the competition), simultaneously with the signing of a credit agreement. In other words, it is providing the project with real money with legal registration of financing obligations.

Providing the project with finance is preceded by a long-term work. The procedure of financial closure, in fact, begins from the very beginning of the project preparation—from financial structuring, that is, construction of a financial model and risk allocation. The financial closure process is usually controlled by a private partner (concessionaire) and may include the following steps:

- assessment of the acceptable amount and cost of borrowed funds taking into account the financial model of the project and the terms of the agreement;
- analysis of the market of credit funds;
- determination of the preliminary list of financing terms and receipt of letters of interest from creditors;
- selection of the Bank—the organizer/underwriter of financing;
- preparation of documents for obtaining financing;
- conducting pre-investment research by creditors;
- preparation and signing of credit documentation (financial closing act);
- fulfillment of preliminary conditions by the project company, achievement of financial closure.

The act of financial closure may be accompanied by:

- direct agreement with creditors;
- loan agreement with annexes;
- creditors' agreement;
- agreement on subordinated debt;
- hedging agreements;
- Bank guarantee for construction (fulfillment of preliminary conditions for construction);
- contract documents;
- auditor's letter on the financial model;
- security package of lenders (agreement on guarantees of the sponsors, collateral agreements).

The chances of successfully attracting funding to the project may increase significantly if the following conditions are met:

- high financial performance of the project, elaboration of the project concept;
- positive social and budgetary effects;
- cash flow guarantee;
- stability of the financial condition of the public partner;
- implementation of the project within the 115-FZ, or 224-FZ;
- availability of security structure;
- share of debt financing does not exceed 80–85% of the total private financing;
- existence of a direct agreement.

One of the main tasks in the organization of financial closure is to determine the most appropriate source of financing. The key types of financial instruments used for the implementation of PPP projects usually include:

- loan financing;
- equity financing;
- mezzanine and subordinated financing;
- project financing;
- infrastructure bonds;
- leasing arrangements;

- export credit financing;
- public funding (full/partial).

The choice of the form of financing depends on many factors, such as the scale of the project, duration of the project, required amount of financing, share of debt financing in the total amount, availability of guarantees from the state, cost of financing, etc.

The form of financing also depends on the payment mechanisms used, on which, in turn, the cost of financing depends (Chart 10.2).

Control and Monitoring of Project Implementation

After signing the agreement, the main task of the public party is to monitor the progress of the private partner's (concessionaire) execution of the terms of the agreement.

Control of PPP project implementation includes:

- control over the operation of the infrastructure object, implemented by the relevant industry authorities, depending on the industry and specifics of the object;
- monitoring and control of implementation of the PPP agreement and project targets;
- monitoring and management of risks and obligations assigned to the public partner.

The organization of control over design, construction, commissioning, and operation of the infrastructure object under a PPP project is carried out by the relevant public and municipal authorities in the framework of standard procedures.

It is recommended to develop procedures for monitoring and control of the PPP project at the stage of structuring the project and preparation of the PPP agreement. The control procedures are based on relevant regulations and legal acts, as well as on the provisions of the agreement.

It is important to distinguish the powers and responsibilities of various public and municipal bodies involved in the implementation of PPP projects.

It is also possible to involve independent expert organizations to improve efficiency and develop specialized solutions.

The authority responsible for finance and budgeting controls spending and monitors effectiveness of the use of budgetary funds.

Sectoral authorities control the project within their powers (including regulation of tariffs and monitoring quality of services of the infrastructure object).

In addition to the formation of a special public body responsible for the control and monitoring of a PPP project, for successful implementation of the relevant functions it is important to develop a procedure for interaction with the private party and between public organizations (at the management level—to solve strategic tasks, and at the executive level—to solve current issues) (Kalinina et al. 2019).

PPP models without transfer of ownership to the private sector (for example, BOT, DBFO, BOOT)				PPP models with transfer of ownership to the private sector (for example, BOO)		
Payment schedule	User-pays PPPs	Government-pays revenue	Availability Payment	User-pays PPPs	Government-pays revenue	Availability Payment
Equity IRR	30% → lower → 15%					
Senior Debt Rate	15% → lower → 12%					
State cash flow	Прямой налоговый денежный поток + косвенный денежный поток					
	- State co-financing of construction (if applicable)	+ part of income that exceeds Government-pays revenue - Government-pays revenue	+ Availability Payment (if applicable) - Operational payment	- Capital grant (if applicable)	+ part of income that exceeds Government-pays revenue - Government-pays revenue	+ Availability Payment (if applicable) - Operational payment
	+ terminal (residual) cost of the project					

Chart 10.2 Key parameters of payment mechanisms

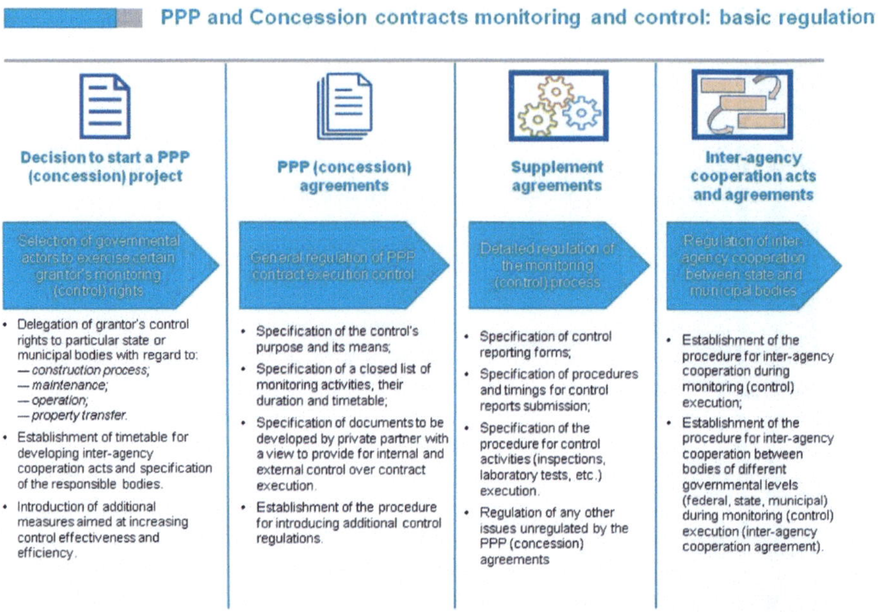

Chart 10.3 General model of regulation of control over the implementation of PPP project (concession agreement)

The general model of regulation of such control is presented in Chart 10.3.

At the same time, general requirements for the public partner to monitor implementation of the PPP agreement by the private partner, under 224-FZ, are established by the Decree of the Government of the Russian Federation of December 30, 2015, No. 1490 "On the implementation by the public partner of control over the implementation of the public-private partnership agreement and the municipal-private partnership agreement".

The General logic of such control is shown in Chart 10.4.

Monitoring and analysis of the private partner's activities in the project can be carried out on the basis of several sources of information:

- data provided by the private partner—the private partner provides the public authorities with information on the implementation of the project. The regularity, format and content of this information is defined in the PPP agreement on the basis of the PPP project control regulations and other legal acts;
- data of independent expert organizations and consultants—independent experts can be involved in collection and analysis of information on the quality of services provided at the relevant PPP project infrastructure;
- end-user data—surveys and customer satisfaction surveys are the most reliable source of information on the quality of infrastructure facility services.

Chart 10.4 General logic of PPP agreements' audit

The results of control over the activities of a private partner may be the basis for management decisions to adjust the terms or early termination of the agreement.

No less important part of the control and monitoring of the PPP project is cost control. As a rule, cost control is carried out in three semantic groups:

- budget costs
  - determination of the cost of work performed during the reporting period;
  - monitoring of the cumulative total of expenses from the beginning of the project and comparison with the initial budget;
  - comparison of initial and current/final budget.

- invoices and payments
  - analysis of compliance of invoices and payments to the time period and cost;
  - analysis of payments to the General contractor based on the results of the work performed.
- borrowed funds
  - analysis of the intended use of borrowed funds;
  - analysis of cash flows for the project.

An integral part of the control and monitoring is the monitoring of risks and obligations assigned to the public partner.

- monitoring of actual and expected indicators of potential threats to the project implementation for the public partner;
- reducing the likelihood of risks transferred to the public party;
- development of measures to eliminate new risks arising in the process of project implementation.

In order to monitor the risks and liabilities of the project, public authorities are recommended to develop a Risk management map of the public partner. This document includes a list of risks and liabilities with relevant indicators and data sources that are monitored. The following information structure is formed in the Risk management map of the public partner for each risk:

- type of liability;
- risk status;
- expected impact of risk on the project;
- current risk status;
- proposed risk mitigation measures.

It is recommended to develop a Risk management map for public and private partners before signing an agreement.

In March 2017, the Government of the Russian Federation established the procedure for monitoring conclusion and implementation of concession agreements, including compliance by the parties to the concession agreement with their obligations to achieve the targets contained in the concession agreement, the timing of their implementation, the volume of attracted investments, and other essential terms of the agreement.

Monitoring is to be carried out using the state automated information system "Management" through the collection, analysis, compilation, systematization, and accounting of information provided by the Concedent on the concession agreements planned, being in the process of implementation and already realized in the reporting period in the territory of Russia. The Ministry of economic development is empowered with the authority to monitor all concession agreements.

Conclusion

Despite the fact that the key terms of PPP projects are determined at the stage of project preparation, the stages of commercial and financial closure, at which the distribution of risks between the parties (as a result of post-competitive negotiations) or the terms of attracting financing (as a result of financial closure) may change, are no less important. In the Russian Federation, less than 5% of PPP projects attract debt financing, which makes the problem of financial closure relevant only for large projects. This situation is due to the fact that the concession mechanism is actively used in Russia in the housing sector, where there are mainly non-capital-intensive projects, and investors are accustomed to invest their own, not borrowed funds.

Another aspect of the successful implementation of PPP projects and the protection of the interests of the public side in such projects is the organization of effective control and monitoring of the performance of private partners of their obligations under the project. Such monitoring, on the one hand, should not create problems and obstacles for the private partner, and on the other hand, should ensure the protection of public interests in the execution of the agreement.

The quality and organization of control and monitoring is often associated with penalties in the project, with terms for ensuring the implementation of the agreement, and as a consequence, with the flow of funds in the project. That is, the approach to the organization of control and monitoring can affect not only the future course of the project implementation, but also its financial parameters at the stage of preparation and launch.

References

Caselli, S., Vecchi, V., & Corbetta, G. (2015). Public private partnerships for infrastructure and business development. Principles, Practices, and Perspectives (p. 384). Palgrave Macmillan US. https://doi.org/10.1057/9781137541482.

Evaluation of Public Private. Partnerships in Infrastructure. (2017). Office of evaluation and oversight (OVE). www.publications.iadb.org/publications/english/document/Evaluation-of-Public-Private-Partnerships-in-Infrastructure.pdf. Accessed 9 Mar 2019.

Federal'nyj zakon "O gosudarstvenno-chastnom partnerstve, municipal'no-chastnom partnerstve v Rossijskoj Federacii i vnesenii izmenenij v otdel'nye zakonodatel'nye akty Rossijskoj Federacii" ot 13.07.2015N 224-FZ. (Federal Law No. 224-FZ of July 13, 2015 "On Public-Private Partnership, Municipal-Private Partnership in the Russian Federation and Amendments to Certain Legislative Acts of the Russian Federation"). https://base.garant.ru/71129190/. Accessed 10 Mar 2019.

Federal'nyj zakon "O koncessionnyh soglasheniyah" ot 21.07.2005N 115-FZ (Federal law No. 115-FZ of July 21, 2005 "On Concession agreements"). https://base.garant.ru/12141176/. Accessed 10 Mar 2019.

Flyvbjerg, B., Bruzelius, N., & Rothengatter, W. (2014). *Megaprojects and risk: An anatomy of ambition* (pp. 1–2017), Cambridge University Press. https://doi.org/10.1017/cbo9781107050891.

Flyvbjerg, B., Holm, M. S., & Buhl, S. (2002). Underestimating costs in public works projects: Error or lie? *Journal of the American Planning Association, 68*(3), 279–295. https://doi.org/10.1080/01944360208976273.

Ghobadian, A., O'Regan, N., Gallear, D., & Viney, H. (2004). *Private-public partnerships: Policy and experience* (p. 318), Palgrave Macmillan UK.

Grimsey, D., & Lewis, M. K. (2004). *Public private partnerships: The worldwide revolution in infrastructure provision and project finance* (pp. 1–268), Edward Elgar Publishing. https://doi.org/10.4337/9781845423438.

Haimes, Y. Y., & Jiang, P. (2001). Leontief-based model of risk in complex interconnected infrastructures. *Journal of Infrastructure Systems, 7*(1), 1–12. https://doi.org/10.1061/(ASCE)1076-0342(2001)7:1(1).

Hart, O. (2003). Incomplete contracts and public ownership: Remarks, and an application to public-private partnerships. *Economic Journal, 113*(486), C69–C76. https://doi.org/10.1111/1468-0297.00119.

Hensher, D. A., & Houghton, E. (2004). Performance-based quality contracts for the bus sector: Delivering social and commercial value for money. *Transportation Research Part B: Methodological, 38*(2), 123–146. https://doi.org/10.1016/S0191-2615(03)00004-3.

Inshakova, A. O., Goncharov, A. I., Kazachenok, S. Y. (2019). legal regulation of the syndicated lending: Banking innovations in contemporary Russia. In *Proceedings of the 5th National Scientific and Practical Conference "Perspectives on the Use of New Information and Communication Technology (ICT) in the Modern Economy": Advances in Intelligent Systems and Computing* (pp. 368–377).

Ivanov, O. V. (2016). *Teoriya i mirovaya praktika gosudarstvenno-chastnogo partnerstva (Theory and world practice of public-private partnership)* (p. 299). Moscow: MGIMO-University.

Ivanov. O. V. (2019). Gosudartsvenno-chastnoe partnerstvo kak instrument razvitiya infrastruktury i modernizatsii ekonomiki. Opyt stran Aziatsko-tikhookeanskogo regiona (Public-private partnership as an instrument of development of infrastructure and modernization of economy. Experience of Asia-Pacific countries) (300 p). Moscow: MGIMO-University.

Kalinina, A. E., Inshakova, A. O., Goncharov, A. I. (2019). Polysubject jurisdictional blockchain: Electronic registration of facts to reduce economic conflicts. Ubiquitous computing and the internet of things: Prerequisites for the development of ICT. In E. G. Popkova (Ed.), *Studies in Computational Intelligence*, Vol. 826, (pp. 205–213). Cham: Springer Science + Business Media.

Kommentarij k Federal'nomu zakonu ot 13 iyulya 2015g. N 224-FZ "O gosudarstvenno-chastnom partnerstve, municipal'no-chastnom partnerstve v Rossijskoj Federacii i vnesenii izmenenij v otdel'nye zakonodatel'nye akty Rossijskoj Federacii". (2016). (Comment to the Federal Law of July 13, 2015N 224-FZ "On Public-Private Partnership, Municipal-Private Partnership in the Russian Federation and Amendments to Certain Legislative Acts of the Russian Federation") (Batrova T.A., Antropceva I.O., Vorobyov N.I., Shapkina E.A., Pushkin A.V., Artem'ev E.V., Ruzanov I.V., Kandelaki G.G., Bogatyreva N.V., Kotuhov S.A.). SPS Konsul'tant Plyus (Consultant).

Konrad, T. S. (2018). Management control in public-private partnerships. Between International Governmental Actors and the Private Sector. Gabler Verlag.

Lessons learned and best practices in public-private partnership projects. (2015). Inter-American Development Bank. www.idbdocs.iadb.org/wsdocs/getDocument.aspx?DOCNUM=39560533. Accessed 8 Mar 2019.

Luchshie praktiki realizacii proektov gosudarstvenno-chastnogo partnerstva v social'noj sfere. (2016). (Best PPP practices in social sphere (2016)). PPP National Development Center. pppcenter.ru/assets/docs/pppcenter_a4_2016_v2_web.pdf. Accessed 11 March 2019.

Mackie, P., & Preston, J. (1998). Twenty-one sources of error and bias in transport project appraisal. *Transport Policy, 5*(1), 1–7. https://doi.org/10.1016/S0967-070X(98)00004-3.

Marques, R. C., & Berg, S. (2010). Revisiting the strengths and limitations of regulatory contracts in infrastructure industries. *Journal of Infrastructure Systems, 16*(4), 334–342. https://doi.org/10.1061/(ASCE)IS.1943-555X.0000029.

Martin, H. (2013). *Value for money analysis-practices and challenges: how governments choose when to use PPP to deliver public infrastructure and services (English)*. Washington, DC: World Bank Group.
Mekhanizmy gosudarstvenno-chastnogo partnyorstva v ekonomicheskoi politike Rossii. (2018). (Mechanisms of public-private partnership in the economic policy of Russia). Ed. by O. V. Ivanov. MGIMO-University, Moscow. (409 p).
Murphy, T. J. (2008). The case for public-private partnerships in infrastructure. *Canadian Public Administration, 51*(1), 99–126. https://doi.org/10.1111/j.1754-7121.2008.00006.x.
O'Donnell, C. J. (2018). *Productivity and efficiency analysis. an economic approach to measuring and explaining managerial performance* (p. 418), Springer Singapore. https://doi.org/10.1007/978-981-13-2984-5.
Osobennosti otbora chastnogo partnera v GChP-proektah v stranah EAJeS. (2018). (Characteristics of the private partner selection process in PPP projects in the EAEU countries (2018)) PPP National Development Center. http://pppcenter.ru/assets/files/18062018analitika.pdf. Accessed 11 Mar 2019.
Ocenka effektivnosti proektov GCHP po sravneniyu s inymi formami realizacii infrastrukturnyh proektov v stranah-uchastnicah EAES. (2018). (PPP projects effectiveness assessment compared to other forms of infrastructure projects in the countries participating in the EAEU (2018)). PPP National Development Center. http://pppcenter.ru/assets/files/issledovanie_100118.pdf. Accessed 11 March 2019.
O pervoocherednyh merah po sovershenstvovaniju koncessionnogo zakonodatel'stva. (2017). (On priority measures for concession legislation development (2017)). PPP National Development Center. http://pppcenter.ru/assets/files/reliz_21092017.pdf. Accessed 11 March 2019.
Public-Private Partnership and Investment in Infrastructure (2010). OECD.
PPP Basics and Principles of a PPP Framework. (2012). PPIAF. www.castalia-advisors.com/files/Note-One-PPP-Basics-and-Principles-of-a-PPP-Framework.pdf. Accessed 9 Mar 2019.
PPP Reference Guide 3.0. (2017). World Bank. www.library.pppknowledgelab.org/documents/4699. Accessed 12 Mar 2019.
Procuring Infrastructure Public-Private Partnerships Report 2018: Assessing Government Capability to Prepare, Procure, and Manage PPPs. (2018). World Bank, Washington, DC.
Public-Private Partnership Handbook. Manila: Asian Development Bank. (2008). Asian Development Bank.
Public–Private Partnership Monitor. (2017). Asian Development Bank.
Rekomendacii po realizacii proektov gosudarstvenno-chastnogo partnerstva. Luchshie praktiki. (2016). (Recommendations for the public private partnership projects implementation. Best practices (2016)). Ministry of Economic Development of the Russian Federation. http://economy.gov.ru/minec/activity/sections/privgovpartnerdev/support/20160829. Accessed 10 March 2019.
Rekomendacii po realizacii proektov gosudarstvenno-chastnogo partnerstva v sub"ektah Rossijskoj Federacii. (2013). (Recommendations for the public-private partnership projects implementation in the subjects of the Russian Federation (2013)). PPP Development Center. www.pppi.ru/sites/all/themes/pppi/img/pppsphere_managment1.pdf. Accessed 10 Mar 2019.
Roumboutsos, A., & Sciancalepore, F. (2014). Public-private partnership tenders: Optimizing on competition. *Transportation Research Record* (pp. 83–90), Vol. 2450. National Research Council. https://doi.org/10.3141/2450-11.
Saussier, S., & de Brux, J. (2018). *The economics of public-private partnerships: Theoretical and empirical developments* (p. 240), Springer International Publishing. https://doi.org/10.1007/978-3-319-68050-7.
Thomas, E. (2013). Water and wastewater treatment facility project. P3 Value for Money Assessment and Project Report.
Jiang, W. (2014). Business partnerships and organizational performance. In *The role of resources and capabilities* (p. 355). Springer, Berlin Heidelberg. https://doi.org/10.1007/978-3-642-539 89-3.

Yescombe, E. R. (2013). *Public-private partnerships: Principles of policy and finance* (2nd ed.). Oxford: Elsevier Science.

Yvrande-Billon, A. (2006). The attribution process of delegation contracts in the French urban public transport sector: Why competitive tendering is a myth. *Annals of Public and Cooperative Economics, 77*(4), 453–478. https://doi.org/10.1111/j.1467-8292.2006.00315.x.

Zakon o gosudarstvenno-chastnom partnerstve: rukovodstvo po primeneniyu. (2015). (Public-private partnerships law: guidelines). Centr razvitiya GCHP (PPP Development Center). Moscow. http://p3institute.ru/netcat_files/23/25/Zakon_Block_28_09_2015_v01__2__003_.pdf. Accessed 10 March 2019.

Part V
PPP Projects in Specific Sectors

Chapter 11
PPP Mechanisms in the Transport Infrastructure of Russia

Vasily A. Marinin and Ellina A. Shamanina

Abstract Current state and major problems of transport infrastructure—one of the largest segments of the Russian economy—are examined. New trends in government approaches to public administration of the sector are explored. Conclusion on the objective need for the use of PPP mechanisms to reach ambitious goals of government transport policies is made. Application of PPP mechanisms in transport infrastructure is explored. It is noted that the transport industry in Russia is the most advanced in terms of the application of public-private partnership mechanisms. Noteworthy that both the sectoral range of PPP projects and the variability of payment mechanisms and forms of PPP are expanding. The most representative cases of implementation of PPP projects in the sector are presented. On the basis of the study, it is concluded that PPP mechanisms are in demand in various sectors of transport infrastructure. The most promising areas of application of PPP mechanisms and key drivers in the sector are evaluated. Specific recommendations on the use of PPP mechanisms in transport infrastructure are made.

Keywords Public-private partnership in russia · Public administration · Concessions · PPP policy · Transport infrastructure

JEL-Codes H43 · H43 · K12 · K15

V. A. Marinin (✉)
Center for PPP Projects, JSC "Avtodor-invest", Malaya Dmitrovka str., 16/6, 127006 Moscow, Russia
e-mail: marininvas@gmail.com

E. A. Shamanina
MGIMO University, Vernadsky Ave., 76, 119454 Moscow, Russia
e-mail: erina008@mail.ru

O. V. Ivanov and A. O. Inshakova (eds.), *Public-Private Partnerships in Russia*, Competitive Government: Public Private Partnerships,
https://doi.org/10.1007/978-3-030-56352-3_11

Introduction

Transport infrastructure is one of the most important components of social and industrial infrastructure in the Russian Federation. The special geographical position of Russia determines the enormous role of transport in the development of competitive advantages of the country. The high level of development of transport infrastructure directly affects both the satisfaction of social and production needs in the country and the implementation of economic relations in the territory of the Russian Federation and abroad.

However, despite the strategic importance of the transport component, Russia is not able to provide its financing in full. The budget for the implementation of all projects is not enough. According to the World Economic Forum, the quality of Russian infrastructure in many important components leaves much to be desired—114th place in the quality of road infrastructure, 66th in the quality of seaports, 59th in the quality of airport infrastructure. (World Economic Forum 2018, pp. 248–249).

The country's leadership is aware of the scale of the problem and is trying to solve it systematically. In the beginning, the government developed a strategic document for the development of infrastructure. Since 2018, the transport system in Russia has been developing within the framework of a Comprehensive plan for modernization and expansion of the core infrastructure for the period up to 2024 and National projects.

Since the state is not able to cover the infrastructure deficit in the transport system, PPP mechanisms are actively used in the country. Most of the concessions in transport are on roads. In fact, this sector is one of the most advanced in terms of PPP application.

Results

Transport Infrastructure in Russia

The Russian market of transport infrastructure is quite large: according to the data of the consulting company EMBS Group, the construction and repair of roads, bridges and railways, airports, ports, and coastal infrastructure in 2017 accounted for 12% of the costs of the construction industry in Russia, amounting to almost 7.6 trillion rubles. Currently, the transport complex employs more than 1.8 million people.

Historically, the transport infrastructure of the Russian Federation is experiencing a lack of investment (Maksimov 2010; Ivanov 2019). The infrastructure deficit causes a low level of accessibility and quality of transport infrastructure in the country and, according to the estimates of the Research Institute of Territorial Development and transport infrastructure, costs the domestic economy more than 1.3 trillion rubles or 3% of GDP annually.

In many respects, the transport infrastructure occupies an important place in the agenda of the government. In 2009, the implementation of the Federal target program (FTP) "Modernization of the transport system in Russia in 2002–2009" was successfully completed. The projects and initiatives launched within its framework were continued in the new sectoral FTP for 2010–2020, implemented within the framework of the Transport strategy of the Russian Federation, which was adopted by the Government in 2008. In 2014, the Government of the Russian Federation approved the State program "Development of transport system for the period 2013–2020", which included financing of two target programs—"Development of transport system of Russia" and "Modernization of Uniform system of the organization of air traffic of the Russian Federation".

Since 2018, the fundamental document for the development of transport infrastructure in Russia is a Comprehensive plan for the modernization and expansion of the core infrastructure for the period up to 2024. Its budget is 6.3 trillion rubles, of which only 3 trillion rubles will be allocated from the Federal budget. It is planned to attract 3.3 trillion rubles from extra-budgetary (private) sources. The comprehensive plan includes nine projects aimed at modernization and expansion of transport infrastructure. These Federal projects envisage the development of the West-East and North-South transport corridors for transportation of goods and improvement of economic connectivity of the territory of Russia through expansion and modernization of railway, aviation, road, sea, and river infrastructure. In particular, the plan includes such projects as: "Europe—Western China", "Sea ports of Russia", "Northern Sea route", "Railway transport and transit", "Transport and logistics centers", "Communications between the centers of economic growth", "Development of regional airports and routes", "High-Speed railways", "Inland waterways".

The priority of the transport part of the Comprehensive plan is the innovative transformation of the infrastructure construction industry. To this end, it is planned to introduce and widely apply advanced technologies and best practices, digitalization of the transport industry and logistics processes (Inshakova et al. 2019).

According to the Russian government, the implementation of the transport part of the Comprehensive plan will significantly improve the transport system by 2024.

Since 2018, road construction has been separately identified in the national project "Safe and high-quality roads". The budget of the national project is 4.8 trillion rubles (Chart 11.1).

Traditionally, the Russian market of transport infrastructure is dominated by road facilities—in 2017 their share was 59%. The remaining costs and investments are borne by railways, airports, and ports (Fig. 11.1).

Despite the increased attention from the government and the slow but still existing growth of the Russian market of transport infrastructure, its quality is still estimated to be low. Thus, in the special annual report of the World Economic Forum, The Global Competitiveness Report[1], Russia has not been in the best positions among almost 140 countries for many years.

[1] The rating is compiled by processing the results of a survey of local businesses for satisfaction with the state and level of development of national infrastructure. This KPI, which reflects the degree of

Chart 11.1 Dynamics of the volume of the Russian transport infrastructure market (2009–2016, billion rubles). *Источник: ПАО "Мостотрест" по данным PMR, EMBS Group, Росстат*

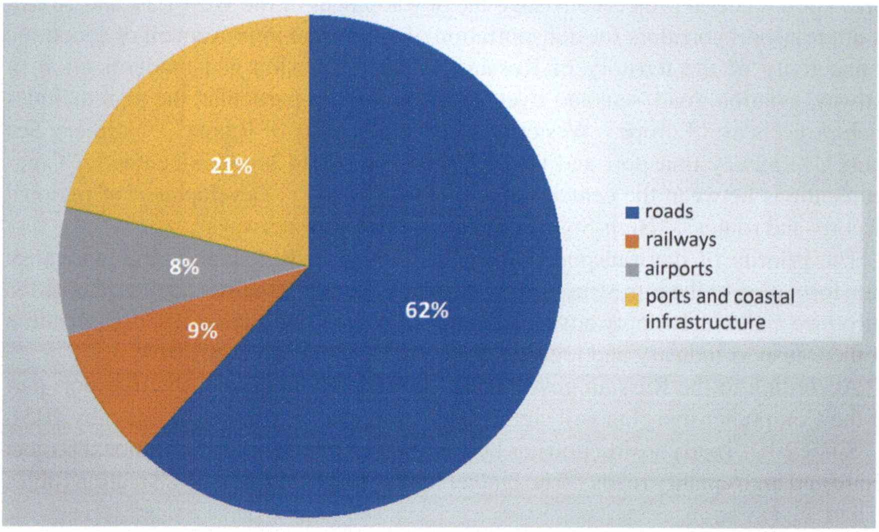

Fig. 11.1 Structure of the Russian transport infrastructure market (2017, % and billion rubles). *Источник: ПАО "Мостотрест" по данным PMR, EMBS Group, Росстат*

Although, as can be seen in Table 11.1, since 2011 Russia has managed to significantly improve its position in the ranking in terms of the overall quality of transport infrastructure, rising from 100 to 35-the place, quality of roads—that is 62% of the total market—is still at a critical level

---

optimism/pessimism of infrastructure users, is recognized by the most informative experts of the WORLD ECONOMIC FORUM.

Table 11.1 Russian Federation in the WEF ranking of quality of infrastructure

Index components	Global competitiveness index	
	2011/2012 142 countries	2017/2018 138 countries
Quality of overall infrastructure	100	35
Quality of roads	130	114
Quality of railroad infrastructure	29	23
Quality of port infrastructure	97	66
Quality of air transport infrastructure	105	59

Source World Economic Forum. The Global Competitiveness Report 2011–2012, 2017–2018

Moreover, according to a World Bank study, Russia ranks 85th in the world in the Logistics Performance Index (Logistics Performance Index), with low scores on all indicators taken into account in the calculation of the index (including the assessment of the customs system, the state of infrastructure, the availability of international transport, etc.).

Thus, despite attempts to rectify the situation, Russia still has the historical problems of the transport sector: lack of investment and low operational efficiency. The use of PPP mechanisms is intended to solve these problems, and it is quite natural that public-private partnership in the transport sector is becoming increasingly common practice.

PPP in Transport Infrastructure

In Russia, there are 148 PPP projects in the field of transport infrastructure at different stages of implementation as of May 2019. Most of them were initiated in the road sector (Fig. 11.2).

As of May 2019, 124 projects have reached commercial closure, the total volume of investment obligations of the public and private parties amounts to 2,051 billion rubles, including the obligations of private investors—1,293 billion rubles.. It is noteworthy that the accumulated volume of private investment attracted to PPP transport projects is greater than the volume of investment in all other areas of public infrastructure combined.

The sectoral structure of projects that have reached commercial closure is shown in Chart 11.1. The share of road projects is 53%, while the share of private investment in these projects in total amounts to 49%. However, if we take into account the

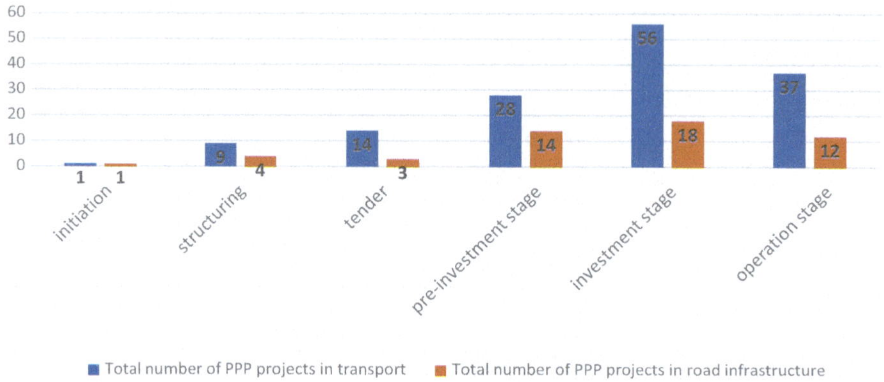

Fig. 11.2 PPP projects in transport by stages of implementation. *Source* National PPP center

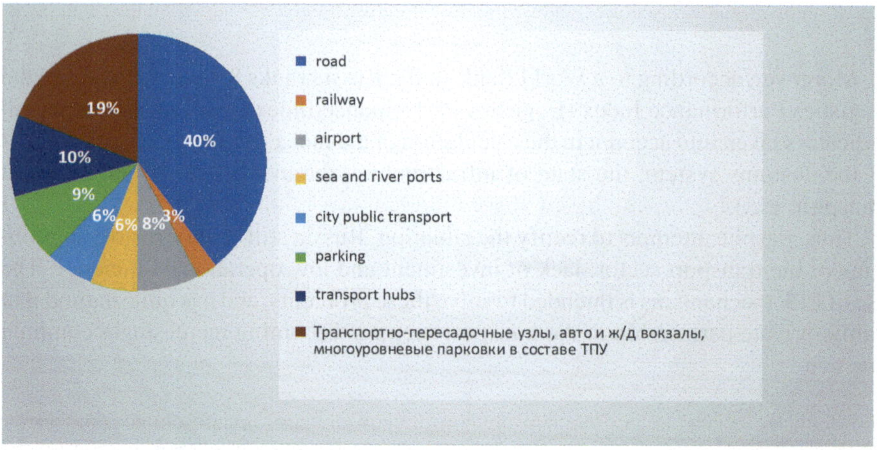

Fig. 11.3 PPP projects in the transport sector that have passed the stage of commercial closure

accumulated budget investments made through PPP, the investment share of road projects will be significantly higher—71% (see chart below) (Fig. 11.3).

Specifics of Concessions in the Road Sector

In toll road construction and operation projects, revenue from toll collection is the main and in most cases the only source of return on investment. That is why one of the key risks of such projects is the risk of demand/traffic. In order to minimize this risk, at the pre-project stage, it is especially important to assess the potential intensity of traffic at the object. The main factors that should be taken into account in its calculation are current traffic intensity in the location of the object, forecasts of socioeconomic development, and data on the development of the road network.

At the same time, the actual traffic intensity is often lower than expected, which should be taken into account in the financial structuring of the project. In this regard, for example, the Ministry of Economic Development of Russia recommends to build financial models of road projects in such a way that the cost of the project at the stage of operation in the amount of 20–30% less than the projected revenue.

Legal structuring of the project should adequately reflect the peculiarities of implementation of projects in the field of construction and operation of toll roads in all material aspects, including distribution of liabilities and risks between the parties, payment mechanism under the agreement, mechanism of enforcement (the procedure for recovery of losses, penalties, conditions and procedure for payment of additional remuneration to the private partner/concessionaire, the procedure for providing Bank guarantees and other security methods) (Estache et al. 2007; Rall et al. 2010).

Thus, in terms of risk allocation, the project should ensure the transfer of specific risks associated with the construction and operation of the road to one of the parties (taking into account which party is most likely to manage such risk). For the construction stage primarily risks of errors in design, detection of additional objects, risks associated with the provision of land as well as environmental risks and risks of commissioning should be paid attention in the legal structuring of the project. For the stage of operation, it is important to take into account the already mentioned demand risk, risk of road changes at the request of the Concedent, etc. Distribution of risks can be made through various legal mechanisms, in particular, mechanism of circumstances (ensuring the economic balance of the agreement), assurances about the circumstances (Art. 431.2 of the Civil Code) and others.

In the case of toll roads, the main factor determining their payback is the efficiency of toll collection. Fee collection, in turn, largely depends on the demand and accordingly, the quality of the final infrastructure services. In this regard, it seems appropriate to link payments in favor of the private partner to the achievement of the established levels of transport and operational indicators (for example, convenience and safety of travel and other operational qualities of the road).

To date, the Russian practice of implementing road PPP projects has been formed within the framework of the concession law (Ivanov 2016). The main types of concession agreements are the direct fee concession and the availability payment concession. The subject of the concession with direct fee collection is the performance by the private partner of a complex of works on construction or reconstruction and operation of the road (or its section) in whole or in part at the expense of own and borrowed funds. This agreement allows participation of the Concedent in the costs of creating the facility of the concession.

The right of ownership of the created object of concession after completion of construction (reconstruction) remains with the Concedent, thus for the period of validity of the agreement the object is transferred to the private partner for temporary use. The main source of return on investment and financing of the concessionaire's operating costs is the direct collection by the private partner of fees from the users of the object of the concession agreement. Such agreements are usually concluded for 25–30 years.

The subject of the concession with the payment of the Concedent is the concessionaire's performance of a complex of works on construction and operation of the concession facility (road, road section) in whole or in part at the expense of its own and borrowed funds. The concessionaire collects fees from the users of the concession facility in favor of the Concedent. In this case, the concessionaire's return on investment is provided in stages within the period specified in the agreement with the agreed rate of return, the actual amount of which depends on the achievement of the private partner's transport and operational targets. Financing of operating costs is provided by operating fees paid by the Concedent. Agreements on this model are concluded, as a rule, also for a period of 25–30 years.

Case. Construction of the Moscow—St. Petersburg Highway (M-11)

This is a high-speed toll road connecting the largest megacities of the country. The total length of the motorway is 669 km, which is comparable to the distance from Paris to Zurich. The road passes through Moscow, Tver, Novgorod, and Leningrad regions bypassing all settlements. The construction period 2010–2019. The highway was put into operation in November 2019.

The M-11 highway is built in parallel to the existing free M-10 highway. According to Russian law, toll roads can be used only if there is a free-of-charge alternative.

Construction of the highway Moscow—St. Petersburg was carried out in several sections, each of which was an independent investment project. All plots were built under concession. The state company "Avtodor" acts as the Concedent, which on behalf of the state concluded agreements. For a long time, Avtodor was the only company in Russia that could act as a Concedent. Since 2018, such an opportunity has appeared at the state Corporation Rosatom, which is engaged in the construction and maintenance of nuclear power plants in Russia, and also owns the world's only nuclear icebreaker fleet.

Concessionaires at M-11 in different sections were: a consortium of investors "North-West concession company" (including the French group Vinci), companies "Magistral of two capitals", "Mostotrest", "Transstroymechanizatsiya".

The total cost of construction of the M-11 resulted in 520 billion rubles, of which about one third (148 billion) are the funds of private investors.

Sources of return on investment for M-11:

- Direct collection of fees from consumers for the use of the object (services)/other commercial activities;
- Availability fee (fixed payments) from the public partner (budget).

According to "Avtodor", the fare throughout the site will be 1800-2000 rubles. (≈25–27 €).

Technical parameters of the Expressway:

- road category—IA (highway);
- design speed—150 km/h;
- number of lanes—4 to 10.
- traffic intersections at different levels—36;
- artificial structures (bridges, overpasses, overpasses, and cattle runs)—325;

Case. Modernization of Pulkovo Airport (St. Petersburg)

Pulkovo airport in St.Petersburg is the first airport in Russia built on the terms of public-private partnership. In 2010, following the results of the tender, the government of St. Petersburg and Pulkovo Airport (owned by St. Petersburg) signed an agreement on PPP with the consortium "Air Gates of the Northern Capital" (VVSS), which includes VTB Capital (subsidiary of VTB state Bank), the German company Fraport managing Frankfurt airport, as well as the Qatar Investment Authority (QIA). The airport was built entirely at the expense of the consortium. The total investment amounted to 50 billion rubles.

Source of return on investment is direct collection of fees from consumers for the use of the object (services).

Under the terms of the agreement, the private consortium received a long-term lease for 30 years of the airport property complex for the large-scale reconstruction of existing and construction of new airport infrastructure. Throughout this period, the consortium will operate Pulkovo airport, provide airport services, and invest in the development of the airport in accordance with the PPP agreement. The consortium has been granted the exclusive right to provide airport services at the Pulkovo airport. In 2011–2015, a new international passenger terminal with an area of 145 thousand square meters, passenger and cargo aprons, a hotel and a business center on the forecourt, a complex of Parking lots and other infrastructure of the airport were built and put into operation, as well as the terminal building of "Pulkovo-1" was reconstructed.

The agreement on PPP "Pulkovo" is considered one of the most successful. The project was awarded international awards. In 2014, the International Financial Corporation, as well as the Infrastructure Journal, selected the best projects out of 40 PPP projects worldwide on the basis of their high innovative level and social significance. The Pulkovo airport reconstruction and development project won a silver award in the categories Europe, Central Asia, Middle East, and North Africa.

Case. Construction of Western High-Speed Diameter (St. Petersburg)

Western high-speed diameter is the first intracity high-speed toll highway in Russia. The road length of 47 km passes through the territory of St. Petersburg. At the same time, more than half of the motorway are artificial structures: bridges, overpasses, etc.

The plans of the government of St. Petersburg to build a high-speed road passing through the city, appeared in 1966. However, the work on the project began only in the 90 s, at the same time it got its name "Western high-speed diameter", because the road runs along the Western part of St. Petersburg along the coast. The project was decided to be implemented on PPP terms and even a tender was held to choose a concessionaire. However, the project encountered many difficulties. Due to the crisis of 2008, the agreement on construction and operation with the winner of the tender consortium "Nevsky Meridian" headed by "Basel" billionaire Oleg Deripaska was never signed. As a result, the city authorities built the southern and northern sections of the road by 2011 independently, without the involvement of a private investor.

However, the most difficult from a technical point of view was the Central section, which runs along the coastline. In 2011, the government again announced a tender, which resulted in signing a PPP agreement with the Northern capital highway consortium for 30 years. The consortium includes VTB Capital, Gazprombank and Astaldi (Italy), Ictas Insaat (Turkey) as construction contractors (Inshakova et al. 2018).

The volume of investments in the Central section amounted to 120 billion rubles, of which the private investor invested 70 billion rubles.

Source of return on investment—direct collection of fees from consumers for the use of the object (services).

According to the PPP agreement, the consortium will maintain all sections of the road and charge tolls until 2042. Under the agreement, if the private partner's annual income is less than 9.6 billion, the city budget pays the investor a subsidy to cover the costs incurred.

Technical parameters of the Expressway:

- road category—IA (highway);
- total length of the highway—46.6 km;
- number of lanes—4 to 8;
- maximum speed—110 km/h;
- average intensity → 100 thousand cars per day;

PPP in Other Transport Sectors

At the first stage, PPP in the transport industry was only in roads. However, afterward the mechanisms of public-private partnership began to be increasingly applied in other sectors too. At the same time, the volume of investment in projects, for example, in the railway industry was not inferior to roads. In 2018, Russia signed two major concessions for construction of railway lines: Kyzyl–Kuragino (Eastern Siberia) and Northern Latitudinal Passage (Western Siberia).

Kyzyl–Kuragino is a section of the road more than 412 km, which is to be built for the export of coal from the Elegest Deposit. Its capacity is up to 15 million tons/year. The construction of the road will be fully financed by a private investor who will invest 127 billion rubles. Construction will be carried out in a mountainous area, which will require the construction of 8 tunnels with a total length of 11 km, the construction of 127 bridges with a length of about 16 km. Source of return on investment—direct collection of fees from consumers for the use of the object (services).

The Northern Latitudinal Passage will be built for the export of oil cargo and gas condensate. The length of the section of the Ob–Salekhard–Nadym is 353 km, total investments—113 billion rubles, the Government will provide a capital grant in the amount of 13 billion rubles, the remaining funds will be invested by private investors. It is also expected to attract debt financing. The main work on both projects will be carried out by the state company—"Russian Railways" (in the case of the Northern Latitudinal Passage, Russian Railways is a co-owner of the project company), which in Russia is a monopoly on the transport of goods by rail. The source of return on investment under the project is the availability fee (fixed payments) from the public partner (budget).

Both projects—Northern Latitudinal Passage and Kyzyl–Kuragino —were under discussion for more than 10 years, because the state could not afford to fully finance them. Construction started in fact only with the use of PPP mechanisms.

In addition to the railway industry, PPP mechanisms have started to be used in the port and airport infrastructure. In 2018, a concession agreement for the construction of the Lavna coal terminal in Murmansk (1500 km North of Moscow) was signed. The capacity of the terminal will be 18 million tons/year. The construction will be carried out entirely at the expense of the private investor, who will invest 16.7 billion rubles, the Source of return on investment will be the availability fee (fixed payments) from the public partner (budget).

The next port concession project is expected to be a dry cargo terminal in Taman (Krasnodar region, South).

The first since the Soviet Union times completely new airport was also built using the PPP mechanism. Renova Group, a private investor, built Platov International Airport in Rostov-on-Don, the largest city in the South-West of Russia. The capacity of the airport is 5 million people/year. "Renova" has fully funded the construction of nearly $20 billion. Source of investment return is a direct collection of payments from consumers for the use of the object (service)/other commercial activities.

In addition to classical concessions and PPP agreements, other forms of public-private partnership are actively used in the transport sector in Russia. For example, Moscow buys subway cars under life cycle contracts (LCC) from a private group of companies Transmashholding. These are large contracts for more than 100 billion rubles. Transmashholding supplies subway cars for Budapest (Hungary) under a similar scheme.

Moscow is also actively using this form of PPP as a corporate model of public-private partnership in the implementation of transport projects. According to the approach of the World Bank (the leading analytical center and aggregator of PPP projects in the world), the corporate model of public-private partnership corresponds to the type of contract called "Partial privatization"/"Joint venture", which means the partial sale of equity in a state-owned asset company to a private investor while maintaining state control over the asset of the company ("Project company"/"Special purpose company"). Moscow is building transport hubs through the corporate model as part of the development of the capital's passenger transport system. As of May 2019, 15 contracts worth 110 billion rubles were signed under the scheme. Funds are invested by a private investor. The contracts provide for different sources of return on investment:

- other commercial activities (sublease, advertising, trade, etc.);
- availability fee (fixed payments) from the public partner (budget);
- direct collection of fees from consumers for the use of the object (services).

Conclusion

- Russian transport industry is the most advanced sector in terms of the use of public-private partnership mechanisms. The most capital-intensive PPP projects are also implemented in the transport infrastructure. Initially, PPP mechanisms were used only in road construction, gradually the spectrum of PPP application significantly expanded to include railways, airports, ports, transport hubs, city public transport, etc.
- Since 2018, Russia has been implementing two large-scale National projects—the "Main infrastructure development plan" and "Safe roads". For these two projects alone, 11.1 trillion rubles will be invested in transport projects over six years, of which 3.5 trillion rubles will be extra-budgetary funds. No doubt, these are significant funds for the country, but these plans will not have a strong impact on the PPP market. According to the estimates of the National PPP Center, most of the projects are planned to be implemented through public procurement, i.e., without the use of PPP mechanisms.
- However, since the implementation of transport projects using PPP forms has already proven itself, especially in the road sector, these tools will continue to be used. Russian governors recognize that Federal budget money provided to implement National projects to improve transport infrastructure is not enough. Therefore, regional authorities will have to look for private investors and use PPP mechanisms. As recognized by the Ministry of Eonomic Development of Russia at the St. Petersburg International Economic Forum in June 2019, "more than 90% of the total network of roads in the country are roads of regional importance. The subjects of the Russian Federation are faced with the urgent task of ensuring both the construction of these roads and bringing them to the normative state.

Here, of course, it is necessary to pay attention, first of all, to projects within the framework of public-private partnership".

- We also believe that PPP mechanisms will be developed in different sectors of transport infrastructure. Budget deficits in the regions will encourage the search for new mechanisms to achieve the goals. This will be the main driver for not rich regions. On the other hand, rich regions, such as Moscow, have already gained good experience in implementing multibillion projects through PPP mechanisms, and will continue to move along this path. So, there is enough ground to believe that public-private partnership will develop in the regions regardless of the level of gross-regional product.
- A significant driver for the PPP market will be the new status of Rosatom State Corporation as a Concedent, granted by a special Decree of the Government in 2019. The company is assigned as the curator of the Federal project "Northern Sea route" with total investments of 735 billion rubles, and with dozens of large enterprises in which more than 400 thousand people work, under its control. Therefore, from our point of view, Rosatom will become no less active player in the PPP transport market than Avtodor state company.

We also believe that if Russia takes the decision to begin construction of such large-scale projects as Europe–Western China and Meridian highways, Moscow–Kazan or Moscow–St. Petersburg high-speed railways, they will be implemented through PPP mechanisms.

References

Aeroport "Pulkovo" priznan odnim iz luchshih GCHP proektov mira. (2013). (Pulkovo Airport is recognized as one of the best PPP projects in the world (2013)). Pulkovo Airport, Saint-Petersburg. https://pulkovoairport.ru/about/news/2013/1740/. Accessed 17 Apr 2019.

Estache, A., Juan, E., & Trujillo, L. (2007). Public-private partnerships in transport: Policy research working paper, [s.1.], №4436. The World Bank.

Federal'nii Zakon ot 21.07.2005. No.115-FZ "O kontsessionnikh soglasheniyakh" (Federal law No. 115-FZ of July 21, 2005 "On Concession agreements").

Federal'nii zakon ot 13.07.2015 № 224-FZ "O gosudarstvenno-chastnom partnyorstve, munitsipalno-chastnom partnyorstve v Rossiyskoy Federatsii i vnesenii izmenenii v otdelnie zakonodatelnie akti Rossiyskoy Federatsii" (Federal Law no. 224-FZ of July 13, 2015 "On Public-Private Partnership, Municipal-Private Partnership in the Russian Federation and Amendments to Certain Legislative Acts of the Russian Federation").

GCHP yavlyaetsya klyuchom dlya investicij v dorozhnuyu otrasl' - gubernator Ryazanskoj oblasti. (2019). (PPP is a key for transport infrastructure investments (2019)). Information Agency "Prime". https://1prime.ru/transport/20190607/830050041.html. Accessed 10 June 2019.

GCHP-zhurnal 2013–2018 (PPP journal, 2013-2018). http://pppjournal.ru/. Accessed 17 Apr 2019.

Guidebook on PPP Frameworks in APEC Region: Investment Experts' Group-May 2015. (2015). Asia-Pacific Economic Cooperation (APEC), Jakarta.

Guidebook on Promoting Good Governance in Public-Private Partnerships. (2008). United Nations Economic Commission for Europe. https://www.unece.org/cicppp/cecipublications/ceci/2008/guidebook-on-promoting-good-governance-in-public-private-partnerships/guidebook-on-promoting-good-governance-in-public-private-partnerships.html. Accessed 14 May 2019.

Inshakova, A. O., Goncharov, A. I., Kazachenok, O. P. (2018). Legal regulation of the syndicated lending: Banking innovations in contemporary Russia. In E. Popkova, & V. Ostrovskaya (Eds.), *Perspectives on the use of new information and communication technology (ICT) in the modern economy* (pp. 368–377). Cham: Springer.

Inshakova, A. O., Goncharov, A. I., & Marchukov, I. P. (2019). Common energy policy and development paths legal regulation of foreign trade turnover of energy resources in the CIS and in the EEU. In O. V., Inshakov, A. O., Inshakova, E. G. Popkova (Eds.), *Energy sector: A systemic analysis of economy, foreign trade and legal regulations* (pp. 207–225). Cham: Springer Science + Business Media.

Ivanov, O. V. (2016). *Teoriya i praktika gosudarstvenno-chastnogo partnerstva (Theory and world practice of public-private partnership (2016))* (p. 299). Moscow: MGIMO-University.

Ivanov, O. V. (2019). Gosudartsvenno-chastnoe partnerstvo kak instrument razvitiya infrastruktury I modernizatsii ekonomiki. Opyt stran Aziatsko-tikhookeanskogo regiona (Public-private partnership as an instrument of development of infrastructure and modernization of economy. Experience of Asia-Pacific countries) (300 p). Moscow, MGIMO-University.

Koncessionnye soglasheniya v kommunal'noj sfere: aktual'naya statistika, izmenenie koncessionnogo zakonodatel'stva i sovershenstvovanie regulirovaniya. (2016). (Concession agreements in the housing and utilities sector: current statistics, changes in concession legislation and legislation improvement (2016)). PPP Development Center, RE Legal. http://pppcenter.ru/assets/docs/re-legal_booklet-kontsessii_v_jkh_24-10-2016.pdf. Accessed: 10 Mar 2019.

Kto vladeet ZSD. (Who owns the Western High-Speed Diameter (ZSD)). Gazeta "Fontanka", Website. https://www.fontanka.ru/2016/10/05/075/. Accessed 17 May 2019.

Logistics Performance Index. (2012–2018). The World Bank. https://lpi.worldbank.org/international/aggregated-ranking. Accessed 10 May 2019.

Maksimov, V. V. (2010). Gosudarstvenno-chastnoe partnerstvo v transportnoj infrastructure. (Public-private partnership in transport infrastructure (2010)) (178 p). Moscow: Alpina Publishers.

Mekhanizmy gosudarstvenno-chastnogo partnyorstva v ekonomicheskoi politike Rossii (Mechanisms of public-private partnership in the economic policy of Russia (2018)). Ed. by O.V.Ivanov. MGIMO-University, Moscow, 409 p.

Nacional'nye proekty: klyuchevye celi i ozhidaemye rezul'taty. (2019). (National projects: key objectives and expected results (2019)). The Russian Government Website. http://government.ru/news/35675/. Accessed 15 Mar 2019.

Ob utverzhdenii Kompleksnogo plana modernizacii i rasshireniya magistral'noj infrastruktury na period do 2024 goda. (2019). (About the approval of the Comprehensive plan of modernization and expansion of the core infrastructure for the period till 2024 (2019)). The Russian Government Official Website. http://government.ru/docs/34297/. Accessed 10 May 2019.

Obzor otraslevikh praktik realizatsii proektov GCHP 2017–2018. (2018). (Review of industry practices of implementation of PPP projects 2017–2018 (2018). PPP Development Center, Moscow.

Obzor rossijskogo rynka infrastruktury. (2018). (Russian Infrastructure market overview (2018)). Mostotrest. http://ir.mostotrest.ru/ru/o-kompanii/obzor-rynka.html?print=1&type=98&no_cache=1. Accessed 15 May 2019.

Oleg Deripaska skhodit s dorogi. (2009). (Oleg Deripaska goes off the road. Oleg Deripaska doesn't finance the Western High-Speed Diameter (2009)). Gazeta "Kommersant". https://www.kommersant.ru/doc/1116943. Accessed 17 May 2019.

Overview of Public Governance of Public-Private Partnerships in the Russian Federation. (2014). OECD. http://www.pppi.ru/sites/all/themes/pppi/img/zana3.pdf. Accessed 22 May 2019.

Procuring Infrastructure Public-Private Partnerships Report. (2018). World Bank, Washington. http://documents.worldbank.org/curated/en/891171523343989736/Procuring-infrastructure-public-private-partnerships-report-2018. Accessed 14 Mar 2019.

Proekt Nacional'nogo doklada o privlechenii chastnyh investicij v razvitie infrastruktury i primenenii mekhanizmov gosudarstvenno-chastnogo partnerstva v Rossijskoj Federacii. (2018). (Draft national report on attracting private investment in infrastructure development and application of Public-Private Partnership mechanisms in the Russian Federation (2018)). PPP National Development Center, 80 p. http://pppcenter.ru/assets/docs/22032019reiting.pdf. Accessed 10 March 2019.

Public–Private Partnership Monitor. (2017). Asian Development Bank. https://www.adb.org/publications/public-private-partnership-monitor. Accessed 25 May 2019.

Public-Private Partnership. Reference Guide. Version 3.0. (2017). World Bank. https://ppp.worldbank.org/public-private-partnership/library/ppp-reference-guide-3-0. Accessed 14 Apr 2019.

Putin nazval "vzdutymi" tarify na trasse M-11. (2016). (Putin called the tariffs on the highway M11 too high (2016)). Gazeta RBK. https://www.rbc.ru/society/25/01/2016/56a6555a9a794771dc2e872e. Accessed 17 April 2019.

Rall, J., et al. (2010). Public-private partnerships for transportation. A toolkit for legislators. Washington.

Rekomendacii po realizacii proektov gosudarstvenno-chastnogo partnerstva. Luchshie praktiki. (2016). Ministerstvo ekonomicheskogo razvitiya Rossijskoj Federacii (Recommendations for the public-private partnership projects implementation. Best practices (2016). Ministry of Economic Development of the Russian Federation). http://economy.gov.ru/minec/activity/sections/privgovpartnerdev/support/20160829. Accessed 10 Mar 2019.

Russian infrastructure in the global context. (2013). Ernst&Young. https://www.ey.com/ru/en/issues/business-environment/ey-road-to-2030-russian-infrastructure-in-global-context. Accessed 13 Mar 2019.

Schwab, K., (Ed.). (2018). The global competitiveness report 2017–2018. World Economic Forum. http://www3.weforum.org/docs/GCR2017-2018/05FullReport/TheGlobalCompetitivenessReport2017%E2%80%932018.pdf. Accessed 11 May 2019.

Simply and honestly about investments in infrastructure and PPP in Russia. Analytical review. Rating of regions 2018–2019. (2019). ROSINFRA. PPP Development Center. http://pppcenter.ru/assets/files/obzor240419.pdf. Accessed10 Mar 2019.

Soglashenie o gosudarstvenno-chastnom partnerstve aeroporta Pulkovo. (2013). (Pulkovo Airport. Public-private partnerships agreement (2013)). Pulkovo Airport, Saint-Petersburg. https://pulkovoairport.ru/about/agreement/. Accessed 17 Apr 2019.

Transportnaya strategiya Rossijskoj Federacii na period do 2030 goda (The Strategy of the Russian Federation transport development till 2030). The Russian Federation Government Resolution of November 22, 2008 №1734-p.

World Economic Forum. (2018). The global competitiveness report 2017–2018. http://www3.weforum.org/docs/GCR2017-2018/05FullReport/TheGlobalCompetitivenessReport2017%E2%80%932018.pdf. Accessed 11 May 2019.

Chapter 12
PPPs in Social Infrastructure. Problems and Perspectives

Elena B. Zavyalova and Agnessa O. Inshakova

Abstract Social commitments account for the biggest share of the Russian budget expenditure. However, there is an evidence of insufficient budget spending both on regional and federal levels, though the demand for better social services is growing. The only way to eliminate this imbalance is to find the alternative source of financing social commitments by private funds, mainly through public-private partnerships. The emphasis should be set on the social infrastructure development. "Social infrastructure" includes such objects as infrastructure objects in health, education, social security, culture, tourism and sports.

Keywords Public-private partnership · PPP in social sector · PPP in health · PPP in education · PPP in sports · PPP in tourism · PPP in social security system · Concessions · PPP agreements · Social infrastructure · Social sphere

JEL-Codes L32 · L30 · M10 · M21

Introduction

The development of social sphere is traditionally the key factor of Russian economic agenda formation. This fact is attested to by total social consumption in budgets of all levels and analysis of regulations, the May decrees of The President of The Russian Federation in particular. Social commitments are traditionally high, however, they

E. B. Zavyalova (✉)
Department of economic policy and public-private partnership, MGIMO University, Vernadsky Ave., 76, 119454 Moscow, Russia
e-mail: e.zavyalova@inno.mgimo.ru

A. O. Inshakova
Department of Civil and Private International Law (the Basic Department of the Southern Scientific Center of the Russian Academy of Sciences), Volgograd State University, Prospekt Universitetskij 100, 400062 Volgograd, Russia
e-mail: gimchp@volsu.ru; ainshakova@list.ru

O. V. Ivanov and A. O. Inshakova (eds.), *Public-Private Partnerships in Russia*, Competitive Government: Public Private Partnerships,
https://doi.org/10.1007/978-3-030-56352-3_12

do not correspond fully to the actual needs for the development of social infrastructure. Furthermore, in conditions of an economic crisis, the reduction of budget spending for developing infrastructure in health, education and culture sectors has occurred. As a result, inflows to capital construction of social facilities has slowed down considerably, which impacts on the accessibility of qualitative services. In this regard in addition to the need for enhancing the effectiveness of budget expenditure the problem of stimulating the inflow of private investments in the social sphere takes place. This problem is particularly severe on the regional level where the social pressure on budget is traditionally larger than on the federal level (Baksheeva 2016).

We may say that a controversial situation takes place in Russia. The long-term stagnation of budget inflows is combined with the growing society demand for a higher quality of social infrastructure. To solve this contradiction, the Federal Law on "Public-Private Partnership" was adopted in 2015. Additionally, the practice of concessions application was enhanced. Because of the given factors share of private investments in the social infrastructure development started to rise. Due to the cooperation of the authorities and the business community, the practice of applications of PPP in developing the social infrastructure of health, sport, elder care, vacation and education sectors has developed. The application of a given method allows us to consider the interests of all parties concerned. Thus the government reduces budget costs on creating and exploitation of social infrastructure facilities, the management of state property enhances and the financial returns from these assets increase (Inshakova et al. 2017). Unlike privatization measures that took place in the 1990 in this case the government reserves the ownership. For their part, the private partners receive guaranteed income from investments for rather long terms. Eventually, the society becomes the main beneficiary as the development of social infrastructure is enhancing the quality of life (Ivanov 2016).

Results

Today we may face two different trends. On the one hand, there is a decline in budget funding, while on the other hand the number of projects funded by private capital under PPP conditions is growing steadily. To prove this statement let us refer to the statistics.

According to the Federal Treasury, the aggregate public expenditure on social infrastructure was steadily declining since 2011. But starting from 2018 the government increased the financing to the sector. According to the current 3-year financial plan, the tendency is to stay for the coming years (Fig. 12.1).

However, the growing demand in creating new social infrastructure facilities provided the trigger for private investors. We may say that unsatisfied public demand on social services proved to be a powerful incentive for the market to find the means of reaching the needed level of infrastructural accessibility. In fact, a new funding system for social infrastructure has occurred through private funding.

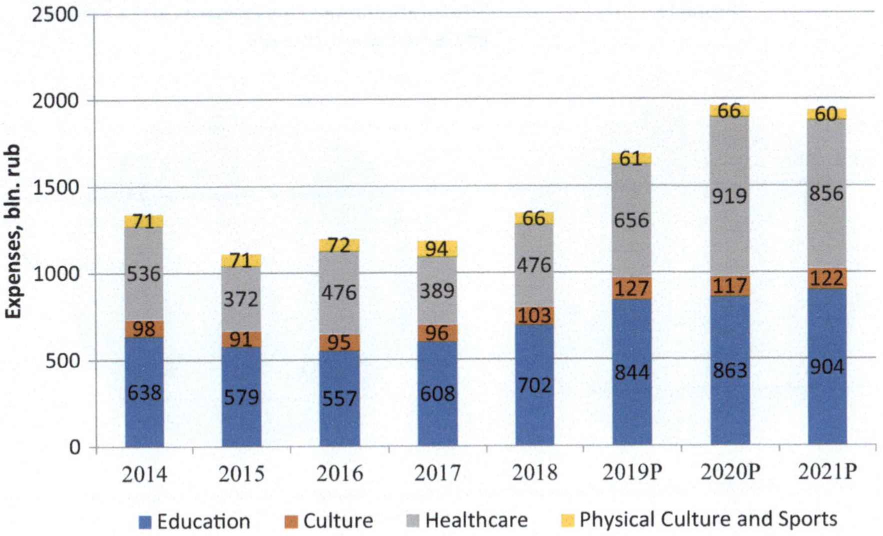

Fig. 12.1 Total government spending on social infrastructure (industries/budgets of appropriate levels). *Source* Ministry of finance of the Russian Federation. https://www.minfin.ru/ru/perfomance/budget/federal_budget/budgeti/2019/ (date of issue: 28.10.2019)

Due to the current economic situation and the decline of effective demand a special place is held by projects that require PPPs. In this case, the government can lend a "budget hand" for private investors by undertaking co-finance of the costs of creating a facility and guarantee a certain load of the facility as well as the returns over the years.

Thus, according to PPP Development Center, the total number of PPP infrastructural projects is steadily growing. The share of human-centred projects is rather high. 307 out of 2586 PPP projects are aimed at the social sector. The aggregate value of social sector projects implemented is 278,2 billion rubles, which is a share of 10,7% of the total investment. As can be seen in Fig. 12.2, the majority of PPP projects are implemented in health and education, while tourism and culture draw less attention of possible investors. Such sectors as a sport and social services draw even less interest in private business (Seleznev 2017).

Main Factors that Influence the Development of PPP in Social Sector

In most cases, analysing possible opportunities and difficulties in implementation of PPP projects the balance tilts towards advantages. However, in practice, the success of a project depends on a way of implementation of a certain PPP project. The given ways happen to be the most common ones: concession agreements, classical agreements on

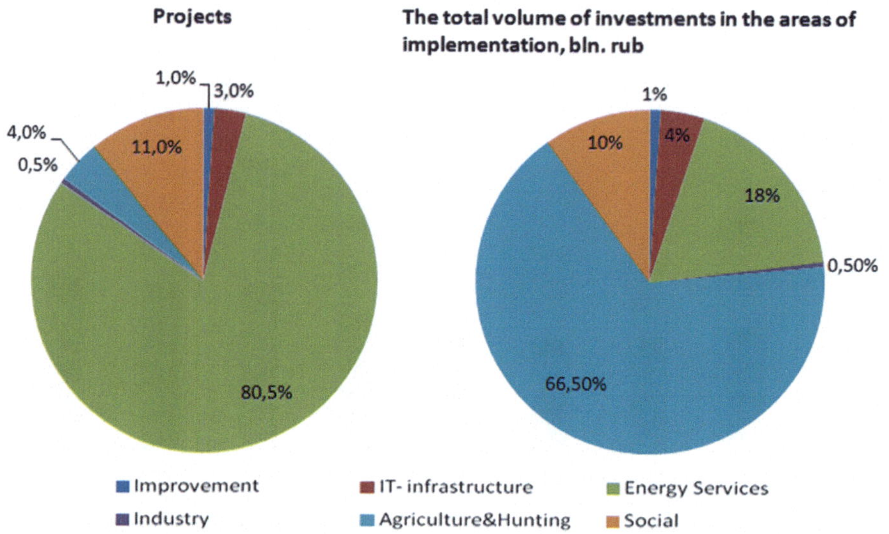

Fig. 12.2 The distribution of the number of projects and the total volume of investments in the areas of implementation. *Source* http://pppcenter.ru/assets/docs/pppcenter_a4_2016_v2_web.pdf (date of issue: 28.10.2019)

PPP and such forms of quasi-PPP as lease agreements with investment commitments. In terms of *concession*, a concessionaire attracts funding for creating/reconstructing an infrastructure facility and provides services according to the terms of agreement. In their turn, the grantor offsets the lost income to the concessionaire or fulfils other obligations according to the agreement. The form of concessions is useful for the creation of healthcare facilities, park projects and social sector projects, for example, creation and development of gerontology centres and rehabilitation centres. Such projects allow us to combine services funded by the government and services based on the commercial framework (Tkachenko and Meteleva 2017).

In terms of the *PPP agreement*, the private partner attracts funding for creation/reconstruction of an object, equipping and maintaining it until the end of the agreement, then conveys the right of property at the end of the agreement (Inshakova et al. 2019). If the costs for the private partner have been below 50% the public counterpart offsets the costs of the private partner according to the terms of the agreement. The public partner also leases land or a real estate for the purposes of the agreement.

In case of *lease with investment commitments* (quasi-PPP), the government leases the infrastructural facility and the private investor obtains finance for equipping, reconstructing, or constructing of a social infrastructure facility, manages and operates it and makes investment commitments. For example, in the Moscow area under the programme "Moscow manors", 18 manors are being restored this way. In Moscow care facilities are created according to such method.

The key issue for all PPP social sector projects is a problem of applying mechanism of reimbursing the private investment (Ivanov and Ivanova 2019). On this matter, all

PPP and quasi-PPP projects in Russia can be divided into four groups depending on a used model:

1. access fee implies full or partial returns for the private investor paid by the public counterpart including compensation of funds spent on creating quipping and maintaining a facility and raising finance.
2. direct collection of charges and other commercial activities according to administrated prices. The private partner provides returns by collecting service fees according to administrated prices. Due to legislation features, a public counterpart may refund private counterpart's costs after the project is completed.
3. minimum guaranteed return. A private counterpart provides a return on investment by collecting service fees according to administrated prices. In this case, the agreement implies a contingent liability on the public counterpart to refund the lost income to the private counterpart.
4. direct collection of charges and other commercial activities without additional assurance from the public counterpart. A private counterpart provides refunds solely through commercial activities without additional assurance from the public counterpart.

Based on the given classification all social infrastructure facilities can be divided into groups depending on whether there are any guarantees provided by the government:

1. projects with a fixed flow of payments—when is the government guarantees minimal return;
2. projects where the flow of payments fully depends on consumer demand.

In the first case, the financial model and the risks are clear to the investors. This attracts more investors for the project. In the second case, the projects appear to be more risky and attract less investors or require additional guarantees. However, in both cases funding social structure facilities seems to be more risky and less marginal than funding other sectors such as transport.

As was stated the interest to social sector among investors is steadily growing; however, there is a number of dimensions that hinder PPP development the in social sector. First of all implementation of Federal Law #224 has shown that the law requires various changes. In particular, one of the main deterrents for a private counterpart is an impossibility of full return from a PPP project from a public counterpart. Also, the experts dispute the procedure of benefits evaluation (Sergi 2019). It compares the budget efficiency of a PPP project and a direct budget financing which is not always within reach especially for projects in education sphere. The amendments to the law are expected soon.

Secondly, talking about actual problems of implementing PPP projects in the social sector we should mention that people-centred business projects are distinguished by high uncertainty of payback periods and future consumer demand. Furthermore, pricing and budget funding mechanisms can differ from the traditional market approach. The whole thing reduces the capacity of effectiveness evaluation.

Such risks as insufficient budget funding of projects that involve budget participation, lack of guarantees from a public partner the complexity of forecasting consumer demand were considered above. However, the way of things in different regions may vary.

The Analysis of Specific Features of the Implementation of PPP Projects in Selected Industries

We will use two methods for the following analysis: the feasibility of attracting private investments into human-centred projects and assessment of current trends towards budget expenditures. In the first case, the official policy is shown in the Government Decree setting the road map "Access of the non-state organizations to social services rendering". Thus in the road map health, education, social protection and culture spheres are regulated. Analysing budget expenditures in recent years, we may see a long-term shortage in the same spheres: health, education, social protection, culture and sport.

Health. According to the State programme "Health development" (26.12.2017 № 1640), the leading directions are focused on primary health care, high-technology medicine, healthy lifestyle, innovative medicine, elder care, medical rehabilitation, spa, etc.

Almost 70% of proposals of PPP implementations in health sector are focused on these directions. Moreover, 80% of such projects are already on the market. Interestingly, high-technology projects are in high demand. Such spheres as delivery care (maternity homes, perinatal centres) and high-technology medicine also have a capacity for PPP (Seleznev and Mihaylova 2017).

According to experts, health is not only the most forward-looking but also the most successful sector in applicating PPP (Sizova 2015). The most known projects are the health centre in Samara region and general practice health care net in Ul'anovsk region, etc.

However, the capacity could be used in a more effective way. Thus, to enlarge the number of PPP projects it could be useful to address the question of mitigation of the law about compulsory health insurance (CHI) and the time frame of concession contract pay-scale agreements in the health sector to decline commercial risks of PPP health investors. According to the requirements of legislations, CHI is not capable of covering investment costs (capital construction, repayments and others). In so doing, a number of regions have to refund PPP investors by capital granting during constructing/reconstructing a health facility and guaranteeing a load of the facility (the number of commercial patients multiplied by rate).

The potential private partner is significant for PPP health projects. It is important to understand what share of the services was provided by compulsory and voluntary insurance or weather all of the services were paid for. In Russia, there are lots of examples of implementation of PPP projects in health sector where the counterpart does not provide medical services but simply makes commitments on maintaining the facility, while the service is provided by the budget facility itself. In such projects, it's important to assess the long-term demand for such facilities as such projects are especially expensive in the long term excluding construction and exploitation cost overruns that occur in classic government infrastructural projects. It is also important to understand that projects that require reconstruction of a health facility should be properly structured in terms of land and property relationships.

Education. First of all, it is important to notice that the officials and private businessmen have the same views on the education sector. Over 90% of all initiatives account for the industries flagged by the State Programme "Education development" (26.12.2017 #1642). The key directions implementing PPP are early childhood education (kindergartens, child development centres), general education (schools, gymnasium, lyceums, boarding schools), additional child education. Building of childhood education and general education facilities in the Yamal-Nenets Autonomous Region can come as a good example of success (Glushko and Kolodina 2017) (Fig. 12.3).

The only form used in the sphere is PPP agreement that doesn't implement education services but only technical maintenance.

Social protection. This sector covers a vast variety of industries and facilities. The main directions are stated in the State Programme of Social Support. They are multifunctional disability service centres; elderly service centres (nursing homes, geriatric centres), minors' residences. The impetus for the private sector involvement was set in 2018 when the government increased the funding of the non-governmental organization's efficiency programme.

It is interesting to mention that in the first stage the majority of PPP projects were involved in this particular sector, however nowadays private companies have

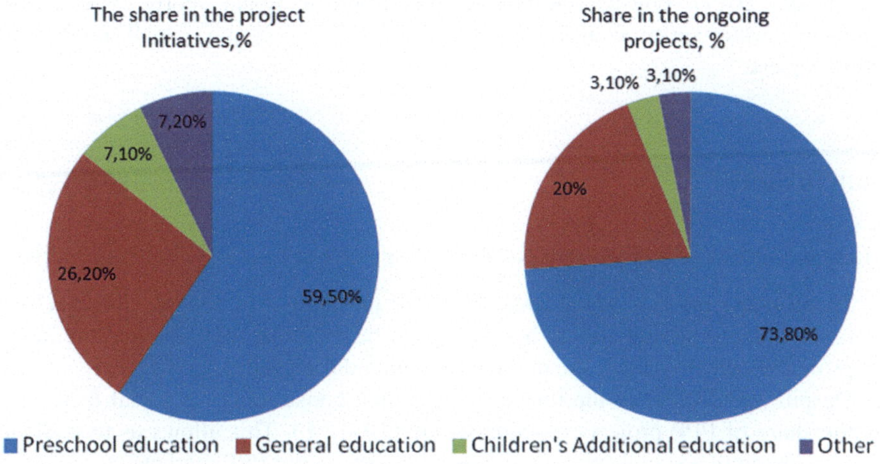

Fig. 12.3 Key areas of the education sector for the application of PPP mechanisms. *Source* http://pppcenter.ru/assets/docs/pppcenter_a4_2016_v2_web.pdf (date of issue: 28.10.2019)

broadened their area of interest. For example, now elderly care service centres attract more attention.

Culture. According to PPP Development Center in today's Russia 34 PPP culture projects are being implemented. Most of them are related to cultural heritage cultural and art centres (creative centres theatres, cinemas) and cultural activity centres (concert halls, entertainment facilities).

The activity in this sphere corresponds to the State Programme "Culture and Sports Development" (15.04.2014 г. № 317, amended 17.08.2019) which shows that developing infrastructure using PPP is quite promising. In practical terms, investors are also active in implementing projects in such directions.

The most well-known of all implemented projects are improvement, maintaining and reconstructing a Baryshnikov Square in Moscow Region, modernization of "Cosmos" cinema in the Perm region and reconstructing a central recreation park in Volgograd.

A tourist sector is also worthy of attention. While in the beginning, the most popular sphere was the creation and development of the recreation tourist centres, now the attention is drawn to the creation of sport and leisure centres (child sport and recreation camps, ski resorts).

Physical education and sports. The most prospective directions are determined by the State Programme "Physical training and sports development" (15.04.2014 #302), expressed in the development of mass sports and sport reserves. Moreover, this project includes a special procedure for subsidies to implement events as a way to undertake finances.

The main sectors of applying PPP are: physical-culture centres; multifunctional sports centres, ice arenas (hockey stadiums, skating rings); water sports facilities (swimming pools, water parks).

The selection of these directions is based on their relevance on the market (Savchenko 2017): physical-culture centres, multifunctional sports centres, ice arenas and water sports facilities account for 3/4 (74%) of the overall number of sport projects.

Conclusions

Within the results of a given analysis the author came to the following conclusions:

1. Today using private capital to solve social problems has become an objective reality. Using private capital has proven to be the most effective and the most profitable way to satisfy the population demand for quality service.
2. Despite the decline in the financing of capital construction of social facilities, the share of PPP projects remains steady (10–12%). This allows us to make a conclusion that social sphere remains a priority on the PPP market.
3. Ineffective demand for the social services has become a powerful incentive for the market to search for new means of social infrastructure development. We may

witness a creation of a new system built on the financing of social infrastructure through private investment.

4. The gap between projects that are planned and are already being implemented is obvious. The market requires new projects on developing social structure. This fact proves the limits of current frameworks that prevent implementing PPP's full capacity in the social sector.

References

Baksheeva, A. D. (2016). Vzaimodeystviya gosudarstva, biznesa i obrazovatelnyih organizatsiy v ramkah gosudarstvenno-chastnogo partnerstva. *Gosudarstvenno-chastnoe partnerstvo* (pp. 63–78).Tom, 3, # 1.

Glushko, Y. V., & Kolodina, N. V. (2017). Osobennosti gosudarstvenno-chastnogo partnerstva v sfere obrazovaniya v Rossii i za rubezhom. Gosudarstvenno-chastnoe partnerstvo (pp. 147–154). Tom, Vol. 4. # 2.

Inshakova, A. O., Goncharov, A. I., Kazachenok, O. P., Kochetkova, S. Y. (2017). Syndicated lending: Intensification of transactions and development of legal regulation in modern Russia. *Journal of Advanced Research in Law and Economics, VIII, 3*(25), 838–884.

Inshakova, A. O., Goncharov, A. I., & Inshakova, E. I. (2019). Innovative technologies of oil production: Tasks of legal regulation of management and taxation. In O. V., Inshakov, A. O., Inshakova, E. G., Popkova (Eds.), *Energy sector: A systemic analysis of economy, foreign trade and legal regulations* (pp. 79–94). Cham: Springer Science + Business Media.

Ivanov, O. V. (2016). Teoriya i mirovaya praktika gosudarstvenno-chastnogo partnerstva (298 p), MGIMO-University.

Ivanov, O. V., & Ivanova, A. O. (2019). *Gosudarstvenno-chastnoe patnerstvo v stranakh Aziatsko-tikhookeanskogo regiona (Paulic-private partnership in the countries of Asia-Pacific region)* (p. 270). Moscow: MGIMO-University.

Luchshie praktiki realizatsii proektov gosudarstvenno-chastnogo partnerstva v sotsialnoy sfere [Elektronnyiy resurs]/Natsionalnyiy tsentr gosudarstvenno-chastnogo partnerstva. (2016). Rezhim dostupa: http://pppcenter.ru/assets/docs/pppcenter_a4_2016_v2_web.pdf.

Savchenko, Y. V., Mihaylova, N. S. (2017). Analiz modeley vzaimodeystviya gosudarstva i biznesa v ramkah GChP v sfere fizkulturyi i sporta v Rossii. Gosudarstvenno-chastnoe partnerstvo (pp. 157–163). Tom 4, # 3.

Seleznev, P. L. (2017). Gosudarstvenno-chastnoe partnerstvo v Rossii 2016–2017: Tekuschee sostoyanie i trendyi, reyting regionov. P. L. Seleznev. M.: Assotsiatsiya "Tsentr razvitiya GChP".

Sergi, B. (2019). *Modeling economic growth in contemporary Russia*, Emerald Publishing Limited.

Sizova, E. S. (2015). Kriterii i metodyi sravnitelnogo analiza variantov realizatsii proekta stroitelstva ili rekonstruktsii ob'ekta infrastrukturyi zdravoohraneniya s ispolzovaniem mehanizmov gosudarstvennogo zakaza i gosudarstvenno-chastnogo partnerstva. Gosudarstvenno-chastnoe partnerstvo (pp. 175–192). Tom 2, # 4.

Tkachenko, I. N., Meteleva, M. A. (2017). Sovershenstvovanie protsessov upravleniya razvitiem gosudarstvenno-chastnogo partnerstva i infrastrukturoy investitsionnoy deyatelnosti na mezourovne, Gosudarstvenno-chastnoe partnerstvo. Tom 4, # 4.

Chapter 13
PPP—A Key to Salvation of Russian Communal Utilities Sector?

Evgeny Y. Moiseichev and Maria A. Ivanova

Abstract Intensive introduction of PPPs in communal utilities sector of Russia in recent years not without reason can be called "a quiet revolution" carried out by the authorities. Mechanisms of public-private partnership in the communal utilities sector, leading in Russia in a number of PPP projects, are investigated and systematized. The paper describes major problems faced by the sector and key measures taken in recent years by the state to attract private investment. Data characterizing quantitative and qualitative changes in the use of PPP mechanisms in the Russian communal utilities sector are also presented. Specific features of PPP projects in communal services are introduced.

Keywords Public-private partnership · Concession agreements · Public-private partnership agreements · Housing and communal utilities services

JEL-codes K12 · K15 · L97 · R31 · R53

Introduction

Housing and communal services are one of the basic sectors of the Russian Federation economy, providing the population with vital services, and industry—with necessary engineering infrastructure. Its share in the country's GDP is 7.2%, annual industry turnover exceeds 3 trillion rubles. Its fixed assets are more than 26% of the total fixed assets of the country (8 trillion rubles) Housing and communal services are provided by 35 746 enterprises and organizations. The number of employees in the housing

E. Y. Moiseichev (✉)
Strategic Development, Analytical and Information Support for PPPs, Center for PPP Projects, AVTODOR-invest, Malaya Dmitrovka str., 16/6, 127006 Moscow, Russia
e-mail: moiseichev@pppcenter.ru

M. A. Ivanova
MGIMO University, 119454 Moscow Vernadsky Ave., 76,, Russia
e-mail: ivmariam@mail.ru

O. V. Ivanov and A. O. Inshakova (eds.), *Public-Private Partnerships in Russia*, Competitive Government: Public Private Partnerships,
https://doi.org/10.1007/978-3-030-56352-3_13

and communal sector is more than 3 million people. The sector consumes more than 20% of the country's energy resources.

Annual investment needs of the housing and communal sector are estimated at 500 billion rubles, including.

- 200 billion rubles in heat supply,
- 100 billion rubles in water sector,
- 100 billion rubles in sanitation, and
- 100 billion rubles in solid waste treatment.

At the same time, the communal utility sector is characterized by systematic underfunding, which has already led to high levels of wear and tear of Russian utility infrastructure and, as a consequence, to an increase in accidents and a decrease in the quality of public services. According to the polls held a few years ago, for example, housing and communal services took the first place in the ranking of personal and family problems of Russians.

Physical depreciation of fixed assets of housing and communal services in the Russian Federation remains at 60%, reaching 70–80% in some municipalities. About 30% of fixed assets of housing and communal services have already fully served the standard terms.

This situation is typical for all sectors of housing and communal utilities. For example, heat supply systems of settlements in Russia include more than 77 thousand boilers, about 24 thousand central heating points, about 160 thousand kilometers of heating networks. More than 60% of the objects are in municipal ownership. The performance of heat supply systems is 20–30% worse than in the Nordic countries. In the past 20 years, the wear of heating systems equipment has grown critically. The number of boilers with a service life of more than 30 years was 75%, one-fourth of them worked for more than 50 years. The situation is similar with heating networks—68% of them have exceeded the critical service life of pipelines. The consequence of these negative factors is the poor quality of heat supply and hot water supply services (mass "under-heating"), significant restrictions in the provision of multi-apartment buildings with heat energy in emergency situations, long outages of hot water during the repair period.

The situation with water supply and sanitation is not much better. Every fifth sample of drinking water from water supply networks does not meet sanitary standards for sanitary and chemical and every tenth–for microbiological indicators. About 30 million people in rural areas use drinking water that does not meet sanitary standards. Annually, 55 billion cubic meters of wastewater is discharged into natural water bodies, of which almost 20 billion cubic meters are contaminated in excess of established standards (Table 13.1).

Today, it is obvious that it is impossible to reverse the situation in the housing and communal services related to the degradation of infrastructure and its critical wear and tear without attracting private investors to the industry.

In terms of attractiveness for the private sector, the communal utilities sector has at least two important features. First, housing and communal services have a huge consumer market, since housing and communal services are in demand by every

Table 13.1 Condition of communal utilities (as of 1 January 2017)

Objects of communal utilities infrastructure	Total length of networks (thousand km)	Share of networks in need of replacement (%)
Heat supply networks	173	29.06
Water supply networks	577	43.6
Sewerage networks	194	44.4

Source Ministry of construction and communal utilities of Russia

resident of the country, which as a result provides a guaranteed demand of more than 145 million people (this does not include industrial sector). Secondly, the sector has significant potential to improve profitability. The existing "unprofitability" is not a natural characteristic, but a consequence of inefficient management and other negative factors. One of the main tools by which the private sector can succeed in terms of efficiency is the introduction of new technologies. Today new technologies, including digital, allowing to optimize the processes, application of energy efficiency technologies, commissioning of automated dispatching systems, mobile services, etc., are increasingly introduced in the Russian communal utilities sector.

Results

Measures to Attract Private Investment in Housing and Utilities

In order to attract private capital into the communal utilities sector for modernization of municipal infrastructure, the Government of the Russian Federation has developed and implemented a range of measures, primarily related to the consolidation of the regulatory framework. On the whole, more than 30 normative legal acts have been adopted (including within the framework of improving the legislation on concession agreements) to create conditions for attracting private investment in housing and communal services (Concession agreements in the municipal sphere: current statistics, changes in concession legislation, and improvement of regulation 2016).

Amendments to the federal concession legislation introduced in 2013 provided, in particular, for the establishment of mandatory requirements for owners, concessionaires, and tenants to achieve targets of reliability, quality, and energy efficiency. Thus, at the conclusion of concession agreements, obligations of the operator to ensure the quality of services and achieve indicators of reliability and energy efficiency of the objects taken in the concession are determined. In case of default, property liability is envisaged.[1]

[1]Indicators of reliability and energy efficiency of heat supply facilities, as well as rules for their determination were approved by Resolution of the Government of the Russian Federation of May

At the same time, conditions that ensure guarantees of return of invested funds were created for investors. In particular, amendments to sectoral legislation synchronizing the rules of the Federal law "On concession agreements" and provisions relating to tariff regulation were adopted. As a result, the size of the tariff began to depend on obligations to achieve the quality of services provided to consumers.

The process of tariff regulation has also undergone changes. In order to increase the attractiveness of investment in heat supply, a number of important amendments were made to the Decree of the Government of the Russian Federation of October 22, 2012 № 1075 "On pricing in the heat supply sector". These changes made it possible to stimulate heat supply organizations to increase the efficiency of their activities, reduce operating costs, increase the number of energy-saving and energy efficiency measures, reduce the level of losses in heat networks, use more efficient types or brands of primary and reserve fuel on heat sources.

In July 2014, amendments to the Law on concessions (115-FZ) regarding the possibility of concluding a concession agreement by the initiative of the concessionaire (private partner) were adopted (came into force in May 2015). This significantly expanded the possibilities of implementing concession agreements in the communal utilities sector. Previously, the conclusion of concession agreements was possible only at the initiative of the Concedent (public partner) through competitive procedures.

Inclusion in July 2016 in the 115-FZ of a special Chap. 5 concerning preparation and implementation of PPP projects in water, heat, and sanitation (entered into force on January 1, 2017) was a real innovation for the PPP market. New provisions

- defined the subject of the Russian Federation in housing and utilities projects as an independent party to the greement (along with the Concedent (municipality) and an investor);
- established a ban on participation of foreign investors in such projects;
- fixed the possibility of holding a joint regional-municipal tender;
- enshrined the right to transfer concession objects of centralized water and heat supply and sanitation with unregistered property in their composition;
- introduced possibility of repayment by the concessionaire of debts of unitary enterprises;
- described in detail preparation and holding of concession tender, conclusion and amendment of the agreement in heat and water supply, sanitation, etc.

The emergence of a new Chapter in the Law had a positive impact on the application of PPP mechanisms in the communal utilities sector, improving the quality and investment volume of projects in this area. The right to take into account—when determining the size of concession fee—outstanding monetary obligations of

16, 2014 № 452, and the list of indicators of reliability, quality, energy efficiency of objects of centralized hot water supply, cold water supply, and (or) wastewater disposal and the procedure for their determination was approved by the Order of the Ministry of construction of Russia of April 4, 2014 № 162/, etc.

state/municipal enterprises made it possible to repay debts of unitary enterprises with the help of investor funds.

At the end of 2017, the Federal law № 503-FZ which clarified powers of state bodies and local governments in solid waste treatment was adopted. In accordance with the Law from January 1, 2019, urban settlements have to ensure the creation and maintenance of places of accumulation of solid municipal waste, to determine places of accumulation of such waste and to maintain a register of such places. Requirements to places (sites) of waste accumulation were established, powers of regional operators on treatment of solid municipal waste and rules of establishment of tariffs were defined (Inshakova et al. 2019).

In addition, over the past year, the legal framework for implementation of PPP projects in water, heat, and sanitation facilities has been significantly adjusted: the procedure for holding a joint regional-municipal tender was described in detail, new measures for financing communal utilities modernization projects have been provided, procedure for adopting, changing investment programs of organizations in heat and water supply, etc., has been updated.

In addition to legislative measures, steps have been taken to financially support investment projects.

Decree of the Government of the Russian Federation of December 26, 2015 № 1451 "On provision of financial support at the expense of the State Corporation—the Fund for promotion of reform of housing and communal services for modernization of municipal infrastructure systems" became the main instrument of such support. The rules approved by Decree № 1451, provided for allocation of funds for each specific project, including financial support for preparation, implementation of the project, and co-financing of the interest rate on the loan for its implementation.

In August 2017, these rules were updated by Decree of the Government of the Russian Federation of August 25, 2017 №997 "On implementation of financial support measures at the expense of the State Corporation—the Fund for the promotion of housing and communal services reform and amendments to some acts of the Government of the Russian Federation". The said Decree provides for financial support from the Fund for the purpose of co-financing the interest rate on loans, bond loans, attracted by resource supply organizations, as well as for the preparation of modernization projects.

Financial support for the modernization of municipal infrastructure systems will be provided to the subjects of the Russian Federation within the limits defined by the decision of the Prime Minister of the Russian Federation, adopted on the basis of proposals of the Ministry of construction of Russia, agreed with the Ministry of economic development of the Russian Federation.

To receive financial support in the subject of the Federation, a "road map" for development of housing and communal services in the region, the procedure for selecting potential modernization projects, the procedure for co-financing the interest rate, including the obligation of the subject of the Federation to conclude an agreement with a resource supply or credit institution on co-financing the interest rate, must be approved.

Table 13.2 Investment support of the Fund of Housing and Communal utilities

Provision of financial support at the expense of Housing and Communal utilities Fund for promotion of reform of housing and communal services				
74 applications (from 32 subjects of the Russian Federation) are registered	Total amount of applications—8726.99 million rubles			
51 application approved by the Board of the Fund (23 applications in heat supply, 23 applications in water supply and sanitation, 5 applications in solid waste treatment	Total amount of approved funds—5669.00 million rubles			
		Project development (RUB million)	Project implementation (RUB million)	Subsidy of interest rate (RUB million)
	2016	16,18	1180,68	122,17
	2017	8,59	4341,37	0
	Total	24,77	5522,06	122,17

Source Ministry of Construction and Communal Utilities of the Russian Federation

Financial support will be provided in accordance with the requests of the regions received by the Fund on the basis of an agreement between the subject of the Federation, the Ministry of Construction, and the Fund.

The agreement should include the indicator of the effectiveness of the use of financial support. It is defined as the ratio of the amount of funds raised by the subject of the Federation under concession agreements to the amount of financial support. This ratio should be more than 10 to 1. If this condition is not met, the subject of the Federation will be obliged to return the funds of financial support in proportion to the failure to meet the target (Table 13.2).

In 2018, the President of the Russian Federation in the "May Decree" outlined national goals and set strategic objectives for the development of the Russian Federation for the period up to 2024 (presidential Decree of May 7, 2018 N 204 "On national goals and strategic objectives of the Russian Federation for the period up to 2024", GARANT 2018). In pursuance of the May Decree, 12 national projects and the Comprehensive Plan of modernization and development of core infrastructure were approved. The national project "Ecology" consists of several Federal projects, including

- The Federal project "Improvement of the Volga river", which provides for construction, reconstruction (modernization) of treatment facilities. 129.7 billion rubles are allocated by budget mechanisms, 31.7 billion rubles is planned to attract from off-budget sources.
- The Federal project "Clean water" is a part of the state program of the Russian Federation "Providing affordable and comfortable housing and public services to citizens of the Russian Federation" and provides for the construction, reconstruction (modernization) of drinking water supply facilities. 146,7 billion rubles are

allocated by budget mechanisms, 85.5 billion rubles is planned to attract from off-budget sources.

Of course, not all the problems of infrastructure activities in the communal utilities sector have been resolved. There is a certain set of issues that are increasingly being addressed when discussing various aspects of improving the legal framework in this area (Draft National report on attracting private investment in infrastructure development and the use of public-private partnership mechanisms in the Russian Federation 2018). First of all, we are talking about finding legal tools to resolve the issue of consolidation of concessions in various settlements, expanding possible ways and forms of transfer of heat and water supply facilities to private investors, finding new mechanisms of financial support for the modernization of housing and communal services, etc. (Inshakova et al. 2017).

Since housing and communal services remain one of the most important and socially significant areas, interest in optimizing PPP regulation will not run out in the coming years.

PPP in Communal Utilities

Thanks to the establishment of conditions for attracting private investment, public-private partnership in the communal utilities sector in terms of the number of annually concluded agreements experienced a period of rapid development, reaching a peak by 2016. Over the following years, the number of projects implemented reduced. (Simply and honestly about investments in infrastructure and PPP in Russia. Analytical review 2019) (Table 13.3).

The atypical increase in the number of projects was due to changes in legislation. According to the Federal law of July 27, 2010 N 190-FZ “About heat supply” and the Federal law of December 7, 2011 N 416-FZ “About water supply and water disposal” since January 1, 2015 the rights of possession and use of the objects which are in municipal property are transferred only under concession agreements providing creation or reconstruction of property.

In fact, these changes affected only noncapital-intensive projects. Therefore, despite the increase in the number of PPP projects, there was no proportional increase in investment volumes. According to experts, by 2018 the effect of these factors was completely exhausted, and the market will continue to develop without sharp fluctuations.

Table 13.3 Dynamics of number and volume of investment of PPP projects in communal services

	2014	2015	2016	2017	2018	Total
Number of PPP projects	244	477	1111	471	240	2890
Volume of investment (RUB billion)	35,3	78,6	89,3	68,9	77,1	601,3

Source data of The National PPP Center

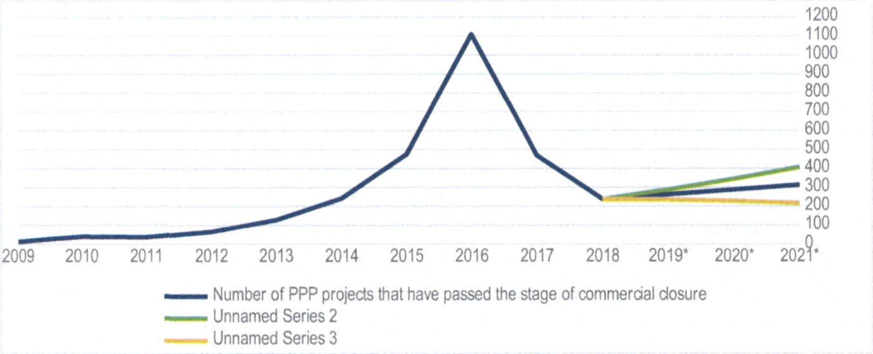

*** Forecast. Basic scenario**. **Optimistic scenario. Pessimistic scenario.**
Source: data, calculations of the National PPP Center

As of April 1, 2019, 2731 projects were being implemented in the communal utilities sector with a total investment of more than 590 billion rubles (of which 560 billion rubles are concessionaire finance).

Similar trends are observed in the heat, water, and wastewater sectors.

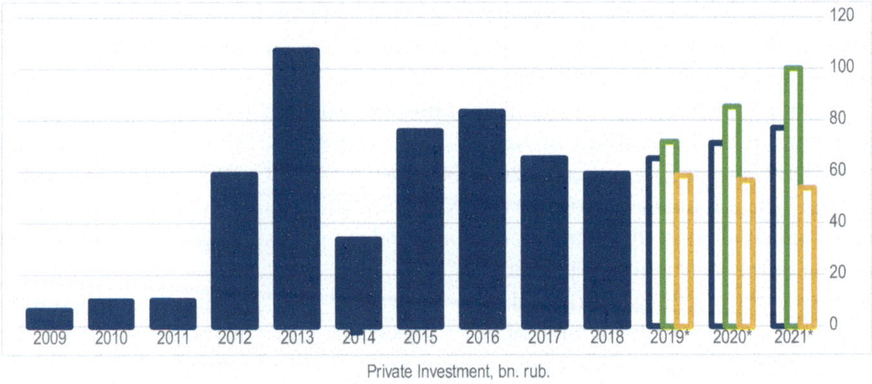

*** Forecast. Basic scenario**. **Optimistic scenario. Pessimistic scenario.**
Source: data, calculations of the National PPP Center

Heat supply

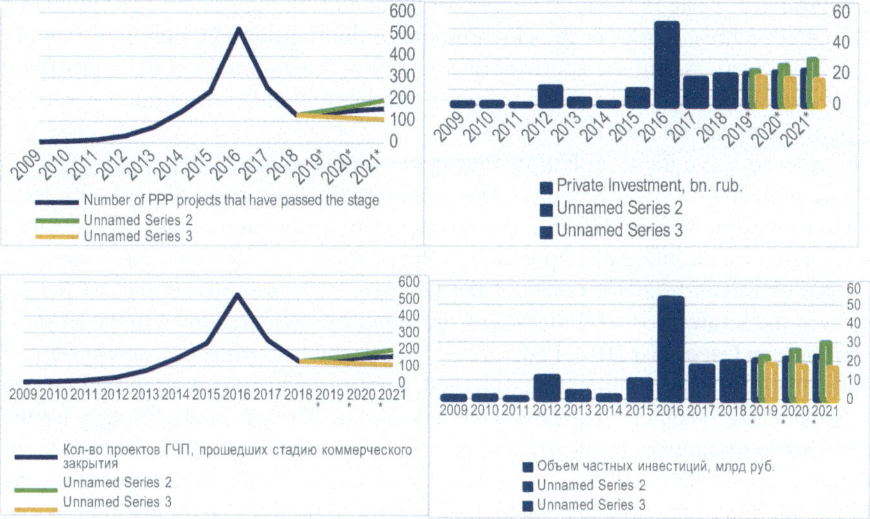

*** Forecast. Basic scenario**. **Optimistic scenario. Pessimistic scenario.**
Source: data, calculations of the National PPP Center

Water and Sanitation

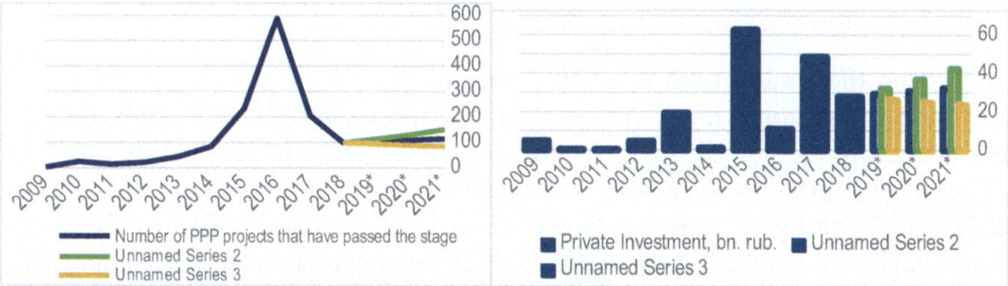

*** Forecast. Basic scenario**. **Optimistic scenario. Pessimistic scenario.**
Source: data, calculations of the National PPP Center

The situation is somewhat different in solid waste treatment. According to official data, in Russia every year the city with a population of about 1 million people throws into the surrounding environment up to 400 thousand tons of solid waste, which corresponds to about 350–400 kg of annual solid waste per capita in the country (Kosolapov 2014). At the same time, the share of municipal solid waste transferred for processing in the total volume of the produced waste is still extremely low and was about 7.5% in 2014, 7.8% in 2015, and 8.9% in 2016. Thus, according to the

Ministry of Natural Resources and Ecology of the Russian Federation, the share of the neutralized waste in the total volume of waste during the past 5 years fluctuated within 46.9–59.6% (Order of the Government of the Russian Federation of January 25, 2018 N 84-p "About the approval of Strategy of development of the industry on processing, utilization and neutralization of production and consumption waste for the period until 2030", 2018).

In order to solve these problems, President of the Russian Federation by Decree of March 29, 2011 № PR-781 ordered the regions to ensure preparation of long-term targeted investment programs for the treatment of solid municipal and industrial waste, based on an integrated approach to the process of collection and disposal of all types of waste. In 2013, Order of the Ministry of Natural Resources of Russia approved the Strategy of solid municipal (household) waste treatment in the Russian Federation. In December 2014, Federal law № 458 which established a new system of solid municipal waste treatment was adopted. Russia seriously took up the solution to the "solid waste" problem. The government decree in 2018 adopted a Strategy for the development of industry for the treatment, utilization, and disposal of solid waste for the period up to 2030. The document noted that sources of financial support for the implementation of the Strategy can include borrowed funds of credit institutions and private investors finance, including in the framework of public-private partnership.

Conditionally "waste reform" can be divided into several stages:

- preparation of territorial schemes of waste treatment in each region of the country;
- selection of regional operators[2] responsible for the entire waste treatment cycle;
- installation of a unified regional tariff for waste treatment services;
- creation of modern high-tech waste disposal complexes in the regions;
- introduction of separate waste collection in the regions.

However, the "waste reform" stalled due to the lack of preparedness for such changes at the regional level. Amendments to the legislation repeatedly delayed the transition to the new system. Nevertheless, the legislation defined that no later than January 1, 2019 in all regions of the Russian Federation regional operators of solid waste should start working. However, the Federal law of 2018 established a transitional period for those regions in which regional operators were not determined subject to all legally established procedures—until 2020, and for regions that are cities of Federal importance—until 2022. As of May 2019, out of 85 subjects of the Russian Federation, only 65 subjects selected regional operators, 5 subjects of the Russian Federation did not even announce the election of regional operators (Regional operators of solid waste treatment 2019).

[2]Regional operators are organizations responsible for the entire technological chain of waste treatment from the container site to the landfill.

At the same time, a positive trend of qualitative changes in legislation in this area, which increases the investment attractiveness of such projects for investors should also be noted. Since January 1, 2018, Federal law No. 503-FZ came into force. Among the key innovations defined by the Law are the following:

- The content and procedure for approval of territorial schemes have been clarified, which will make the obligations of public partners (Concedents) on PPP projects more transparent, and for private partners (concessionaires) it will become an additional guarantee of return on investment (through the forecast tariff). Territorial schemes should undergo a procedure of public discussion, which should improve the quality of their preparation;
- The procedure for the adoption of regional programs and priority directions of the collected funds from the payment of the environmental fee have been clarified. Now the funds from the environmental collection are prioritized for the implementation of recycling standards and the renewal of treatment facilities, waste disposal;
- Some aspects of the regulation of waste treatment activities of operators have been changed. In particular, it is provided that the status of a regional operator shall be granted for a period not exceeding 10 years.

In November 2018, the powers on solid waste treatment were transferred from the Ministry of Construction to the Ministry of Natural Resources of the Russian Federation. In January 2019, the company "Russian environmental operator (REO)" was created by the decree of the President of Russia. The main task of the company is to coordinate the reform of solid waste treatment, to carry out necessary expertise and to monitor territorial schemes of waste treatment, including by involvement of leading scientific institutions. The company will formulate proposals to change the legislation, develop projects of Federal state programs to support investments, issue bonds, buy land, enterprises, equipment, and acquire equity of other companies. REO will also form a database of best projects in the sector, develop and promote new technologies. 240 million rubles were allocated for the organization of the company's activities and the start of work (Alexey Gordeev held the first meeting of the Supervisory Board of the Russian environmental operator 2019).

Solid waste treatment

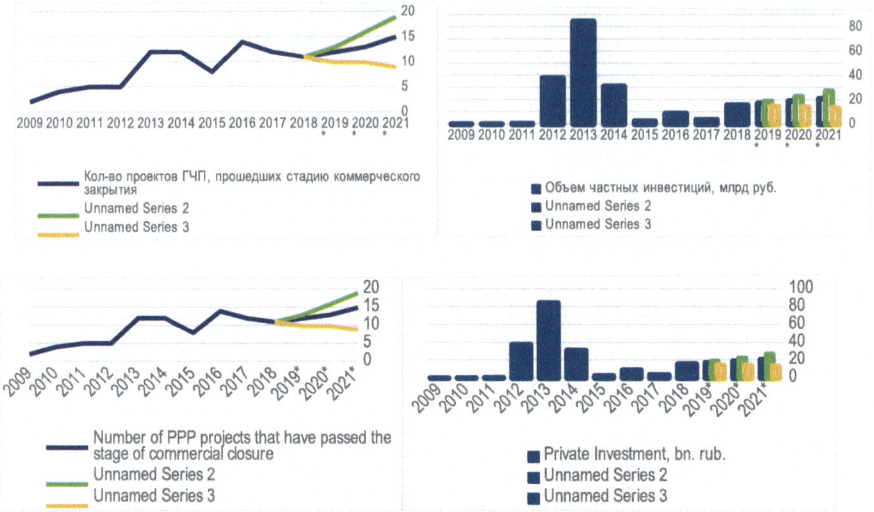

* **Forecast. Basic scenario**. Optimistic scenario. Pessimistic scenario.
Source: data, calculations of the National PPP Center

Table 13.4 Accident reduction (2012–2016)

	2012	2013	2014	2015	2016
Number of accidents (water supply)	142893	109114	106913	86709	74412
Number of accidents (heat supply)	9397	8082	6782	5794	5738

Source Ministry of construction and communal utilities of the Russian Federation

Involvement of the private sector in communal services has already borne fruit: from 2012 to 2016, the accident rate at heat supply facilities decreased by more than 1.5 times, at water supply facilities—by almost 2 times (Table 13.4).

Specific Features of PPP Projects in Communal Services

Today, taking into account the accumulated experience, the best tool for the application of PPP in communal services is the transfer of public infrastructure facilities to private operators under concession agreements. The existing regulatory and institutional framework ensures a balance of interests of all parties of public-private partnership—the state, the private sector and end-users (Recommendations for the implementation of public-private partnership projects. Best practices/Ministry of economic development 2016).

The use of concession mechanism in the communal sector has a number of specific features, which include the following:

- *no obligation to establish a concession fee*

The amount of such fee may not exceed the level calculated on the basis of the principle of reimbursement to the Concedent of the costs of mandatory payments related to the right of ownership of the object of the concession agreement.

- *criteria of the contest*

The preferred bidder is the participant who offered a minimal amount of discounted revenue. If the value of discounted revenue of the two best contestants differs by less than 2%, the participant who offered the highest number of the best planned indicators of the activities of the concessionaire is declared the winner.

- *Harmonization of long-term regulatory parameters and targets for quality, reliability and energy efficiency*

Heat supply, water supply, and sanitation are the areas of public utilities, the prices in which are regulated by the state, and until 2016 the legislation provided for a gradual transition to long-term regulation of all tariffs in these areas. Pursuant to the principle of transition to long-term regulation, the Federal law "On concession agreements" was amended in July 2014. According to amendments only long-term tariffs using long-term parameters of concessionaire's activities can be set, and long-term parameters are essential conditions of concession agreements. If the tariff is not based on the long-term parameters of the concessionaire's activities included in concession agreement, the Concedent is obliged to compensate the concessionaire lost revenue (Tuktarov and Dubinchina 2016).

- *Obligatory participation of the subject of the Russian Federation as an independent party in municipal concessions related to heat supply facilities, centralized hot water supply systems, cold water supply and (or) water disposal, individual objects of such systems if the authority for state regulation of tariffs in the relevant area is not transferred to the municipality.*
- *Possibility of transfer to concession of property, part of which was not registered in accordance with the established procedure. In addition, in accordance with the law on concession agreements, the transfer of municipal infrastructure objects to the concession can be carried out in one of three ways:*
- as a result of a tender;
- on a noncompetitive basis through private initiatives;
- on a noncompetitive basis through the transformation of the existing lease agreement of municipal infrastructure.

Standardization of PPP Projects Implementation Practices in Communal Services

On August 18, 2017, the Ministry of Construction of Russia published a standard form of concession agreement for modernization of municipal infrastructure, developed jointly with Sberbank of Russia (*Recommended form of concession agreement for a Standard industry decision in heat supply 2017*). The so-called "package approach" can now be used by regions and investors to prepare, finance, and support regional and municipal public-private partnership projects. To date, 41 regions of Russia have prepared proposals on concluding concession agreements using "package approach".

A set of document templates for preparation, maintenance, and financing of concession projects in the housing and communal utilities sector has become available to the regions.

"Package approach" suggests that if the concession is developed according to the proposed form, the Bank can provide project financing up to 15 years at 11–14% per annum. The rights under the concession agreement can be a collateral. The parameters specified in the form can be adjusted depending on region, investor, and object of the concession agreement. The concession agreement itself already includes a step-in agreement, where the Bank acts as a fourth party.

For the project to become bankable, it is necessary to fix in the concession agreement the long-term parameters of regulation, as well as to describe in detail the procedure for payment and calculation of the amount of compensation for early termination. This provision allows banks to be confident in the security of the loan.

The first agreement with the use of this form was signed in relation to the reconstruction of heat supply systems in Yasnogorsk, Tula region in June 2017 between the Government of the Tula region, PJSC "Sberbank" and CJSC "Regional generating company № 1". The total cost of the project in Yasnogorsk is 453.05 million rubles. Under the concession agreement, it is planned to re-equip 5 boilers in the amount of 175.3 million rubles and reconstruct heating networks of 277.8 million rubles. "CJSC Regional Generating Company No.1" is a project company created especially for investment in projects of modernization and development of generating and network infrastructure of heat and power supply in the territory of the Russian Federation.

Cases of PPP Projects in Communal Utilities

Most of the municipal concessions (92% of total investment and 85% of total project number) belong to the communal utilities sector. Such projects are traditionally small in volume: 130 municipal projects in communal services belong to the segment from 100 million rubles to 1 billion rubles, and only 34 remaining ones are more than 1 billion rubles. However, municipal-level agreements can also be capital-intensive—for example, a concession for water supply and sanitation in Volgograd, which in volume (58 billion rubles) exceeds even the largest concessions at the regional level.

In 2015, JSC "Water supply concessions" in Volgograd began work on the replacement of dilapidated and in-emergency-condition pipelines of the city water utilities. According to Volgograd city administration estimates, wear of urban water supply networks exceeded 75%, water losses reached 100 million tons per year, which is 50% of the total volume of water pumped from the Volga River. The concessionaire has developed a 2-year program that will dramatically reduce these losses and significantly reduce the degree of wear of water supply networks.

Under the terms of the agreement, the investor must invest 7.1 billion rubles in networks and public infrastructure facilities within 2.5 years. In total, for the 30-year period of the concession, the company undertakes to invest 58 billion rubles in the modernization of the city's water and sanitation facilities.

Another landmark project for the entire communal utilities sector is the concession agreement between the Arkhangelsk region and "RVC-Center" Co., which provides for a comprehensive modernization of water supply and sanitation system of the capital of the region. The agreement was signed in autumn 2018 for 49 years.

Under the term of the agreement, total investment in construction and reconstruction of water supply and sanitation facilities in Arkhangelsk will amount to 12.8 billion rubles. Concessionaire takes over 85% of the debt of municipal enterprise "Vodokanal", which is about 1.2 billion rubles. The priorities include work on the construction of the second and third stage of the ring water pipeline as well as reconstruction of the main water pipe with a diameter of 1000 mm. This will significantly improve the current situation in public services.

Concession agreement fixed key targets for water quality, continuity, reduction of accidents. It is planned that by 2022 the number of accidents on water supply and sanitation networks will be reduced 3 times. The proportion of wastewater that does not meet requirements will be reduced fourfold. Drinking water losses will be reduced from 52.3% to 12%. In the meantime, more than half of the water literally "goes into the sand" because of pipes wear and high accident rate.

One more example—the project of construction of an integrated inter-municipal landfill for placement, disposal and treatment of solid municipal waste for cities of the Khanty-Mansi Autonomous district-Yugra—is of interest from the point of view of its financial model. It is a concession agreement for 22 years, which was concluded in 2017. Private partner is JSC "KhMAO resource saving", which assumes to invest in the project at least 875 million rubles.

As part of the project, the concessionaire will create

- two landfills for solid municipal waste treatment located on plots of 16.2 and 21.5 hectares;
- waste sorting complex with a capacity of 100 000 tons per year.

The specifics of the project is the use of the mechanism of the minimal guaranteed income (MGI). In case of discrepancy between the actual gross revenue and the MGI, the Concedent shall pay each year a compensation payment to the concessionaire.

In other words, under the terms of concession agreement the Concedent guarantees the amount of gross revenue received by the concessionaire. MGI is calculated on the basis of concessionaire's estimated tariff for the relevant year in accordance with the terms of concession agreement and the difference between the projected capacity of the facility (in percent) and the volume of underutilization of the capacity of the facility.

Conclusions

- Implementation of PPP projects in communal utilities sector has a number of specific features, primarily associated with the application of tariff regulation and the need to find a balance of interests between all parties of public-private partnership—the state, the private sector, and users.
- Key problems facing the sector in Russia include problems of inefficient management, especially in the regions, use of outdated technologies, and lack of funding.
- To overcome these problems, measures to improve both special legislation on PPP and sectoral legislation in heat supply, water supply, sanitation are taken. They include
    - procedures of transfer into the concession of objects of heating, water, and wastewater are specified;
    - the subject of the Russian Federation is defined as an additional party to concession agreements of municipal level;
    - under concession agreements repayment of debts of unitary enterprises by incorporating their outstanding monetary obligations into concession fee became possible;
    - possibility of private concession initiatives (unsolicited proposals) is fixed in legislation;
    - transition to long-term regulation of tariffs in heat supply, water supply, and sanitation has been carried out, the Concedent's obligation to ensure tariff setting on the basis of these long-term obligations has been established;
- Along with the adopted legal and regulation acts, additional legislative initiatives aimed at development and improvement of this sphere are under consideration. In particular, a bill limiting the creation of state and municipal unitary enterprises in order to reduce cases of bankruptcy of these organizations is being considered.
- Financial support mechanisms, including different types of funds, etc., are developed.
- The Russian Federation is implementing a large-scale reform to create a system of solid municipal waste treatment. Despite the existing lag behind the originally set deadlines, the reform is being implemented consistently. In order to implement the tasks of creating a solid waste treatment system relative legislation is also

being improved, establishing transparent rules, which positively affect the PPP market and help to attract investors.

- PPP in the communal utilities sector is one of the largest segments of the Russian PPP market in terms of both the number of projects and investment volume. A large part of municipal concessions are projects of municipalities (92% of investment and 85% by number). Such projects are traditionally small in volume: 130 municipal projects in housing and communal services belong to the segment from 100 million rubles to 1 billion rubles, and only 34 remaining ones are more expensive than 1 billion rubles. However, municipal-level agreements can also be capital-intensive—for example, a concession for water supply and sanitation in Volgograd in volume (58 billion rubles) exceeds the largest concessions at the regional level and is one of the largest in Europe.

References

Aleksej Gordeev provyol pervoe zasedanie Nablyudatel'nogo soveta « Rossijskogo ekologicheskogo operatora » (Alexey Gordeyev held the first meeting of the Supervisory Board of the Russian Ecological Operator (2019)). http://government.ru/news/36511/. Retrieved June 7, 2019.

Approaches to Private Participation in Water Services. A Toolkit. (2006). The World Bank.

Agnessa O. Inshakova, Alexander I. Goncharov, Maxim V. Sevostyanov. (2017). Institutional ambiguity of regulation of possessory relations in modern Russia. In *Overcoming Uncertainty of Institutional Environment as a Tool of Global Crisis Management* (Vol. 1, pp. 207–212).

Agnessa O. Inshakova, Alexander I. Goncharov, Elena I. Inshakova. (2019). Innovative technologies of oil production: tasks of legal regulation of management and taxation. In Oleg, V., Inshakov Agnessa O. Inshakova, Elena G. Popkova (Eds.), *Energy Sector: A Systemic Analysis of Economy, Foreign Trade and Legal Regulations* (p. 79–94). Cham: Springer Science + Business Media.

Draft national report on attracting private investment in infrastructure development and application of Public-Private Partnership mechanisms in the Russian Federation. (2018). PPP Development Center, Moscow. http://pppcenter.ru/assets/docs/22032019reiting.pdf. Retrieved March 10, 2019.

Infrastructure to 2030 (Volume 2): Mapping Policy for Electricity, Water and Transport. (2007). In *International Futures Programme, OECD.* https://www.oecd.org/futures/infrastructureto2030/infrastructureto2030volume2mappingpolicyforelectricitywaterandtransport.htm. Retrieved March 10, 2019.

Koncessionnye soglasheniya v kommunal'noj sfere: aktual'naya statistika, izmenenie koncessionnogo zakonodatel'stva i sovershenstvovanie regulirovaniya. (2016). (Concession agreements in the housing and utilities sector: current statistics, changes in concession legislation and legislation improvement (2016)). PPP Development Center, RE Legal. http://pppcenter.ru/assets/docs/re-legal_booklet-kontsessii_v_jkh_24-10-2016.pdf. Retrieved March 10, 2019.

Kosolapov, N. A. (2014). Statistika TBO v Rossii (Household Waste data in Russia (2014)). In *Nauchno-Metodicheskij Elektronnyj ZHurnal "Koncept" (Scientific Oline Journal "Koncept")* (Vol. 26, pp. 562–563).

Mekhanizmy gosudarstvenno-chastnogo partnyorstva v ekonomicheskoi politike Rossii (Mechanisms of public-private partnership in the economic policy of Russia). (2018). In Ivanov, O. V. (Ed.) (p. 409). Moscow: MGIMO-University.

Rasporyazhenie Pravitel'stva RF ot 25.01.2018 N 84-r "Ob utverzhdenii Strategii razvitiya promyshlennosti po obrabotke, utilizacii i obezvrezhivaniyu othodov proizvodstva i potrebleniya na period do 2030 goda". (2018). ("About the approval of the Development Strategy of industrial and household till 2030 waste neutralization" (2018)) The Russian Federation Government Resolution of January 21, 2018 N 84-p. http://www.consultant.ru/document/cons_doc_LAW_289114/. Retrieved June 7, 2019.

Regional'nye operatory po obrashcheniyu s TKO. (2019). (Regional household waste handling operators (2019)). https://investinfra.ru/regionalnye-operatory/. Retrieved June 7, 2019.

Rekomendacii po realizacii proektov gosudarstvenno-chastnogo partnerstva. Luchshie praktiki. (2016). Ministerstvo ekonomicheskogo razvitiya Rossijskoj Federacii (Recommendations for the public-private partnership projects implementation. Best practices (2016). Ministry of Economic Development of the Russian Federation). http://economy.gov.ru/minec/activity/sections/privgovpartnerdev/support/20160829. Retrieved March 10, 2019.

Rekomenduemaya forma koncessionnogo soglasheniya dlya Standartnogo otraslevogo resheniya v teplosnabzhenii. (2017). (The recommended for of concession agreement for heat supply system (2017)). http://www.minstroyrf.ru/docs/14083/. Retrieved March 10, 2019.

Simply and honestly about investments in infrastructure and PPP in Russia. Analytical review. Rating of regions 2018–2019 (2019). ROSINFRA. PPP Development Center. http://pppcenter.ru/assets/files/obzor240419.pdf. Retrieved March 10, 2019.

Tuktarov, Yu. E., Dubinchina, S. V. (2016). Koncessionnoe soglashenie: pravovaya priroda, sfera primeneniya, poryadok zaklyucheniya i ispolneniya: Rukovodstvo dlya praktikuyushchih yuristov, gosudarstvennyh i municipal'nyh sluzhashchih (Concession agreement: legal nature, scope of application, procedure for conclusion and execution. A guide for lawyers, civil servants and local government employees). Statut, Moscow.

Ukaz Prezidenta RF ot 07.05.2018 N 204 "O nacional'nyh celyah i strategicheskih zadachah razvitiya Rossijskoj Federacii na period do 2024 goda" (s izmeneniyami i dopolneniyami) (The Russian Federation Presidential Decree of May 07, 2018 No 204 "On the national goals and strategic objectives of the development of the Russian Federation for the period till 2024" (2018)). GARANT. https://base.garant.ru/71937200/. Retrieved June 7, 2019.

Zakonoproekt: Sistema obespecheniya zakonodatel'noj deyatel'nosti (2019) №554026–7 (Administration Bill: Legislative Support System (2019). https://sozd.duma.gov.ru/bill/554026-7 Retrieved June 7, 2019.

Chapter 14
IT—New Horizons in Application of PPP Mechanisms in Russia

Maxim V. Tkachenko and Ellina A. Shamanina

Abstract Innovative information and communication technologies penetrate all spheres of public life in the modern world. IT technologies are one of the basic factors of competitiveness not only for an individual company but also for a country in the world market. At the same time, the development and implementation of digital technologies require significant financial investments, as well as professional, specialized knowledge and skills in this area. In the conditions of economic and financial instability observed in many countries of the world today, the financing of IT projects is becoming a heavy burden for the state budget. Consequently, in many countries, the role of mechanisms of public–private partnership (PPP), particularly, in the development of IT infrastructure, is growing. The inclusion of IT projects in the PPP perimeter is becoming a profitable solution for the participants of such a partnership. On the one hand, the public sector, which receives a ready-made solution with the ability to pay for it by installments, on the other hand, a business that is secured with a guaranteed return on investment. This chapter discusses the features and key areas of PPP mechanism application in IT infrastructure projects, including the infrastructure of "smart cities" in Russia. A description of some features of the legislative regulation of PPP mechanisms in the IT sector of the Russian Federation, as well as typical models for the implementation of such projects with the latest legislative changes, is presented.

Keywords Public–private partnerships · Information and communication technologies · Digital economy · "Smart cities" infrastructure · The russian federation · PPP regulatory framework · Private investment

---

M. V. Tkachenko (✉)
Executive Director of the National PPP Center, Potapovskaya Roshcha str. 7, building 1, 119454 Moscow, Russia
e-mail: tkachenkomv.mos@gmail.com

E. A. Shamanina
MGIMO University, Vernadsky Ave., 76, 119454 Moscow, Russia
e-mail: erina008@mail.ru

O. V. Ivanov and A. O. Inshakova (eds.), *Public-Private Partnerships in Russia*, Competitive Government: Public Private Partnerships,
https://doi.org/10.1007/978-3-030-56352-3_14

JEL-Codes H54 · K11 · O33 · O34

Starting from the end of the twentieth century, the global economy is undergoing a massive transformation caused by the process of the information revolution, accompanied by the implementation of information technologies into the economy.

The development of such a trend indicates the formation of a new model of economic development, a model of so-called digital economy, the production factor of which is data in digital form (Chinaeva 2018; Drath and Horch 2014).

For the first time, this term, like the very concept of the digital economy, appeared in the paper of D. Tappscott, Doctor of Law, Professor of Management at the University of Toronto "The Digital Economy: Promise and Peril In The Age of Networked Intelligence." The author highlights the emergence of new business models and the strengthening of the relationship between people and organizations due to access to the information space of the Internet and the absence of intermediaries due to the establishment of direct contacts between producers and consumers (Tappscott 1996).

Currently, there is no unified generally accepted approach to the definition of "digital economy." However, summarizing the definitions provided by international organizations and consulting companies such as Deloitte (Cassar et al. 2017), McKinsey & Company, IMF (Measuring the Digital Economy, IMF 2018), and OECD (Gestrin and Staudt 2018), one may think of the digital economy as the "part of the socio-economic relations associated with the production, exchange, distribution, and consumption of information technologies" (Basaev 2018).

In accordance with the national program "Digital Economy of the Russian Federation" drawn up by the Ministry of Communications and Mass Media of the Russian Federation and adopted in 2017, the digital economy in Russia is represented by *three levels*:

- markets and industries (fields of activity), where the interaction of specific subjects (suppliers and consumers of products, works, and services) is carried out;
- platforms and technologies, where competencies for the development of markets and sectors of the economy (fields of activity) are formed; and
- environment that creates conditions for the development of platforms and technologies, as well as effective interaction of market entities and sectors of the economy (fields of activity) and covers regulations, information infrastructure, personnel, and information security.

Along with such key objectives of the above program are as follows:

- increasing competitiveness of the Russian economy in the global market; creating an ecosystem of the country's digital economy, in which data in digital form is a key factor of production in all spheres of social and economic activity, where effective interaction, including cross-border one, between business, scientific and educational community, the state and citizens is ensured;

  the *need to create sufficient infrastructural conditions* for the creation and (or) development of high-tech businesses or inadmissibility of the emergence of new

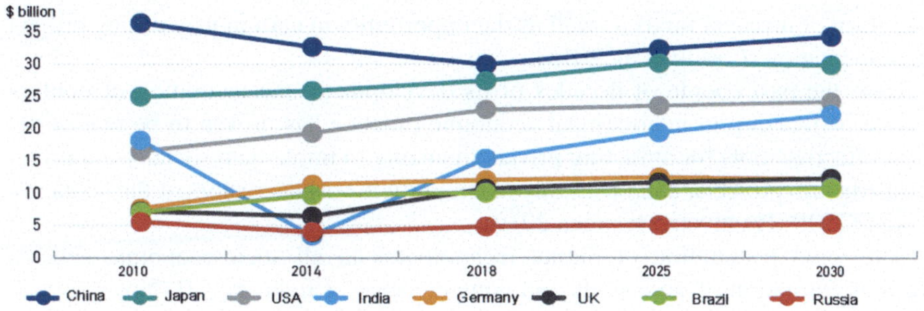

Chart 14.1 Dynamics of IT infrastructure investments by country (2010–2030, $billions) (Reproduced from ROSINFRA (2019), PPP Development Center, Moscow. http://pppcenter.ru/assets/files/obzor240419.pdf)

obstacles and restrictions both in traditional sectors of the economy and in new industries and high-tech markets is outlined (National Program "Digital Economy of the Russian Federation", 2019).

The widespread introduction of the latest information and communication technologies in all spheres of public life, including the activities of a number of individual companies, is becoming one of the main factors of competitiveness of both firms and the state as a whole (Kolodnyaya 2018; Kozhevina 2018). However, typically, the costs of creating and implementing IT technologies are high (Chart 14.1).

Today, Russia is lagging behind the leading world economies in terms of digitalization, which is vividly demonstrated by the positions it holds in international rankings. Particularly, according to the ICT Development Index (IDI 2017 Rank. ICT Development Index, 2017) for 2017, Russia ranks 45th, and in the IMD World Digital Competitiveness Index (IMD World Digital Competitiveness Index 2018) for 2018 the country ranked 40th. Such low positions of Russia are explained by the minor amount of IT infrastructure financing.

For example, in 2018, Russia's investments in this area amounted to $5 billion, while, for example, in the United States for the same period of time, financing was at around $24 billion and in China, the IT infrastructure costs for the same period of time amounted to $30 billion.

Accordingly, the uncovered prospective need for investment in the infrastructure of the information and communications sector in Russia for 2024 is 2 trillion rubles. At the same time, the total cost of the National Program for the Digitalization of Russia for the period 2018–2024 accounts for 1.634 trillion rubles (National Program "Digital Economy of the Russian Federation", 2019).

In this regard, as well as due to the unstable global economic environment, government financing of large-scale and costly fields becomes problematic and even burdensome, which conditions the need in search for alternative methods and models for financing and managing such projects. In such conditions, public–private partnerships become an attractive tool both for the state, which, when receiving a ready-made solution, reduces the budget burden and for the private sector, which guaranteed the return of invested funds as well as the opportunity to earn money during project implementation (Caselli et al. 2015).

Over the past couple of decades of its development, the institution of public–private partnership in international economic practice has proven to be one of the most effective tools for attracting private financing to implement socially important infrastructure projects, demonstrating its viability in various sectors of the economy (Ivanov 2019; Ivanov and Ivanova 2019).

The rapid penetration of digital technologies in all socio-economic spheres requires formation of new skills and competencies in Industry 4.0 (Nosova et al. 2019). No doubt, the change of technological structures affects the development of the institution of public–private partnership as well. The digital economy is putting forward to the institute of public–private partnership new requirements for the development of the intellectual, scientific, and technological activity (Gromova 2018). The creation of sufficient infrastructural conditions mentioned in the National Program "Digital Economy of the Russian Federation" for the development, implementation, and commercialization of digital technologies is conditioned not only by the need to find additional sources of investment but also the need to attract innovative management potential.

The public–private partnership, which, according to international practice, has proven to be an effective mechanism for creating the infrastructure of the digital economy, is becoming the ideal tool for solving the tasks set (Sulejmanov 2017). In Russia, the aforementioned program on the digital economy recognizes the public–private partnership as one of the basic tools for attracting alternative sources of financing for implementing the main fields of the program, as well as for structuring new projects in the sphere of information technologies and communications emerging in the market (Inshakova et al. 2017).

Thus, it is assumed that the use of PPP mechanisms in creating the IT infrastructure of the digital economy will provide an opportunity to attract both the required funds and technologies, which will undoubtedly have a positive socio-economic effect. At the same time, the use of PPP tools in the IT sphere will allow to increase efficiency of state information systems (SIS), which amount to about 1,000 in Russia today.

PPP in IT: Regulation and New Prospects

The adoption of the Federal Law No.173-FZ dated 29.06.2018 "On Amendments to Certain Legislative Acts of the Russian Federation" contributed to the active development of public–private partnerships in the field of information technologies in Russia, which significantly expanded the boundaries of PPP tools.

The law makes significant changes to the Federal Law No. 224-FZ dated 13.07.2015 "On Public-Private Partnership, Municipal-Private Partnership in the Russian Federation" and to the Federal Law No.115-FZ dated 21.07.2005 "On

Table 14.1 IT infrastructure facilities, in respect of which the conclusion of concession agreements and PPP/MPP agreements is possible (PPP experience of creating the "Smart Cities" infrastructure: overview (2018). National PPP Center, Moscow. http://pppcenter.ru/assets/files/10122018.pdf.)

Objects of information technologies (IT objects) (First group)	Technical means of support of IT object functioning (Second group)	Data processing centers (Third group)
• Computer software; • Databases; • Information systems (including public ones); • Websites on the Internet or in other networks (which include computer software, databases); • A set of the specified objects	• IT objects; • Property technologically related to IT objects, intended to secure their functioning or to implement other activities	*A set of:* • Buildings; • Parts of buildings; premises – Combined by common purpose with movable property technologically related to IT objects; – And intended for: • Process automation information processing (using computer software and databases); • Providing access to information; • Presentation and distribution of information

Concession Agreements." The main innovation proposed by the law is the inclusion of IT infrastructure objects in the lists of objects of concession agreements and PPP/MPP agreements (Table 14.1).

At the same time, prior to the amendment, the conclusion of relevant agreements with respect to IT infrastructure objects was burdened by the binding to real estate items or real estate items and technologically related movable property, which significantly affected the investment attractiveness of such projects.

Currently, IT infrastructure objects, in respect of which the conclusion of concession agreements and PPP/MPP agreements is possible, are divided into three general groups.

Thus, the conclusion of concession agreements and PPP/MPP agreements is possible with respect to the following types of property:

- *exclusively, intellectual activity outcomes (intellectual rights),* to which intellectual rights are recognized, which include the exclusive right being a property right, as well as personal non-property rights (first group);
- *intellectual activity outcomes (intellectual rights) and movable property items* (second group)*; and*
- *real estate items and movable property items* (third group).

At the same time, the project perimeter may include objects both individually and in their entirety. The legislation allows implementing not only the so-called "informational" projects but also launching projects with a mixed object. For example, a project may include the creation of and/or upgrading an object of education, health care (preschool institutions, schools, hospitals, laboratories) along with the creation of training, research, or other information systems, information banks, i.e., associated IT infrastructure (Belousova et al. 2018).

Taking into account the legal nature of information technology objects and intellectual property outcomes (IPO) as a part of technical means, the conclusion of concession agreements or PPP/MPP agreements in respect of IPO leads to the need to distribute the arising property rights, the exclusive rights.

The exclusive right is a kind of "analog" of the right of ownership, the holder of which may use IPO at its discretion, in a manner not contrary to the law, including alienating or granting the right to use (license) to third parties. The right to use gives the holder the opportunity to use intellectual activity outcomes (information technology object) within the limits established by the agreement (Table 14.2).

Thus, the Law 173-FZ not only added IT objects to the lists of objects of concession agreements and PPP/MPP agreements, having regulated the procedure for their involvement in a sectoral project, but also described in detail the features of regulation of relations arising from the implementation of such projects, which has significantly reduced the likelihood of additional risks for the public and private parties of the project.

Amendments made by the Law 173-FZ have become a tremendous step not only toward the development of domestic legislation in the field of regulation of mechanisms of public–private partnership but also actually allowed forming a new market for sales of PPP projects—the IT market—due to the addition of such IT objects to the list of allowable objects of concession agreements and PPP/MPP agreements. It is predicted that making such amendments will not only increase the number of concession agreements and PPP agreements but also increase the quality of projects implemented (Zusman and Shcheglov 2018).

PPP Projects in the Field of Information Technologies in the Russian Federation

Despite the fact that, until recently, IT facilities were not included in the list of objects, in respect of which the conclusion of concession agreements was not possible in accordance with Federal Law No.115-FZ dated 21.07.2005 "On Concession Agreements" and PPP agreements in accordance with Federal Law No.224-FZ dated 13.07.2015 "On Public-Private Partnership, Municipal-Private Partnership in the Russian Federation and Amendments to Certain Legislative Acts of the Russian Federation," it did not mean that there had been no projects under PPP agreement, as well as projects within the framework of concession agreements in the IT field.

PPP projects in the field of IT infrastructure were being implemented and are being implemented at present. Except for the fact that the conclusion of such agreements before the adoption of 173-FZ "On Amendments..." was possible only in respect of real estate items or real estate items and technologically related movable property.

Table 14.2 Distribution of rights to IT and intellectual property outcomes (IPO) objects as a part of technical means depending on the legal model and project conditions

Types of agreements/rights to the object of agreements	Concession agreement	PPP/MPP agreement
Exclusive right	***Acquired by the concessor*** at the time of the creation of IPO (always owned by the concessor)	*Acquired by the private partner* at the time of the creation of IPO, except for the following cases: – The PPP agreement establishes the *obligation of a private partner to alienate* an exclusive right to a public partner after a certain period, but no later than the day of termination of the PPP agreement; – *The volume of financing* by the public partner of the creation of the object *or the market value* of the exclusive rights transferred by the public partner to the private partner *exceeds in the aggregate the amount of financing the creation of the object* by the private partner
		Moreover, alienation of the exceptional right by the private partner with the written consent of the public partner is possible before the expiration of the PPP agreement
Right to use	*May be owned by the concessionaire* based on license agreements and (or) sublicense agreements, if there is an appropriate conditions in the concession agreement	*May be owned by the public partner* in the case, if in the PPP agreement establishes the obligation of the private partner to provide the public partner with the right to use after a certain period of time, but no later than the day of termination of the PPP agreement
Possibility to pledge the right	No	yes

Source PPP experience of creating the "Smart Cities" infrastructure: overview (2018). National PPP Center, Moscow. http://pppcenter.ru/assets/files/10122018.pdf

In this regard, until recently, all implemented projects were structured as industry projects (transport, housing and public utilities, health care, education, etc.) with IT systems as part of the object (other property).

As of the end of 2018, according to the analytical review of the National PPP Center and data from the ROSINFRA portal, in the field of the Russian IT infrastructure, about 80 PPP projects have already been implemented or are at the implementation stage. 20 more projects, for which it is planned to attract 24.1 billion rubles, are at the stage of tender procedures.

The leader in the number of implemented PPP projects in the IT field, as well as in terms of the volume of investments attracted in this field, is the Central Federal District of the Russian Federation. There are 41 projects being implemented with the aggregate amount of attracted private investment of 12.8 billion in the subjects of the Central District Russia (Chart 14.2).

In the sectoral context, according to Table 14.3., the leader in the number of projects is the industry of the creation of automated lighting systems for the road network. On the other hand, in terms of capital intensity, the leaders are projects for the creation and operation of an automated system for integrated road traffic safety, including a vision-based inspection system of road conditions, photo and video recordings of administrative road traffic offenses, as well as weight and dimensional monitoring of vehicles.

More than 60% of the total investment in projects of the Automated System for Integrated Road Traffic Safety (ASIRTS) falls on the federal project for the creation and operation of the Platon fee collection system designed to ensure compliance with the procedure for fee collection to compensate for road damage caused by vehicles with a gross vehicle weight of over 12 tons.

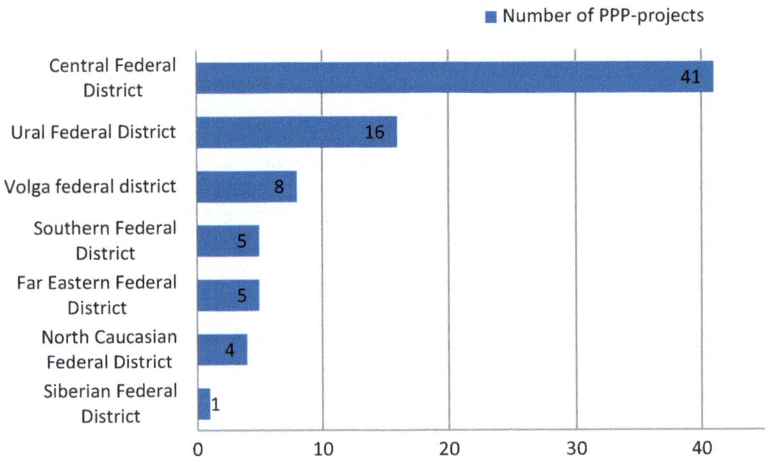

Chart 14.2 Allocation of PPP projects by Federal Districts of the Russian Federation. http://pppcenter.ru/assets/files/10122018.pdf). *Source* PPP experience of creating the "Smart Cities" infrastructure: overview (2018). National PPP Center, Moscow

Table 14.3 Implemented PPP projects in the IT sector in Russia

No.	Project implementation sectors	Number of projects	Total investment (million rubles)
1.	Automated System for Integrated Road Traffic Safety (ASIRTS) (photo and video recordings of road traffic offenses, weight and dimensional monitoring)	17 + Platon	42.8
2.	Automated lighting systems for the road network (lighting in cities and on regional roads)	39	11.67
3.	Systems of organization and operation of parking space	3	1.17
4.	Automated traffic control systems (traffic lights, monitoring systems, etc.)	3	0.663
5.	Smart public transport stops and information systems on public transport (including for collecting fees)	5	3.46

Source Tkachenko (2018) National PPP Center, Moscow

At present, the Platon project is the largest and the most expensive PPP project implemented in the Russian IT sector. The total cost of the project is estimated at 28.9 billion rubles, and at the same time, the capital costs for the creation of the object fall on a private partner. This project is being implemented in the form of a concession agreement concluded on September, 29, 2014 by the Federal Road Agency (Rosavtodor) with the special project company RT-Invest Transport Systems LLC. The total project implementation period since the signing of the Concession Agreement is 13 years.

The company RT-Invest Transport Systems LLC acts as the operator of the fee collection system, for its own and borrowed funds ensure the full cycle of creation of the Platon state system, from design to operation and upgrade of the system. All funds raised from the system go to the Road fund of the Russian Federation, from where they are then sent to build and repair roads and artificial road structures, as well as to implement PPP projects. Through fees from the Platon system, the Road fund of the Russian Federation has already received more than 73 billion rubles. Thanks to the funds allocated from the system, more than 2,000 km of roads and 30 bridges have been repaired. Of this amount, 22.9 billion rubles were allocated for the construction of roads and bridges; more than 2,000 km of roads and 30 bridges have been repaired ("Platon": The state charge system 2018).

Despite the difficulties encountered during the project implementation, the Platon system in Russia proved its reliability as a source of replenishment of the Road fund of the Russian Federation, which caused the authorities to expand the scope of the Platon system to regional and municipal roads (Hovavko 2018).

The Russian IT infrastructure is not limited to the implementation of large federal mega-projects only. PPP projects in this sphere are being implemented in other 32 regions of the Russian Federation. Smolensk region is the leading region in the number of projects (13) on creation of automated lighting systems in the framework of energy service contracts with features of PPP. (Infrastructure Projects Support Platform ROSINFRA 2019) PPP mechanisms are actively and most successfully used to create road traffic safety monitoring systems, regional navigation and information systems, automated centralized warning systems for the population, etc. Moscow, Nizhny Novgorod, and Voronezh regions show priority development in this field.

Undoubtedly, the experience of implementing IT projects using PPP mechanisms and quasi-forms of PPP in the Moscow region seems to be more interesting and diverse. For example, in education, within the framework of the investment agreement, a project to create, implement, and support the operation of a hardware and software complex of a unified information system for accounting and monitoring educational achievements of students of general education organizations, particularly, schools of Moscow region, is being implemented.

The information portal (platform) "school.mosreg.ru" created within the project has already covered 1,500 schools, 776,500 students and 56,000 teachers throughout Moscow region. Two years since the implementation of the system in 2015, more than 80% of schools in the region have abandoned paper grade book and school diaries ("Homework Diary"—Digital educational platform, 2018).

Table 14.4 reflects the main obligations of the parties to the investment agreement for the implementation of the project of the school information portal. It should be noted that the investor is not only responsible for creating and financing of the project but also obliged to ensure the further technological support of the platform.

Table 14.4 Model of interaction between the investor and the state (Dnevnik—Cifrovaya obrazovatel'naya platforma 2018 ("Homework Diary"—Digital educational platform))

Investor	Subject of the Russian Federation
• Will invest in the creation of a unified information educational platform;	• Will determine the subordinate organization responsible for the comprehensive support and development of the project;
• Will teach the work with the platform to responsible officers of the region and schools;	• Will publish methodological recommendations on the implementation and use of the platform in the region;
• Will ensure support and reliable operation of the platform for the entire duration of the investment project (at least 10 years);	• Will organize the monitoring of the active operation of the platform and contribute to the achievement of target indicators of the use of key free services of the platform;
• Will undertake to upgrade the platform in the case of the emergence of new federal requirements for the platform without costs from the regional budget during the entire term of the investment project	• Will confirm the investor's right to develop and manage the platform with the possibility of providing additional (optional) commercial services on its basis to ensure return on investment

It is worth noting that every year, each region of the Russian Federation spends 3–17 million rubles on various information systems in education. And the total cost of the budget is about 255 million rubles per year, excluding the cost of maintenance (Unified procurement information system, http://zakupki.gov.ru/epz/main/public/home.html. Access 28 June 2019).

Moreover, the SIS "Regional navigation and information system of Moscow Oblast" has been created and upgraded in the format of an investment contract (according to 39-ФЗ "On investment activity in the Russian Federation, Carried Out in the Form of Capital Investments"). The system allows monitoring the movement of vehicles in real time, controlling tasks and routes on a "plan/fact" principle.

The parties to the contract are the Ministry of Transport and Road Infrastructure of Moscow region (MTRIMO), the Mostransavto State Unitary Enterprise of Moscow region, the Mosavtodor State Budgetary Institution, the State Public Institution Road Traffic Safety Center of Moscow region, and T-1 Group JSC. The cost of the project amounted to more than 249 million rubles. Financing of the project was in full provided by a private partner, T-1 Group JSC. At the same time, the return of invested funds is not being carried out at the expense of the budget, but through payment for additional services of the Regional Navigational and Information System by private enterprises, state and municipal departments, and carriers. The implementation period of the project is 7 years.

Immediately after the creation of the Regional Navigational and Information System, it became the property of MTRIMO. More than fifteen thousand vehicles have been already connected to the system, which regularly transmits their data; these vehicles, particularly, are school buses, ambulances, passenger transport, etc. (Paramonov 2018).

Currently, one of the interesting, innovative projects, which is at the stage of structuring, is the project of creating the SIS "Product Labeling." The agreement on this project, which is being finalized, will be the first PPP agreement in the IT sphere in Russia concluded within the framework of Federal Law No.224-FZ "On Public-Private Partnerships, Municipal-Private Partnerships in the Russian Federation". The aim of the project is to introduce a system of labeling and tracing products in the territory of the Russian Federation and EAEU countries.

The data in Table 14.5 show that the project has its advantages for all stakeholders: for the state, consumers, and business. It is expected that the introduction of the system will create prerequisites for economic growth in Russia (the projected increase in the efficiency of market participants and the state is 6–7%), as well as will help to deepen the integration of the EAEU, increasing the transparency of trade flows and promoting the growth of trade between countries through the unification of regulation and information about products in a uniform catalog (CRTP 2019. https://p3week.ru/images/2019/12.pdf. Access 28 June 2019).

Currently, the most popular form of project implementation in Russia's IT infrastructure is the so-called quasi-PPP, particularly, energy service contracts; the total number of projects is 35. Among other forms, concession agreements in a total of 19 projects, as well as government contracts with investment component in a total of 5, prevail. Structuring of projects takes place within the framework of other contractual

Table 14.5 Aims and objectives of creating a system of labeling and tracing products

State	Consumers	Business
✓ Increase in customs and tax collection, including excise payments; ✓ Saving of budget costs for control of commodity markets; ✓ Real-time, nationwide statistics	✓ Protection of life and health of citizens; ✓ Public control; ✓ Consumer protection	✓ Increase in the competitiveness of legal market participants by reducing the share of illegal traffic; ✓ Access to data on the movement of products along the supply chain in real time

Source CRTP, 2019. https://p3week.ru/images/2019/12.pdf

models, particularly, lease agreements with investment commitments, investment agreements, and PPP/MPP agreements. Currently, about 20 projects in the IT sphere are at the finalization and initiation stage (Infrastructure Projects Support Platform ROSINFRA, 2019. http://www.pppi.ru/projects?sphere=748. Access 28 June 2019).

As can be seen from Chart 14.3, the main player in the Russian market of PPP projects in the IT sphere is currently Rostelecom PJSC, Russia's largest provider of digital services, which implements about 13 PPP projects in this sphere, both within the traditional forms of PPP and within the quasi-PPP format.

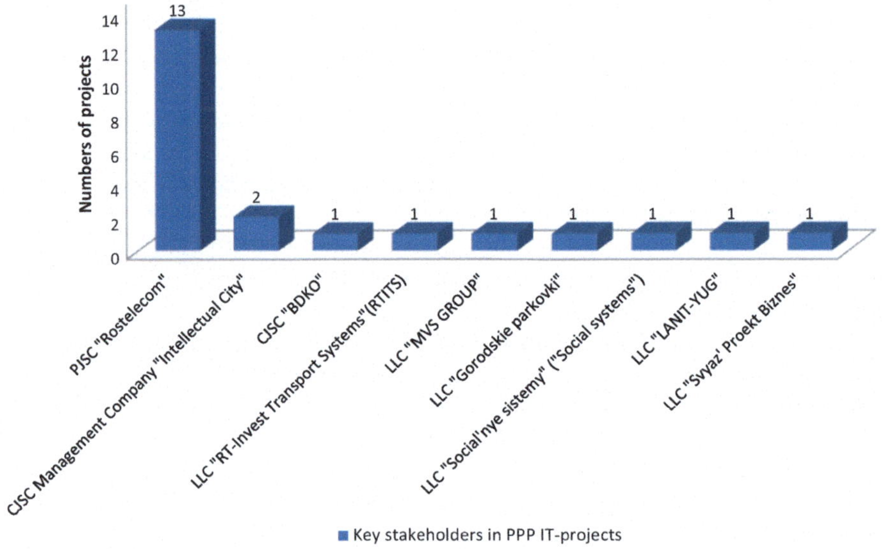

Chart 14.3 List of major investors (and concessionaires) participating in PPP IT projects (You&Partners 2018, Moscow)

In the last 3 years alone, Rostelecom PJSC has invested more than 23 billion rubles in IT projects (Kostryukova 2019). Among the most significant IT projects implemented by the company are projects to design, construct, and operate automated-vision-based inspection system of road conditions, photo and video recordings of road traffic offenses in the Zabaykalsky Krai, Astrakhan region, Nizhny Novgorod Oblast to organize paid parking in Kursk, to create a corporate regional educational communication networks of state and municipal educational organizations of Samara Oblast, to create and support a unified information and analytical utilities system in Moscow Oblast, and others (PJSC "Rostelecom", Moscow, 2018).

Applying PPP Mechanisms to Create the IT Infrastructure of the Digital Economy and Smart Cities in the Russian Federation

The creation of "smart cities" is an integral part aimed at raising the standard of living of the population and achieving sustainable development goals, including in Russia. This direction of the digital economy has been actively developing since the end of the twentieth century in many countries of the world and it is the basis of urbanization (Dameri 2017).

In accordance with the report of the International Telecommunication Union in 2014, "a smart sustainably developing city is an innovative locality, in which information and communication technologies and other means, which provide the satisfaction of the economic, social, and environmental needs of present and future generations, are used for the purpose of the improvement of quality of living of the population and services provided, the effectiveness of urban management, and the increase in competitiveness" (Smart and Sustainable Cities Indicators, UNECE 2015).

According to another interpretation, a smart city is a concept aimed at developing modern methods and strategies for managing cities (urban areas), using the up-to-date advanced technologies (including IT), in accordance with the principles of environmental safety and maintaining the trend toward saving resources and achieving expected results (Sikora-Fernandez and Stawasz 2016; Camero and Alba 2019).

And these are far from all definitions characterizing the concept of a "smart city," which suggests that this term today does not have a strict, unified definition. However, after analyzing the diversity of approaches to the term "smart city," it may be noted that the focus of the definition shifts toward one or another aspect depending on the level of socio-economic development, at which the state is. As a consequence, it is worth noting that governments and stakeholders need to work together to develop a common understanding of what smart city means in their specific national contexts and at the level of individual cities.

Digitalization projects and the implementation of smart city technologies, both abroad and in Russia, may often be introduced in the form of public–private or municipal–private partnerships. This approach allows municipalities to implement advanced technologies without investing in their development. For technology companies, PPP projects provide a guaranteed sales market and a return on investment.

Projects cover such areas as street lighting, parking space monitoring, traffic video recording and management, air quality monitoring, monitoring of filling rate of garbage cans, navigation for household waste disposal, data on the movement of passenger traffic, and analysis of social media data (Center for Strategic Research "North-West", 2019).

In Russian reality, the creation of "smart" cities is directly connected with state initiatives in the field of the development of the digital economy. In 2018, the Ministry of Construction Industry, Housing and Utilities Sector of the Russian Federation approved the project of digitization of the municipal economy "Smart City," which will be implemented within the framework of the national project "Housing and Urban Environment" and the national program "Digital Economy." The project is aimed at improving the competitiveness of Russian cities, the formation of effective mechanisms for managing the urban economy, and providing safe and comfortable conditions of living for citizens ("Smart City": official project of urban economy digitalization 2019).

The goal of "Smart City" lies not only in digital transformation and automation of processes but also in a comprehensive increase in the efficiency of urban infrastructure (McClellan et al. 2018; Votzel and Kuznetsova 2018). The departmental project "Smart City" is the basis, according to which the subjects of the Russian Federation are recommended to approve their own projects "Smart cities of the Subject of the Russian Federation," taking into account the specifics of the development (PPP Development Center, Moscow, 2018).

The implementation of the "smart city" concept implies the use of ICT, digital resources, modern technological management solutions, and more, and other IT infrastructure objects, for the development and implementation of which significant amounts of investments are required (Eliseev 2018). The lack of financing, as well as the managerial capacity and experience, in the IT sphere in the state conditions the objective need to find additional resources, both financial and managerial. Attracting alternative sources of public financing is feasible only if there are legal mechanisms accessible for and understandable to investors. The public–private partnership may serve as such a mechanism (PPP Development Center, Moscow, 2018).

Currently, almost all of the PPP projects being implemented in Russia in the IT sphere may be attributed to the projects of creation of the infrastructure of "smart cities." (Chart 14.4).

Thus, at the end of 2018, about 90 such projects are being implemented in the Russian Federation with the total accumulated capital investment of 34.6 billion rubles, of which budget financing amounts to 7.1 billion rubles and private financing amounts to 27.5 billion rubles.

Table 14.6 presents the leading ongoing projects in terms of attracted investments.

22 out of 90 PPP projects on "smart cities" are being implemented in the form of concession agreements, and another four projects are being implemented within

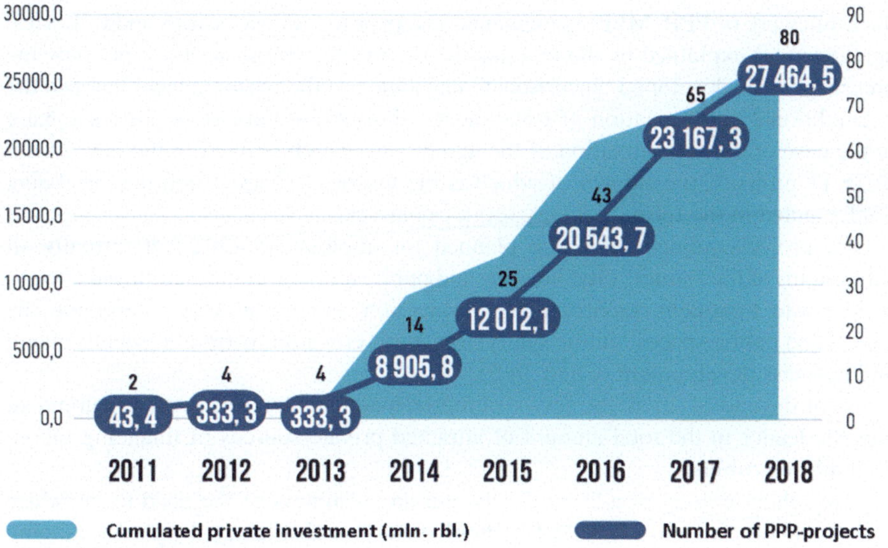

Chart 14.4 Number of PPP projects for smart cities infrastructure development and the cumulated private investment (PPP experience of creating the "Smart Cities" infrastructure: overview 2018. PPP Development Center, Moscow.)

Table 14.6 Top 5 projects in terms of attracted investments (PPP experience of creating the "Smart Cities" infrastructure: overview, 2018. PPP Development Center, Moscow)

Project name	Form of implementation	Private investments (million rubles)
Creation and operation of the safety control system for road traffic of Moscow Oblast	Concession agreement (115-FZ)	4,960
Creation of the cashless payment of fares for passengers in the territory of Moscow Oblast (Strelka)	Investment agreement	3,357
Range of works for the design, construction, and further technical maintenance of objects of outdoor lighting in Nizhny Tagil, Sverdlovsk Oblast	Lifecycle contract (44-FZ)	1,870
Creation of information and dispatch center and transport stop pavilions with multimedia scoreboards for information display in Nizhny Novgorod	Concession agreement (115-FZ)	1,600
Creation and operation of a set of elements of motor road development in the territory of Sevastopol	Concession agreement (115-FZ)	1,534

the framework of PPP (MPP) agreements. The priority of concessions and PPP/MPP agreements is explained by the fact that the use of other forms requires not only the presence of the developed "investment" legislation at the regional level but also the unconditional compensation of investments of a private partner or concessionaire in the case of early termination of the agreement, which is fixed in the law. 24 out of 28 IT projects, the subject of which is the upgrade of street lighting, are being implemented in the form of energy service contracts.

The projects implemented and planned for implementation cover virtually all subsystems of the "smart" city: housing and public utilities, construction and energy; solid waste treatment, environmental protection and monitoring; upgrading the streets and public spaces; public safety; transport; city administration; social sphere; and business development (Chart 14.5).

As of the end of 2018, the sector of motor road and street network development was the leader in the total amount of attracted private sources of financing (about 14.5 million rubles).

Thus, the ideology of a "smart" city and an awareness of the need to introduce smart technologies into everyday life should penetrate absolutely all spheres, ranging from government and business to the life of a particular individual (Il'ina 2018). In the conditions of a lack of budget financing, the necessity and practical value of introducing smart technologies under the PPP model is manifested.

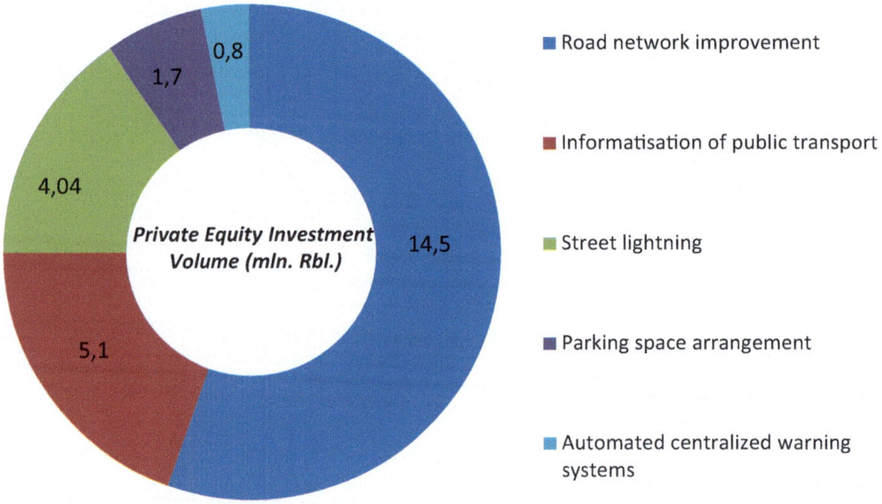

Chart 14.5 Top 5 IT largest industries in terms of private investments in Russia in 2018 (PPP experience of creating the "Smart Cities" infrastructure: overview, 2018. National PPP Center, Moscow)

Conclusion

The solution of fundamentally new tasks, which in the modern world concern all spheres of life, economics, and politics, is inextricably linked with the level of informatization of these areas. Today, around the world, in which Russia is no exception, all sectors of the economy are actively passing the informatization stage. Such a dynamic development of digital infrastructure, of course, imposes an additional burden on the budgets of all levels. Nevertheless, digital transformation not only imposes a heavy burden on the state but also brings additional opportunities for IT business, for example, due to the development and provision of new IT infrastructure services.

In this regard, it becomes necessary to develop such legal mechanisms that ensure business involvement in the field of information technologies. When creating new and developing existing IT technologies, it is the synergy of the state and business that provides the key to successful, mutually beneficial processes of informatization of all spheres of life.

PPP mechanisms are becoming one of the most effective forms of such synergy since not only the successful creation and launch of the relevant product but also its further development lie in the field of relations between the state and business, in the format of such a partnership. The relationship of such nature determines the direct interest of a private partner in the effectiveness of its obligations, and accordingly in the quality of the infrastructure created by it, ensuring its long-term operation. At the same time, the state obtains legal grounds to support IT projects, which makes the agreement mechanism mutually beneficial from the point of view of the economy (Tarakanov et al. 2019).

Of course, despite significant progress in the development of PPP in the field of information technologies, there still are some bottlenecks. It would be expedient to further improve federal legislation in this area due to the need to structure a number of practical aspects that are not covered within the framework of Federal Law No.173-FZ "On Amendments to Certain Legislative Acts of the Russian Federation." Moreover, the absence of active law enforcement and judicial practice or its ambiguity currently serves as a deterrent to the development of PPP in the IT sphere in Russia.

Another challenge facing the Russian IT infrastructure market is the need to increase the investment attractiveness of projects, to ensure which is necessary to improve the mechanisms for commercializing IT products, providing the development of sectoral legislation to create opportunities for the implementation of commercial services based on IT systems being created.

Summing up, it may be said that as for 2019, there are quite a lot "gray areas" in the legislation that regulates the procedure for the conclusion of concession agreements and PPP/MPP agreements in the field of IT, as well as "pressing issues" in the course of implementation of these agreements, with which parties of such agreements encounter.

Nevertheless, the adoption of the law that allows concluding concession agreements and PPP agreements with respect to IT objects has opened up new opportunities not only for the state but also for the private sector with respect to the global trend toward digitalization of the economy. The involvement of private capital in the modernization of the IT infrastructure of the country, secured by the legal guarantees of the state, may serve as an incentive for the growth of the entire market since it opens access to large-scale projects not only for the already proven leaders of the IT industry but also for a number of new actors. An additional advantage of using new tools is the ability to improve the quality and availability of public services for the population.

Thus, the potential of the project market, which has opened after the recognition of IT objects as independent objects of concession agreements and PPP/MPP agreements, is enormous, which conditions further prospects for the development of partnership mechanisms and the formation of diverse sources of monetization of projects.

References

Basaev, Z. V. (2018). Cifrovizaciya ekonomiki: Rossiya v kontekste global'noj transformacii (Digitalization of the economy: Russia in the framework of global transformation). Ekonomika XXI veka, № 4, 32–38. https://doi.org/10.26794/2220-6469-2018-12-4-32-38.

Belousova, O. Y., Mokin, S. V., Ogorodova, U. S., & Orekhovich, A. V. (2018). GCHP v IT: novye vozmozhnosti (PPP in IT: New Opportunities. Analytical review. Internet Initiatives Development Fund) Fond Razvitiya Internet Iniciativ, P&PUnity. http://ppunity.ru/files/files/%D0%93%D0%A7%D0%9F%20%D0%B2%20IT.pdf. Access 29 June 2019.

Camero, A., & Alba, E. (2019). Smart City and information technology: A review. *Cities, 93,* 84–94. https://doi.org/10.1016/j.cities.2019.04.014.

Cassar, C., Heath, D., & Micallef, L. (2017). What is digital economy? Delloitte. https://www2.deloitte.com/mt/en/pages/technology/articles/mt-what-is-digital-economy.html. Access 27 June 2019.

Caselli, S., Vecchi, V., & Corbetta, G. (2015). Public private partnerships for infrastructure and business development. In *Principles, practices, and perspectives* (p. 384), Palgrave Macmillan US. https://doi.org/10.1057/9781137541482.

Chinaeva, T. I. (2018). Informacionno-kommunikacionnye tekhnologii i razvitie cifrovoj ekonomiki (Information and communication technologies and the digital economy development). Ekonomist, № 6, 61–67.

Dameri, R. P. (2017). Smart city implementation. In *Creating economic and public value in innovative urban systems* (154 p), Springer International Publishing. https://doi.org/10.1007/978-3-319-45766-6.

Defining and Measuring the Digital Economy, BEA. (2018). https://www.bea.gov/system/files/papers/WP2018-4.pdf. Access 29 June 2019.

Doklad o mirovom razvitii "Cifrovye dividendy". (2016). (World Development Report "Digital Dividends" (2016). Review). International Bank for Reconstruction and Development, World Bank, Washington DC. https://openknowledge.worldbank.org/bitstream/handle/10986/23347/210671RuSum.pdf, https://doi.org/10.1596/978-1-4648-0671-1.a. Access 28 June 2019.

Drath, R., & Horch, A. (2014). Industrie 4.0: Hit or hype? *IEEE Industrial Electronics Magazine, 8*(2), 56–58.

Eliseev, D. O. (2018). Tekhnologicheskoe razvitie megapolisov na osnove koncepcii "umnogo goroda" (Megacities technological development based on the concept of "smart city"). Problemy teorii i praktiki upravleniya, № 9, 20–29.

Federal'nyj zakon ot 29.06.2018 № 173-FZ "O vnesenii izmenenij v otdel'nye zakonodatel'nye akty Rossijskoj Federacii" (Federal law 'On amendments to certain legislative acts of the Russian Federation' of 29.06.2018 N 173-FZ (2018)). http://www.consultant.ru/document/cons_doc_LAW_301312/. Access 29 June 2019.

Federal'nyj zakon "O gosudarstvenno-chastnom partnerstve, municipal'no-chastnom partnerstve v Rossijskoj Federacii i vnesenii izmenenij v otdel'nye zakonodatel'nye akty Rossijskoj Federacii" ot 13.07.2015 N 224-FZ. (Federal Law No. 224-FZ of July 13, 2015 "On Public-Private Partnership, Municipal-Private Partnership in the Russian Federation and Amendments to Certain Legislative Acts of the Russian Federation"). https://base.garant.ru/71129190/. Accessed 28 June 2019.

Federal'nyj zakon "O koncessionnyh soglasheniyah" ot 21.07.2005 N 115-FZ (Federal law No. 115-FZ of July 21, 2005 "On Concession agreements"). https://base.garant.ru/12141176/. Access 28 June 2019.

Forecating infrastructure needs and gaps. Outlook, Global Infrastructure Hub. https://outlook.gihub.org/?utm_source=GIHub+Homepage&utm_medium=Project+tile&utm_campaign=Outlook+GIHub+Tile. Access 28 June 2019.

Gestrin, M. V., Staudt, J. (2018). The digital economy, multinational enterprises and international investment policy. OECD, Paris. http://www.oecd.org/investment/investment-policy/The-digital-economy-multinational-enterprises-and-international-investment-policy.pdf. Access 27 June 2019.

Glaz'ev, S. Y. (1993). *Teoriya dolgosrochnogo tekhniko-ekonomicheskogo razvitiya (Theory of long-term technical and economic development)* (p. 310). Moscow: VlaDar.

Gosudarstvennaya sistema "Platon", Klyuchevaya statistika. (State system "Plato". Key indicators) http://dorogi.platon.ru/. Access 28 June 2019.

Gromova, E. A. (2018). Gosudarstvenno-chastnoe partnerstvo v cifrovuyu eru: poisk optimal'noj pravovoj formy (Public-private partnership in the digital era: the search for the optimal legal form). Yurist: nauchno-prakticheskoe i informacionnoe izdanie (Publishing Group "Yurist"), №10, 34–40.

Guidelines on private public partnerships for infrastructure development. (2000). UN/ECE BOT expert advisory group. https://www.mfcr.cz/assets/en/media/Guidelines-on-Private-Public-Partnership-for-Infrastructure-Development.pdf. Access 29 June 2019.

Hovavko, I. Y. (2018). Sistema "Platon": Internalizaciya eksternalij ili "kara nebesnaya"? (State system "Plato": internalization of externalities or "visitation") Ekonomicheskaya politika, № 2, 78–99.

Il'ina, I. N. (2018). Umnye zhiteli dlya umnyh gorodov (Smart residents for smart cities) Byudzhet, № 5, 52–54.

IDI 2017 Rank. ICT Development Index 2017. https://www.itu.int/net4/ITU-D/idi/2017/index.html.

IMD World Digital Competitiveness Index (2018). IMD World Competitiveness Center. file:///C:/Users/prepodgchp/Downloads/imd_world_digital_competitiveness_ranking_2018.pdf.

Infrastruktura Rossii. (2017). (Russian infrastructure. Analytical review) Analiticheskoe issledovanie, Gazprombank. http://www.gazprombank.ru/upload/iblock/209/gpb_infrastructure_09072014.pdf.

Inshakova, A., Goncharov, A., Smirenskaya, E., & Dolinskaya, V. (2017). Modern communication technologies in notification of Notarial Actions in Russia. *Journal of Advanced Research in Law and Economics, VIII*, 7(29), 2144–2151.

Ivanov, O. V. (2019). Gosudartsvenno-chastnoe partnerstvo kak instrument razvitiya infrastruktury i modernizatsii ekonomiki. Opyt stran Aziatsko-tikhookeanskogo regiona (Public-private partnership as an instrument of development of infrastructure and modernization of economy. Experience of Asia-Pacific countries) (300 p). Moscow, MGIMO-University.

Ivanov, O. V., & Ivanova, A. O. (2019). *Gosudarstvenno-chastnoe patnerstvo v stranakh Aziatsko-tikhookeanskogo regiona (Public-private partnership in the countries of Asia-Pacific region)* (p. 270). Moscow: MGIMO-University.

Kolodnyaya, G. V. (2018). Cifrovaya ekonomika: Osobennosti razvitiya v Rossii (Digital economy: Features of development in Russia) Ekonomist, № 4, 63–69.

Kostryukova, N. S. (2019). Prakticheskie voprosy i perspektivy ih resheniya: koncessionnye proekty v IT (2019) (Concession projects in IT: Practical issues and prospects for their solution). PJSC "Rostelecom". Moscow. http://www.p3week.ru/images/2019/11.pdf. Access 29 June 2019.

Kozhevina, O. V. (2018). Cifrovye faktory razvitiya umnyh gorodov (Digital factors in the development of smart cities). Menedzhment v Rossii i za rubezhom (Management in Russia and Abroad), № 3, 36–40.

McClellan, S., Jimenez, J., & Koutitas, G. (Eds.). (2018). Smart cities. In *Applications, technologies, standards, and driving factors* (239 p), Springer International Publishing. https://doi.org/10.1007/978-3-319-59381-4.

Markirovka i proslezhivaemost': kratkij obzor GCHP-proekta (Marking and traceability: a brief overview of the PPP project. Advanced Technologies Development Center). CRTP. https://p3week.ru/images/2019/12.pdf. Access 28 June 2019.

Measuring the Digital Economy. (2018). IMF, Washington DC. https://www.imf.org/en/Publications/Policy-Papers/Issues/2018/04/03/022818-measuring-the-digital-economy. Access 27 June 2019.

Mekhanizmy gosudarstvenno-chastnogo partnyorstva v ekonomicheskoi politike Rossii (Mechanisms of public-private partnership in the economic policy of Russia) (409 p). O. V. Ivanov (Ed.). Moscow: MGIMO-University.

Metodicheskie rekomendacii po podgotovke regional'nogo proekta « Umnye goroda » programm cifrovogo razvitiya ekonomiki sub"ekta Rossijskoj Federacii. (2018). ("Smart Cities" regional projects and digital development programs of the constituent entity of the Russian Federation: guidelines). http://asmo45.ru/menu/manual/accomplishment/mr_msrf_umnye_goroda.PDF. Access 28 June 2019.

Nacional'naya programma "Cifrovaya ekonomika Rossijskoj Federacii". (2019). (National Program "Digital Economy of the Russian Federation" Approved by the Russian Federation Government order dated July 28, 2017 No. 1632-p.). Official Website of the Russian Government. http://static.government.ru/media/files/9gFM4FHj4PsB79I5v7yLVuPgu4bvR7M0.pdf. Access 28 June 2019.

Nosova, S. S., Askerov, P. F., Rabadanov, E. R., Dubanevich, L. E., & Voronina, V. N. (2019). The role of digital infrastructure in the digital transformation of the modern Russian economy. *International Journal of Innovative Technology and Exploring Engineering, 8*(7), 2311–2318.

Obzor praktiki primeneniya mekhanizmov GCHP dlya sozdaniya infrastruktury "umnyh gorodov". (2018). (PPP experience of creating the "Smart Cities" infrastructure: overview). PPP Development Center, Moscow. http://pppcenter.ru/assets/files/10122018.pdf. Access 29 June 2019.

Ob"ekty IT stali ob"ektami koncessionnyh soglashenij i soglashenij o GCHP/MCHP Analiticheskij obzor. (2018). (IT facilities are the subject of concession and PPP-agreements. Analytical review). You&Partners, Moscow.

Ocenka perspektiv realizacii GCHP i koncessionnyh proektov v sfere informacionnyh tekhnologij i svyazi. (2018). (PPP and concession projects implementation in the field of information technology and communications: prospective assessment. Analytical survey). Analiticheskoe issledovanie. https://www.iidf.ru/upload/images_articles/PPP_IT_V1.pdf. Access 29 June 2019.

Otchet "Rossiya onlajn: chetyre prioriteta dlya proryva v cifrovoj ekonomike". (2017). (Report "Russia Online: Four Priorities for a Breakthrough in the Digital Economy"). The Boston Consulting Group. http://image-src.bcg.com/Images/Russia-Online_tcm27-178074.pdf. Access 29 June 2019.

Paramonov, L. S. (2018). *Cifrovizaciya transportnoj otrasli regiona za schyot investicionnyh kontraktov (Investment contracts as a tool for digitization of the transport industry in the country region).* Moscow: T-One Group.

Pasport vedomstvennogo proekta cifrovizacii gorodskogo hozyajstva "Umnyj gorod". (2019). ("Smart City": official project of urban economy digitalization). Ministry of Construction, Housing and Utilities of the Russian Federation. http://www.minstroyrf.ru/upload/iblock/ecf/Pasport-proekta-umnyygorod.pdf. Access 29 June 2019.

Platforma podderzhki infrastrukturnyh proektov ROSINFRA (Infrastructure Projects Support Platform ROSINFRA). http://www.pppi.ru/projects. Access 29 June 2019.

Pokazateli "umnyh" ustojchivyh gorodov. (2015). (Smart and Sustainable Cities Indicators, UNECE). UNECE. http://www.unece.org/fileadmin/DAM/hlm/documents/2015/ECE_HBP_2015_4.ru.pdf. Access 29 June 2019.

Prakticheskie voprosy i perspektivy ih resheniya: koncessionnye proekty v IT. (2019). (Concession projects in IT: Practical issues and prospects for their solution). PJSC "Rostelecom", Moscow. http://www.p3week.ru/images/2019/11.pdf. Access 29 June 2019.

Prioritetnye napravleniya vnedreniya tekhnologij umnogo goroda v rossijskih gorodah (Priority areas for the "Smart city" technologies introduction in Russian cities) Centr strategicheskih razrabotok "Severo-Zapad" (Center for Strategic Research "North-West"). https://www.csr.ru/wp-content/uploads/2018/06/Report-Smart-Cities-WEB.pdf. Access 29 June 2019.

Primer sozdaniya regional'noj sistemy obrazovaniya. SHkol'nyj portal Moskovskoj oblasti. (2018). Opyt realizacii investicionnyh proektov v regionah RF. (An example of a regional education system. School portal of the Moscow Region (2018). Investment projects implementation in the regions of the Russian Federation. "Homework Diary" - Digital educational platform.). Dnevnik – Cifrovaya obrazovatel'naya platforma.

Prosto i chestno ob investiciyah v infrastrukturu i gosudarstvenno-chastnom partnerstve v Rossii. Analiticheskij obzor (2019) (Simply and honestly about investments in infrastructure and PPP in Russia. Analytical review. Rating of regions 2018–2019). ROSINFRA, PPP Development Center, Moscow. http://pppcenter.ru/assets/files/obzor240419.pdf.

Public-Private Partnerships: Reference Guide, Version 2.0. (2014). The World Bank, Asian Development Bank, Inter-American Development Bank, Washington DC. https://openknowledge.worldbank.org/handle/10986/20118. Access 30 June 2019.

Saussier, S., & de Brux, J. (2018). The economics of public-private partnerships: Theoretical and empirical developments (p 240)), Springer International Publishing. https://doi.org/10.1007/978-3-319-68050-7.

Sikora-Fernandez, D., & Stawasz, D. (2016). The concept of smart city in the theory and practice of urban development management. *Romanian Journal of Regional Science*, *10*(1), 1–19. http://www.rrsa.ro/rjrs/V1015.Sikora.pdf.

Smart cities and infrastructure. (2016). Economic and Social Council, UN. https://unctad.org/meetings/en/SessionalDocuments/ecn162016d2_en.pdf. Access 30 June 2019.

Smart cities: digital solutions for a more livable future. (2018). McKinsey Global Institute. https://www.mckinsey.com/industries/capital-projects-andinfrastructure/our-insights/smart-cities-digital-solutions-for-a-more-livablefuture. Access 30 June 2019.

Stelling, C. (2014). Public-private partnerships & the need, development and management of trusting. A processual and embedded exploration. Copenhagen Business School, Denmark. https://openarchive.cbs.dk/bitstream/handle/10398/8942/Christiane_Stelling.pdf?sequence=1. Access 29 June 2019.

Sulejmanov, T. (2017). Rol' mekhanizmov gosudarstvenno-chastnogo partnerstva (The role of public-private partnerships in creating the infrastructure of the digital economy). *IT-News Journal*, №11 (265), 16–17.

Tapscott, D. (1996). The digital economy: Promise and peril in the age of networked intelligence (342 p).

Tkachenko, M. V. (2018). Retrospektiva GCHP-proektov v sfere IT: statistika po Rossii, opyt zarubezhnyh stran, perspektivnye napravleniya (Retrospective review of PPP projects in the field of IT: statistics, foreign countries experience, prospective for development) PPP Development Center, Moscow.

Tarakanov, V. V., Inshakova, A. O., & Goncharov, A. I. (2019). Interactive demo on-line maintenance foreign trade deals of business entities of BRICS jurisdictions. In *Competitive Russia: Foresight Model of Economic and Legal Development in the Digital Age: Proceedings of the International Scientific Conference in Memory of Oleg Inshakov (1952–2018)* (pp. 319–327). Cham: Springer Nature.

Votzel, J., & Kuznetsova, E. (2018). (in Rus.) Tekhnologii umnyh gorodov: chto vliyaet na vybor gorozhan? (Smart city solutions: What drives citizen adoption around the globe?). McKinsey Center for Government. https://www.mckinsey.com/ru/~/media/McKinsey/Industries/Public%20Sector/Our%20Insights/Smart%20city%20solutions%20What%20drives%20citizen%20adoption%20around%20the%20globe/smartcitizenbook-rus.ashx.

Zusman, E., & Shcheglov, A. (2018). GCHP v sfere IT (PPP in ICT sector). D-Russia. http://d-russia.ru/gchp-v-sfere-it.html. Access 25 June 2019.

Part VI
International Aspects of Public-Private Partnership in Russia

Chapter 15
Public–Private Partnership in the Post-soviet Space: Can It Play the Role of an Integrator?

Oleg Ivanov

Abstract Public–private partnership is of increasing interest in the post-Soviet space. The countries of the former USSR see PPP as an effective tool for infrastructure development solving many socio-economic problems, promoting sustainable economic growth, and improving the living standards of the population. At the same time, PPP development in the former USSR countries is still mainly of the "vertical" model, providing for combining of efforts of the state and business in the national framework. Development of PPP "horizontally," i.e., giving it a supranational, multilateral character could be useful for these countries not only in terms of promoting development of national infrastructure, but also in terms of expanding the field of their economic cooperation both bilaterally and within the framework of economic associations in which they participate (EAEU, SCO, etc.), to consolidate their efforts in the implementation of mutually beneficial transnational infrastructure projects, as well as to cooperate in achieving the UN sustainable development goals. Based on the study of relevant experience, it is concluded that it is possible and expedient to strengthen mutual cooperation of former USSR countries in the field of PPP by harmonizing their legal and methodological framework, establishing practical cooperation in the implementation of transnational projects of mutual interest.

Keywords Infrastructure gaps · Public–private partnership · Transnational infrastructure projects · Sustainable development · Regional interconnectedness

JEL codes F15 · H10 · H41

O. Ivanov (✉)
Department of Economic Policy and Public-Private Partnership, MGIMO University, Vernadsky Ave., 76, 119454 Moscow, Russia
e-mail: ivanov_ov@mail.ru

O. V. Ivanov and A. O. Inshakova (eds.), *Public-Private Partnerships in Russia*, Competitive Government: Public Private Partnerships,
https://doi.org/10.1007/978-3-030-56352-3_15

Introduction

Over the past decades, public–private partnership (PPP) has become an effective tool for infrastructure development in different countries of the world and has proved its viability in countries with different systems and levels of socio-economic development. Through PPP mechanisms the state engages a private partner in financing, construction, operation, maintenance, reconstruction, and modernization of public infrastructure on the terms of long-term cooperation, sharing of risks and responsibilities. The results of PPPs are clearly embodied in the objects of transport infrastructure, energy supply, utilities, communications and telecommunications, public and municipal administration, health care, education, and culture.

Public–private partnership is beneficial to all the parties involved. It gives the public partner the opportunity to provide better quality of service, to complete projects on time and within budget, to access improved technology and innovation, to ensure the proper allocation of risk, optimization of resources and greater service coverage for users, to promote lower tariffs for users, to achieve clear separation between regulation and operations, and to increase foreign investment in the economy (APEC, USAID, p. 9–10).

The private sector considers it beneficial to participate in PPPs, given the expansion of business opportunities and access to new, previously inaccessible market segments. Attractive for business are the long-term nature of PPP, the availability of direct government support and participation, which reduce risks for the private entrepreneur as well as the relative autonomy in making operational decisions (Ivanov 2016).

In view of the above, public–private partnership is of increasing interest in the post-Soviet space. The countries of the former USSR see PPP as an effective tool for infrastructure development, solving many socio-economic problems, promoting sustainable economic growth, and improving the living standards of the population. The interest of the former USSR countries in PPP and importance they attach to this institution in improvement of infrastructure are becoming even more clear in the light of assessments by authoritative international experts of infrastructure condition in these countries. According to the World Economic Forum (WEF) estimates, the state of infrastructure in the main sectors is estimated to be no more than "medium" and "medium-low" (see Table 15.1).

Table 15.1 Quality of infrastructure in former USSR countries

Country	Quality of overall infrastructure rank/137	Quality of roads (score 1–7)	Quality of railroad infrastructure (1–7)	Quality of air transport infrastructure (1–7)	Quality of electricity supply (1–7)
Armenia	80	3.7	2.9	4.8	4.8
Kazakhstan	68	2.9	4,1	4,0	4,6
Kyrgyz Republic	109	2.7	2,4	3,1	3,6
Russia	35	2.9	4,5	4,6	5,1
Tajikistan	99	4.1	3.7	4.3	3.7
Uzbekistan	n/d available				
Ukraine					
Azerbaijan	26	4.8	4.7	5.6	5.5
Moldova	102	2.5	2.7	4.1	4.3
Georgia	76	3.8	3.8	4.3	5.0

Source Compiled on the basis of World Economic Forum (2017). The Global Competitiveness Report 2017–2018

Results

Specifics of Approaches of the Former USSR Countries to the Establishment and Development of Public–Private Partnership

The countries of the former USSR started using PPP mechanisms at different times, on different scales, and having different legal and institutional frameworks of PPP. As a result, the development of PPP in them today has a multi-level character. According to the World Bank estimates, the degree of the former USSR countries' "PPP maturity" in the main thematic areas is as follows (Table 15.2).

In general, Russia and Kazakhstan are significantly ahead of other countries according to the degree of maturity of the institutional environment for PPPs, which is understood as a complex political, economic, legal, and institutional conditions that shape incentives for its development: political support of the state, receiving expression in formulation of PPP policies and programs, legal framework—adoption of relevant legislation and regulations, system of PPP governance including creation of PPP units fulfilling functions of coordination, assistance, and control. Ukraine, Ukraine, Belarus, and Kyrgyzstan, who started development of PPP later, are trying to force formation of its legal and institutional framework. Many countries, including Armenia, Tajikistan, and Uzbekistan, are at the very beginning of the road and are only taking the first steps (Inshakova et al. 2019).

Table 15.2 Assessment of former USSR countries' activities in PPP key thematic areas

	Preparation of PPPs	Procurement of PPPs	PPP contract management	Unsolicited proposals
Armenia	47	77	12	0
Azerbaijan	16	38	32	Not regulated
Belarus	75	53	60	58
Georgia	41	57	33	Not regulated
Kazakhstan	59	51	59	58
Kyrgyz Republic	33	40	49	50
Moldova	48	62	49	Not regulated
Russian Federation (concessions)	34	63	78	58
Russian Federation (PPP)	31	67	63	54
Tajikistan	23	51	52	67
Ukraine	78	57	42	75

Source Compiled on the bases of WB (2018). Procuring Infrastructure Public–Private Partnerships Report 2018

Nevertheless, analysis of the activities aimed at development of PPP in the countries of the former USSR allows to highlight some general points that can be attributed to the specifics of their approach to PPP.

PPP Conceptual Design

In the countries of the former USSR (as, indeed, in the world as a whole), there is no single, unified definition of public–private partnership. Nevertheless, regardless of the peculiarities of national legislation, all countries are united in the understanding that PPP has its own system characteristics that distinguish it from other forms of interaction between government and business, which primarily include the long-term partnership, the distribution of risks and responsibilities between partners, full or partial financing of the creation of a public infrastructure facility by a private partner, as well as the involvement of a private partner not only in the creation of the facility, but also in its subsequent operation or maintenance.

In the practice of the countries of the former USSR, the conceptual foundations of PPP are usually enshrined in fundamental political documents, as well as special legislation. Doctrinal design of public policy of PPP in these countries is quite variable and has the form of concepts, strategies, plans, programs, and other documents.

Thus, in *Armenia,* with the help of the UN Development Program (UNDP), the concept of PPP was developed, which fixed the concept of PPP, its system characteristics, scope, main goals, and scope of application. In 2017, the PPP Policy of the Republic of Armenia was also developed and approved, which defined the legislative and institutional principles for the implementation and promotion of PPP taking into account local conditions and international practice, as well as set the task of transferring public–private partnership to a qualitatively new level.

In 2013, the Cabinet of Ministers of *Ukraine* approved the concept of public–private partnership development for 2013–2018, the main purpose of which is to form a national model of public–private partnership development, taking into account the institutional features and modern conditions for attracting investment and developing the national economy on an innovative basis. As the main tasks in the field of PPP, the concept defines the following:

- development of a unified approach to the development of the institutional environment of PPP, identification of priority areas of PPP development, as well as features of PPP development in certain areas;
- improvement of legal regulation of PPP;
- establishment of a clear distribution of powers between the executive authorities in the public administration of PPP;
- identification of ways to improve the efficiency of interaction between the state and the private sectors regarding the initiation and implementation of PPP projects;
- improving the institutional capacity of public authorities and local governments to use modern PPP mechanisms; and
- definition of directions of improvement of mechanisms of the state support and guarantees of the state.

The concept provides for the modernization of the national economy through cooperation between the public and private sectors, support for energy and resource—saving technologies and attracting investment in housing and communal services. The next step is expected to be the adoption of the PPP development strategy in Ukraine, which will outline the main objectives, characteristics, and principles of further PPP development.

In *Russia*, in March 2018, the Russian government approved the "Roadmap for the development of public-private partnership tools"—in fact, the first systematic and planning document aimed at stimulating the use and development of PPP mechanisms. According to the document, it is planned to implement a set of measures aimed at developing mechanisms for the construction and reconstruction of infrastructure in Russia, improving legislation in the field of PPP for the implementation of long-term infrastructure projects and increasing their investment attractiveness for private investors. A road map, in particular, provides for the development of concepts for new mechanisms of construction and reconstruction of infrastructure, the establishment of a government commission, the competence of which will include the coordination of interested bodies and organizations on issues of public policy in field of PPP mainstreaming of government programs in the development of the infrastructure and control of the implementation of activities of the road map will be updated in guidelines of the Ministry of Economic Development on the implementation of PPP projects. In addition, as priorities are development of the "infrastructure map" and opening the single register of projects on construction and reconstruction of infrastructure in key sectors, the formation of the list of pilot projects of PPP and MPP and concessions, and also a complex of measures to ensure competition, encourage the use of modern technologies, and the reduction of costs during design and construction.

In 2017, the implementation of the National Sustainable Development Strategy of *Kyrgyzstan* for 2013–2017 was completed. Through the prism of PPP mechanisms development the tasks of ensuring economic growth, enterprises of material and financial resources of the state and private sectors for implementation of investment projects, reducing the burden on the state budget, and redistribution of budgetary funds were set in the strategy.

In their PPP conceptual documents, governments of many countries of the former USSR define the main goals that they would like to achieve through implementation of PPP programs and plans. The list of these goals and their alignment in a certain priority give an idea of the direction of PPP policy and its interconnection with other areas of government economic policy. These objectives include the following:

- Attracting additional investment resources to the infrastructure through involvement of the private sector;
- use of new approaches to infrastructure development, in particular, the management of infrastructure facilities on the basis of a life cycle;
- improving quality of services provided to end users;
- leveraging management, technical and technological capabilities of the private sector;
- use of innovation and greater efficiency of the private sector;
- achieving optimal value for money of infrastructure projects;
- increased openness and accountability in the provision of infrastructure services; and
- stimulating economic growth and development in the country.

Long-Term Planning of Infrastructure Development

In recent years, more and more countries of the former Soviet Union are moving in their economic policies to long-term planning of infrastructure development. That generally corresponds to the leading trends in the world practice. This phenomenon reflects the growing desire of governments to form a clearer vision of infrastructure development vector, to calculate quantitative and qualitative parameters of this development, and to establish guidelines for funding sources. It is obvious that importance of long-term planning especially increases when infrastructure projects with a horizon of 20 years or more are numbered in hundreds, they cover a wide range of infrastructure areas, and there is a need for their cross-sectoral balancing.

Setting infrastructure development on a long-term planned basis makes the following possible:

- to determine strategic direction of movement;
- to develop sectoral and regional priorities;
- to define quantitative and qualitative target parameters;
- to form tools for achieving goals; and
- to develop guidance on sources of funding.

In this regard, the experience of *Belarus*, where the "National infrastructure strategy for 2017–2030" was developed and approved, reflecting the government's assessment of the country's infrastructure needs and the gap in budget funding for the long term is of special interest. The National Infrastructure Strategy (NIS) is considered an important document designed to guide the business community on public infrastructure development plans and aimed at engaging the private sector in financing, construction, and reconstruction of infrastructure on PPP principles. The NIS identified priority areas for infrastructure development up to 2030 (energy, transport, social infrastructure, and housing and communal services) and approved a list of 100 priority infrastructure projects with guidelines on the amount of funding required.

In order to create a favorable environment for development and successful implementation of the PPP mechanism, the program of development of public–private partnership for 2016–2021 was developed in the *Kyrgyz Republic*. This program is a road map for development of public–private partnership in Kyrgyzstan. The document defines main conditions and tasks for implementation of PPP mechanisms and will contribute to the modernization of existing and the creation of new infrastructure facilities and services to ensure long-term economic growth and efficiency of the country.

Kazakhstan has successfully implemented the PPP development program for 2011–2015, which provided for the expansion of the scope of PPP mechanisms, the development of public support measures, the introduction of new types of contracts, changing approaches to planning budget investments, and improving the procedures for planning and implementation of projects. Later national and regional road maps for development of PPP in 2016–18 were adopted, providing, in particular, the expansion of the use of PPP mechanisms and attracting private investment in such areas as education, health, physical education and sports, housing, agriculture, environmental protection and transport, etc.

In September 2018, the Government of the *Russian Federation* approved a comprehensive plan for development of core infrastructure until 2024. The plan includes objects of transport and energy infrastructure with a total cost of 6.3 trillion, 3 trillion of them will be provided by the Federal budget, the rest—by extra—budgetary sources. The plan includes projects for construction of High-Speed Railways (HSR), development of existing major transport hubs and the creation of new transport and logistics centers, development of sea ports of the Azov–Black Sea Basin, reconstruction of a number of leading highways, bypasses of major cities—Nizhny Novgorod, Krasnodar, Ivanovo, Ryazan, reconstruction of more than 60 airports, etc.

The importance of a strategic, long-term vision of infrastructure and PPP development has been repeatedly emphasized by the World Bank. In the report on PPP in Ukraine, the WB noted, in particular, that Public Investment Management in Ukraine is missing a number of the key elements that would otherwise classify it as a good practice country in an international context. It lacks a strategic view on public investment priorities, clarity about the definition of what private company project proposals can be considered as public investments, a consistent legal framework for PPPs, and clear criteria for selection and capacity for effective management of traditional public investments and PPPs (World Bank (2015) Public–Private Partnerships in the Context of Public Investment Management in Ukraine. An Assessment. p.6).

Strengthening PPP Legal Framework

Given the fact that PPP is risky for business and is associated with its long-term interests, the countries of the former USSR attach particular importance to the establishment of a solid regulatory framework and the development of "rules of the game" on the PPP field. It is noteworthy that legal framework of PPP in the majority of these countries is based on the model of special legislation.

Belarus has adopted the Law on Concessions of 2013 and the Law on Public-Private Partnership of 2016, as well as a wide range of normative legal acts (government resolutions, resolutions of the Ministry of Economy, etc.) regulating procedural issues and, thus, designed to promote the practical implementation of the above legislative acts.

The legislation of the Republic of *Kazakhstan* in the field of PPP includes the law "On concessions" of 2006, the Law "On public-private partnership" of 2015, and other regulatory legal acts. Special attention is paid to the variability of forms of public support for PPP projects, including partial compensation of investment costs, public guarantees of demand, in-kind grants, guarantees for loans, guarantees for infrastructure bonds, and other forms. The law on PPP regulates conceptual apparatus, the range of participants, and the scope of PPP and establishes different forms of PPPs, including concession agreements, service contracts, and trust management contracts. In accordance with the PPP Law, potential private partners are subject to clear qualification requirements. Depending on the complexity of the object, there are two scenarios for the competition—a simplified version for small projects based on standard tender documentation and a model PPP contract, as well as a two-stage competition for unique and technically complex projects. The law is focused on the broad development of partnership—PPP projects are allowed in all sectors except strategic ones.

The PPP law of 2010 in *Ukraine* contains detailed regulation of the wide range of issues related to the use of PPP mechanisms. It introduced the basic concepts of PPP, fixed organizational and legal principles of interaction between public and private partners; rights and obligations of partners; the scope of PPP; the forms in which partnership can be carried out; and formulated provisions related to state support, state guarantees, and state control over PPP projects.

The law defines the main forms in which public–private partnership can be carried out in Ukraine: concessions, joint activities, distribution of products, and others. The choice of a particular form for a particular PPP project is carried out by the body authorized to make a decision on the implementation of such a project, based on the results of the analysis of the effectiveness of the project. Attention is drawn to the rigid fixation of the impossibility of transferring ownership of these objects to a private partner. PPP facilities cannot be privatized for the duration of the relevant PPP project. Such objects shall be returned to the state partner after the termination of the contract concluded under the PPP. The state partner also owns the ownership of completed, rebuilt, and reconstructed PPP facilities. Objects of PPP cannot be objects in respect of which the decision on privatization is made.

The law on PPP also reflected one of the most important issues—the land issue. The law not only establishes the obligation of the public partner to provide land, necessary for the implementation of a project, but also the obligation to provide the private partner the possibility of using such land for the period required by applicable PPP contract, as well as to coordinate land acquisition with the state authorities or bodies of local self-government (article 8). Given the problems faced by private companies in obtaining permits for the use of land, this provision greatly facilitates the tasks of the private partner.

A special regulatory framework for PPP has been formed in *Kyrgyzstan*. The Law "On public-private partnership in the Kyrgyz Republic" established the scope of application of PPP mechanisms, defined competent authorities operating in the field of PPP, their powers and competences, types of public support, implementation procedures for PPP projects, and provisions for the selection and implementation of PPP projects. Pursuant to the law on PPP a wide range of regulatory acts (government resolutions, orders of the Ministry of Economy, etc.), regulating numerous specific issues relating to the PPP activities of the competent authorities, conduct of competitions, content of tender documentation, keeping the register of PPP projects, etc. was adopted.

Russian legislation on PPP consists of the PPP law, the law on concessions, other Federal laws, and other normative legal acts of the Russian Federation and regulatory legal acts of constituent entities of the Russian Federation. All legal norms contained in regulatory legal acts of the subjects of the Russian Federation and municipal legal acts must comply with the national laws on PPP and concessions.

The key difference between the PPP law and the law on concessions is the possibility of private ownership of public infrastructure. At the same time, it is possible for a private partner to perform only maintenance of the object of the agreement without the operation of the object (in concessions it is impossible), which could potentially be more interesting for private investors.

In the interests of investors, the PPP and concession laws provide a mechanism to guarantee the immutability of the main parameters on the basis of which the decision to implement the project was made. In the event of a change in macroeconomic conditions or legislation directly affecting the project (taxes, benefits, etc.), made reasonable changes to the agreement to the return of investment of the concessionaire (it may be extension of the implementation of concessions, increase in co-financing by public side, granting state, or municipal guarantees).

Although special laws on PPP in the former USSR differ significantly from each other both conceptually and substantively, reflecting political approaches, specifics of national jurisdictions, legal traditions, etc., all these acts are united by the desire of legislators to form a single conceptual apparatus, to consolidate necessary terminological base, to formulate common "rules of the game." As a rule, the structure of special laws on PPP has the following main blocks: objectives, definitions, concept, main directions and principles of public policy, key parameters of projects, project selection procedures, competitive selection of private operators, and measures of public support. Of particular importance for private partners are provisions of the legislation that fix the guarantees of their rights, procedure for settlement of disputes between the parties, issues of recovery of collateral, and compensation in case of early termination of a PPP contract.

PPP Institutional Framework

The level and quality of public–private partnership development are largely determined by the efficiency of the public administration system in the PPP sphere, including formation of various types of government bodies and their respective functions, creation of PPP development institutions, development of public support tools for the implementation of PPP projects, etc.

The *Republic of Belarus* has formed an appropriate institutional framework for PPP governance with a clear distribution of powers between different institutions of power. The President defines the general state policy in field of PPP and the Government ensures its implementation and determines the order of interaction of subjects in the field of PPP (preparation, review and evaluation of proposals for PPP projects, organization and conduction of the tender and conclusion of the PPP agreement, etc.).

The Ministry of Economy is the main body responsible for implementation of state policy and coordination of activities of state bodies and organizations subordinate to the government, as well as local executive and administrative bodies in the field of PPP. It also establishes the requirements for feasibility study of PPP projects and the methodology for evaluating proposals for PPP projects, and together with the National Agency for investment and privatization (PPP center is part of the agency) provides methodological and advisory support in preparation and implementation of PPP projects.

Other ministries and departments, as well as local executive and administrative bodies within their competence implement state policy in the field of PPP. As a rule, the following state bodies and departments take part in the implementation of specific PPP projects: the Ministry of economy, the Ministry of Finance and the State property committee, as well as other state bodies within the competence, if necessary. They evaluate PPP projects proposed for implementation, coordinate tender documentation, and participate in the work of the tender commissions.

The PPP center prepares a comprehensive assessment of proposals for PPP projects, as well as evaluates tender documentation.

The Interdepartmental Infrastructure Coordination Council (IICC) makes decisions on approval of PPP project proposals and tender documentation for PPP projects.

In *Kazakhstan,* the Government of the Republic is engaged in development of the main directions of PPP state policy and its implementation. The Ministry of National Economy, the Ministry of Finance, as well as the authorized state bodies of the relevant industries implement state policy in the field of PPP within its competence. Inter-sectoral coordination and methodological guidance in the field of PPP is carried out by the Ministry of National Economy.

At the local level, the state PPP policy is implemented by local executive bodies of regions, cities of republican significance, and the capital within their competences. Local executive bodies also monitor PPP contracts and implementation of local PPP projects.

In *Kyrgyzstan,* a Public–Private Partnership Council has been established to ensure coordination of PPP development activities, with the following functions:

- coordination and ensuring interaction of state executive authorities, local governments, business entities, non-profit and research organizations on the search, initiation, preparation and implementation of PPP projects;
- approval of action plans for PPP development; preparation of proposals for the development of concepts, strategies, programs, and other documents related to PPP development in the Kyrgyz Republic;
- preparation of recommendations for improvement of regulatory legal acts in the field of PPP;
- analysis of existing and newly proposed measures to stimulate PPP development;
- monitoring activities of state executive bodies on the search, initiation, preparation, and implementation of PPP projects; and
- identification of priority sectors and areas for initiating PPP projects.

In the *Russian Federation,* the institutional framework of the PPP sector has not yet acquired a final and holistic character, but many of its elements have already been formed and are functioning. An important role in this system is played by the Ministry of Economic Development, responsible for drafting PPP policy and legal and regulatory acts, selection of PPP projects and preparing opinions on effectiveness and comparative advantages of PPP projects, assessing the level of PPP development in the regions, and preparation of PPP rating of Russian regions.

Some Federal executive bodies (Ministry of health, Ministry of construction and housing, Ministry of transport, Ministry of culture, etc.) are engaged in preparation and implementation of PPP projects within their competences.

An important role in supporting the development of PPP in the country is played by the National PPP center, which performs a wide range of functions—from examination of project initiatives and assistance in finding private partners for them to advising the subjects of the Federation and assisting them in training.

The Ministry of Economic Development and Trade (MERT) plays a leading role in the system of PPP management in *Ukraine*. The Ministry is working to create conditions for development of PPP. It approved a number of normative acts determining the procedure of implementation of PPP projects, submission form of proposals for the implementation of PPP projects, the form of feasibility studies of PPP, the method of analysis of the effectiveness of PPPs and the regulation on the assessment and competitive selection proposed by ministries, other central and local executive bodies of the investment projects providing attraction of means of the state budget, about creation of the Commission of the Ministry on assessment and competitive selection of investment projects, etc.

Since 2016 the Ministry of Infrastructure of Ukraine has a Project Office on Public-Private Partnership in Infrastructure “SP3ILNO.”

As part of the reform of the PPP legislation, consideration is given on the possibility of establishing a separate PPP agency in which responsibilities will include improvement of the institutional and regulatory framework (training, development of methodological recommendations, PPP market monitoring, etc.), ensuring preparation of PPP projects (providing methodological support to public partners in the process of preparation and implementation of PPP projects), etc. In turn, the Ministry of Economic Development will be responsible for approval of PPP projects and monitoring of their quality (participation in the analysis of project effectiveness, participation in competitive commissions, keeping a register of PPP projects, etc. (Realization of Public-Private Partnership Projects in Ukraine. Guideline. November 2017 p.22).

Public Support for PPP Development

One of the most important functions of PPP units in the world practice is to promote the development of this institution.

The legislation of *Kazakhstan* regulates a large variability of forms of public support for concession projects—partial compensation of investment costs, guarantees of demand, co-financing of projects, provision of in-kind grants (in the form of land plots, structures, machinery and equipment, computers, measuring and regulating parting and devices, vehicles, production and economic equipment, etc.), guarantees for loans, guarantees for infrastructure bonds, and other forms.

To assist development and launch of PPP projects, Kazakhstan created a number of institutions performing important functions. The government has established a PPP development center to conduct research and develop recommendations on PPP issues to conduct expertise and evaluation of PPP projects, as well as to train specialists in the field of PPP and to maintain a list of PPP projects.

At the national level, Kazakhstan Project Preparation Fund carries out activities on Advisory support of PPP projects, as well as assistance in the preparation and launch of PPP projects.

One of the forms of support for PPP projects in Kazakhstan are preferences in obtaining land and other necessary properties. According to the law on PPP of the Republic of Kazakhstan, the provision of land is one of the forms of participation of state bodies in PPP. Land plots on the right of temporary gratuitous land use may be provided to citizens and legal entities of the Republic of Kazakhstan for the duration of the public–private partnership agreement, including the concession agreement. The legislation also provides that a private partner for the implementation of PPP projects or a concessionaire for the implementation of concession projects can obtain a land plot without bidding (tenders, auctions) in respect of the land plot.

A similar rule applies to concession and PPP agreements in the *Russian Federation*. This simplified procedure for the provision of land reduces the time for the implementation of the PPP project and reduces land risks for investors.

Kyrgyzstan is more advanced than other former USSR countries in terms of creating special structures to provide financial support for PPP projects. Based on the best international practices, the country has created a whole range of financial support instruments, including

- infrastructure finance fund for the provision of long-term borrowings in national currency due to the limited capacity of the domestic banking sector to provide such financing;
- guarantee fund (guarantee fund) in order to reduce exposure to the risks of private sources of financing, including the provision of currency risks, risks of increasing the cost of lending, risks of insufficient profitability, and political risks; and
- subsidized funding fund (viability gap fund) to finance the lack of viability of PPP projects that are economically sound and attractive, but are not financially viable due to income from user payments.

Rather active support for development of PPP in Ukraine is provided by non-governmental structures. In 2010, a non-profit organization "Ukrainian center for public–private partnership" was established, the main purpose of which is to promote the development of PPP for the implementation of socially significant infrastructure projects to enhance scientific and technical potential and innovative technologies for the modernization of life support systems, to promote investment attractiveness of the Ukrainian economy and its regions, etc.

Advisory assistance from the United States, in particular, in the framework of the development of public–private partnership (Public–Private Partnership Development Program, P3DP) funded by the U.S. Agency for international development (USAID) contributes to establishment and development of PPP in Ukraine. The program is aimed at helping Ukraine to create a favorable institutional environment for PPP in five areas: improving legislation, supporting activities of the national PPP units, training and information, implementation of PPP pilot projects in key sectors, and promotion of clean energy.

The program selected and implemented pilot projects in areas such as health care, management of pre-school education, disposal of solid waste, energy efficiency, maintenance of the parks, transportation, etc. (http://www.ukrproject.gov.ua/ru/page/mezhdunarodnoe-sotrudnichestvo-1).

In 2014, the USAID PPP Development Program and the American Chamber of Commerce in Ukraine established an expert center on public–private partnership and infrastructure, which is designed to provide technical expertise for the development of infrastructure and public–private partnership in Ukraine. The center assists stakeholders in development of a new program of reforms in infrastructure and PPP. In the future, the center will become a platform for consultations and exchange of views and experience between business and government of Ukraine, local authorities, and the international expert society.

Conclusions

Analysis of PPP in the former USSR countries allows to draw the following conclusions and make some recommendations:

- The scope and level of use of PPP mechanisms in the former Soviet Union countries vary significantly: Some of them (Russia and Kazakhstan) have already accumulated considerable theoretical and practical experience of PPP, in general, formed the legal framework of PPP, built organizational and institutional basis of partnership, gained experience in practical implementation of PPP projects in various fields. Others (Ukraine, Belarus, and Kyrgyzstan) have made progress at the very first stage of PPP formation, and have developed fundamental legislative and regulatory acts, have created PPP units and started implementing PPP projects. Armenia, Uzbekistan, and Tajikistan are at the very beginning of the road, forming institutional base of PPP and trying their hand at implementation of pilot projects.
- In almost all countries of the former USSR today there is a problem of deterioration of infrastructure, which necessitates implementation of socially significant infrastructure projects. One of the best solutions to this problem is seen in these countries in PPP mechanisms.
- The countries of the former USSR seek to put development of PPP on a systemic basis. To this end, they form national public administration systems in the field of PPP, develop strategic goal-setting documents, try to put development of infrastructure on a long-term planning basis, form PPP units, and create a system of state support for PPP projects.
- However, PPP development in the countries of the former Soviet Union is mostly of "vertical" model, involving joint efforts of government and business within a national framework. Development of PPP "horizontally," i.e., giving it a supranational, multilateral character could be useful for these countries not only in terms of promoting development of national infrastructure, but also in terms of

expanding the field of economic cooperation both bilaterally and multilaterally, joining efforts in implementation of mutually beneficial transnational infrastructure projects, as well as cooperation in achieving the UN sustainable development goals.

- However, despite the declared within the framework of the EAEU and SCO desire to deepen cooperation, at the moment there has not been much progress in multilateral supranational coordination of PPP development. So, back in 2015 on the premises of the international conference "On the path to success public-private partnership in the Republic of Belarus: retrospective and perspectives," proposals to create a supranational PPP center of excellence in the EAEU by analogy with the European EPEC center were welcomed. But at the moment similar no such structure has been established yet. The main work on supranational coordination of efforts on PPP development in EAEU is carried out by the expert group on PPP issues.
- Nevertheless, it still seems that public–private partnership could become an effective tool for establishing and deepening economic cooperation between the countries of the former USSR, especially in the field of infrastructure. There are a number of objective prerequisites and enabling factors for that, including substantial interest in PPP in almost all these countries, experiences of many countries gained in PPP field, including the experience of PPP public governance, formation of public support system, practical implementation of PPP projects in various infrastructure sectors, common commitment to multilateral cooperation in the implementation of major transnational infrastructure projects, primarily in the field of transport, the availability of a rich methodological database related to PPP, developed by international institutions and forums in which most of the former Soviet Union countries participate (APEC, ESCAP, UNECE), the beginning of the work of a number of powerful financial institutions, the assistance of which could be expected in the implementation of joint infrastructure projects (Asian Infrastructure Investment Bank—AIIB, New BRICS Development Bank, Asian Development Bank) (Inshakova and Goncharov 2019).
- Integration of PPP issues with UN sustainable development goals should not be underestimated as an aspect of PPP cooperation. Adoption in 2015 by the UN of the 2030 agenda for sustainable development ("2030 Agenda"), which set out the sustainable development goals, marked the transition to a new paradigm of financing for development, in which PPP has an important role to play as a tool for mobilizing knowledge, technology, know-how and financial resources for the creation and development of sustainable energy, infrastructure, transport and information and communication technologies (11).
- Some Shanghai Cooperation Organization (SCO) countries have already started practical activities in this direction. In particular, in 2017, China and ESCAP signed an agreement on strengthening public–private partnership (PPP) in the Asia-Pacific region, with a view to focusing on improving access to infrastructure services in the water, energy, and transport sectors. Considering that China has become the largest PPP market in the region, the partnership of UNESCAP and the PPP Center of China could help strengthen business ties between PPP units

in SCO countries to expand the exchange of best practice "PPP experiences", to facilitate member countries of the organization of the region to promote regional connectivity in the framework of the UN Agenda for sustainable development until 2030 and in the context of the organization's activities (12).

- It seems that the motion vector in the direction of establishing former USSR countries' cooperation in the field of PPP could be the following: formation of expert groups on PPP consisting of representatives of the government and the business community in bilateral or multilateral format—organization of discussion forums (possibly in the framework of the annual Russian PPP week)—exchange of experiences and information on PPP development at the national level to disseminate best practices, facilitate training of personnel in the public sector and improvement of methodical work—establishing "road maps" of development of PPP cooperation—formation of the list of priority infrastructure development projects and supranational instruments to attract financing for pilot infrastructure projects implementation on the territory of the former USSR that bears maximum effects from the point of view of development and deepening of mutual economic cooperation.
- In thinking about joint pilot projects, it would be possible to rely on the concretization of the Chinese initiative "Silk Road Economic Belt." Although a clear route of the Silk Road has not yet been developed, according to preliminary data, the project is based on the construction of three railway corridors (northern, central, southern), which will connect the eastern provinces of China with many countries of the former USSR (13, 14).
- No doubt that taking into account the interest shown by the vast majority of the former Soviet Union countries in public–private partnership, the methodological developments and experience of practical implementation of infrastructure projects based on PPP mechanisms, as well as the desire and willingness to deepen economic cooperation declared in the statutory documents of organizations in which many of these countries take part, PPP could become another promising direction for deepening mutual cooperation in the field of infrastructure in the post-Soviet space.

References

Akobirov S. PPP development in Uzbekistan. http://www.lib.knigi-x.ru/23ekonomika/645499-1-so-akobirov-sardor-odilovich-akobirov-aspirant-kafedri-ekonomicheskoy-teorii-ekonom.php. Accessed 24 Aug 2019.

APEC, USAID. (2017). Public-Private partnerships for transportation in the APEC region. *An Analysis and Literature Review*.

Asian Development Bank. (2012). *Enabling identification of public-private partnership (PPP) projects and capacity building in kyrgyz republic*. Consultant's Report.

Asian Development Bank. (2017). *Public–Private partnership monitor*.

Asia-Pacific Economic Cooperation (APEC). (2015). *Guidebook on PPP frameworks in APEC region: Investment experts' group-may 2015*. Jakarta: APEC.

Delmon, J. (2017). *Public-private partnership projects in infrastructure* (2-nd edn). Singapore.

Economist Intelligence Unit (EIU). (2015). E*valuating the environment for public–Private Partnerships in Asia-Pacific: The 2014 infrascope.*

Estache, A., & Garsous, G. (2012). *The impact of infrastructure on growth in developing countries.* IFC Economics Notes, Note 1. Washington, D.C.: International Finance Corporation.

Evraziiskaya ekonomicheskaya komissiya. (2018). Gosudarstvenno-chastnoe partnyorstvo v stranakh Evraziyskogo ekonomicheskogo soyuza. Prakticheskoe rukovodstvo dlya investorov. 2-e izdanie (Eurasian Economic Commission (2018). Public-private partnership in the countries of the Eurasian economic Union. A practical guide for investors. 2-nd edition).

Federalnii Zakon ot 1 iyulya 2015 goda No.224-FZ "O gosudarstvenno-chastnom, munitsipalno-chastnom partnyorstve v Rossiiskoi Federatsii" (Federal law No. 224-FZ of 1 July 2015 "On public-private partnership, municipal-private partnership in the Russian Federation").

Federalnii Zakon ot 21 iyulya 2005 goda No.115-FZ "O kontsessionnikh soglasheniyakh" (Federal law No. 115-FZ of 21 July 2005 "On concession agreements").

Gosudarstvenno-chastnoe parnyorstvo v Ukraine (Public-Private Partnership in Ukrain*).* Arzinger. Kiev. 2010.

Ian Hawkesworth, Ihssane Loudiyi. Overview of public governance of public-private partnerships in the Russian Federation. OECD Journal on Budgeting. 2015.

Inshakova, A. O., & Goncharov, A. I. (2019). Innovation as an integral condition for the development of modern foreign trade turnover of energy resources and its legal regulation. In O. V. Inshakov, A. O. Inshakova, E. G. Popkova (Eds.*), Energy sector: A systemic analysis of economy, foreign trade and legal regulations* (pp. 67–78). Cham: Springer Science + Business Media.

Inshakova, A. O., Goncharov, A. I., & Marchukov, I. P. (2019). Common energy policy and development paths legal regulation of foreign trade turnover of energy resources in the CIS and in the EEU. In O. V. Inshakov, A. O. Inshakova, & E. G. Popkova (Eds.), *Energy sector: A systemic analysis of economy, foreign trade and legal regulations* (pp. 207–225). Cham: Springer Science + Business Media.

Ivanov, O. V. (2016). Teoriya i praktika gosudarstvenno-chastnogo partnyorstva. MGIMO, Moskva. (Theory and world practice of public-private partnership. MGIMO. Moscow).

Kudelich, M. I., Khachatryan, A. V. (2018). "Uchastie finansovikh organov Respubliki Armeniya v protsessakh gosudarstvenno-chastnogo partnyorstva", Finansovii zhurnal. ("Participation of financial bodies of the Republic of Armenia in the processes of public-private partnership". Financial journal), №4, pp. 76–89.

Llanto, G. M., Navarro, A. M., Ortiz, M. K. P. (2015). *Infrastructure financing, public-private partnerships and development in Asia-pacific region. Asia-Pacific Development Journal, 22*(2), 27–69.

Mekhanizmy gosudarstvenno-chastnogo partnyorstva v ekonomicheskoi politike Rossii (Mechanisms of public-private partnership in the economic policy of Russia). Ed. by O.V.Ivanov. MGIMO-University, Moscow. 2018. 409 p.

National PPP Center. (2019). Analytical review. Simply and honestly about investments in infrastructure and PPP in Russia. ROSINFRA. PPP Development Center. URL: http://pppcenter.ru/assets/files/obzor240419.pdf. Accessed 24 Aug 2019.

Natsionalnaya infrastrukturnaya strategiya 2017–2030. Minsk, 2017. (National infrastructure strategy 2017–2030. Minsk 2017).

Osobennosti otbora chastnogo partnyora v GCHP-proektakh v stranakh EAES. Obzor. Natsionalnii tsentr GCHP, EAEK. 2018 (Selection of the private partner in PPP projects in the countries of the EAEU. Review. National PPP Centre, Eurasia Economic Commission. 2018).

Otsenka effektivnosti proektov GCHP po sravneniyu s inymi formami realizatsii infrastrukturnikh proektov v stranakh-uchastnitsakh EAES. Analiticheskoe issledovanie. Natsionalnii tsentr GCHP, EAEK. 2018 (Assessment of the effectiveness of PPP projects in comparison with other forms of implementation of infrastructure projects in the EAEU member States. Analytical study. National PPP Centre, Eurasia Economic Commission. 2018).

Postanovlenie Ministerstva ekonomiki Respubliki Belarus ot 27 iyulya 2016 goda No.49 "O merakh po realiazatsii Zakona Respubliki Belarus ot 30 dekabrya 2015 goda "O gosudarstvenno-chastnom partnyorstve" (Resolution of the Ministry of economy of the Republic of Belarus No. 49 of 27 July 2016 "On measures to implement the Law of the Republic of Belarus of 30 December 2015 "On Public-Private Partnership").

Postanovleniye Pravitelstva Kyrgyzskoi Respubliki ot 14 sentyabrya 2012 goda No.616 "O Strategii realizatsii gosudarstvenno-chastnogo partnyorstva v Kyrgyzskoi Respublike" (Resolution of the Government of the Kyrgyz Republic of September 14, 2012 №616 "On the Public-Private Partnership Strategy in the Kyrgyz Republic").

Postanovleniye Pravitelstva Kyrgyzskoi Respubliki ot 16 iyunya 2016 goda No.327 "Ob utverzhdenii Programmi razvitiya gosudarstvenno-chastnogo partnyorstva v Kyrgyzskoi Respublike na 2016–21 godi" (Resolution of the Government of the Kyrgyz Republic of June 16, 2016 №327 "On approval of the Program of development of Public-Private Partnership in the Kyrgyz Republic for 2016–21").

Postanovleniye Pravitelstva Kyrgyzskoi Respubliki ot 16 iyunya 2016 goda No.328 goda "Ob obrazovanii Soveta po gosudarstvenno-chastnomu partnyorstvu v Kyrgyzskoi Respublike" (Resolution of the Government of the Kyrgyz Republic of June 16, 2016 №328 "On the formation of the Public-Private Partnership Council in the Kyrgyz Republic").

Postanovleniye Pravitelstva Kyrgyzskoi Respubliki ot 17 marta 2014 goda No.147 "O finansirovanii podgotovki proektov gosudarstvenno-chastnogo partnyorstva" (Resolution of the Government of the Kyrgyz Republic of March 17, 2014 №147 "On financing of Public-Private Partnership projects' preparation").

Postanovleniye Pravitelstva Respubliki Armeniya ot 9 noyabrya 2017 goda "Ob osnovnikh napravleniyakh gosudarstvennoi politiki Respubliki Armeniya v sfere gosudarstvenno-chastnogo partnyorstva" (Resolution of the Government of the Republic of Armenia of November 9, 2017.

PPIAF. (2014). *Institutional investment in infrastructure in emerging markets and developing economies*. Washington.

Realization of Public-Private Partnership Projects in Ukraine. Guideline. (2017).

Transforming our world: the 2030 Agenda for Sustainable Development. https://documentsddsny.un.org/doc/UNDOC/GEN/N15/285/75/PDF/N1528575.pdf?OpenElement. (United Nations, 2015). Accessed 24 Aug 2019.

UNECE. (2013). *UNECE PPP assessment report. Green PPPs in Kazakhstan*. UNECE International PPP Centre of Excellence.

United Nations Economic Commission for Europe. (2008). *Guidebook on promoting good governance in public-private partnerships*.

World Bank, PPIAF. (2011). *How to engage with the private sector in public-private partnerships in emerging markets*. Washington.

World Bank. (2015). *Public-private partnerships in the context of public investment management in Ukraine. An assessment*.

World Bank. (2017). *Public-private partnership*. Reference Guide. Version 3. Washington.

World Bank. (2018). *Procuring infrastructure public-private partnerships report 2018*.

World Economic Forum. (2017). *The global competitiveness report 2017–2018*.

Zakon Kyrgyzskoi respubliki "O gosudarstvenno-chastnom partnyorstve v Kyrgyzskoi respublike" ot 22 fevralya 2012 goda (Law of the Kyrgyz Republic "On Public-Private Partnership in the Kyrgyz Republic" of 22 February 2012).

Zakon Respubliki Belarus "O gosudarstvenno-chastnom partnyorstve" No345-3 ot 30 dekabrya 2015 goda (Law of the Republic of Belarus "on public-private partnership" No. 345-3 of 30 December 2015).

Zakon Respubliki Kazakhstan "O kontsessiyakh" No.167 ot 7 iyulya 2006 goda (Law of the Republic of Kazakhstan "On concessions" No. 167 of 7 July 2006).

Zakon Respubliki Kazkahstan "O gosudarstvenno-chastnom partnyorstve" ot 31 oktyabrya 2015 goda (Law of the Republic of Kazakhstan "on public-private partnership" of 31 October 2015).

. 习近平"一带一路"构想战略意义深远 (XI Jinping: "One belt and one road" is of great strategic importance). http://news.cri.cn/gb/42071/2014/10/10/882s4720906.html.
习近平提战略构想:"一带一路"打开"筑梦空间". 人民网. 2014年08月11日 (XI Jinping: "One belt and one road" will open new horizons of dreams. http://politics.people.com.cn/n/2014/0811/c1001-25439028.html.

Chapter 16
Public–Private Partnership as an Instrument to Implement the Sustainable Development Goals in the Developing Countries

Evgenia A. Starikova

Abstract The 2030 Agenda for Sustainable Development (the 2030 Agenda) actualized the necessity to employ the effective and innovative mechanisms of development financing. The global community has currently faced the task of searching for new formats of cooperation between the state and business that will prove to be most effective in terms of attracting private investment in the interests of the Sustainable Development Goals (SDGs) implementation in the developing world. The chapter concentrates on the problem of framework formulation for interaction between the state and the private sectors in the interests of SDGs implementation in developing and least developed countries. In this study, the state is understood to be the authorized state agencies specializing in providing foreign aid to recipient countries (donor agencies). It also reviews the current practice of collaboration between the private sector and the donor government agencies and implementation of the corresponding public–private partnerships in the recipient countries aimed at the achievement of the SDGs in the developing world.

Keywords Public–private partnership · Sustainable development · Sustainable development goals (SDGs) · The 2030 agenda · Shared value

JEL Codes F23 · F63 · Q01

Introduction

With the adoption of the "2030 Agenda for Sustainable Development" by the United Nations in 2015 (hereinafter referred to as the "2030 Agenda"), which contains the 17 Sustainable Development Goals (SDGs), the transition to a new paradigm for financing development was also designated. As noted in the updated global agenda, public sources of finance in the form of Official Development Assistance (ODA)

E. A. Starikova (✉)
MGIMO University, Vernadsky Ave., 76, 119454 Moscow, Russia
e-mail: evan3132@gmail.com

O. V. Ivanov and A. O. Inshakova (eds.), *Public-Private Partnerships in Russia*, Competitive Government: Public Private Partnerships,
https://doi.org/10.1007/978-3-030-56352-3_16

continue to serve an important function in promoting the development of the least developed countries that have limited domestic resources, however, the attraction of "*additional resources from other sources, both public and private*" (2030 Agenda, United Nations 2015) is gaining an ever-increasing role. In particular, the very interpretation of the functions of official financing for development has changed in the donor countries community: at the current time, the most sought-after idea is that the funds allocated from public sources first of all need to be used as a tool to attract resources from private sources to finance priority areas that ensure sustainable and subsequently independent economic development in the aid-recipient countries (OECD 2018).

In this regard, the governments of developed countries and international organizations have begun to search for new formats of state–business interaction, which would be more focused on the implementation of the SDGs and solving the most serious global challenges that humanity faced in the twenty-first century.

This trend is reflected in the majority of official documents adopted by international organizations in the context of the proclamation of the "2030 Agenda", in which PPP is considered as the most essential tool of implementing the SDGs in practice. In particular, in the report of the ECOSOC Commission on sustainable development, that was prepared back to 2003, notes that in modern conditions, PPP projects should be linked to economic, social, and environmental aspects of sustainable development (United Nations 2003). According to the United Nations Development Program (UNDP), infrastructural PPP projects have fundamental importance from the point of view of achieving sustainable development (UNDP 2015). In the Addis Ababa Action Agenda, PPP is presented as a tool of financing "sustainable, affordable, acceptable cost and failure-free functioning qualitative infrastructure" to achieve sustainable development that implies strong accountability mechanisms and is aligned with national priorities of socio-economic development.

The direct interconnection between the SDGs and PPPs is indicated directly in the "2030 Agenda" itself—notably in SDG 9, aimed at creating a "resilient" infrastructure and developing innovations for sustainable development, and in SDG 17, in which asserted the need to stimulate PPP as an instrument mobilizing knowledge, technology, know-how, and financial resources in order to create and develop sustainable energetics, infrastructure, transport, as well as information and communication technologies.

Thus, at the current time, the creation of public–private partnerships (PPPs) between governments of donor countries and the private sector is one of the most promising and sought-after financing mechanisms for the SDGs in developing and most vulnerable countries (Ivanov 2019). *This chapter focuses on* a review of the practice of creating public–private partnerships in order to realize the SDGs using the example of cooperation between government agencies and departments operating in developed countries that specialize in providing external assistance to the private sector.

Public–Private Partnerships (PPPs) as a Financing Instrument of the Sustainable Development Goals (SDGs) in the Developing World

According to UNCTAD's calculations, annual incremental investments of $2.5 trillion only in developing countries are needed for the timely achievement of the SDGs and to create an appropriate infrastructure for this purpose (UNCTAD 2014). At the same time, it is pointed out that the funds currently allocated in the format of ODA and through public sources of financing can cover only half of this deficit (UNCTAD 2014) (see Fig. 16.1).

Thus, with the adoption of the "2030 Agenda", the ever-increasing importance acquired the search for new financing mechanisms for development. One of these innovative mechanisms is the so-called "*blended finance*" is a tool that, according to estimates by the Global Commission on Economy and Climate, can attract additional private capital in the amount of up to $1-1.5 trillion annually (Brookings Institution 2015). Blended finance is the strategic use of public or philanthropic development capital for the mobilization of additional external private commercial finance for SDG-related investments (Business & Sustainable Development Commission 2018).

In the "Addis Ababa Action Agenda" of the "Third International Conference on Financing for Development" (Addis Ababa Action Agenda, United Nations 2015)

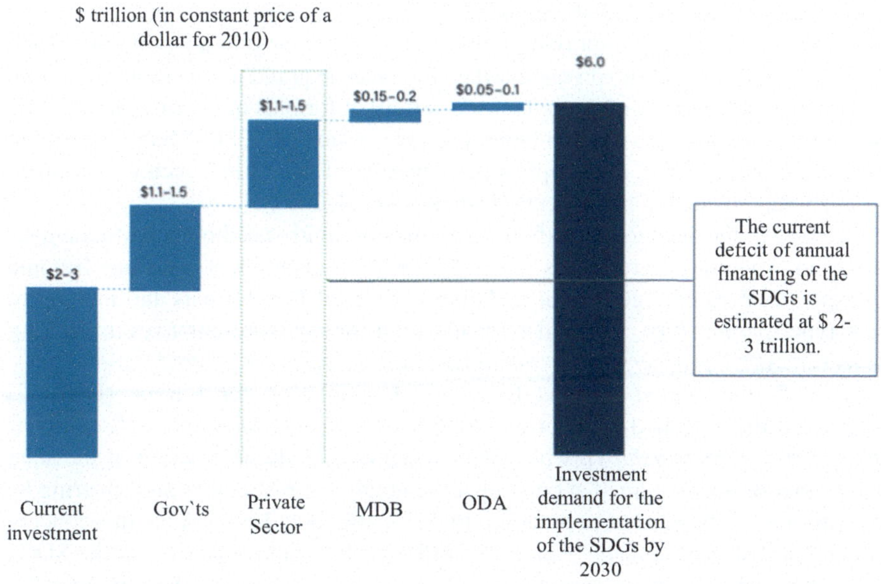

Fig. 16.1 Deficit of infrastructure financing to achieve the SDGs in developing countries. *Source* Compiled based on data from the report of the Global Commission on Economy and Climate (Brookings Institution 2015)

is indicated that the key role in financing infrastructure projects is played by both public and private investments, which are the most important from the point of view of promoting international development, "including through development banks, development finance institutions and tools and mechanisms such as public–private partnerships, blended finance, which combines concessional public finance with non-concessional private finance and expertise from the public and private sector." At the same time, public–private partnerships are mentioned in this document as an important tool that allows "to lower investment-specific risks" and stimulating "additional private sector finance across key development sectors" (Addis Ababa Action Agenda, United Nations 2015). Thus, the phenomenon of "blending" of capitals, carried out in the framework of public–private partnerships, occurred long before the term "blended finance" appeared (Zavyalova et al. 2018).

Obviously, that cooperation between the government and business in the framework of jointly implemented public–private projects in developing countries is one of the most sought-after and promising mechanisms of financing development. If the state is traditionally charged with providing services in socially important areas (health care, education), creating the appropriate infrastructure, ensuring security, practical implementation and dissemination of scientific knowledge and new technologies for social development, monitoring compliance with the law in the field of environmental protection (Ivanov 2016), then the private sector is called upon to provide financial, technological, managerial, and expert resources for the realization of the SDGs that repeatedly emphasizes in documents such as the "Addis Ababa Action Agenda" and the "2030 Agenda."

At the same time, it is important to note that in the context of adopting the "2030 Agenda," the term "public–private partnership" has acquired a broad interpretation, under which it began to understand a wide variety of formats of interaction of public and commercial partners. In particular, even the notion of "PPP+" has appeared in foreign literature, which also implies participation of the "third" sector (non-profit organizations) in such joint projects (Inshakova et al. 2019).

The idea of the need to intensify the activities of multi-stakeholder partnerships,[1] which are voluntary agreements between various stakeholders, also has become widespread, ideas emerged about updating traditional PPP formats and moving to "new type" partnerships, which also involve civil society representatives in working projects *("ABC" partnerships - "administration", "business", "civil society").*

In 2015, the United Nations Economic Commission for Europe (UNECE) proclaimed the so-called concept of *"PPP for the benefit of people" (People-first Public-Private Partnerships)*, which was interpreted as the interaction of the state and the private sector, aimed at creating a sustainable infrastructure and ensuring its accessibility for the general population. In 2018, after detailed work on, this concept was interpreted as a separate "variety" of PPP to achieve the objectives of the SDGs that is directed to invest in appropriate infrastructure, in doing so these partnership projects must not only meet the set out cost-effectiveness criteria, but should also

[1] The concept of multi-stakeholder partnerships got its development after the Johannesburg Summit in 2002.

be more focused on providing "value for people" (UNECE Guiding Principles on PfPPPs 2019).

It is important to note that the "2030 Agenda" focuses not only on economic efficiency in the implementation of projects, but also on their "target effectiveness" (achieving specific SDGs and objectives within these goals) and "inclusiveness" (focus on satisfaction of interests of society as a whole and the most vulnerable segments of the population).

In this regard, the thesis is widely spread in modern scientific literature that the population becomes the "main beneficiary" of PPP projects under current conditions seemed fair, and the key results of PPP projects will be evaluated in terms of improving the quality of life of society in a broad sense. The main goal of such partnerships is to increase public access to quality public services and provide people with the necessary resources (water, food, energy, transport, health care, and education).

At the same time, any assertions about the fundamental transformation of the PPP concept in connection with the adoption of the SDGs are premature and declarative before the development and implementation of the state–business interaction principles updated in accordance with the SDGs into national laws and international legal acts.

The Practice of Interaction Between Government Agencies and the Private Sector: A Contribution to the Sustainable Development of Developing Countries

Since the "2030 Agenda" still devolves a large share of responsibility on developed countries for promoting global development and implementation of the SDGs in the developing world, the author found it appropriate to provide an overview of the practice of involving the private sector in joint programs with key international development agencies in the USA, Great Britain, and Germany.

* * *

Founded in 1961, USAID agency serves as the key institution of the American government, responsible for international development and foreign aid. USAID has the status of an independent government agency, but works closely with the US State Department, which determines the political course and priority areas of agency activity. In 2017 fiscal year, USAID received funding of $29.5 billion, which is 8% higher than the total budget of the agency for 2016 (USAID 2017).

Taking into account the changing specificity of promoting international development, the US government claims a leading role in creating projects of public–private partnerships in the donor countries community. Thus, starting in 2001, USAID has signed over 1,800 partnerships with more than 3,900 private sector partners. At the same time, the cumulative investment from the private sector at a rough calculations is estimated at $38 billion (USAID 2017). In general, there is an approximately equal balance of costs between public and private partners in joint projects.

The vast majority of public–private partnerships, created with the participation of the agency, are aimed at creating and developing infrastructure. Four key partner initiatives that are related to the agricultural (Feed the Future), energetic (Power Africa) industries, the health sector (Global Health Initiative) and the environmental protection (Global Climate Change Initiative) deserve special attention. It is important to note that all these projects are aimed at achieving the main socio-economic and environmental SDGs (Goals 2, 3, 7, 13) in the least developed countries.

In 2014, USAID launched a new platform for innovation and multilateral initiatives—the Global Development Lab. The Center for Transformational Partnerships (CTP), created as part of the laboratory, establishes contacts with companies interested in cooperating with USAID and provides overall management of the agency's partnership initiatives.

The largest PPP project implemented by USAID since 2006 is the program aimed at treating neglected tropical diseases (Neglected Tropical Diseases (NTD) Program) (see Fig. 16.1). Under the program, the largest pharmaceutical TNCs—Eisai, GlaxoSmithKline, Merck & Co., Merck KGaA, Johnson & Johnson and Pfizer—provide delivery of six essential medicines. The aggregate amount of cost of the partners amounted to over $19 billion for more than a decade of project existence (USAID 2019a, b).

In general, USAID considers public–private partnerships as a strategic element of its activities, which naturally reflects the tendency of foreign aid format transformation. If 30 years ago, 70% of cash flow from the United States to the developing world was provided through ODA, now 80% of the funds come in the form of foreign direct investment, private donations, remittances, and other non-governmental sources. At the same time, ODA accounts only 14% of total foreign aid, which indicates the ever-increasing role of the private sector in promoting development.

It is important to note that when implementing joint projects with business, USAID adheres to the principle of creating "shared value" both for the population of aid-recipient countries and for participating companies. For example, as part of the implementation of energetic projects in developing countries, US companies are given an opportunity to significantly expand the export of equipment and software in the energetic sector (USAID 2018). In particular, in 2015, US exports of equipment necessary for energy supply to USAID aid-recipient countries amounted to $3.6 billion. Another very good example that demonstrates business benefits from participation in partnership programs is the case of the American energetic company Azure Power, which, with the assistance of USAID, provided technical support for the solar energetics development project in India and won the tender for the creation of solar panels which are installed on rooftops. Currently, the American company is a key business player in the Indian National Program for the Development of Solar Energy (USAID 2018). It is also worth noting that most partnerships are implemented in middle-income countries with fast-growing economies, which opens up opportunities for the private sector to enter new markets (Fig. 16.2).

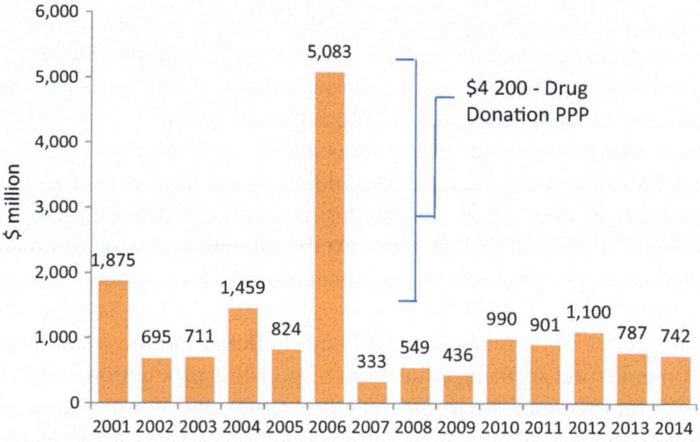

Fig. 16.2 USAID investment in public–private partnership projects, $ million *Source* Compiled by the author based on data from the Devex report (Devex 2018)

* * *

The *German* government is also pursuing an active policy of engaging the private sector to mobilize additional financing and support the implementation of the SDGs in developing countries. In particular, the Ministry of Economic Cooperation and Development of Germany (BMZ) provides co-financing and expert support for investment business projects in the least developed countries. Companies are obliged to compensate at least half of the total costs for the project implementation within this cooperation format, and the share of financial participation of BMZ can reach €200,000. The maximum duration of such partnership projects is 3 years.

At the initiative of BMZ in 1999, a special program of cooperation between the state and business "develoPPP.de" was launched. Projects implemented in cooperation with private German and European companies on the "develoPPP.de" platform are implemented with the participation of one of the three authorized government partners—the Financial Development Institute—which is a subsidiary of the state development bank KfW Group (DEG-Deutsche Investitions-und Entwicklungsgesellschaft mbH), German Development Agency (Deutsche Gesellschaft für Internationale Zusammenarbeit (GIZ) GmbH) and the international non-profit organization sequa gGmbH, sponsored by the largest German business associations, as well as the German Agency of Development (GIZ).

Besides the financial support, a public partner represented by one of the three authorized organizations helps private companies to overcome the barriers associated with the underdevelopment of legal and regulatory institutions; infrastructure; the lack of qualified specialists and lack of knowledge about local conditions when entering markets of developing countries; and also provides dialog with local authorities, companies, and non-governmental organizations (Inshakova et al. 2017).

The main organization that provides technical advice and strategic planning in the field of international cooperation for the Ministry of Economic Development and Cooperation (BMZ) of Germany is the German Agency for Development GIZ. In 2015, the amount of funds allocated for the activities of GIZ exceeded $2.3 billion (€2.1 billion). Since the launch of the "develoPPP.de" platform in 1999, the work of GIZ has been strategically focused on building public–private partnerships. From 1999 to the present, over 1,500 partnership projects for development have been implemented on the basis of this program. At the same time, the selection of companies interested in cooperation with government partners takes place on a competitive basis.

The priority areas of partnership are all key challenges to the concept of sustainable development (food security, education, responsible production, working conditions, decent employment, environmental protection and conservation of natural resources, combating climate change, implementation of sustainable technologies), which reflects the priorities of external assistance, which are indicated by German government.

Together with private partners, GIZ launched over 2000 partnership projects over the period 1999–2016. The total amount of public–private investment under the develoPPP.de program amounted to more than €1.1 billion, while 37.7% of funds ($443 million) came from the public sector and 62.3% ($732 million) from the private sector. According to data on the official website of the program, the following distribution of investments by sectors is observed: 36.22% was allocated in order to achieve "sustainable economic development" in the recipient countries, 18.96% invested in agriculture, 12.84% for environmental purposes, 8.08% in health care, 6.63% to energetics, 6.55% in education, and 6.38% in water resource management (develoPPP.de 2018).

The largest number of projects was implemented in the East Asian region (496 projects with total amount of financing of $226 million), second in the number of projects and allocated financing for the period from 1999 to 2015 were countries from sub-Saharan Africa (303 projects with total value of $176 million).

All projects within the develoPPP.de program are aimed at finding solutions in response to global challenges identified in the SDGs in more than 100 countries (develoPPP.de 2018). In doing so, GIZ provides active support to business, helping companies that participate in the program to expand their sales markets in developing countries.

To establish communication with companies and promote partnerships for development under the auspices of the GIZ agency, a special Private Sector Cooperation Unit was created. Furthermore, Business Development Units (BDUs) have been formed in a number of developing countries that can independently participate in local partnership projects.

* * *

The Department for International Development of the United Kingdom (DFID) also stated that partnerships with the private sector are a key priority of its activities:

from 2012 to 2016 financing of private sector in joint projects with the Ministry was increased ninefold, reaching $715 million in 2016.

The main tools of DFID to promote partnerships are specialized funds to deal with certain challenges (the so-called "challenge funds") and partnerships involving several donors. Challenge funds are established in more than 30 countries of the world: their main task is to provide financial support to companies that offer their own innovative solutions through the provision of grants, loans, and other financial instruments on a competitive basis.

As part of ongoing partnerships, DFID provides technical and expert support and provides co-financing for projects. DFID partnership programs are open to all companies; however, most projects are currently being implemented in partnership with British companies.

In 2011, in order to activate business participation in partnerships, DFID established a special unit, the Private Sector Department (PSD). Currently, companies can initiate cooperation with the Ministry by requesting to a special department—Business Engagement Hub (BEH).

Besides bilateral partnerships with the private sector, DFID actively promotes multi-stakeholder partnerships with the involvement of several donors, among which the most famous are initiatives such as the Business Call to Action alliance, the Global Innovation Fund, and entrepreneurial funds to deal with challenges in Africa and the Caribbean (Africa Enterprise Challenge Fund, Enterprise Innovation Challenge Fund for the Caribbean).

The DFID has allocated 494 million pounds to create alliances and partnerships with British and foreign companies during the period from 2012 to 2015. Among the most financed partnerships can be identified network for the development of socially responsible business in Africa (Business Action for Africa) partnership to enhance the rights of women (Safety, Health and Education and Employment for Girls and Women Alliance), cooperation projects with British non-profit organization "Water and Sanitation for the Urban Poor", aimed to increase access to water and sanitation for urban slum dwellers in countries of Asia and Africa, as well as food fund (Food Retail Industry Challenge Fund) (DFID 2018) (Table 16.1).

The examples reviewed demonstrate the ever-increasing role of cooperation with the private sector in the activities of state agencies for international development. Bilateral state agencies, providing foreign aid currently play an important role in attracting private funding. Analysis of the practice of government interaction in the form of authorized donor organizations and the private sector showed that partnerships are a form of cooperation that is promising in terms of attracting private funding necessary for the SDGs implementation in the developing and least developed countries.

In Russia, the Federal Agency for Affairs of the Commonwealth of Independent States, Compatriots Residing Abroad and International Humanitarian Co-operation (Rossotrudnichestvo) is the federal government body responsible for providing foreign aid and International Development Assistance (IDA). On April 20, 2014, by Decree of the President of the Russian Federation No. 259, a new concept for

Table 16.1 Cooperation between state agencies for international development and private sector

Government donor agencies	The total amount of provided external assistance 2016–2017	Investments from government sources allocated through partnership programs	The total amount of private investments within partnership programs	Number of partnerships with private sector
USAID	$29.5 billion	$19.9 billion (from 2001 to 2017)	$79.9 billion (from 2001 to 2017)	More than 1800
DFID	$12 billion	$715 million + $740 million (the budget of PSD within the Ministry)	Not specified	Not specified
GIZ	€2.6 billion *(within the develoPPP.de program* €1.2 billion) (from 1999 to 2018)	€443 million (from 1999 to 2018)	€732 million (from 1999 to 2018)	More than 2000

Source Compiled by the author based on data from the Devex report and statistical data from the official sites of the agencies under review (Devex 2018)

the state policy of the Russian Federation in the field of promoting international development was approved.

Within the framework of this document, the task was set to intensify interaction between the state and business in two areas: firstly, to support Russian companies entering the markets of developing countries; secondly, to attract domestic business to foreign aid programs implemented by the state. However, it should be noted that to date, no effective system of interaction between government bodies and Russian TNCs in the implementation of joint Community Programs abroad has been developed yet; there are no integrated data on already implemented or planned public–private partnership programs in the framework of IDA.

One of the few well-known cases of cooperation between Russian business and the state in the field of providing foreign aid abroad is the project of public–private partnership to combat Ebola in Guinea, implemented by Rospotrebnadzor together with UC Rusal. As a result of the implementation of this PPP project, the management of Rusal addressed to Rospotrebnadzor and the Ministry of Finance with a proposal on the subsequent institutionalization of the PPP mechanism in the control of especially dangerous infections and epidemics, that is, the creation of a "mixed" funding fund in this area in cooperation with public authorities. If such fund is created, this institution will be the first official mechanism for the participation of Russian business in IDA programs (RUSAL 2016).

Thus, it seems possible to assume that today large domestic business players are interested in reducing risks in the countries of their presence and express their willingness to formalize cooperation with the state and other stakeholders in the implementation of the SDGs at the global level, which, first of all, will be implemented within the framework of IDA programs of the Russian government.

Conclusion

Today government donor agencies are playing an ever-increasing role in financing for development: in addition to traditional ODA programs, they are increasingly participating in innovative mechanisms such as partnerships with the private sector. Using this area of their activity as an instrument of "soft power" in foreign economic policy, donor agencies ensure the attraction of additional private capital by reducing investment risks for commercial partners, providing technical support to business within the framework of ongoing projects and creating a "shared value" for all participants of the partnership.

Therefore, state agencies, providing foreign aid, can play a significant part in attracting private investment and expertise in the interest of SDGs implementation in the developing world. These institutions provide advisory services to government authorities, contribute to the improvement of political climate in order to facilitate access to private investment and use risk mitigation instruments, as well as co-investment instruments and other innovative financing mechanisms in collaboration with the private sector. The above measures contribute significantly to the mobilization of additional financial, innovative, and expert resources from companies and institutional investors.

A distinctive feature of creating such partnerships is observance of the principle of "shared value": companies participating in joint projects with the state gain significant competitive advantages by expanding sales markets and reducing the risks of their operating activity in the aid-recipient countries. Thus, it seems appropriate to assume that, in the context of the adoption of the "2030 Agenda," public–private partnerships will be an increasingly popular tool used by government donor agencies to help achieve the SDGs in the developing world.

In Russia, sustainable development issues are also becoming the subject of wide discussion at the political level and in the business community. In the context of the formation of the state policy of the Russian Federation in the field of IDA, the task of harmonization of official programs carried out by Russian authorities in the interests of achieving the SDGs in recipient countries and CSR projects carried out by Russian business abroad is becoming increasingly relevant.

References

Addis Ababa Action Agenda of the Third International Conference on Financing for Development. (Addis Ababa Action Agenda). Resolution 69/313. https://unctad.org/meetings/en/SessionalDocuments/ares69d313_ru.pdf (United Nations, 27 Jul 2015). Accessed 05 Jul 2019.

Business & Sustainable Development Commission: Better Finance, Better World. Consultation paper of the Blended Finance Taskforce. (2018). http://s3.amazonaws.com/aws-bsdc/BFT_BetterFinance_final_01192018.pdf p. 10. Accessed 05 Jul 2019.

Commission on Sustainable Development: 11th session of the Commission on Sustainable Development. Economic and Social Council Official Records, 2003 Supplement No. 9 (United Nations, New York, 28 Apr–9 May 2003). https://www.un.org/ga/search/view_doc.asp?symbol=E/CN.17/2003/6&Lang=E.

Decree of the President of Russia of 20.04.2014 No 259 (rev. 24.05.2016) On approval of the concept of state policy of the Russian Federation in the field of international development assistance. http://www.consultant.ru/document/cons_doc_LAW_162006/bad5a39384f9c1e3296a15cd3d7fa25c867b3864/.

DeveloPPP.de. (2018). Our programme. Facts and figures. Joint achievements: Working together to take political, social and economic responsibility. https://www.developpp.de/en/our-programme-funding-for-development-partnerships-with-business/facts-and-figures-about-the-developppde-programme. Accessed 05 July 2019.

Devex Reports. (2018). Biateral donor agencies. A closer look at 5 development leaders. https://pages.devex.com/rs/685-KBL-765/images/Devex_Reports_Biateral_Donor_Agencies_A_Closer_Look_at_5_Development_Leaders.pdf.

Driving Sustainable Development Through Better Infrastructure: Key Elements of a Transformation Program. (2015). Global Economy & Development Working Paper 91, the Brookings Institution (p. 26). https://newclimateeconomy.report/workingpapers/wp-content/uploads/sites/5/2016/04/Driving-sustainable-development-through-better-infrastructure.pdf. Accessed 05 Jul 2019.

Inshakova, A. O., Goncharov, A. I., Sevostyanov, M. V. (2017). Institutional ambiguity of regulation of possessory relations in modern Russia. In *Overcoming Uncertainty of Institutional Environment as a Tool of Global Crisis Management* (1st edn, pp. 207–212).

Inshakova, A. O., Goncharov, A. I., & Inshakova, E. I. (2019). Innovative technologies of oil production: tasks of legal regulation of management and taxation. In O. V. Inshakov, A. O. Inshakova, & E. G. Popkova (Eds.), *Energy sector: A systemic analysis of economy, foreign trade and legal regulations* (pp. 79–94). Cham: Springer Science + Business Media.

Ivanov, O. V. (2016). *Teoriya i mirovaya praktika gosudarstvenno-chastnogo partnerstva (Theory and world practice of public-private partnership)* (p. 299). Moscow: MGIMO-University.

Ivanov, O. V. (2019). Gosudartsvenno-chastnoe partnerstvo kak instrument razvitiya infrastruktury I modernizatsii ekonomiki. Opyt stran Aziatsko-tikhookeanskogo regiona (Public-private partnership as an instrument of development of infrastructure and modernization of economy. Experience of Asia-Pacific countries) (300 p). Moscow: MGIMO-University.

OECD. (2018). *Making blended finance work for the sustainable development goals.* Paris.

Statistics on International Development. Final UK Aid spend. (2017). https://assets.publishing.service.gov.uk/government/uploads/system/uploads/attachment_data/file/760175/Statistics-International-_Development-Final-UK-Aid-Spend-2017.pdf (DFID, Nov 2018). Accessed 05 July 2019.

Transforming our world: the 2030 Agenda for Sustainable Development. https://documentsddsny.un.org/doc/UNDOC/GEN/N15/285/75/PDF/N1528575.pdf?OpenElement. (United Nations, 2015). Accessed 05 July 2019.

UC RUSAL Sustainability Report 2016. https://s3-us-west-2.amazonaws.com/ungc-production/attachments/cop_2018/451911/original/UC_RUSAL_SUSTAINABILITY_REPORT_2016.pdf?1515578024 Accessed 05 July 2019.

UNDP: World leaders adopt Sustainable Development Goals. (2015). http://www.undp.org/content/undp/en/home/presscenter/pressreleases/2015/09/24/undp-welcomes-adoption-of-sustainable-development-goals-by-worldleaders.html. Accessed 05 July 2019.
USAID FY 2017 Agency Financial Report. (2017). https://www.usaid.gov/sites/default/files/documents/1868/USAIDFY2017AFR.pdf. Accessed 05 July 2019.
USAID. (2018). Shared Interest: How USAID Enhances U. S. Economic Growth. https://www.usaid.gov/sites/default/files/documents/1870/FINAL_Version_of_Shared_Interest_6_2018.PDF. Accessed 05 Jul 2019.
USAID. (2019a). Drug Donation Partnerships. Neglected Tropical Diseases Program. https://www.neglecteddiseases.gov/about/drug-donation-partnership. Accessed 05 July 2019.
USAID. (2019b) Global Development Alliances. https://www.usaid.gov/gda. Accessed 05 July 2019.
World Investment Report 2014. Investing in the SDGs: an Action Plan. https://unctad.org/en/PublicationsLibrary/wir2014_en.pdf (United Nations, New York and Geneva, 2014). Accessed 05 Jul 2019.
Zavyalova, E. B., et al. (2018). Economics for political scientists: Textbook. MGIMO University. Moscow, Publishing House 'Scientific library',.

Conclusion

Over a relatively short period of 10–15 years Russia has accumulated vast experience in Public–Private Partnerships. In fact, a fundamentally new area of state-business economic relationship has been established in the country.

During this time PPP has come an impressive way from a fragmented set of individual projects to a single integrated market. A huge breakthrough in PPPs has been made, as evidenced by the growth in the number of projects and their capital intensity. As of the beginning of 2020, there are more than 3,500 PPP projects at different stages of implementation in Russia, and the cumulative volume of private contracted investments has exceeded 3 trillion rubles. Infrastructure investments are 70% covered by extra-budgetary funds. It can be concluded that PPP market as a major economic phenomenon has taken place in Russia.

The sectoral spectrum of PPPs is becoming more and more diverse. There is a steady growth of PPP projects in traditional sectors like road infrastructure and energy. At the same time, an explosive growth of concessions in the communal utilities sector has been recorded. Along with them, PPP has been established in infrastructure sectors that were previously a "preserved zone" of the state—social infrastructure, primarily healthcare, pre-school and school education, sports, culture, and social security. In recent years, PPP is increasingly opening up both completely new markets and markets that are being formed within traditional infrastructure sectors. These include high-tech medicine, public transport, site improvement (parks, public spaces, embankments, city lighting systems), photo and video recording of traffic offenses, organization of weight and size control on roads, handling of solid municipal waste, railway and airport infrastructure, and seaports. One of the most prospective PPP areas promises to be the IT sector, recently included by lawmakers in the list of permitted PPP objects. In just a year and a half, about a hundred smart city projects have been launched, providing for the creation of automated systems of comprehensive road safety, traffic management, city lighting and lighting of the road networks, information systems on public transport, educational platforms in schools,

O. V. Ivanov and A. O. Inshakova (eds.), *Public-Private Partnerships in Russia*, Competitive Government: Public Private Partnerships, https://doi.org/10.1007/978-3-030-56352-3

etc. Implementation of the country's largest innovative IT PPP project—introduction of a national system for marking and tracing goods—has begun.

The use of various forms of PPP is becoming more and more variable. Along with the "classic"—concessions and partnership agreements—alternative forms (life-cycle contracts, lease agreements with investment obligations, institutional PPPs, special investment contracts, etc.) are increasingly used. They allow flexible structuring of projects, "fine-tuning" of the terms of agreements as well as of the criteria for selecting a private partner, easier changes to the concluded agreements, more rapid conclusion of agreements and launch of projects. These forms of PPP now account for a one-third of all private investment in PPP projects in Russia and about 12% of their total number.

The approach of the state to PPP governance is distinctly becoming more and more systematic in recent years. This is reflected in strategic goal setting, long-term planning of infrastructure and PPP development, measures to further improve and strengthen PPP legal framework, expansion of the tools of public support for PPP projects, and adoption—and, if possible, improvement—of the best international practices of PPP governance. In this context, at least two recent Russian innovations deserve special mention.

The first one—so-called "project finance factory"—is a mechanism for financing of investment projects in priority sectors of the Russian economy, including infrastructure, that provides for extending of syndicated loans to borrowers. Launched under the auspices of Russia's largest development institute, Vnesheconombank (VEB.RF), this fundamentally-new-for-Russia mechanism is designed to promote the development of syndicated lending in Russia, to increase availability of credit resources for investors, to reduce the overall cost of project financing, to mitigate risks by attracting additional participants, and eventually to ensure economic growth through the implementation of new projects. The "factory" has already started its operation and has launched a number of mega-PPP projects, including the abovementioned project of the national system for marking and tracking goods.

The second is the creation of the ROSINFRA infrastructure project support platform. ROSINFRA is a unique digital platform designed to facilitate the launch of infrastructure projects with state participation. A wide range of user tools and services allows to simplify the process of preparing projects, to find partners, and to increase the level of competence of specialists in attracting infrastructure investments. Thanks to the new platform, Russian regions have the opportunity to place investment proposals for private partners, as well as to receive blitz expert assessment of initiatives and assistance in forming a portfolio of projects. Investors and funding institutions can find promising initiatives and get acquainted with the activities of public partners. The expert community provides itself with up-to-date information about the market and participates in the evaluation of promising projects. The creation of such a platform is in line with one of the main global trends—digitalization of infrastructure development governance, and by its functionality the platform even exceeds those that operate in many of the most "PPP-mature" countries.

What will be the further development of PPP in Russia? What awaits him on this path? Will PPP—from a new and promising area of state-business interaction in Russia—develop into the mainstream of the government economic policies?

It is not easy to give an unambiguous answer to these questions because in the equation about the prospects of PPP in Russia there are still many introductory unknowns of both endogenous and exogenous nature.

A number of systemic problems in the PPP sector need to be addressed, such as the further adjustment of the regulatory environment, including legal framework, the streamlining of the institutional basis of the PPP sector, the creation of a comprehensive infrastructure planning system, the expansion of the range of financial support tools for PPP projects, etc.

Numerous existing external factors that can influence the prospects for PPP development in Russia are added by the new ones, which appeared just during the preparation of this monograph—the pandemic, the collapse of world oil prices, the decline in state budget revenues, and the weakening of the ruble. If we evaluate these only factors through the prism of the direct current impact on the PPP market, the answer is obvious: the projects that are being prepared and launched are hit hard. The National PPP center estimates that more than 10% of all PPP projects at various levels are "at risk" due to the pandemic, the fall of the ruble, and the slowdown in economic growth. If there is no rebound in the oil price and the lifting of restrictions due to the pandemic, the overall negative consequences for the PPP market (loss of revenue and excess project cost) may amount to at least 25–30 billion rubles in the first 6 months. The National PPP center identifies several industries where PPP projects under construction or operation will suffer the most. These are, first of all, social and consumer services, health care and spa treatment, culture, leisure, sports, tourism and other socio-cultural facilities, and urban transport and transport infrastructure in cities.

If the epidemiological situation persists for a long time, general uncertainty of the economic situation can lead to an investment pause in the infrastructure market. Preparation for the conclusion of new agreements will be slower due to the desire of investors and authorities to wait for a more stable state of the economy. Projects whose financial closure has not yet occurred may have their deadlines pushed back. The factor of falling oil prices and a radical reduction in budget revenues may force the government to reconsider many infrastructure investment plans for the near future and even the "drawdown" of the PPP market can be foreseen.

However, "every cloud has its silver lining." All these negative factors can also work to ensure that the government will pay even more attention to PPP than before and will look at it as a leverage that can be used to get out of the difficult situation the country's economy and its infrastructure find themselves in, as a driver of economic development and recovery from the crisis.

It is important that all governmental long-term plans for infrastructure development are based on the principal inevitability and expediency of combining its efforts with the private sector and using PPP mechanisms. The authorities cannot ignore the fact that there is a significant potential for PPP today. The PPP portfolio contains more than 300 PPP projects, including major federal projects as well as projects at the regional and municipal level, that are being prepared for launch. In general, there are more than a thousand potential projects at the initiation stage, where it is possible and desirable to use PPP mechanisms, with a total cost of more than 3 trillion rubles, which is comparable to the current size of the PPP market in Russia.

All this still gives reason even in these difficult times to look at the prospects for PPP development in Russia with optimism.

Oleg V. Ivanov, Agnessa O. Inshakova

Index

O. V. Ivanov and A. O. Inshakova (eds.), *Public-Private Partnerships in Russia*, Competitive Government: Public Private Partnerships,
https://doi.org/10.1007/978-3-030-56352-3

The manufacturer's authorised representative in the EU is Springer Nature Customer Service Centre GmbH, Europaplatz 3, 69115 Heidelberg, Germany. If you have any concerns regarding our products, please contact ProductSafety@springernature.com

Printed and bound by CPI Group (UK) Ltd, Croydon, CR0 4YY
30/09/2026
02225452-0012